The Rise and Fall
of the
South African Peasantry

PERSPECTIVES ON SOUTHERN AFRICA

The Rise and Fall
of the
South African Peasantry

COLIN BUNDY
Research Fellow
Queen Elizabeth House, Oxford

UNIVERSITY OF CALIFORNIA PRESS
BERKELEY AND LOS ANGELES

University of California Press
Berkeley and Los Angeles, California

© Colin Bundy 1979
First published 1979

ISBN 0–520–03754–5
Library of Congress Catalog Card Number 78–62841

Printed in Great Britain

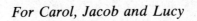

For Carol, Jacob and Lucy

Contents

Aftermath and Conclusions

List of Tables

Preface

This book is about people definable as peasants and about their place in South African history. The nature of peasants and peasant societies, on the one hand, and South Africa's economic and social history, on the other, are areas of study in which substantial changes and advances have been registered since 1970, making work on this project (in the eight years since it was begun) at once highly rewarding and somewhat taxing. Some of the developments in the study of peasants, and their application to the South African case, are discussed in Chapter 1; use of the term peasant and the definition arrived at in that chapter are not incidental to the investigation and argument of this book, but crucial.

Before stating the main concerns and intentions of my own work, I want to give a very brief account of the shifting focus of research and the process of reinterpretation in South African historical writing (as I understand them). I do so because I believe that this sets my own exposition and conclusions within their broader context, but also because it gives an intimation of how and when I came to ask the questions that the exposition and conclusions attempt to answer. The redefinition of the focus of historical enquiry and the recasting of the terms in which to explain South Africa's past can be viewed in two ways: as a specific 'late developing' instance of a general phenomenon – the explosion of African historical scholarship since 1960 – and as a debate being conducted between historians of (broadly speaking) two schools.

The belated entry by South Africanists into the swift-swelling current of African social sciences is spotlighted by two observations in a retrospective survey of *African Studies since 1945*. The overall conclusion is that 'In the last fifteen or twenty years there has been a revolution in the study of African history', while the commentator on post-war South African scholarship was 'immediately struck by the apparent dearth of any analytical breakthrough until comparatively recently .... since the early fifties it would seem that South Africa remained outside the advances being made to the north of the Limpopo, in almost every field [of the social sciences]'.[1] In 1972 Richard Gray remarked that 'to an extraordinary degree, South African historical research has fallen behind that of other African countries, let alone that of other modern industrial countries'.[2]

The gap remains, but has begun to close. The last few years have seen the commencement and consolidation of a vigorous body of research by South African historians, sociologists, archaeologists and others. Most of this work has been carried out by scholars based outside South Africa; much of it has consciously re-examined and revised prevailing accounts of the making of contemporary South Africa. In a way, the very belatedness of this research in respect to that elsewhere in Africa has influenced its content and emphasis. Like much African history of the sixties, it includes research on the dynamics and inter-relations of precolonial societies, the nature of resistance to conquest, and the rise of 'nationalist' politics; but it has come to concentrate rather more upon other aspects, especially upon the nature of capitalist development and industrialization in South Africa and upon the extent to which those processes were conditioned within the broader context of the expansion of a world economic order. In this, it reflects a new emphasis in African scholarship more generally. The committed enthusiasm of the pioneer columns for the 'African voice' and for the nationalist revolutions has been joined by a committed concern about the persistence of poverty in and the continuing subordination of Africa. There has been a movement by scholars into problems of political economy: the formation and structure of classes, the penetration of new relationships of exchange and production, the processes of accumulation and expropriation. A most important conceptual contribution has come from underdevelopment theory, especially as it has been formulated, refined and amplified during the past decade. Underdevelopment theory seeks to explain the incorporation and subordination of peripheral (colonial) economies to those of the metropolitan (imperialist) centres of capitalist development; the transformation of precapitalist economic and social structures; and also the processes whereby 'external' dominance and 'internal' dependence are maintained and reproduced.[3]

Then, too, the reinterpretation of South Africa's past has been shaped by the prior existence of a body of scholarship and by a reaction to the ideological consensus represented and sustained within its canons. It was not simply that the prevailing interpretations had been so little affected by the eddies and tides that swirled through the social sciences in the rest of the continent; in addition, developments in South Africa in the decade after Sharpeville called acutely into question their perspectives and prescriptions. In the 1960s very rapid economic growth was concomitant with the extension and modernization of *apartheid* measures and the elaboration of the apparatus of repression. Shula Marks has pointed out that it was in the 1930s and 1940s that the intellectual foundations of the thinking of South Africa's most influential social scientists were laid and that, by and large, their assumptions and preoccupations were those of classical liberalism. 'Deeply concerned, as many of these scholars were, with the tension and conflict arising in the course of industrialisation and urbanisation in twentieth-century South Africa, they saw these as arising essentially from the irrational heritage of the past.'[4] In particular, Walker, Macmillan and de Kiewiet brought new standards and techniques to the writing of history in South Africa and were the creators of the mainstream liberal historical tradition. They found their heroes in missionaries and Cape liberal politicians, and in imperial policy-makers of 'high motives and worthy ends'; they mourned the defeat of these elements and the 'triumph of the frontier'. De Kiewiet concluded his *The Imperial Factor* with an elegy for an ideal: that of 'a social and economic order in South Africa in which a greater tolerance of race, a more ardent trusteeship, a more inspired social wisdom should be the mark of the peace and unity and liberty for which the [nineteenth] century had suffered so grievously'.[5]

The humane vision of de Kiewiet and the sensitivity to injustice and suffering that illumines the work of Macmillan are unmistakable. So is their firm ideological locus and in particular the assumption that economic development (that is, the growth of the 'modern' sector of a dual economy) has served, and serves still, to minimize social conflict and to ameliorate social and economic disabilities. This approach posits a fundamental and historical dissonance between racism (usually described as Dutch or Boer or Afrikaner racism) and economic growth (which is taken to occur most freely within the framework of liberal institutions). The premise is then extended to suggest that the distance between the races in South Africa – cultural, economic, and political – is steadily diminished by the development of the economy, which development is in turn made possible by freeing South Africa's institutions and statutes from 'archaic' or 'irrational' preoccupations with segregation, miscegenation, colour bars and the rest. Thus, in classically polarized form, Macmillan described 'the alternatives ... one the way of freedom accepted in the old Cape Colony, the other the road of repression chosen in the Trekker Republics'. The 'Cape way of freedom' drew on a heritage that stretched back to the abolition of slavery, and is manifestly the preferable tradition: it 'would hasten more slowly, striving to safeguard the development of civilization among the native peoples, convinced that the only way to safety for white and black alike is to promote a general economic progress'. The logic is extended by other social scientists: they stress the disjunction between racism and economic growth and discern 'an inflexible assertion of the prerogative of political authority over the course of economic development' as a prime force in producing a repressive society.[6]

De Kiewiet, the most influential historian in the intellectual lineage under discussion chiselled some typically lapidary phrases on this topic. The Anglo-Boer War was 'the seedbed of nationalist feeling and racial passion', and it sustained 'the slow and persistent rise of an aggressive Afrikaner nationalism'. This nationalism was 'cultural defence against the English and ... racial defence against the natives':

racial discrimination had roots deep in Afrikaner experience and history, and was continued despite being 'politically unwise, economically unprofitable, and morally reprehensible'. Thus *apartheid* is seen as extrinsic and inimical to economic growth; racism as an obsolete and dysfunctional element in capitalist society. South Africa's rulers (defined by language, not class) are castigated for their 'historical deafness', their 'perverse conviction' (and the 'perverse economics of *apartheid*'); they have 'created a paradise without history and in defiance of economics' – more, they have 'declared a war . . . against the law of economics'. They have failed to recognize an ultimate 'confluence and congruency of economic interests' between white and black, failed to perceive that 'an expanding use of the benefits of income and property are the indispensable pillars of prosperity and social peace', and hence have failed to scrap the 'Alice in Wonderland economics of *apartheid*' in favour of 'investment, industrialisation and urbanisation' which would confer 'material satisfaction and dignity', a 'better future', and would move South Africa through 'economic necessity' away from racism to 'greater liberalism and cooperation'.[7]

More recently, the two volumes of the *Oxford History of South Africa* have appeared. Despite editorial suggestions of a location somewhere on an academic new frontier, this work represents a summation rather than a departure, the full flowering of an academic variant of Cape Liberalism.[8] It served as a precipitating agent for historical debate: a reviewer remarked that its 'editors could scarcely have anticipated the scope and extent of the scrutiny to which the volume would be subjected, nor how soon would be the call for revision'. Certain reassessments themselves took firmer shape when measured against the scholarship in the Oxford volumes: as one of the most influential of the 'revisionist' scholars puts it, 'both the strengths and weaknesses of the Oxford History are a spur to further research'.[9] A thoughtful critique saw the Oxford histories as the apogee of the 'liberal school of South African scholarship' and argued that the focus of research – especially in Britain – had altered:

> The standpoint of this new generation of scholars has been to re-evaluate the structural characteristics of the Southern African political economy and to ask whether the 'dynamics of modernization' will in fact tend to dissolve racial oligarchy. . . . They have also asked whether it is not more fruitful to see South African history in terms of class conflict than in terms of the traditional racial dichotomy. . . . Underlying all these arguments is the basic assumption that all of Southern Africa is involved in *one* economy. . . . Such questions have led historians not only towards a reappraisal of contemporary history but to a re-examination of the dynamics of contact and conflict between precolonial modes of production in the 'tribal' economies and the growth of capitalism.[10]

Among the topics investigated by this 'new generation' are: the nature and relationships of pre-industrial societies, the development of the mining industry, the history of migrant labour, the changing role of the state, tensions and accommodations between international and national capitalist interests, the complex interaction between race and class conflict, and the historical nature and function of segregation and *apartheid*.

There has also been some attention paid to social change in the rural areas, mention of which makes this a suitable moment to say something about the scope, nature and intention of this volume. It chronicles the history of African agriculture in South Africa (no systematic account exists elsewhere) concentrating upon the years 1870 to 1913. It begins with a description of agricultural practices before conquest and incorporation, and the concluding chapter brings the chronology up to the present day, but the years between the beginning of the 'mineral revolution' and the passage of the Natives Land Act are the core of the study. This was the crucial period in the transformation of the bulk of the rural African population from their precolonial existence as pastoralist–cultivators to their present existence as sub-subsistence inhabitants on eroded and overcrowded lands, dependent for survival upon wages earned in 'white' industrial areas and on 'white' farms.

Other historians have stressed the destructive impact of colonial rule upon 'traditional' African agriculture (typified as unscientific, negligent and technologically backward), telling a 'story of continuous depression and disintegration'.[11] They overlooked or underestimated a phenomenon to which Monica Wilson has recently drawn attention: an initial period of early prosperity in regions of peasant production in South Africa, followed only later by the symptoms of agrarian decay and underdevelopment. I argue, and demonstrate as fully as possible, that there was a substantially more positive and successful response by black agriculturists to market opportunities than has usually been indicated, and that hundreds of thousands of African peasants met the new demands of the state and of landowners by adapting their existing farming methods rather than by entering wage labour on the terms of the white colonists.

Those responses and adaptations are defined in a particular manner: as the formation in the nineteenth century of an African peasantry. The emergence of a peasantry – a class of petty agricultural producers who sought to sell a portion of what they raised in order to meet the demands of a cash economy and a colonial state – is described in terms that permit examination of the changing relations over time between the peasant and the land he farms, the peasant and the market, and the peasant and the wielders of economic and political power. A definition of peasant that draws notice to his relations with other groups in the political economy at a given time has an analytical and expository purpose: to distinguish peasants individually and the peasantry as a class from precolonial cultivators, from capitalist farmers and from the rural proletariat.

While the positive response to market conditions by African growers and graziers was a starting point for this investigation, it very soon became clear that this could hardly be studied without reference to the subsequent checking or failure of that response. The emergence of a peasantry and the proletarianization of some of its members are social processes that overlapped and commenced more or less simultaneously. Within the emergent peasantry, an important internal dynamic was its propensity to stratification, the breakdown of redistributive tenets and institutions, and the generation of new social antagonisms. At one 'end' of the process large peasants became successful landowners and farmers; at the other end, small or marginal peasants were separated from the means of production – crucially, they lost access to enough land to subsist – almost as soon as the peasantry emerged as an identifiable element in the political economy. The pace of peasantization and proletarianization was affected by the political intervention of non-peasants, of groups with superior access to power in the colonial state. For example the 'Cape liberal' merchant/missionary axis favoured the creation of a class of black rural producer-consumers. Absentee proprietors relied upon rent from African tenants and permitted the growth of a sizeable sector of squatter-peasants. By the turn of the century, those who favoured the development of a black peasantry lost ground to those who sought to undermine peasant production and peasant 'independence'. The interests of these latter were translated into political action: between roughly 1890 and 1913, an employers' offensive directly undercut the position of large numbers of peasants.

The commercialization of 'white' agriculture, an increasing demand for cheap labour (plus the legislative devices and state actions that these gave rise to) and the changing marketing arrangements combined to effect a deterioration in the peasant's access to markets, his terms of trade and his command over the disposal of his surplus. These factors reinforced and perpetuated peasant disabilities due to geophysical, natural and demographic causes. At the same time that the peasant's capacity to generate a surplus and his opportunities for accumulation were diminished, his further integration into the national (and international) economy raised the impositions on him in the shape of taxes, rents and other fees.

In sum, the formation of a peasantry did not *cause* African proletarianization and poverty in South Africa, but did vitally affect their nature and timing. The emergence and existence of a peasantry, its initial productive boom and its relative economic sufficiency, tend to have been obscured by the decisiveness of its later decline. In the pages that follow both the rise and the fall of the peasantry are described in the belief that they contribute to the investigation and explanation of the course and causes of South Africa's level of development as well as the course and causes of its level of underdevelopment.

The Cape Colony (later Province) has been selected for the closest study, not only because the transition from precolonial cultivator to peasant to rural proletarian is clearly observable there but also because of the more abundant printed source material available. The book might well have been restricted to the Cape alone (and at many stages in its compilation the temptations so to curtail it were strong), but I felt that it was important to outline a comparative survey of the process as it took place in different parts of Southern Africa. The heartland of the Cape peasantry is also the region of clearest focus in my work: that portion of the Cape lying east of an imaginary line drawn along the Sunday River and its continuation northwards – in contemporary terms, most of the eastern Province and Border, and the whole of the Ciskei and Transkei.

The chronological period and the geographical area covered, let alone the diversity and complexity of the human experiences involved, have determined the nature of this book. Its scope is broad and its purpose essentially that of an initial survey. The principal source has been the voluminous series of printed papers for the Colony of the Cape of Good Hope. Missionary archives have been another important source: missionaries were strategically placed to observe and report on social change, and their records (although subject to their own biases and preconceptions) offered a valuable alternative set of perceptions to those of the 'official mind'. Contemporary reportage – colonial newspapers, travellers' accounts and the like – contained invaluable details. Some limited use was made of the Cape archives, usually to test a hypothesis or to seek data known to exist in a specific file, but detailed studies using the material available in South African archives are still to be written.

The material in Chapter 1 and elsewhere indicates the extent to which my work could be built upon existing foundations, the studies by Macmillan, de Kiewiet, Robertson, Van der Horst, Goodfellow and Wilson. I have already mentioned – and it is a pleasure to acknowledge – how valuable have been the insights, perspectives and syntheses of other scholars, and how fruitful have been many of the directions pointed and methods employed by those active in recent years in re-interpreting South Africa's history. It is not simply that one has been able to read published articles and books; there has also been the zest and sense of engagement derived from participating in seminars, conferences and other less formal debates. Intellectual indebtedness is not confined to the formalized commerce in ideas and details and its audit in footnotes; it also exists, on the most liberal of terms, whenever discussions and other exchanges take place. This book has been undertaken with a sense of involvement in an academic exercise less lonely, less parochial and less exclusive than research is sometimes held to be. For this I am grateful.

Particularly, I want to thank Stanley Trapido – who supervised with such stimulating criticism and encouraging enthusiasm the thesis upon which this book is based – for the aid, advice and friendship he gave at every stage. After the thesis was completed, it was read by Shula Marks, Robin Palmer and Terence Ranger: from each of them, I received not only helpful suggestions and pointers as to revision, but also additional personal kindness and generosity. There is another to whom my debt exceeds any acknowledgement I can make: my wife, Carol, who over eight years has borne my research, her work and our children. It is not just that she has been a perceptive and stringent reader of my work in all its stages or that she masterminded the index· to this book, nor even that she was the only mother in her maternity ward proofreading a typescript – it is all these and more.

NOTES

1 C. Fyfe (ed.), *African Studies since 1945* (London, 1976). The quotations are from T. O. Ranger, 'Towards a Usable African Past', 17, and S. Marks, 'South African Studies since World War Two', 186.

2 Cited by Marks, 'South African Studies', 186.

3 There is already a sizeable literature on underdevelopment. Two essays are exceptional in their clarity and perception: A. Foster-Carter, 'Neo-Marxist Approaches to Development and Underdevelopment', in E. de Kadt and G. Williams (eds.), *Sociology and Development* (London, 1974), 67–105; and the Introduction of C. Leys, *Underdevelopment in Kenya: The Political Economy of Neo-Colonialism* (London, 1975), 1–27. A splendid critical bibliography with particular reference to Africa is C. Allen, 'A Bibliographical Guide to the Study of the Political Economy of Africa', in P. C. W. Gutkind and I. Wallerstein, *The Political Economy of Contemporary Africa* (London, 1976), 291–314.

4 Marks, 'South African Studies', 188.

5 C. W. de Kiewiet, *The Imperial Factor in South Africa* (London, 1965, 1st ed. 1937), 5; *A History of South Africa: Social and Economic* (London, 1941), 150–1; *The Imperial Factor*, 328. An incisive critique of the stress upon 'frontier' influences as an explanation for racialism is M. Legassick, 'The Frontier Tradition in South African Historiography', ICS, CSP, Vol. 2.

6 W. M. Macmillan, *Complex South Africa* (London, 1930), 17–18; R. Horwitz, *The Political Economy of South Africa* (London, 1967), 3.

7 C. W. de Kiewiet, *The Anatomy of South African Misery* (London, 1956), 16, 18–19, 21–2, 28, 38–9, 45, 47, 52, 67, 70, 73.

8 M. Wilson and L. Thompson (eds.), *The Oxford History of South Africa*, 2 vols. (Oxford, 1969, 1971). The premises and conceptual approach of the Oxford history, particularly the second volume, have been examined in a number of reviews, including: A. Atmore and N. Westlake, 'A Liberal Dilemma: A Critique of the Oxford History of South Africa', *Race*, XIV, 2 (1972), 107–36; M. Legassick, 'The Dynamics of Modernization in South Africa', *Journal of African History*, XIII, 1 (1972), 145–50; S. Marks,

'Liberalism, Social Realities and South African History', *Journal of Commonwealth Political Studies*, X, 3 (1972); S. Trapido, 'South Africa and the Historians', *African Affairs*, Vol. 71, No. 285 (October 1972), 444–8.

9 Trapido, 'South Africa and the Historians', 444; Legassick, 'The Dynamics of Modernization', 150.

10 P. Kallaway, 'What happened in South African history?', *Concept*, June 1975 (published for the Convocation of the University of Natal).

11 C. W. de Kiewiet, 'Social and Economic Developments in Native Tribal Life', *Cambridge History of the British Empire*, VIII (Cambridge, 1936), 828.

1

Introduction

From a comparatively free husbandman the Native has been converted into a modern wage-slave, with only his labour-power to sell. . . . This is the change in South Africa, the transformation of the Native farmer into a landless proletarian.

Clements Kadalie, 'The Aims and Motives of the I.C.U.', 1925

But if the men of the future are ever to break the chains of the present, they will have to understand the forces that forged them.

Barrington Moore, Jr., *Social Origins of Dictatorship and Democracy*

At the core of South Africa's social history lies the transition of a majority of her people – the rural African population – from their precolonial existence as pastoralist-cultivators to their contemporary status: that of sub-subsistence rural dwellers, manifestly unable to support themselves by agriculture and dependent for survival upon wages earned in 'white' industrial areas or upon 'white' farms. The transition is a striking one, and its external aspects have been described often enough: the diminution of Africans' lands by conquest and annexation, the creation of 'Reserves', the deterioration of these into eroded, overstocked and overcrowded rural ghettoes that function as the supply source of migratory labour.

The most widely accepted explanation of the 'failure' of African agriculture to provide a living for people who were once herders and farmers is found in the work of Macmillan, de Kiewiet, Marais and others. They stress, on the one hand, the destructive impact of white rule, especially the hammer-blow of sweeping land expropriations and sudden land shortage, and on the other hand, the dislocation of the traditional economy and social order, the vulnerability and frailty of a primitive tribal economy with unscientific, negligent and technologically backward agricultural techniques, in the face of the imperatives and dynamism of a more advanced, commercialized market economy. They were consciously writing corrective history, replacing the pro-settler complacency and misrepresentation of Theal and Cory and challenging the justificatory hagiography of certain Afrikaans

1

histories; de Kiewiet was at pains to dispel the comfortable fiction that Africans continued even after the Frontier Wars to enjoy an agreeable *dolce far niente*, stressing that rural Africans underwent hardships 'of a much greater degree than is normally conceded'.[1]

The 'devastating effects of the colonial advance on the social and economic life of the dispossessed Bantu' expressed themselves most directly in the loss of land: this loss was too severe a blow for the tribal economy or traditional mode of production to resist or to survive through adaptations. Without available land for all, 'one of the corner-stones of tribal life had been wrenched away'; the cash nexus dissolved the old self-sufficient economic order, while rising consumption needs 'threw upon the tribes a burden their subsistence economy could not bear'.[2] The frailty of the subsistence economy was in large measure due to the 'unscientific and wasteful' agriculture and 'the ignorance and neglect' of 'native life'. Similarly, Hancock blames the soil deterioration and human wretchedness arising from 'native congestion' upon the fact that the 'Europeans had left the natives too little land', an evil compounded by the 'inertia of native custom' and by the fact that neither labour nor 'squatting' on white-owned land could 'stimulate change and progress in the economic methods of the Bantu'.[3]

The gulf between the economic and agricultural practices of colonists and Africans is further emphasized in the works of D. Hobart Houghton, who has written widely upon the economic history of the 'Reserves'. His explanation derives more explicitly from a theoretical insistence upon the dual nature of the South African economy, the parallel existence of 'subsistence' and 'market' sectors of that economy.[4] Palmer and Parsons have drawn a useful distinction between the concept of the 'dual economy' and 'dualism theory'.[5] The former is used loosely as a convenient label to describe uneven economic development within national boundaries, especially where a system of socio-legal segregation is based on reserved land categories. The central concept in 'dualism theory' typifies an economy divided into two sharply distinguished and largely independent sectors, and predicts a number of specific economic phenomena that flow from the division. The capitalist (or modern or industrial) sector is characterized by high productivity, is market-oriented, receptive to change, and pursues rational and maximizing aims. The precapitalist (or primitive or traditional or subsistence) sector is stagnant, and displays little market awareness, high leisure preferences, and the dominance of 'tradition' or 'custom' over rationality – that is, the description 'reflects the opinion that small peasants will not respond to ordinary economic incentives'.[6] The chief link between the two sectors is the flow of unemployed labour from the traditional to the modern sector.

Hobart Houghton argues that, for a variety of reasons, Africans failed to adapt the tribal economy to the novel conditions of relative land scarcity, or to learn from their white neighbours more modern methods of farming. The 'failure to adapt their economy' is the 'root cause of their distress', and that failure is accounted for in terms of the shortcomings of the traditional or subsistence sector: the lack of technical knowledge, the inhibiting forces of social custom, a consequent hostility to innovation and a low level of responsivity to market incentives. The thesis is underscored that these flaws stem from the nature of African society, that they are so deeply rooted there as to resist the enlightenment and economic rationality of 'farsighted administrators ... missionaries ... and agricultural demonstrators'. The failure to effect significant change in agricultural methods 'should not be attributed to lack of zeal on the part of a noble band of dedicated workers, but must be explained in other ways'.[7] Or, as another influential South African economist put it:

> Three-quarters of the population is in the process of emerging from a primitive culture in which the distribution of labour between different uses is effected not by the pecuniary incentive upon which a capitalist economy chiefly relies, but by totally different arrangements. Among these natural obstacles are traditional attitudes of Natives towards land and cattle; conservatism; family ties; ignorance of conditions prevailing or opportunities offering.[8]

These approaches – which is to say, the dominant prevailing liberal tradition of South African historiography – posit the fundamental and inherent weaknesses of the tribal economy, the disadvantages that it imposed on Africans when they encountered the cash nexus and market relations, and the inability of Africans either to adapt that economy, or to forsake it, so as to participate 'successfully' in the market economy. Such an explanation overlooks or underestimates a phenomenon to which Monica Wilson has drawn attention: an initial period of 'early prosperity' in the reserve areas of South Africa (and in the territories that are today Botswana, Lesotho and Swaziland), followed only later by the symptoms of underdevelopment and sub-subsistence living standards.[9]

This book is also concerned with the transition experienced by the rural African population, and it defines it in a particular manner, in terms of the emergence of an African peasantry in the nineteenth century. In other words, it holds that the creation of an African peasantry was a significant aspect of the 'early prosperity', and that the emergence, and the decline, of African peasants was a crucial element in the transition of farmer-pastoralists into a reservoir of cheap, rightless and largely migrant labourers. As the term peasant is going to be used in the argument that follows, and a specific meaning attached to it, it remains to ask what is meant by peasant? Were there peasants in South Africa? And if so, what analytical and expository purpose is served by the definition and employment of the term?

1 PEASANTS

Historical and anthropological research into peasantries (particularly by British, American and West European scholars) lapsed into virtual insignificance between the world wars: those few studies that emerged were individual ventures, their impact blunted by the prevailing political and intellectual climate. Within a conceptual framework that divided societies into 'pre-industrial' or 'primitive' as against 'industrial' or 'modernized', and awaited with complacency or impatience the passage of the former to the state of the latter, peasants 'disappeared as a specific entity: [and were] bound together in a common category with neolithic tribesmen, Chinese gentry, and so on'. Since about 1948, however, and especially during the 1960s (the years of the Chinese Revolution, the Vietnam War and of formal independence but continuing dependence in much of Africa and Asia) there has been a great resurgence of interest in peasants, and a recognition that the little understood peasant majority was 'one of the major structural determinants which make the so-called "developing societies" into what they are'.[10] Scores of articles and monographs in a number of disciplines broadened empirical foundations and sharpened analytical approaches; by 1972 the study of peasants and rural problems had become 'one of the biggest growth sectors in the social sciences';[11] and in 1973 the appearance of the *Journal of Peasant Studies* simultaneously celebrated and furthered this renascence.

Post-war peasant studies in English may fairly be said to have been rooted in the work of Kroeber and Redfield. Kroeber characterized peasants as forming a part-segment of town-centred societies ('they form a class segment of a larger population which usually contains town centres.... They form part-societies with part-cultures').[12] Redfield elaborated upon this: he attributed four main features to a peasantry. First, they are involved in exchange and markets, although, he argues, the 'local, traditional world' and the market principle are in peasant society 'maintained in some balance; the market is held at arm's length, so to speak'. Secondly, peasants are involved in a wider administrative and political hierarchy, one beyond the village community in which they live and labour; thirdly, they therefore exist in a 'country-wide network' and not merely in the immediate or 'closed' community; finally, peasants display a 'folk' or 'little' version of the 'great' cultural tradition in the containing society. The peasantry's system of values is consistent 'in the main, with those of the city people who constitute, so to speak, its other dimension of existence'.[13]

The concentration upon cultural characteristics and the sociological typology used by Redfield has been criticized by Post. The essence of Redfield's treatment 'seems to be the proposition that the crucial process in a hypothetical transition from a society of "primitive" cultivators to a society based on peasants' is one by which self-sufficient, kin-based communities 'are "turned outwards" as it were, and made dependent in various ways upon external structures and forces'. Post objects that this approach fails to 'focus specifically enough upon the dynamic which moves individuals and communities along this axis'[14] – it fails to examine the *process* by which such an intermediate society comes into being, or to examine the location of peasant societies within the relevant political economies (that is, in terms of the control of economic resources and the distribution of power and goods determined by that control).

Post and Shanin have attempted to move beyond the Redfield typology of peasant, to broaden the analysis by incorporating other aspects; and both are indebted to the work of Eric Wolf, whose brief, challenging general survey was a milestone in peasant studies.[15] Wolf peasant/non-peasant social duality. Peasants, says Wolf, are 'rural cultivators whose surpluses are transferred to a dominant group of rulers that uses the surpluses both to underwrite its own standard of living and to distribute the remainder to groups in society that do not farm but must be fed for their specific goods and services in turn'. The existence of the 'dominant group of rulers' means that the peasant is subject to 'asymmetrical power relations which [make] a permanent charge on his production'. This charge (whether paid in labour, produce or cash) Wolf defines as rent: 'Where someone exercises an effective superior power, or domain, over a cultivator, the cultivator must produce a fund of rent. *It is this production of a fund of rent which critically distinguishes the peasant from the primitive cultivator.*' He also questions the existing identification of peasant production and cities: it is not the city, he argues, but the *state* that marks the threshold of the transition between food cultivators in general and peasants. Thus, 'it is only when a cultivator is integrated into a society with a state – that is, when the cultivator becomes subject to the demands and sanctions of power holders outside his own social stratum – that we can appropriately speak of peasantry'.[16]

Shanin finds Wolf's attempt to define peasants in terms of 'asymmetrical' power relations within a class-structured society preferable to the 'Durkheimian' tradition of Kroeber and Redfield, with its functionalist and cultural emphases, but argues that it is not inclusive enough. He suggests four basic facets which one would look for in constructing a general type of peasant society: (i) the peasant family-farm as the basic unit of social organization*; (ii) land husbandry as the main means of

---

* Elsewhere he defines the peasant family-farm as 'a small production/consumption unit which finds its main livelihood in agriculture and is manned chiefly by family labour. Family consumption needs and dues to the holders of political-economic power define to a major degree the character of production.' ('The Nature and Logic of the Peasant Economy', *Journal of Peasant Studies*, I, 1 (October 1973), 63–80, 67.)

livelihood, directly providing the major part of consumption needs; (iii) a specific traditional culture related to the way of life of small communities; (iv) the 'underdog' position: domination of the peasant by outsiders, with political subjection interlocked with economic exploitation and cultural subordination.[17]

Other questions arise in connection with the use of the concept 'peasant' in the African context. Post has commented on the 'marked uncertainty' on the part of scholars in applying the term to Africa's rural population in either historical or contemporary analysis. Some writers have rejected the term and preferred concepts like 'husband-men', 'rural capitalists', 'protopeasants', and so on;[18] while others use the term without any discussion or else define it so loosely as to include all petty cultivators. In an influential article, Fallers addressed himself in 1961 to the question 'Are African Cultivators to be called "Peasants"?', and came up with a qualified affirmative.[19] Basing himself quite closely on Redfield, he used economic, political and cultural criteria. In economic terms, he said, peasants (producing mainly for household consumption but also for exchange) 'abound in Africa'; and inasmuch as they are involved in a vertical political hierarchy, African cultivators are also peasants in the political sense. But he did not discern in Africa the juxtaposition of high and low cultures essential to the existence of peasants; and it was preferable, he concluded, to refer to 'protopeasants' or 'incipient peasants'.

Shortly after Fallers' article, Dalton spoke of peasants in Africa, relying heavily upon a broad economic distinction between 'subsistence' and 'peasant' economies; in the latter the majority of people had 'come to depend on production for sale as their primary source of livelihood', and commercial production had become more important than subsistence production.* [20] Middleton reconsidered the question briefly, concluding that there seemed no good reasons *not* to refer to as peasants those cultivators 'who produce partly for an external market, and so are subject to controls and incentives of that external system, as well as living and producing largely in terms of the requirements and sanctions of their own, local communities.'[21]

This particular debate was carried a good deal further with the essay by Saul and Woods published in 1971. They drew upon the systematic general categorization of Wolf, but also aimed to take into account the African context, so as to provide 'effective concepts within an analytical framework which does usefully structure such an explanation'.[22] Like Wolf, they view a peasantry as a stratum within a wider political and economic system; with Shanin (and Chayanov before him) they emphasize the peasant family household as a production-consumption

* Not even Dalton's later rider about a low technological level successfully avoids the difficulty which his distinction creates: that peasants seem virtually synonomous with commercial farmers. His footnote on page 387 indicates his own awareness of the problem.

unit. They point out that 'predominantly pastoral people' are in Africa subject to the same kinds of political and economic forces as their predominantly agricultural brethren (and that they are based on a similar 'homestead' principle) and argue cogently enough for their inclusion in any study of African peasantries. They stress the historical context of the emergence of peasants in Africa: 'despite the existence of some prefigurings of a peasant class in earlier periods, it is more fruitful to view ... the creation of an African peasantry ... as being primarily the result of the interaction between an international capitalist economic system and traditional socio-economic systems'.[23] That is, the creation of African peasantries is most meaningfully analysed in the historical context of the colonial period.*

Saul and Woods define peasants at one stage as 'those whose ultimate security and subsistence lies in their having certain rights in land and in the labour of family members on the land', as well as being involved in a wider economic system. Post grasps boldly at a definitional nettle whose existence Saul and Woods really only indicate: the subject of land tenure and usufruct. He concludes that 'in both the pre-colonial and colonial periods it would seem that, from the point of view of the individual, land *use* rights must be treated as more important than property rights'. This formula, as he intimates, means the inclusion of important forms of peasant existence (especially in the colonial era) such as renting, sharecropping or 'squatting' without payment and without security of tenure, on land *owned* by others.[24]

Finally, Monica Wilson's essay on 'The Growth of Peasant Communities', a chapter of the *Oxford History of South Africa,* was (when it appeared) the only attempt to examine systematically the history of black cultivators in South Africa in terms of a peasant class. It is a stimulating piece, drawing together several strands of the work of a long-serving anthropologist-cum-historian, and full of rewarding details, but is ultimately disappointing. A pervading weakness is the absence of firm chronological structure: evidence and description are heaped up (dates from the early nineteenth, late nineteenth, early

---

* Henry Slater has objected to the 'general equation of the period of production for the European colonial market with the total existence of the peasantry as an identifiable social formation' in South Africa, and argues that in the definitions used by Saul and Woods (and following them, by me) 'the peasantry is accorded too short a history'. He suggests that in Natal during the precolonial era peasantries developed for the first time during a transition from a 'Germanic' or 'homestead' mode of production to a 'feudal' epoch 'not later than the 16th century and probably a good deal earlier'. He is clearly correct to stress that the development of peasantries in Southern Africa did not follow 'a regular pattern confined to the era of formal colonial rule'; but it still seems to me that a number of analytical distinctions and difficulties arise in using 'peasant' for the sixteenth century or earlier as well as for the colonial period (during which local African economic systems became enmeshed within the capitalist world economy). (H. Slater, 'Peasantries and Primitive Accumulation in Southern Africa', in *Southern African Research in Progress: Collected Papers, 2,* University of York, 1977.)

twentieth and mid-twentieth centuries crowd the pages) as each of a succession of phenomena is described: population density, food production, herding, individual tenure, migrant labour and so on, and the cumulative effect is to blur the outlines of the historical process(es) being described.

More relevant in the present context is the definition of peasant used by Professor Wilson. 'Peasant communities, in the sense in which the term is used in this [*Oxford History*] book, began in 1783 with the foundation of the first mission station in South Africa.' There was a basic similarity between the missions of different denominations; on all of them 'families were urged to settle; the hunters were pressed to become herders; the herders were taught to cultivate; the cultivators were taught to use a plough and irrigate; and all came into much closer relationship with the outside world'. Then, more formally, the characteristics of peasants are defined:

(i) They were 'landowners or tenants, producing on a small scale for their own consumption, and for trade with a town', not tribesmen living 'in isolation with only a trickle of trade' nor farmers engaged in 'larger-scale production for a market'.

(ii) 'Literacy and adherence to a church had begun'.

(iii) 'Some political authority existed wider than that of a chief ruling an independent unit ... and some portion of the peasants' surplus helped to maintain a dominant group.' And finally the process of the development of a peasantry is described as 'a study of increase in scale' in 'economic, religious, intellectual, political, domestic and symbolic aspects'.[25]

Clearly, Professor Wilson's treatment is firmly based on Redfield and Fallers (she adopts Fallers' economic, political and cultural characteristics with little change, merely altering the order so as to 'promote' the cultural category). The predominantly cultural frame of reference is even more strongly reflected in the discussion that precedes the formal definition, where peasants are seen as synonymous with the inhabitants of mission stations. The major shortcoming of this approach is that it excludes from consideration as peasants those cultivators who held land as tenants or as sharecroppers: this distinction seems not merely unhelpful, but analytically inadequate. It is argued in this book that peasants with access to land that they did not own formed an historically important and economically significant proportion of the peasantry (they are called squatter-peasants, so as to distinguish them from peasants enjoying usufruct rights on communally owned lands, or those who owned their plots). In the *Oxford History*, tenants and sharecroppers are described in the chapter on 'white' farming, but not as peasants.

Another consequence of the cultural stress in the Wilson chapter, and the absence of any examination of the changing nature of the demands by the 'dominant group' that expropriated 'some portion of the peasants' surplus' is that one is left in some confusion as to the historical fate of the peasantry. Is a rural community 'so dependent on urban earning ... indeed a peasant community' or 'an industrial proletariat domiciled in the country?' the reader is asked at one stage. The answer to an extremely important question is obscured by the assertion that follows: that any family 'still having a fragment of land or the hope of inheriting one' is classified as peasant. The difficulties that her formula imposes are demonstrated by Professor Wilson's own hesitancy: 'before the end of the chapter [she] has qualified her unsatisfactory definition to the extent that peasants have become "peasants" (p. 59)'.[26]

In the chapters that follow below, a good deal of attention is paid to the proletarianization of African peasants; the process by which the transition from tribesman to peasant was continued as a process by which peasants became members of a rurally based proletariat. Another feature of Monica Wilson's chapter is that little notice is taken of differentiation or stratification *amongst* the peasantry. Although the evidence quoted is full of glimpses of social stratification, this is not examined: not only is sight lost of a most significant aspect in the history of peasant communities, but statements are also made which are misleading, as, for instance, the suggestion that the Bunga 'for nearly fifty years discussed the issues which most concerned the peasantry of the largest African reserve, the Transkei': which peasants, and how many were they, had access to the Transkeian Territories General Council?[27]

Drawing heavily on Saul and Woods, and on Wolf, Shanin and Post, one arrives at a definition of peasant to typify Africans in the Cape (and South Africa generally) during the nineteenth century. An African peasant was a rural cultivator, enjoying access to a portion of land, the fruits of which he could dispose of as if he owned the land; he used his own labour and that of members of his family in agricultural or pastoral pursuits and sought through this to satisfy directly the consumption needs of his family; in addition he looked to the sale of a portion of what he raised to meet the demands (taxes, rents, and other fees) that arose from his involvement in an economic and political system beyond the bounds of his immediate community. Like peasants elsewhere, he had recourse to a specific traditional culture; and under colonialism, with the sudden introduction of the religious, educational and ideological aspects of the colonists' culture, the peasant could not but have a different cultural identity from that of his immediate forebears. Like peasants elsewhere, he was dominated economically, politically and culturally by outsiders in a wider society – involved in relations of coercion and obedience – but under colonialism the extent to which the state or its representatives could enforce these relations differed sharply from time to time and from place to place.

This last point introduces an essential consideration: the need to recognize (in Shanin's phrase) the 'peasantry as a process', especially the structural changes in the peasantry determined or triggered off by the pressures and demands of other social classes. Shanin suggests that the major factors promoting structural change are the spread of market relations, monetization and technological change, the rise in the division of labour, the assertion of an 'external' culture and political changes effected by (non-peasant) power-holders.[28] By comparative historical standards, the impact of these factors (the whole pattern of social and economic change) has been very rapid in the colonial situation. A peasant society emerging during the era of the integration of a peripheral economy to the metropolitan capitalist economy is subject to rapid structural change; under the capitalist development of Africa, stratification within the peasantry means that some agriculturists 'have moved out of the peasant category' and must be redefined, perhaps as capitalist farmers; other peasants have been proletarianized; in other words, 'the further development of capitalism has begun to phase out the very peasantry it defined and created ... the existence of a peasantry could be viewed all the more as a transitional phenomenon'.[29]

Rather than 'peasantry as a process', some prefer the term 'peasantization', defined as a process referring 'essentially to the widening and depersonalization of market relations consequent to the introduction of a pervasive cash economy and a colonial state'. Post suggests that in historical study of peasantization one is concerned with: first, the process of change from communal cultivator to peasant, and secondly, the process of the incorporation of communal and peasant structures into a world capitalist network; both processes have occurred simultaneously.[30] The latter process hastens the speed and intensity of the former, but in an uneven way: a critical feature of the creation of a peasantry in the era of imperialist incorporation has been its propensity to internal stratification. In the South African case, a portion of the peasantry was proletarianized almost as soon as the peasantry emerged as an identifiable element in the political economy.*

Clearly, then, it is important to take account of the differentiation between members of a peasantry and of the generation within peasant society of new social groups. One approach is to point out that at one end of a continuum 'large' peasants became successful commercial farmers and proprietors; that at the other end, small or marginal peasants were proletarianized, and that an infinite series of gradations lay between these extremes. It may be more useful to distinguish, even in broad and imprecise terms, several categories between these

---

* Robin Cohen expresses this in another way: he discusses peasantization and proletarianization as 'interrelated social processes' that are 'set in train more or less simultaneously' by 'the introduction and spread of capitalist social relations'. (In P. C. W. Gutkind and I. Wallerstein (eds.), *The Political Economy of Contemporary Africa* (Sage, London, 1976), p. 156.)

margins. Galeski has provided a rough 'common sense' division of a peasant class into three categories;[31] he speaks of:
(i) the poor or little peasant: he owns a dwarf farm (or in the South African context he often owns very poor or infertile land) and possesses insufficient means of production to assure the family's subsistence; some member(s) of the family will have to dispose of labour power in return for wages. (There is a thin but perceptible line between he whose main income is derived from peasant labour but must be supplemented, and he whose labour for others is becoming the major means of his subsistence.); (ii) the middle peasant: he has a large enough farm or plot to assure the family's maintenance, but not large enough to permit or require the employment of hired labour (in the South African context it should be added that the surplus-generating capacity of this peasant would be subject to considerable variations in years of favourable or unfavourable climatic or natural conditions). (iii) the large peasant: he has a little more land, produces more surplus for sale and needs occasionally to hire outside labour.

Another internal division between South Africa's peasants has already been suggested: that between peasants on land communally owned but where each raises and disposes of his own product, squatter-peasants living on land leased from absentee proprietors, and peasants with individual land tenure. This distinction has not only economic divisions, but social and cultural ones as well: in very broad terms, it will be observed that the first of these categories is culturally 'more traditional' and the last of them 'less traditional' or more receptive to the 'great' culture. Another distinction between South African peasants existed, but cannot yet be accurately enough reconstructed for the period covered in this work to be consistently applied: it is the difference between those who were predominantly 'pastoral peasants' and those who were predominantly 'agricultural peasants'. The difference could involve both types in significantly different relationships with respect to land allocation and usage and to agricultural innovation (some aspects of this are dealt with in Chapter 5).

The definition of peasant arrived at above, together with the comments on the processes of change or 'peasantization', serves certain expository functions. It distinguishes peasants from precolonial (or 'tribal' or 'primitive') agriculturists by the integration of the former into a more complex social structure with novel economic and political obligations. It distinguishes peasants from capitalist farmers or agrarian entrepreneurs in terms of the latter's ability to accumulate, to hire non-family labour and to break with the material and ideological confines of peasant society. It distinguishes peasant from rural proletarian in that the former retains access to the means of subsistence, and sufficient control over the disposal of his surplus to feed and clothe his family through agricultural exertions, while the latter must sell his

11

labour power to subsist. It provides for the study in the South African case of the numerically and historically significant sector of squatter-peasants. It assumes no permanence in the status of peasant, but is concerned with the decline or disappearance of peasants – their transition into agricultural labourers or migrant workers – as much as with their emergence.

The main implications of this usage have affected the direction and contents of this book. Its aim is to chronicle the history of African agriculture during a period of important economic changes in South Africa and especially to record the complex and various responses evinced by Africans to a series of economic pressures and opportunities. It is not a history of agricultural technology, it is not an account of reactions to conquest, nor is it a history of the agricultural policies of the white rulers of South Africa. It is a history, first, of the relations between the peasant and the land he farmed, his crops, cattle, ploughs and pastures; secondly, of the relations between the peasant and the market, his experience of new systems of trade and transport, prices and debts; thirdly, of the relations between the peasant and the wielders of economic and political power outside his own social class, the transfer of surplus in rents, taxes and labour, and his response to the pressures of legislators, administrators and employers.

The attention paid to the definition of the term peasant in the South African context will have been worthwhile if the concept enables one to explain and analyse the behaviour of various individuals and groups in other than an impressionistic, atomized way. For a given year – say, 1890 – the term peasant will have to be flexible enough and yet precise enough to include: a Mpondo, still a member of an independent African kingdom, who has bought his first metal plough by the sale of some livestock; a Bhaca who has picked up a little Dutch, some second-hand clothing, and half a dozen ploughing cattle during a spell in service on a colonist's farm in the Gatberg, and who now sells to the local trader a bag of grain so as to pay his hut-tax and to buy sugar, paraffin and some furniture; and a literate Thembu who attends meetings of an African Farmers Association, has hired help this year to harvest the wheat he sells directly to a merchant in a frontier town. All these and many others are the subject of this book; if the approach adopted helps to discover and to understand their different situations and responses, it will be justified.

No systematic treatment of the history of African agriculture in South Africa exists, nor of the particular responses and initiatives by African food-producers after 1870 and until 1913. The nearest is Monica Wilson's chapter in the *Oxford History,* already discussed, but a handful of earlier works drew attention to African responsivity to market opportunities in the period under review. H. M. Robertson's pioneer article merits great respect; it is bold in scope and a model of clarity in execution. S. T. Van der Horst and D. M. Goodfellow also provide valuable insights into the nature and timing of African economic responses.[32]

Building upon these foundations, this book argues that there was a substantially more positive response by African peasants to economic changes and market opportunities than is usually indicated; that an adapted form of the prevailing subsistence methods provided hundreds of thousands of Africans with a preferable alternative to wage labour on white colonists' terms in the form of limited participation in the produce market; that a smaller group of black farmers made considerable adaptations, departing entirely from the traditional agricultural economy and competing most effectively with white farmers. The transition from tribesman to peasant saw a breakdown of customary redistributive tenets and institutions (although of course not their complete disappearance) and the emergence of new patterns of behaviour and social relations amongst peasants. The formation of a peasant class was accompanied by social differentiation among its members and a portion of the peasantry was rapidly proletarianized. The transition from tribesman to peasant – or the positive response by Africans to market opportunities – is the starting point of the investigation, but it should be clear that this could hardly be studied without reference to the subsequent checking, or failure, of that response. One is also involved with explaining the transition from peasant to proletarian. In its narrative chapters, this book indicates the chronological and spatial incidence of a characteristic early prosperity in the peasant response, as well as the nature and timing of the subsequent decline, or blunting, of that response. Implicit in these concerns is a dissatisfaction with dualism theory as an explanation of Southern Africa's history, and a reluctance to project into the past the underdevelopment and disabilities of a particular region or sector of the contemporary economy. It will be argued that the underdevelopment which occurred in African peasant regions is historically related to the development of the capitalist economy in the form which it took in South Africa.

To understand the nature and the extent (and the limits) of the transition from tribesman to peasant, it is essential to have some idea of the precolonial mode of production of those African agriculturists who became peasants. The next section of this chapter is therefore devoted to a brief account of the precolonial agricultural economy of the Cape Nguni.

2 THE AGRICULTURE AND ECONOMY OF THE CAPE NGUNI

While there were variations in the structure and organization of the different Nguni states, the 'Cape Nguni exhibit a picture of considerable cultural homogeneity'[33] which permits a fairly general description of their agricultural and economic organization. In details of crops and herds, agricultural techniques and resources, the division of labour and the extent and nature of extra-agricultural activities, there was a broad similarity amongst the major groupings of the Cape (or southern) Nguni: namely the Xhosa (sub-groups Ngqika, Gcaleka, Ndlambe), the Thembu, the Mbo (sub-groups Mpondo, Mpondomise, Xesibe, Bomvana), and later immigrant groups such as Bhaca, Mfengu, Hlubi and Qwati.³⁴ Some of what follows is equally applicable to other Southern Bantu-speaking peoples, including the northern Nguni and the Sotho-Tswana peoples, although these latter differed from the Nguni not only in aspects of their kinship system but also in certain respects of their economic organization.

The description that follows of the agricultural practices of the African inhabitants of what are today the Ciskei and Transkei is not historical, but is located at a non-specific point in time (which would vary from place to place) prior to the major impact of the colonial economy. Ideally a description of the agriculture and economy of precolonial Nguni societies would constantly indicate shifts in resources, technology, products and methods, and would relate these to the social and political sources of change such as fission, clan formation, migrations, population growth and military conflict. To cite no other examples, a satisfactory account of precolonial agriculture would describe the arrival and uneven spread of maize as a major grain crop, or the manner in which the workings of a redistributive economy were affected by the range in scale or size of the clans at different times. Failing this, it is acknowledged that a description of the type undertaken below is in danger of presenting a static or synchronic view; in mitigation of this shortcoming the plea is entered that its presence should not be taken to imply that Cape Nguni societies were static or lacking in internal dynamics of change.

By 'tribal societies' anthropologists and economists seek to give a general description to certain communities (also called 'primitive societies', 'pre-literate peoples' and so on). Tribesmen are distinguished from the simpler hunters who preceded them; and tribes are crucially distinguished from more highly organized sócieties (including peasant societies) by the absence of the state. 'The tribal condition ... is transcended at the moment a state apparatus is differentiated from and imposed upon society at large'. Tribes range from segmentary groups (socially and politically fragmented, economically undiversified and very modestly endowed) to tribes under chiefs, a 'development ... towards integration of the segmentary system', and one that anticipates statehood.³⁵

The Cape Nguni were tribesmen of the latter sort, with rudimentary state apparatuses fairly clearly articulated. Politically, they were arranged in lineages, clans and chiefdoms (it is possible to think of these as a series of concentric circles, with the extended family at the core). Observance of hierarchy and political obligations in tribal society are largely conterminous with kinship. The Nguni, typically, were socially ordered by kinship ties: property rights and the social relationships of the individual were determined by his membership of a particular, permanent kinship group.

Sahlins reminds one that the 'tribal economy' is not strictly separable from the social and political arrangements of tribal societies; that the economy is 'embedded' in such generalized institutions as families and lineages; that kinship and chieftainship regulate economic functions such as the accumulation and distribution of goods. Epigrammatically, 'in tribes, production, polity, and piety are not as yet separately organized, and society not as yet a holy alliance of market, state, and church'.[36] Nevertheless it is possible at a level of abstraction to define a tribal economy – as, indeed, Sahlins has done elsewhere:

> In primitive economies, most production is geared to use of the producers or to discharge of kinship obligations, rather than to exchange and gain. A corollary is that *de facto* control of the means of production is decentralized, local, and familial in primitive society. The following propositions are then implied: (1) economic relations of coercion and exploitation and the corresponding social relations of dependence and mastery are not created in the system of production; (2) in the absence of the incentive given by exchange of the product against a great quantity of goods on a market, there is a tendency to limit production to goods that can be directly utilized by the producers.[37]

Dalton defines a 'primitive economy' within a different analytical framework and with different emphases, but makes essentially the same points. In such an economy, he says, market exchange transactions are absent or negligible; no appreciable amounts of land or labour are hired or sold. The distinctive feature is the pervasive social control of production and distribution, and the guarantees of subsistence livelihood through resource allocation and the rights – enforced through kinship – to receive aid in time of need.[38]

Production in tribal society, then, is a domestic function; the family is the productive unit. This does not necessarily imply totally self-sufficient family units, or totally self-contained work units: a family may depend marginally upon exchange for certain goods and labour will be expended collectively upon certain occasions. Nevertheless, production within the tribal economy is principally organized by and for the family. It is the family household that organizes the growing and sharing of food, its processing and its storage; its members decide how much land to cultivate, and labour for cultivation is drawn from the various members of the family for different purposes. To express this in another way: the division of labour is not *between* families, but *amongst* the members of a family; it is based primarily upon the sexual division in each family.

15

As indicated, trade and production for a market play only a very limited part in the tribal economy; and so specialization or craft production are almost wholly absent. Production is essentially production to meet consumption needs. The low level of the social division of labour means that the society is unlikely to accumulate much surplus. The growth of the surplus product beyond narrow limits – beyond the immediate reserves of the family or clan – is not the result of an independent development of the tribal economy. It results from the intervention or penetration of outside pressures, either economic (in the form of exchange and market relations) or political (the demand for tribute by a dominant group outside tribal society).[39]

Reference has been made to the reallocation of resources through kinship links and by the chief. The existence of certain redistributive tenets and mechanisms was a crucial feature of tribal economies. (Legassick has even characterized the precolonial economy in South Africa as a 'redistributive mode of production'.)[40] Kinship obligations are expressed in a series of traditional duties, such as support for the ailing, the aged or the indigent within a clan; kinship ties are the channels for the redistribution of resources from haves to have-nots. They powerfully reinforce the egalitarian and non-stratified nature of tribal society; they are ordained and expressed through custom, religious beliefs and tribal affiliation.

Even more central to the redistributive aspects of tribal society is the economic role of the chief. Sahlins principally calls redistribution by the chief 'the economic basis' of tribal society; a chief's allocation of resources is 'at one stroke an act of positive morality and a laying of indebtedness upon the underlying population'; redistribution is 'chieftainship said in economics'.[41]

Nguni society, it will become apparent, is adequately subsumed within this general type of 'tribal economy' although it must be noted that efficient exploitation of varied local resources made possible the production of a certain surplus over and above the subsistence needs, permitting rather fuller development of local trade and of a state apparatus than in the ideal type outlined above. The Cape Nguni were Iron Age tribesmen with a mixed subsistence economy; they were pastoralists-cum-hoe-cultivators at a modest technological level and at a relatively undifferentiated level of economic activity. The details that follow are of their agricultural and pastoral techniques and methods, of the organization of the homestead, of the sexually based division of labour, the patterns of land ownership and those institutions inhibiting private accumulation.[42]

The Cape Nguni belonged to clans made up of a number of lineages whose members claimed descent from a common ancestor and did not inter-marry. New clans were formed by fission, usually as a result of a dispute between (half) brothers. Members of a clan owed political allegiance to the chief of the clan; in their turn clans were grouped in loose subordination to a dominant or paramount chief. By chiefdom, therefore, one means a political unit occupying a defined area under a recognized leader. By the late eighteenth century, the Nguni kingdoms ranged in size from a thousand to perhaps thirty-five thousand people. Centuries of gradual westward movement meant that Nguni peoples occupied much of the broad swathe of territory between the Indian Ocean and the mountain ranges that lie roughly parallel to the coast (the Winterberg, Stormberg and Drakensberg), bounded in the north by the Mzimkulu River and in the south by the Fish River. It was in this southern region, along that hotly disputed shifting 'frontier' between the Winterberg–Amatola front and the sea that the Cape Nguni peoples came into contact successively with the Khoi-Khoi, San and white colonists.

The Nguni clan system interlocks with the ownership of cattle. Nguni tribesmen looked to cultivation to meet some of their subsistence needs and they also hunted the relatively abundant varieties of wild game for food; but much of the distinctive coloration of their existence and identity derived from their role as herders. The possession of herds of cattle – and estimates are that Nguni cattle probably outnumbered the human population by at least two to one – affected the tribal economy, diet, social customs and legal system. The Nguni were expert herdsmen with a loving and detailed knowledge of animal husbandry. Their beasts were eaten only on ceremonial occasions, but the milk that they provided (drunk in various stages of fermentation) formed a major part of the Nguni diet. The security of the Nguni family as an economic unit was bound up with milk-based products; in the existing technological limits crops were more unreliable and more difficult to store than milk-based foodstuffs.

The relatively low level of agricultural production meant that a large proportion of the land occupied by each clan was given over to pasturage for the herds. The care of livestock was strictly confined to male hands. Cattle comprised the tribesman's wealth; they were the medium of exchange, particularly in the form of marriage prestation; the number held affected an individual's social standing (although there were influences that regulated the accumulation of stock, described a little later). Cattle also provided an important source of products for clothing and items of household manufacture; before contact with traders and European goods was established, the Cape Nguni wore hide karosses, supplemented by the skins of goats and game; they fashioned shields and gourds from ox-hide, as well as various articles from the horns.

Less social and economic importance was attached to agricultural production. The division of labour between the sexes meant that tillage – in all its aspects – was commonly entrusted to women.* The men

* But not exclusively. In the case of the Mpondo, Beinart has written that 'the men participated in agriculture long before the introduction of the plough.' (W. Beinart,

cleared new ground and broke up the hard surface; women hoed, sowed, weeded, gathered and threshed the crops. The raising of crops was regarded as a necessary occupation, but one 'inferior' to the raising of cattle. Agriculture nevertheless provided vital elements – bulk and variety – of the Nguni diet; the degree of dependence upon grain or milk or wild produce varied from group to group and altered within groups with the passage of time and shifts of circumstance. Cattle loss, whether through disease or raiding, would reduce the area needed for grazing and permit an increase in agricultural output during the period of rebuilding the herds. The raising of crops had important implications for the relative permanence of settlements and is of special interest in the context of this book as the agricultural base upon which later peasant enterprises rested.

The most important grain crop was sorghum* although it was being supplanted throughout the eighteenth century (and possibly ever since the sixteenth century) by maize (variously described in the literature of the period as Indian corn, corn, mealies, green mealies). Sorghum and maize were planted by the women on the arable lands – the 'gardens' or 'plots' – allocated to the head of each household. The number of lands was basically determined by the number of wives a man had in the polygamous Nguni society; as a rule each wife had her own garden or gardens. The land sown by a household was commonly subdivided according to the crops on it: a typical usage by the late eighteenth century was a plot of three areas, one each for maize and sorghum and a third for other vegetables, tobacco, wild sugar-cane or fruit.

The Cape Nguni practised a form of shifting cultivation, permitting tilled land to regain its fertility through a period of disuse. When (fairly frequently) additional land was required for agriculture a new area would be cleared. As forest lands provided richer yields than grass veldt, 'there is good reason to suppose', writes Monica Wilson, 'that the Nguni [had] long cultivated at the edges of forest or bush, pushing it back and back, and utilizing the ash from the trees that were burned as fertilizer'.[43]

The men assisted in the clearing of land, by using rough axes made by local smiths, as well as by burning. The main tilling instrument was a primitive hoe or pointed spade (Xhosa *ikuba*) shaped out of a hard wood or made of iron. The women used these to loosen the top-soil and also for weeding the lands; they kept the soil soft and moisture-retentive during the growing period by turning the surface. Children assisted in protecting the gardens from birds and animals (herdsmen

'Economic Changes in Pondoland in the Nineteenth Century', ICS, CSP, 7, p. 27.) And see p. 24 below.

---

* Two varieties were raised, distinguished by the amaXhosa as *imfe* and *amazimba* (*amabele*). The correct designation of sorghum appears very rarely in nineteenth- or early twentieth-century sources: it is usually called kaffir corn or millet; the *Oxford History of South Africa* usage is followed in these pages.

took especial care in the crucial summer months to keep the cattle out of cultivated lands) and finally the women reaped and threshed the grain crops. The grain was stored in flask-shaped pits, from which it was taken as needed for grinding or cooking in a number of ways or fermenting. Other traditional crops included pumpkins, gourds, calabashes, melons, wild peas and several varieties of beans, the coco-yam, guavas, mangoes and some citrus. Tobacco, grown in increasing quantities by the end of the eighteenth century, was particularly favoured as a trade item among the Nguni. There was also a range of edible tubers, roots, berries and leaves that were resorted to in times of shortage. In general the Nguni relied less upon cultivation and more upon herding than did the Sotho-Tswana peoples to their north. Nutrition was reflected in social usage and ceremony: in Sotho societies there were gardens set aside for chiefs, upon which all the members of the clan hoed and sowed at the first rains.

Production in Nguni society was mainly for subsistence, but this is not to say that no trade took place in Nguni communities. On the contrary, the exchange of goods between neighbouring chiefdoms, as well as within smaller units, occurred continually although irregularly. There were no formal, fixed markets such as were common farther north in Africa; and no specialization of individuals as traders or dealers in produce. Trading bulked larger in Tswana societies where craftsmen, smiths, tanners and specialist hunters might depend entirely upon their skills to produce exchange commodities, and where economic differentiation made possible life in larger 'urban' agglomerations.

The only significant article for longer-distance trade was ivory. Trade in metal 'must have been small because even iron remained so scarce until the nineteenth century'.[44] Exchange, typically, was in the form of small quantities of medicine, cosmetics, ornaments and tobacco, bartered in return for grain or livestock. By the beginning of the eighteenth century, of course, a slightly larger trickle of trade goods such as cloths, trinkets and metal items came from Cape-based travel-lers and hunter-traders. Certain Nguni peoples, favoured by climate and topography, naturally produced more grain than others; the Mpondo not infrequently produced grain in surplus to their own requirements. (Bain, on a visit in 1829 described Pondoland as the 'granary of the Eastern part of Caffreland', noting that the Mpondo supplied their neighbours with maize and sorghum in return for hides, cattle and beads.[45]) Early accounts reveal that they also received copper rings from tribes farther east in exchange for grain and that they exchanged maize and tobacco with the San for ivory.[46]) Within a Nguni clan, a family that had a corn surplus might part with a few baskets of grain to purchase an axe-head or other metal object; as a rule house-hold objects like baskets, pots, mats, spoons, pestles and so on, were made by their users, although they could be exchanged for food.

19

The primary social unit in Nguni society was the household (all those who recognized a common family head, and who lived in a single settlement or 'kraal' – Xhosa *umzi*). In a polygamous family, each wife had her own garden and grain storage place; thus in a sense each hut with a married woman was the centre of an independent economic unit. At the same time, all the members of the household (the family head, his wives and their offspring, and any other dependent kinsfolk living with them) shared in the produce of the whole *umzi*. The household was the essential unit for the production and consumption of food.[47]

There was in Nguni society a practice that modifies (although it does not in the final analysis conflict with) the characterization of the household as the primary unit of consumption and production: it was the 'work party'. This was a brief period of communal labour on the fields of one household by the members of neighbouring households, in exchange for foodstuffs and beer provided by the recipient of the labour. These work parties were the principal means whereby numbers of people co-operated in the performance of difficult work; they were a principal medium for the investment of human capital in agriculture, and they also served as an occasional alternative grouping for consumption.[48]

In Nguni society, then, men cared for livestock, cleared and broke up arable land, made the frames for the houses and built the animal shelters of wood or stone; the women sowed, tilled, weeded, harvested, threshed and prepared the crops; children were accorded duties as bird-scarers or herders. Labour was family labour. There was little or no specialization or division of labour in agricultural production outside the family unit. Each family possessed roughly equal skills, technical means and access to the means of production. The household was

> the unit to which a chief look[ed] for his revenue. . . . It is the unit as regards land tenure, both of arable and grazing land; it is the unit which co-operates with others in such productive enterprises as building and sometimes field cultivation; it is also the unit which gives feasts, thus effecting a distribution of food over a large area.[49]

Such a system of production operated against sharp economic stratification or the differentiation of the society into classes. A situation of rough egalitarianism was maintained by kinship obligations and by the economic functions of the chief, particularly in relation to land and to cattle. This does not mean, of course, that Nguni society was completely egalitarian or wholly lacking in social gradations. Inequality was, for one thing, structurally determined by age; in addition, 'client' and 'patron' relationships could exist within a kinship network, with dependent groups 'tucked on' to the household in a subordinate position. Moreover, the development of the centralized institutions of rudimentary states clearly meant that Nguni chiefs and paramounts were able to appropriate a certain amount of surplus in the shape of tribute or labour or military service. The rate and methods of appropriation, however, were relatively undeveloped; the emergence of a wealthy aristocracy was 'precluded by the absence of the means to translate formal rights of land allocation into monopoly control, and especially by the social and geographical dispersal of accumulated property' through inheritance patterns.[50]

The principal resource in Nguni society was land, but the relationship between man and land was not purely economic. The members of the society depended upon land not only for subsistence, but also for recognition as members of the social group: the allocation of land to an individual was a badge of his membership of clan or tribe. Land was the communal 'property' of the political community, although property 'rights' *vis-à-vis* other communities were barely defined as long as land was a relatively plentiful resource. Land occupied by a tribe 'belonged to' rather than being 'owned' by the tribe; it was treated as theirs by usage. Within the community property rights were formally vested in the chief: he acted as the allocator of land to his followers. Conversely, it was on his generosity and equity in the distribution of land that his following depended. Once a piece of land had been allocated to a member of the community it was defined in terms of the claims of that particular family's rights of cultivation. Individual *rights* in property were not recognized: individual *usage* was; it was a system of communal ownership, central allocative powers and individual cultivation.

Goodfellow reminds us that it is fallacious to suppose that arable land was ever a 'free good' to members of Nguni societies. Apart from the cost of labour expended in clearing such land, there was the social cost of other activities forgone in preparing the land for cultivation; in addition, part of the 'price' for obtaining land lay in obedience to the chief. There was a strong sense of individual proprietorship towards one's plot of land, strongly implemented by the legal and supernatural sanctions.[51] Arable lands were distinguished from those of neighbours by stretches of common pasturage. Once allocated, arable land was alienable only by dispossession: if a man lost his land he lost his membership in the community.

It has been mentioned that the only form of wealth that could be accumulated was cattle. Here too there was machinery for vesting the wealth in the chief and permitting its redistribution by him. Private ownership of cattle was loosely regulated; at the death of a particularly well-to-do household head, his herds would be redistributed to all his distant matrilineal relatives. This system did not preclude the temporary accumulation of large herds in one man's hands, and particularly in the hands of older men. The institution of 'eating up' operated against the ostentatious accumulation of wealth by an individual and against political ambitions which might accompany such enrichment: 'eating up' saw the confiscation and redistribution of a too wealthy stock-owner's beasts after legal-religious ceremonies.

Having described the externals of Nguni agriculture, an important issue remains: how 'good' or 'bad' were these Africans as food-raisers; how productive, how efficient and how skilled? The question and its answer have obvious implications for the colonial era: the agricultural methods and capacity of the peasantry developed from the methods and productive levels in precolonial society.

The traditional agriculture of Africans in South Africa has had, by and large, a resoundingly bad press; a few examples culled from a great number will convey the tone and content. In the early years of this century we find Maurice Evans, widely quoted as an 'expert' on 'native affairs', quite unequivocal: the 'Abantu are probably the worst cultivators and the most wasteful occupiers of the land in the world', he complained, adding that their lands were 'just scratched with the plough, unmanured, weeded in slovenly fashion, and yielding scanty and irregular crops'.[52] The missionary Bernard Huss, writing on African agriculture, concurred: 'They do but scratch the ground with hoes. When the ground is prepared they scatter seed over the soil quite at random.... The Native is surely the worst cultivator of the soil in the world.'[53] C. T. Loram, an educationist and 'friend of the Natives', mourned that 'it would be difficult to imagine a more haphazard and wasteful method of cultivation than that practised by the Natives'.[54] More recent and more temperate, although scarcely less critical, is de Kiewiet's conclusion: 'Mediaeval agriculture, poor as it was, gave more rest to its soil than did the tilling of the Eastern Frontier. The unscientific and wasteful methods of the natives and the heavy demands which their gardens and their cattle made upon the fertility of the countryside' did violence to the ecology and harm to the economy.[55]

At their crudest, the assorted criticisms of African agriculture amount to little more than a denunciation of 'primitive' and 'barbarous' methods with a heavy stress upon the laziness of its practitioners and a moral disapproval of the allocation of tilling duties to women. At a more sophisticated level, the critiques commonly focus upon the unscientific aspects (the crude tools, absence of rotation, irrigation or fertilization), or on the 'uneconomic' or 'irrational' aspects (reluctance to cull cattle, hostility to innovation, reliance on supernatural beliefs and so on).

Such criticisms are, in a crucial sense, predictable. Built into all of them is a model of what agriculture should be: productive, efficient, rational, enterprising and 'modern'. They are ahistorical in that they fail to appreciate the limits imposed by the prevailing mode of production and the social relations and technological levels that characterized it. Considerations of 'efficiency' must take account of the appropriate technology, scale of production, and individual and communal profit and loss. The absence of a social division of labour made the production of a sizeable surplus unlikely, and there were neither economic nor political pressures in precolonial society towards the production of such a surplus. The relevant question in viewing an agricultural economy is the measure of its proficiency within a particular mode of production, and whether resources were efficiently deployed within the constraints of the physical and social environment.

A society (like the Cape Nguni) that possesses tools of limited range, that does not use animals as a source of labour power, that has little or no control over water storage or irrigation, that has only limited defences against plant and animal diseases, that has modest storage and transport facilities and that raises crops that are basically low in yield[56] does not win its subsistence easily. For such a society to survive and particularly for it to expand, presupposes a full exploitation of available natural resources. It is forty years since Goodfellow pointed out (although even today he is not always heeded) that we should abandon the 'exploded fiction' that the 'carefree nature' and 'natural' improvidence of the African (sanctioned by custom) prohibited the rational and effective disposal of resources in primitive society. As he made clear, Nguni subsistence agriculture absorbed a large amount of labour.[57] Given the limits of the water supply and the prevailing technology, the potentially available labour time within a familial unit of production had to be fully and efficiently deployed in production. The physical environment itself included certain daunting aspects: even the 'better watered eastern third of South Africa and its grass-lands' was subjected to fluctuations in rainfall and to periods of puni-tive drought.[58] South Africa's soils – with a few exceptions, such as the Cape peninsula and the basalt highlands – are sandy and poor in mineral content, easily exhausted, and possessed of a fragile crumb structure that makes them peculiarly vulnerable to erosion by water and wind.

The response to these physical factors by the Cape's African societies was the adoption of a form of shifting cultivation, or 'bush fallow' technique, in which land was cleared, cultivated until its fertility decreased, and then allowed to regenerate fertility through disuse. This was a 'simple and sensible adaptation' to the exigencies of climate and soil.[59] Shifting (or recurrent) cultivation with natural soil regenera-tion possessed a logic of its own, and a modern study of the system argues that in wooded areas (as much of the Transkei and Ciskei were in precolonial times) shifting cultivation was 'the best that could have been devised', and was 'in general well adapted to produce the means of subsistence with the minimum of labour'.[60]

African agriculturists were not as innocent of ideas about tillage as many of their observers decreed. In fact, an impressive corpus of knowledge and technique was deployed at every stage of the agricul-tural cycle. The cycle began with the decision of which land to use for cattle kraals and granaries and which to clear for cultivation ('in selecting which great care is taken').[61] The decision was based on a knowledge of soil-types, with a soil's fertility closely judged according to grasses and other flora found in it. The choice of sowing time was made in conjunction with climatic conditions as well as certain indications of flora and fauna. Amongst Sotho groups studied by Schapera the chiefs 'ensured that operations would be performed at a time which the experienced elders of the tribe knew to be most suitable';[62] it seems highly probable that a similar pooling of expertise was achieved among the Nguni in the form of their reliance upon 'field magic' under the guidance of doctors or priests.

Nor was the sower's relationship with nature as haphazard and as superstitious as was often assumed. On the contrary (and as was necessary for people whose subsistence was so closely bound up with environmental factors) their observation of and knowledge of their surroundings were wide-ranging, subtle and fruitful. A study of the southern Sotho people, the Pedi, contains the following assessment, which could equally be applied to the Cape Nguni:

> Practically every adult person knows the name of all the trees, shrubs, grasses and other plants in their environment, of the insects, birds, and reptiles, and other wild-life. They also know the customs and habits, how they grow and reproduce, and to what uses they can be put. In fact their empirical knowledge of nature closely resembles a science.[63]

Another recent judge of traditional agriculture in Southern Africa, Professor J. Phillips, wrote:

> I have often been impressed with the ecological flair of African pastoralists, cultivators and ... farmers. Without ... formal education and almost invariably without any training in the elements of either science or agriculture, a fairly high proportion of simple rural people shows a remarkable sense of awareness of the suitability of particular localities and soils for specific crops or varieties thereof.[64]

Finally, the conservatism of precolonial societies, the 'weight of tribal practice', was never so restricting as to preclude changes: 'when it is really advantageous or necessary to do so, the people could make considerable adjustment'.[65] The traditional division of labour that allocated land husbandry to women was sensibly amended when livestock was depleted. Thus Boyce, Steedman and Bain commented in the early nineteenth century that agriculture bulked larger in the economy of the Mpondo than in Xhosa or Thembu societies, and that men shared tilling duties with the women.[66] As Beinart has pointed out, they were all describing the pastoral-agricultural balance in the period immediately after the shock of the *mfecane* (see p. 31), in which the Mpondo experienced heavy cattle losses.[67] The particular instance of the Mpondo illustrates the general point made earlier: that the precolonial economy was able to shift its balance between the two main sources of subsistence, between agriculture and herding.

In sum, much that was decried as primitive in African agriculture was a rational deployment of prevailing techniques in a relatively inclement climate and soil; much described as inefficient was the provision of subsistence in circumstances of low yield; much that was seen as ignorance was actually based upon experience and an awareness of needs and capabilities. Within the traditional family-based mode of production, African agriculture was rationally directed, informed by experience, and possessed of definite skills, adequate to supply the wants of a society that in any case placed far greater importance in the possession of livestock. Its organization, its tempo and its rewards were related to and inseparable from the social and economic structure of precolonial Nguni society. While aware of the danger of romanticizing the precolonial past, subject as it was to privations, violence and uncertainties, the findings of this section are in accord with a general judgement of precolonial African society made by Simons: 'In spite of their technological backwardness, Africans could cope with their environment, and achieved a fair amount of security against famine, disease, disorder and aggression'.[68]

To conclude: the Nguni peoples prior to the colonial era practised an Iron Age subsistence economy of mixed pastoralism and agriculture, with marginal internal trade. Their societies were based on a familial mode of production, with little social division of labour and limited production of a permanent surplus. Kinship and chieftainship provided the social basis for the redistribution of wealth and the allocation of the means of production. A continual disposal of the material product maintained a working economic equilibrium of the society, although the increasing development of state apparatuses permitted a greater diversion of surplus. It was this kind of society that was disrupted in the latter half of the eighteenth century, but more especially during the first half of the nineteenth century, by developments on the (then) eastern frontier of the Cape. The Frontier Wars were the intensified and violent expressions of a much lengthier process of competition for land, resources and labour power. One aspect of that disruption, and of the competition, was the creation through economic and political forces of a new character in the *dramatis personae* of the Cape: the African peasant. In subsequent chapters he takes his place in the centre of the stage.

NOTES

1 C. W. de Kiewiet, 'Social and Economic Developments in Native Tribal Life', *Cambridge History of the British Empire*, VIII (Cambridge, 1936),

811. Cf. W. M. Macmillan, *Bantu, Boer and Briton: The Making of the South African Native Problem* (Oxford, 1963, revised edition, originally 1929), ix–x, 74–5.

2 Macmillan, op. cit., 74; de Kiewiet, op. cit., 812, 819.

3 C. W. de Kiewiet, *The Imperial Factor in South Africa* (Cambridge, 1937), 150; *A History of South Africa: Social and Economic* (Cambridge, 1941), 197; K. W. Hancock, *Survey of Commonwealth Affairs*, Vol. II, 'Problems of Economic Policy, 1918–1939', Part 2 (London, 1942), 25, 71, 17.

4 For Hobart Houghton's writings on reserves and the dual economy see his *Some Economic Problems of the Bantu in South Africa*, South African Institute of Race Relations Monograph Series No. 1 (Johannesburg, 1938); *The Economy of a Native Reserve*, Vol. 2 of the Keiskammahoek Rural Survey (Pietermaritzburg, 1952); (ed.) *Economic Development in a Plural Society* (Cape Town, 1960), esp. 11; *The South African Economy* (2nd edition, Cape Town, 1967), 70–1 *et passim*; 'Economic Development in the Reserves', *Race Relations Journal*, 29 (January 1962).

5 R. Palmer and N. Parsons (eds.), *The Roots of Rural Poverty in Central and Southern Africa* (London, 1977), 4.

6 K. B. Griffin, *Underdevelopment in Spanish America* (London, 1969), 21. For a classic exposition of dualism theory see W. A. Lewis, *Economic Development with Unlimited Supplies of Labour* (Manchester, 1954).

7 D. Hobart Houghton, *The Economy of a Native Reserve*, 2–3, and 'Economic Development in the Reserves', 10–11.

8 N. N. Franklin, *Economics in South Africa* (Cape Town, 1948), 83.

9 M. Wilson, 'The Growth of Peasant Communities', OHSA, II, 55.

10 T. Shanin, 'Peasantry: Delineation of a Sociological Concept and a Field of Study', *European Journal of Sociology*, XII (1971), 289, 290.

11 K. Post, 'Peasants and Pundits', *European Journal of Sociology*, XIII (1972), 337.

12 A. L. Kroeber, *Anthropology* (Chicago, 1948), 284.

13 R. Redfield, *Peasant Society and Culture* (Chicago, 1956), 46–70; *The Primitive World and its Transformation* (Ithaca, N.Y., 1953), 40.

14 K. Post, '"Peasantization" and Rural Political Movements in West Africa', *European Journal of Sociology*, XIII (1972), 225–6.

15 E. Wolf, *Peasants* (Englewood Cliffs, 1966).

16 ibid., 3–4, 9, 10, 11 (emphasis in original).

17 Shanin, 'Peasantry', 294–6.

18 Post, '"Peasantization"', 223 and footnote 1; 233, footnote 28.

19 L. Fallers, 'Are African Cultivators to be called "Peasants"?', *Current Anthropology*, II (1961), 108–10.

20 G. Dalton, 'The Development of subsistence and peasant economies in Africa', *International Social Sciences Journal*, XVI, 3 (1964), 379.

21 J. Middleton, *The Effects of Economic Development on Traditional Political Systems in Africa South of the Sahara* (Surveys of Research in the Social Sciences, Vol. VI), (The Hague, 1966), 14.

22 J. S. Saul and R. Woods, 'African Peasantries', in T. Shanin (ed.), *Peasants and Peasant Societies* (Harmondsworth, 1971), 104.

23 ibid., 106–7.

24 Post, '"Peasantization"', 228.

25 Wilson, OHSA, II, 49, 50–51, 54.

26 ibid., 67; S. Trapido, 'South Africa and the Historians', *African Affairs*, Vol. 71, No. 285 (October 1972), 445.
27 Wilson, OHSA, II, 54.
28 Shanin, 'Peasantry', 298–9.
29 Saul and Woods, op. cit., 107.
30 Post, '"Peasantization"', 227.
31 B. Galeski, *Basic Concepts of Rural Sociology* (Manchester, 1972), 110–11.
32 H. M. Robertson, '150 Years of Economic Contact between Black and White', *South African Journal of Economics*, 2, 4 (December 1934) and 3, 1 (March 1935); S. T. Van der Horst, *Native Labour in South Africa* (London, 1942), esp. 103–5; D. M. Goodfellow, *A Modern Economic History of South Africa* (London, 1931).
33 W. D. Hammond-Tooke, 'The "other side" of frontier history: a model of Cape Nguni political progress', in L. Thompson (ed.), *African Societies in Southern Africa* (London, 1969), 235.
34 For more systematic discussion of the southern Nguni see: S. Marks and A. E. Atmore, 'The Problem of the Nguni', in D. Dalby (ed.), *Collected Papers of the London Seminar on Language and History in Africa* (London, 1970), 120–33; N. J. van Warmelo, *Preliminary Survey of the Bantu Tribes of South Africa*, Dept. of Native Affairs Ethnological Publications, Vol. 5 (Pretoria, 1935); M. Wilson, 'The Early History of the Transkei and Ciskei', *African Studies*, 18, iv (1959); 'The Nguni People', OHSA, I, 75–130; J. H. Soga, *The South-Eastern Bantu* (Johannesburg, 1931); W. D. Hammond-Tooke, *The Bantu-Speaking Peoples of South Africa* (London, 1974: 2nd ed., revised, of I. Schapera (ed.) *The Bantu-Speaking Tribes of South Africa*).
35 M. D. Sahlins, *Tribesmen* (Englewood Cliffs, 1968), 15, 20.
36 ibid., 74, 75–87, 15.
37 Sahlins, 'Political Power and the Economy in Primitive Society', in *Essays in the Science of Culture*, ed. by G. E. Dole and R. L. Carneiro (New York, 1960), quoted by Wolf, op. cit., 3.
38 Dalton, 'Development of Subsistence and Peasant Economies', esp. 387 ff.
39 For a discussion of the concept of surplus and of its limitations within primitive societies see E. Mandel, *Marxist Economic Theory* (London, 1968), 26–63.
40 M. Legassick, 'South Africa: Capital Accumulation and Violence', *Economy and Society*, 3, 3 (August 1974), 288.
41 Sahlins, *Tribesmen*, 87.
42 The description of Nguni pastoralism and agriculture is derived from a number of secondary sources, some of which treat the subject more fully than is possible here. Important modern works include Wilson, OHSA, I, 75–130; M. Hunter, *Reaction to Conquest* (London, 1936); I. Schapera, 'Economic Changes in South African Native Life', *Africa*, 1, 2 (April 1928), 170–88. Nineteenth-century accounts include: J. Barrow, *An Account of Travels into the Interior of Southern Africa* (London, 1801); S. Kay, *Travels and Researches in Caffraria* (London, 1833); J. Maclean, *A Compendium of Kafir Laws and Customs* (Mount Coke, 1858); W. C. Holden, *The Past and Future of the Kaffir Races* (London, 1866).

43 Wilson, OHSA, I, 110.
44 ibid., 114.
45 *Journals of Andrew Geddes Bain*, ed. by M. H. Lister (Cape Town, 1949), 104, footnote.
46 Hunter, *Reaction to Conquest*, 134.
47 See Schapera, 'Economic Changes'.
48 D. M. Goodfellow, *The Principles of Economic Sociology: The Economics of Primitive Life as Illustrated by the Bantu Peoples of South Africa* (London, 1939), 242.
49 ibid., 145–6.
50 R. Moorsom, 'Underdevelopment and Class Formation: The Origins of Migrant Labour in Namibia, 1850–1915', in *Perspectives on South Africa*, ed. by T. Adler (Johannesburg, 1977), 24.
51 Goodfellow, *Principles of Economic Sociology*, 76–8, 217, 230.
52 M. S. Evans, *Black and White in South East Africa* (London, 1916), 131.
53 B. Huss, 'Agriculture among the Natives of South Africa', *International Review of Missions*, XI, 42 (April 1922).
54 Quoted in J. T. Jabavu, *The Black Problem* (Lovedale, n.d.), 101.
55 De Kiewiet, *The Imperial Factor*, 150.
56 Middleton, *Economic Change in Sub-Saharan Africa*, 1–4.
57 Goodfellow, *Principles of Economic Sociology*, 11–12, 237.
58 N. Pollock and S. Agnew, *An Historical Geography of South Africa* (London, 1963), 16.
59 ibid., 14.
60 P. H. Nye and D. J. Greenland, *The Soil under Shifting Cultivation*, 134, quoted in B. Davidson, *The Africans* (London, 1969), 65.
61 W. C. Holden, *The Past and Future of the Kaffir Races*, 228; cf. Kay, *Travels and Researches*, 86, 143, for similar observations.
62 Schapera, 'Old Bantu Culture', in *Bantu-Speaking Tribes*, 12.
63 H. O. Monnig, *The Pedi* (Pretoria, 1967), 147.
64 J. Phillips, 'Could Traditional Agriculture in Southern Africa be Modernised?', unpublished paper (originally a series of broadcast lectures).
65 Goodfellow, *Principles of Economic Sociology*, 238.
66 W. B. Boyce, *Notes on South African Affairs* (Grahamstown, 1838, reprinted Cape Town, 1971); *Journals of A. G. Bain*, 104; A. Steedman, *Wanderings and Adventures in the Interior of Southern Africa*, 2 vols. (London, 1835), I, 282.
67 W. Beinart, 'Economic Change in Pondoland in the Nineteenth Century', ICS, CSP, 7, 26–8.
68 H. J. Simons, *African Women* (London, 1968), 15.

2

Early Peasants:
The Cape Before 1870

1 FRONTIER TRADE

In a study devoted primarily to the economic status of white colonists upon the Cape's frontiers, Neumark has demonstrated that the initial entry of African pastoralist-cultivators into the market economy established at the Cape peninsula and ramifying north and east into the South African interior, was by trade.[1] There are indications that trade in cattle between Africans and colonists (outside, that is, the formally permitted trade by the monopolistic merchant-butchers) went on intermittently through the eighteenth century: hunter-traders and farmer-traders amongst the Dutch colonists exchanged beads, buttons, knives, arms and ammunition for cattle. During the second half of the century, there was a great expansion in the demand for meat, and this promoted a more frequent bartering of cattle by Africans.

Because cattle have a limited rate of reproduction, and because of the particular part played by cattle in Nguni society, the relative number of cattle voluntarily disposed of by tribesmen was probably never very large; certainly, the demand for European merchandise was to be met by the exchange of other products as well as livestock. The hides and horns of cattle were an important trade commodity; others were products of the hunt (especially ivory), as well as certain natural uncultivated items like gum arabic and timber. Even if trade of this nature was in the long term carried out on terms unfavourable to the tribesmen,[2] in the short term it seemed to pose no threat to their political, social and economic well-being. By disposing of what were not vital resources – and it is significant that the voluntary trade in cattle diminished with the passage of time – the pastoralist-cultivators were able to accumulate those items of a technologically advanced society that they desired; they were able to enter the exchange economy without affecting the basic material structure of their own society. In other words, participation in trade at this limited and discretionary level did not affect their mode of production nor the economic organization of their society. While the Cape was under Dutch control it was only in the Zuurveld (later the Eastern Province district of Albany) in the 1780s and 1790s that substantial political and economic pressures were put upon Nguni societies by white colonists:

the contest for land and resources was mainly directed against the Khoi and San; imported and 'apprenticed' slaves provided much of the labour supply.

When the Cape fell under British control, with the abolition of the mercantilist monopolies of the Dutch period, with the infusion of British capital and settlers (particularly the growth of colonial population in the Eastern Cape after the 1820 settlement) there was a marked change in the trade between frontiersmen and tribesmen. As indicated, 'for nearly a century before the British took the Cape in 1795, communication between the Xhosa and colonists had been growing'.[3] Skirmishes foreshadowed the large-scale conflicts known as the Frontier Wars; barter preceded the greater economic involvement of the nineteenth century; cattle raids and boundary beacons prefigured the competition over resources and land. Interdicts on trade, restrictions on 'trekking' and the prohibition of employment of Africans by Dutch farmers were all promulgated – and all disobeyed. 'When successive governments – Dutch, British, Dutch and again British – failed to stop interaction they sought to regulate it': trade was established on a formal footing, with regular fairs, and trading licences.[4] Frontier trade passed out of the hands of non-specialist Boer traders into those of professional traders from among the British settlers and of itinerant traders or *smouse*.

In 1817, bi-annual trade fairs were set up at Grahamstown, and for their duration permission was extended to Xhosas to enter the colony to participate. By 1824, the fair was being held thrice weekly, and had shifted to Fort Willshire, on the Keiskamma River, in the heart of the Xhosa Ciskei.[5] Africans were no longer disposing freely of many cattle: Mrs John Ross, a missionary's wife, noted in the mid-1820s that the fairs had seen the price of African produce rise, and that they could 'scarcely get an ox to slaughter without sending to Tambookieland' [Tembuland], although formerly Xhosas had been keen to sell cattle.[6] Stephen Kay, a Wesleyan missionary, commented a decade later that an African would only rarely sell a good cow 'at any price', but 'almost always selects for the market such as are no longer likely to be useful to him, in consequence of age or some other defect'.[7]

By 1830, traders were permitted to journey into 'Kaffraria' (east of the Keiskamma River) independently of the fairs; and only two years later the Annual General Meeting of the Wesleyan Methodist Church in Grahamstown noted that its (white) congregation had been greatly diminished by the departure of many members travelling beyond the colonial borders to trade with Africans. In August 1832, Mrs Ross wrote that there were traders 'all over Caffreland': 'Beads, buttons, brass wire and red clay are the chief articles of exchange for hides, horns and corn.' In 1834, she estimated that there were a hundred traders active in Xhosa territory, although by the following year Kay asserted that there were 200 traders in Kaffraria.[8] Fifteen hundred wagons of produce were taken to the Grahamstown market each year by the early 1830s, and the district of Albany exported over £50,000 of goods a year by 1832. By 1835, when Port Elizabeth was handling £80,000 of export produce, Kay estimated that from £50,000 to £60,000 of this was in goods obtained from Xhosa producers.[9] Kingwilliamstown had become, by the late 1830s, a brisk centre for trade in animal products, gum arabic, and silk (the Xhosa spun silk from cocoons on thorn trees);[10] but while these natural resources continued to bulk large in frontier trade, there was also a growing element of trade in agricultural produce, especially corn and milk. Almost every traveller's account of the 1820s and 1830s makes mention at some point of encounters with Africans who sought to exchange baskets of grain or fruit, or gourds of milk, for goods or (by the mid-thirties) occasionally for currency.

Ordinance 49 of 1828 provided for the entry of Africans seeking work within the Colony, a measure aimed not only at coping with greater demands by white employers, but also reflecting an attempt to control the influx of Africans over the boundary between 'white' colony and 'black' Kaffraria. This influx was due not only to the desirability of manufactured goods, but also because of pressure on Nguni societies (in the Transkei and Ciskei) from the East and North. This sprang from the violent upheaval amongst Bantu-speaking peoples of Southern Africa known as the *mfecane**, a process which began with the development of a powerful military state in Zululand, and which produced a series of conquests, population movements, political realignments and state formations in South, Central, and East Africa.[11] The success of the Bhaca and Mpondo in withstanding Zulu attacks meant that Cape Nguni tribes were saved from dispersal or absorption by their northern Nguni neighbours, but they were recipients of groups of refugees. The impoverished state of these latter, and their considerable numbers, meant an increased pressure on the lands of the southern Nguni at the same time that pressure was emanating from west of the Nguni lands, from the Colony. The *mfecane* provided the Cape with its first regular supply of African labourers.[12]

Roughly conterminous with the replacement of Dutch control by the British administration (and hence with the increased activity in trade, land speculation and production for the market) came the period of frontier warfare and of direct competition between colonists and indigenous African societies for land and resources, a conflict which was also one between two mutually incompatible economic systems. The traditional economy of the Cape Nguni described in Chapter 1 could only persist if expansion did not take place of the market economy of the Cape Colony which was, of course, an extension of the expanding activities and commercial vigour of post-Waterloo British capitalism.

* In Nguni languages *mfecane* and in Sotho *difaqane*, translated variously as 'the hammering', 'the crushing' or 'forced migration'.

The import – export sector of the Cape economy demanded an increased production of agricultural and natural resources in return for an expanded sale of manufactured goods, and the potential producers of agricultural commodities – cattle, wine and (increasingly important throughout the second quarter of the century) sheep – needed a greater labour force. Increased trade, freer access to land (artificially scarce because of the activities of land speculators[13]) and an expanded labour supply would only be forthcoming if the relative self-sufficiency of the Nguni economy were disturbed, if the existing balance were disrupted so as to release cattle, land and labour from their non-commercial employment in Nguni homesteads and villages.

Between 1812 and 1853, while on the one hand military conquest, dispossession and expropriation of territory undermined the political position of the African peoples of the Eastern Province, on the other hand – and simultaneously – their social and economic life was subjected to pressure and penetration. There was a steady growth of the presence of *smouse* and of the network of small country storekeepers or traders, 'backed' by the merchant houses in Cape Town or Port Elizabeth. As the volume of trade by barter increased, so did the volume of agricultural production for export, especially with the growing demand by Britain for South African wool, a spectacular feature of the 1830s and 1840s.[14] The increase in the value of land gave rise to land speculation and the concentration of large holdings of land in white hands. On these lands, too, members of Nguni societies were embroiled in new economic and social relations: the payment of rent-tribute was exacted by white landowners, in kind or in labour. There began to emerge a class of Africans who found access to land (the primary means of production) denied to them, and they – like the Khoi before them – were forced to enter the labour sector of the colonial economy. Others entered service for colonists on a more voluntary basis, for limited periods, sometimes travelling considerable distances.

Before examining the adaptations made by some pastoralist-cultivators and their participation in the emerging capitalist economy of the Cape as peasants, an account is given of two significant elements in the developing political economy of the nineteenth-century Cape: the Mfengu* people and Christian missionaries. Each played a considerable role in the events and processes described in this book.

2 MFENGU AND MISSIONARIES

In 1835, some 16,000 Mfengu made formal entry into the Cape Colony, crossing the Kei River at Governor D'Urban's bidding, and

---

* Referred to almost always in nineteenth-century documents as the 'Fingo' people or the 'Fingoes'. While 'Mfengu', 'Mpondo' and 'Thembu' are used throughout to refer to the peoples concerned, in accordance with approved orthography, I have used the contemporary forms to refer to administrative areas or territories: Fingoland, Pondoland, Tembuland.

under the missionary James Ayliff's watchful eye; this followed earlier, more desperate migrations into southern Nguni territories. The Mfengu were among those Natal Africans displaced by the rise of the Zulu kingdom, who emigrated – sometimes in scattered bands, sometimes in larger homogeneous groups – into southern Nguni lands. Mfengu, drawn mainly from the Hlubi, Bhele and Zizi clans, as well as from smaller units, arrived in the Transkei over a period of several years during the second and third decades of the nineteenth century. Small groups of Mfengu had been entering the Ciskei from as early as the 1820s, but the main body settled in Gcalekaland where they arrived poor in resources, especially in cattle.

The Mfengu entered a client–patron relationship with the Gcalekas, and much has been written that stresses their subordination, ill-usage, and unhappiness among the Gcalekas. Research in recent years[15] has substantially revised the earlier (and mainly missionary-inspired) version. The Mfengu were, in fact, in the process of becoming 'rehabilitated' among the Gcaleka; that is, they were recovering morale and group cohesion, as well as regaining a measure of material prosperity. This latter factor, indeed, seems to have been so pronounced as to have operated against the integrative forces of their clientship, and to have estranged them from the Gcaleka patrons. In particular, the Mfengu while in Gcalekaland appear to have enjoyed considerable freedom of movement in carrying on an extensive trading system. Ayliff and Whiteside describe a trade network that began with Mfengu cultivation of tobacco which was exchanged in neighbouring and even more distant tribes for cattle and coats. Some of the stock was disposed of to buy implements and goods from missionaries and traders, which goods they could employ themselves, or exchange again.[16]

When D'Urban agreed to the settlement of the 16,000 Mfengu (who brought with them 22,000 head of cattle) near Grahamstown, he was candid about his intentions. The 'Fingo community' would supply military support against Hintza, the Xhosa paramount chief; the colony would gain the labour of 'sober, industrious people, well skilled in the tasks of herding and agriculture'; the land in the Peddie district to which they were moved was 'worse than useless' but, he confidently expected, would be turned into a 'flourishing garden' by the newcomers; finally, and this was at the heart of the strategy, the Mfengu would form a human buffer between the colonists and the Xhosa foe.[17]

Several commentators have remarked that the Mfengu responded efficiently, even spectacularly, to the opportunities and incentives of the market economy. Upon their arrival in the Cape, says Moyer, 'their whole existence was guided by the quest for funds'.[18] Having arrived in the colony with a fair number of cattle (noted Robertson), the Mfengu entered agricultural service and by a combination of hard work, parsimony, and concessions 'soon became the chief economic power among the Bantu tribes'.[19] Ayliff and Whiteside are among several

33

nineteenth-century observers of the shrewd bargaining powers of the Mfengu, and dubbed them 'the Jews of Kaffirland'.[20] In the years immediately subsequent to their migration into the colony, Mfengu involvement in the capitalist economy seems to have been largely confined to the role of agricultural labourers on white-owned farms. The men not only served as cattle herds and shepherds, but also engaged in tilling, ploughing, reaping and the like. This experience was very rapidly transformed into agricultural activities on their own behalf: by the 1840s and 1850s the Mfengu were not only selling tobacco, firewood, cattle and milk, but were raising grain in increasing quantities, and disposing of the surplus for cash or stock.

Various explanations have been offered for the receptivity of the Mfengu to economic opportunity. Omer-Cooper argues that 'their early association with the missionaries, their alliance with the British, and the degree to which traditional ways had been undermined by the *mfecane*' meant that the Mfengu 'adopted western ideas much more rapidly than their settled neighbours', the adoptions including new agricultural techniques. Moyer suggests that their very status as 'refugees in a relatively hostile land' provided the Mfengu, while in Gcalekaland, with the motivation and singleness of purpose that permitted accumulation; once in the colony they had the initial advantage of the cattle they had taken from Gcalekaland, as well as greater scope for the acquisition of wealth.[21] A crucial factor seems to have been that the emigrant groups were often bereft of dynastic leadership, their chiefs dead or dispersed. This weakened the sanctions, embodied in allegiance to the chief, against private accumulation of wealth. The more enterprising members of the Mfengu were in an important sense freer to turn their hands to trade and to agricultural enterprise. It is also noteworthy that during their stay with the Gcalekas, Mfengu men were active in tilling and other agricultural duties:[22] this must have made the subsequent adoption in the colony of agricultural pursuits by the men less an innovation than a continuation of a flexibility already exercised.

Once in the colony, the Mfengu were hastened along the path to fuller involvement in a capitalist economy by their close association with the Methodists, a group of missionaries who keenly favoured the spread of peasant agriculture. Service on white farms provided example and experience; wages (frequently paid in cattle) were retained as cattle or invested in farming as sheep, wagons, or tools. Finally, reinforcing those factors that had favoured Mfengu acquisition in Gcalekaland and in the colony, there was the cumulative advantage derived by the community from their role as allies or collaborators with the British in the Cape. The Mfengu did more than serve as a buffer: they were active combatants in the wars of 1846, 1850–53, and 1877–8, on the imperial side.[23] For these services, the Mfengu were rewarded in land. Apart from the original grant in the Ceded Territory (1835), by 1879 the Mfengu had been awarded territory in Victoria

East and Kingwilliamstown districts and in the Wittebergen Reserve (later Herschel district). They were granted the considerable area of 'Fingoland' (the magisterial districts of Butterworth, Nqamakwe, and Tsomo in the Transkei), amounting to 45 per cent of the former Gcaleka territory, as well as areas in Tembuland and East Griqualand. In addition to these 'communal' grants, individuals and smaller groups of this highly mobile people were found in every frontier town and on small holdings on mission stations and elsewhere, in trade, transport and agricultural enterprises. In addition to the material gains that accrued from collaboration with the colonial power, there was also a cultural flow of values and ideas; most of the earliest instances of individual land tenure were recorded amongst Mfengu.*

A single episode illustrates the extent to which the Mfengu had shifted the balance of their economic activities from pastoralism in favour of agriculture, the manner in which they had broken with their African neighbours and how far they operated in union with the administration, and their promptness in turning circumstances to their own economic advantage. At the time of the cattle-killing in 1857 (*see* pp. 49–51 below) the Mfengu did not act upon Nonquase's prophecy, and when the opportunity to buy Xhosa cattle at reduced prices presented itself, they seized it. After the slaughter, when famine and death fell upon the Xhosa, and the Cape government was impelled to institute relief feeding, the Mfengu response was brisk and profitable: 'As the Fingoes are a very thrifty people . . . and the prices being so high they were induced to sell extensively. In the past sowing season a much greater extent of ground has been broken up,' wrote John Ayliff from Healdtown in 1858. He calculated that the Mfengu in Fort Beaufort district had raised 30,000 bushels of corn (or double their own requirements) and that they had sold 15,000 bushels to the government commissariat and to traders 'to supply the wants of the starving multitudes'.[24]

Ayliff's approbation of the Mfengu response introduces another topic that runs throughout this book: the relationship between missionaries and missions on the one hand and the spread of peasant enterprise amongst the Nguni peoples on the other. The role of the missionary as standard-bearer for the commercial economy and western manners was one which missionaries themselves were not slow to point out, and they left no doubts as to the over-riding influence of missionary endeavour, precept and enterprise: 'These stations were centres of trade and improved agriculture. The first plough that turned

* Once their standing and relative prosperity had been secured, another way in which the Mfengu could consolidate their power was by assimilating other groups of Africans; in 1856 in the Fort Beaufort district, Kona (a son of Maqomo) asked the Mfengu to 'give him land so that he might settle among them and he and they become one people'. (Cape Archives, G. H. 8/48, *Letters from Native Chiefs and Others, 1854–1884*, Extract from the Chief Commissioner's Report, 30 September 1857, on Conduct of Chiefs of British Kaffraria.)

up soil north of the Kei was guided by the hands of a Wesleyan missionary. The first store opened in Kaffirland for the sale of clothing and agricultural implements was at Wesleyville.' And in the same vein, 'the first cotton grown in South Africa ... the first waggon ... the first European type of house ... the first tilled lands and gardens' in Kaffraria were Methodist.[25] More recently, an essentially similar assessment has appeared in the *Oxford History of South Africa*; missionaries take the credit for the establishment of an African peasantry: 'Peasant communities, in the sense in which the term is used in this book, began in 1783 with the foundation of the first mission station in South Africa. ... Peasant communities began around mission stations.'[26]

In this, as in later chapters, it will be seen that there was a correlation between missionary activity and the spread of African peasant agriculture; that 'stations' or 'schools' served as foci of social change. It will also be argued, however, that other important factors operated independently of the 'missionary factor' in prompting and dispersing peasant activity, and that missionary enterprise was not the *sine qua non* of a peasantry that Professor Wilson suggests. One obvious alternative source for the technological knowledge that missionaries offered was work on the land of secular employers. There were also important transmissions of ideas, methods, motives and opportunities from one African community to another: to cite in advance only one of the examples that will be mentioned later, an important side effect of the 1866 migration of 30,000 Mfengu into the Transkei was the 'percolating' effect of their agricultural pursuits into neighbouring tribes. Peasant skills and values were spread through a variety of non-missionary agents and channels: these included chiefs and other individuals, a variety of tenurial systems and other changes in economic and social relations.

The transmission of skills from missionaries to Africans was not the one-sided process that mission (and other) sources suggest: there was present, in varying degrees at different times and places, an active decision by Africans (individually or collectively) to partake of new skills, implements or life styles. What were hailed in the vigorous ecclesiastical press of the day as 'missionary successes' might justifiably be described in retrospect as 'African successes', in that the initial decision to invite the missionary and the subsequent cultural adaptations were conscious and deliberate choices by chiefs, clans or individuals. Anglican missionaries regarded it as quaint proof of the backwardness of the 'native mind' when chiefs welcomed mission schools, with the stipulation that reading, writing and manual skills be offered, but that religion be strictly excluded from the syllabus; yet viewed in terms of the threat that Christianity posed to the religious and political authority of the chiefs, and of the visible benefits accruing from a lay education, this was a discerning attempt by traditional African leadership to channel western education along selected lines.[27]

Two linked features of the missionary presence in African societies are worth emphasizing: first, the role of the missionaries as torch-bearers of capitalist social norms and the market economy, as advocates of increased trade and commercial activity, and secondly, their contribution to class formation in African society. Missionary enterprise, ultimately, was concerned to transform social institutions and practices that were alien or incompatible with capitalist society into ones that were compatible, and hence to encourage a total change in the world-view of the people in whose midst they lived. As far as the extension of commerce is concerned, Professor Wilson has written that in South Africa trade 'was welcomed by missions but did not arise from them'.[28] This seems a less than satisfactory proposition; it understates the very close connection between missionary advocacy of 'civilization' and 'modernization' and trade. It overlooks the expression of an explicit and consistent missionary ideology in the nineteenth century, in terms of which the mission societies and their most influential spokesmen sought consciously to restructure African societies along lines that would attach them securely to the British capitalist economy. Missionaries should 'make a combined effort to effect a social revolution', exhorted the editor of the *Kaffir Express*: the same missionary publication had spelled out the links between the civilizing mission and trade a little earlier. Why encourage Africans to live in square houses? the paper asked; and it answered its query thus:

> with a proper house, then comes a table, then chairs, a clean table-cloth, paper or whitewash for the walls, wife and daughters dressed in clean calico prints, and so forth.... The church-going Kaffirs purchase three times as much clothing, groceries, and other articles in the shops as the red Kaffirs; but with a change in their habitations the existing native trade would soon be doubled.[29]

The missionary's insistence on European dress, his propensity for measuring civilization in terms of the consumption of manufactured goods, his zeal for square houses* and so on, all indicate a more potent link between the missionary and the trader than Monica Wilson allows.

* The frequency of references in missionary correspondence and publications to the superiority of square over round dwellings is striking – descriptions of square houses in straight streets ring with pride – and I was amused to find in the *Kaffir Express* of May 1875 an article on 'Social Reform among the Kafir People' earnestly suggesting an intermediate stage between round and square buildings: 'a new form of hut, oblong and rounded at the ends'. Recently Kate Crehan has explored what seems at first glance an almost mystical preference for an angular life style. She relates the preference to 'certain key elements of capitalist society' (the notions of private property, the individual as the basic unit of society, and the nuclear family), and argues that the 'African house expressed values that were quite alien to those that the missionaries saw as so crucial. It did not cut nuclear families off from one another, privacy within it was virtually impossible, it did not manifest the owner's industriousness', nor did it mirror the notions

As far as missionaries and class formation are concerned, it is clear that missionaries set out consciously and actively to promote economic differentiation and the formation of social classes, and that the mission stations provided auspiciously positioned vantage points, or pioneer columns, in this process. The strategy for ensuring conversions in 'savage' lands involved an explicit need to 'tame', to alter such societies to a degree whereby their members would be receptive to the Gospel as well as to the benefits of western civilization. Only by restructuring African societies in the rough likeness of their own European society could the necessary links be forged that would attach the African community securely to the Home Country, and permit all the benefits of religious, economic and social intercourse to flow between the two. From the conjunction of these processes – the establishing of the cash nexus and the restructuring of 'savage' society – missionaries believed that a whole constellation of beneficial results would flow. These were: a stimulated demand for the consumption of British goods, the increase of commerce, of civilization and of learning, the spread of Christianity and the defeat of heathenism, polygamy, and barbarism – in short, the extension of British control, protection, culture, economy, religion and language.

It is not that missionaries were hypocritical or Machiavellian in their easy identification of the virtues of Christianity with the virtues of the British Empire: empire and the sway of the church were seen as two sides of the same coin. Duty and self-interest coincided.

The story of the establishment in the nineteenth century of missions amongst the Southern Nguni is available in considerable detail elsewhere.[30] Of particular note were the 'chain of stations' established by the Methodists in the Ciskei and Transkei by 1840, the missions of the Scottish societies in the Ciskei and western Transkei, and the later, vigorous exertions by Anglicans in the late 1850s and afterwards. From the earliest mission establishments, evangelical labours were seen within the context of a civilizing mission, that is, the introduction of western values and relationships into pre-capitalist societies. Social reform, suggests Ajayi, is implicit in the teaching of any new religion, but was present especially in the nineteenth century when missionaries saw Christianity and civilization as interdependent and inseparable goals.[31] The doyen of South African missionaries, the Rev. John Philip, wrote to the Lieutenant Governor of the Cape in 1820, outlining very clearly the secular and economic tactics and strategy of missionary endeavour:

---

of social order and hierarchy as did square buildings. ('The Leaves and the Tree: the ideology and practices of the early LMS missionaries', unpublished paper, African History Seminar, Manchester University, 1977.)

Tribes in a savage state are generally without houses, gardens, and fixed property. By locating them on a particular place, getting them to build houses, enclose gardens, cultivate corn land, accumulate property, and by increasing their artificial wants, you increase their dependency on the colony, and multiply the bonds of union and the number of securities for the preservation of peace.[32]

The championship of fixed settlements, of the sale of farm produce and of the purchase of 'artificial wants' are the keynotes to all subsequent nineteenth-century mission practices; Philip's argument that the resultant integration of 'tribes in a savage state' into the colonial economy would bring stability and peace remained the major single secular justification in missionary writings for the rest of the century.

Philip also gave expression to another central tenet in missionary ideology: that by 'scattering the seeds of Civilization' missionaries would extend British trade, influence and Empire:

Wherever the missionary places his standard among a savage tribe, their prejudices against the colonial government give way; their dependence upon the colony is increased . . . confidence is restored; intercourse with the colony is established; industry, trade, and agriculture spring up; and every genuine convert . . . becomes the friend and ally of the colonial government.

He also specified that 'a more liberal system of policy' towards the Khoi and the Africans would make them more productive farmers, better customers of manufactured goods, reliable tax payers and willing labourers.[33]

But how were these devoutly wished for consummations to be achieved, and what particular weight did the missionaries attach to farming? In South Africa, as in Nigeria, 'it was not so much agriculture that the missionaries considered the civilizing influence, as the commerce which resulted from it'.[34] Agriculture was recommended to the tribesman as a means of producing articles of trade that would link him with Christian Europe. But in South Africa, far more than in Nigeria, there was also pressure upon the governing authorities to impel tribesmen to enter the capitalist economy as labourers.

Missionary ideologues addressed themselves to this problem in South Africa. Philip argued that the abolition of slavery and of the commando system would improve, not worsen, the labour market. He put the case for a workforce freed from coercion other than market forces (they would 'prefer labour, in a state of freedom'): 'allow them to bring their labour to a fair market' and farmers would 'no longer have occasion to complain of the want of servants'.[35] Methodist teaching, especially, favoured the creation of wage-earners and stressed the dignity of labour and desirability of manual skills. W. R. Thompson, first missionary to the Ngqikas, noted in 1819 that it was 'the particular wish of the colonial government to introduce among the natives a knowledge of the useful arts of civilized life, and to train them to habits of industry' and to this end he took with him plough, harrow and spades.[36]

It was not enough merely to accustom black hands to the necessary skills to equip them as labourers; they had also to be induced to supply their labour power to white employers. Here, the ecclesiastical Benthamism of the early nineteenth century is seen in characteristic optimism. The missionary societies desired conversions – and thereto a class of small proprietors, wedded to the cash nexus – and the colonists wanted labourers: missionaries looked to both Providence and the beneficent laws of Political Economy in their attempts to merge these aims. The settled nucleus of 'respectable proprietors' would generate the necessary labour supply, they argued. Explicitly, William Boyce (extremely influential in the Methodist Church in South Africa, and the General Secretary later in the century of the Methodist Missionary Society) stated in 1835 the benefits that would flow from the encouragement of a middle class: its members 'would be attached to the soil by the enjoyment of a property in it', they 'would have a *stake* in the colony, and . . . an *interest* in the execution of the laws framed for the protection of life and property'. They would meet 'the want so much felt, of a class of small proprietors, producing articles of consumption neglected by the more extensive grazing farmers'. Moreover, they

> would furnish a most valuable supply of labourers to the neighbouring farmers, because, consisting of a respectable class of men, the supply could be depended upon, as the cultivation of their own locations would not occupy all the time of the settlers, and they would gladly embrace the opportunity of earning a little ready money at intervals. Under the judicious management of sensible missionaries or lay agents, all the useful and necessary arts connected with rural life might be taught.[37]

Is there something of a hiatus here in the missionary argument? Philip and Boyce do not seem to have considered that members of the land-owning class they envisaged might prefer to seek profits under their own employ rather than as wage labourers. A pronounced shift in emphasis by missionaries towards the need to create a labouring class came later, in the closing years of the nineteenth century (a theme taken up in Chapter 4).

Despite their own confidence and optimism, despite the enthusiasm and funds generated by the evangelical revival, and despite government assistance, the initial success rate of the mission societies was low. By 1850, a total of 16,000 Africans in the Eastern Cape (out of perhaps 400,000) lived on 32 mission stations, and as we shall see, missionaries had good cause to doubt the sincerity and ardour of the convictions of many of these. Particularly between 1836 and 1857, the mission records are a chronicle of abandoned stations, dispersed congregations, despondency and a fair measure of disillusionment. This failure to effect a mass conversion was in part due to the missionaries' own mistakes and to their susceptibility to diseases and death, but more particularly due to the fact that most missionary effort was expended in the area where frontier wars were endemic for half a century, and most of all due to the political resistance of the Cape's Xhosa-speakers and their leaders.

Donovan Williams concentrates upon the conflict between the 'cake of custom' and missionary disapproval of Xhosa customs like polygamy, *lobola*, and so on.* He concludes that it was the missionary attack on Xhosa rites that provoked the hostility of the chiefs in particular and of the Xhosas in general: 'There was a fundamental and unrelenting antagonism which was rooted in the instinctive realization that once rites and customs went, Kaffir society would disintegrate and their own power be nullified'.[38] Evidence in mission sources themselves suggests that African opposition to missionaries sprang indeed from fears that their 'society would disintegrate' and 'their own power be nullified', but that other considerations than the defence of rites, and other modes of apprehension than 'instinctive realization' were in operation.

It was the creation of the mission stations or villages themselves that seems to have been a major factor in transmuting the cautious acceptance by the chiefs into (by and large) overtly hostile resistance. The station settlements dramatized the political, religious and economic threat to the old order, they made conspicuous the political disloyalty of converts, they served as a base for the missionary's assault on rites and social practices, and they meant the physical absence of clan members, the withdrawal of their economic output as well as of their obligations. A chief summed up the challenge posed by the missions succinctly enough in telling Calderwood 'When my people become Christians, they cease to be my people.'[39] Equally to the point was the chief who told a Select Committee in 1851 'I like very much to live with [the missionaries] if they would not take my people and give them to the government.'[40] Missionaries were also resented for their role as 'the eyes and ears of Government'; they participated, and were seen to do so, in the process of annexation and conquest.[41]

Nor did it escape the notice of Africans that the material benefits of mission life might be offset by new obligations and impositions. Traditionalist (or 'red'†) opposition to 'school' practices is typified by the reluctance of the traditionalists to become enmeshed in the novel dues of rent, taxes and other fees which were higher on mission stations

---

* *Lobola*: prestation gift of cattle made at time of marriage by kin of bridegroom to kin of wife.

† Nineteenth-century commentators defined – and social scientists have found it convenient to continue the usage – Africans as 'school' or 'red': 'school' people attended mission schools and wore 'European' clothes; 'red' people had rejected Christianity and continued to anoint themselves with red clay.

than in surrounding areas. As peasants told an African preacher later in the century, 'We are taught two things – the word of the Lord and the payment of rent.'[42] An accurate and sympathetic assessment by a missionary of the political resistance to Christianity came from the Anglican A. G. S. Gibson:

> The natives fear the formation of a mission is the thin end of the wedge, and that they will be forced to give up all their customs (harmless or not), will have their country inundated either with Fingoes (who are very grasping) or with white people, and will eventually come under European laws and administration, which they cannot understand and do not like, and which are in their practical working here inferior to the native government, the general effect of which is good and orderly. The chiefs, on the other hand, fearing to lose their position, not unnaturally do not look with a very favourable eye upon that which they think is the beginning of the end. So that we have in the scale against us the strong influences of personal feeling, patriotism, and conservatism.[43]

Against this defensive reaction, it might appear surprising that the missions won any converts, let alone that they prospered to the extent that they did. There were however powerful secular forces at work that aided evangelization. First, and corollary to the political resistance of some African leaders, there were others who perceived in the missionaries political allies, go-betweens, diplomatic agents and the like. Co-operation with a missionary might assist in coming to terms with external powers such as the British government, Boer republics, or rival kingdoms. Entire communities or clans that were clients, refugees, or in other ways subordinated in the existing political structure, would attach themselves to missionaries (the Mfengu, Thembu, and Barolong all did this).

Apart from such political considerations, at the level of chief or headman, there were other attractions for individual converts. Hutchinson indicated three secular reasons prompting 'conversions': the draw of technological innovations and material goods; the provision by mission stations of access to land (by 1848, title deeds had been issued by the Cape administration to mission stations for 70,000 acres of land, while another 155,000 acres were held by virtue of 'tickets of occupation'); the role of missions as a sanctuary or refuge to those fleeing tribal justice.[44] The political attractions summed up in the third of these categories are complex and manifold. Most simply, sanctuary might be sought by people fleeing from local quarrels or customary law; one missionary observed that 'No Kaffir goes to a station unless he is for some reason an outcast from a kraal, often to escape punishment from his native *inkosi*.'[45] Another frequent instance was the arrival in mission stations of those who sought to evade traditional sanctions against the accumulation of wealth.[46] Africans also moved to mission stations to avoid the threat of political turbulence[47] or the reality of military

42

disruptions. Missionaries recognized – although not always with the exasperated good humour of D. W. Dodd – that conversions could be expedient and temporary:

> My Kaffir guardian, a small chief appointed to assist me in any emergencies that I may fall into with the Red Kaffirs, was accused of witchcraft, and had to flee for his life to the station ... he has since returned to his own place, asserting however that he is still a member of the station, when in reality he is the most troublesome, deceitful old heathen I have to deal with.[48]

Perhaps the most telling comment of all came from the missionary who wrote 'As far as I know, the only people inclined to be Christians are those who despair of their own nation ever becoming anything by itself.'[49]

Nor were the secular lures of mission life only material. Education (and the assistance it gave in coping with the demands of a cash economy and colonial rule) was a powerful magnet: the most common grounds for the unsolicited invitation to a missionary were the need for a school. There was a minor crisis in the Wesleyan Missionary Society in the early 1870s because numbers of Methodist Mfengu were defecting to the Anglican church, whose schools were held to be better as well as cheaper.[50] The missionary's knowledge of medicine and superior building techniques were also powerful attractions. Cultural gains might also be imagined rather than actual: if the missionary could convince Africans that his prayers were more effective in producing rain or ridding the area of locusts than the competing charms of the traditional priest or diviner, he could win new adherents.[51]

Mention of this last point – ground lost by traditional priests or doctors – makes relevant a return to the chronological outline. By 1850 fewer than three dozen stations were the only survivors of fifty years of evangelical effort. In 1857 there occurred the destruction by the amaXhosa of their cattle and crops in response to the urgings of prophets (especially the girl Nonquase) among them, in a desperate attempt to halt or reverse the process of conquest. The aftermath of the cattle-killing was famine and the loss of land, while perhaps 30,000 Xhosa lives were lost. The authority of chiefs and priests was suddenly and drastically reduced, and their loss was the gain of the missionaries. 'From being feeble and despondent Christianity in Kaffirland became aggressive and triumphant'; in 'hitherto untouched areas' a period 'of steady and afterwards rapid expansion began'.[52] An Anglican Bishop at the time was briefer: 'With this, our whole kaffir difficulty vanishes.'[53] By 1884, there were fifty-two stations in the Transkei and about fifty in the Ciskei. Their presence, and their relevance for the peasant response, will be evident in subsequent chapters.

3 INCIDENCE AND DISPERSAL OF PEASANTS: 1840–70

The emergence of peasants was a piecemeal and hesitant process at first. Being described here are adaptations by pastoralist-cultivators who responded to the political and economic pressures sustained by their societies by their forcible integration in the Cape's colonial economy. One is concerned, that is, with those Africans whose response was not cattle raiding, military resistance or flight; whose relations with the newcomers were not confined to the barter of hunt products, and who did not become labourers on land once theirs by ancestral prescription, now owned and policed by whites; who did not lose access to their land and their herds to become perforce herdsmen, porters, roadmakers or domestic servants. The point is not that theirs was a 'better' or more 'rational' response – that they involved themselves in the cash-based economy of the Cape by disposing of a surplus of their produce – but that it was a qualitatively different response, and one that involved its participants in novel political, economic and social relations.

The main features of the period described in this section can be summarized before they are discussed in detail. First, there was a steady spread of agricultural innovation and diversification, frequently but not entirely among mission-oriented peasants. Secondly, the cattle-killing of 1857, together with the dual policy of land expropriation and civilization pursued by Governor George Grey, accelerated the integration of colonial and Xhosa societies, on terms largely of the former's choosing. Thirdly, between the mid-fifties and 1870, the annexation of the Ciskei and the extension of control over large parts of the Transkei brought an increasing number of Africans into ineluctable relations with traders, magistrates and employers. The same forces that pressed some into bondage enabled others to escape; land expropriation during the wars was accompanied by grants to loyalists; the influx of traders into the Ciskei and Transkei was also an index of the increased sales of animal and agricultural products by peasants. Mfengu, Thembu, Gcalekas, Ngqikas, and others demonstrated in the fifties and sixties how effectively peasants could adjust to the new circumstances. In general terms, the adoption of the plough and other implements, of new crops and methods, increased productivity, so that Africans could respond to the imposition of taxes and the desirability of trade goods by disposing of a surplus. The 'labour shortage' that prompted so much complaint by colonists during these years is often attributed to the lack of responsiveness by tribesmen to the opportunities opened by cash wages. Part, at the very least, of this shortage was due to the preference of the land-based African for meeting the new wants by selling his produce, a preference reinforced by his resistance to a qualitative change in his social relations.

Fourthly, even the drastic effects of large-scale land expropriation were cushioned, as the Cape did not possess the coercive instruments, nor its economy the need, to clear all white-owned land of African occupiers. In the absence of a developed commercial agriculture, and with large tracts of land in white hands, land speculators and 'farmers' alike found it more profitable to have black tenants upon their lands. These might be cash tenants (relatively rare before 1870), or they might have paid a tribute in kind, or they might have rendered a certain amount of labour – commonly ninety days in the year – to the owner of the land on which they lived. The leasing of land to Africans for cash or kind was known as 'kaffir-farming', an inelegant phrase that nevertheless conveys accurately the source of non-producing white land-owners' profits. The appropriation of surplus, then, commonly occurred in the form of these quasi-feudal relationships on extensive lands of low cash value, relationships that provided a short-term answer to white labour needs, afforded a rent income to absentee proprietors and permitted the development of a numerically significant sector of the African peasantry, the squatter-peasants.

In the 1840s, it was the Mfengu of the Ciskei (along with the Khoi and mixed race population at the Kat River Settlement[54]) who set the briskest pace in the practice of peasant agriculture. In that decade, we are told, the Peddie Mfengu 'began to cultivate wheat, while in their gardens they grew many of the vegetables that we [colonists] consume. Many of them possess wagons and oxen in which they carry produce to the towns for sale.'[55] Another striking instance of peasant activity in the 1840s, under the aegis of Methodist missionaries, occurred at Farmerfield (near Salem in the district of Albany). Six thousand acres of land were bought by the Society in 1838, divided into lots and let to converts at a fixed annual rental (the aggregate rents covering repayments on the purchase price). Tenants built houses and enclosed lands, and non-rent-paying 'squatters' were firmly excluded. Some of the tenants rose to comparative wealth, and were able to buy, from their agricultural proceeds, wagons and oxen. When Archdeacon Merriman visited Farmerfield in August 1850, he was struck by the amount of land under cultivation, and noticed that there were from thirty to forty wagons on the station. He indicated the extent to which the peasants had entered agricultural production on a commercial basis: 'the natives bring in so much firewood, poultry, and other things to market at Grahamstown, as materially to alter our prices there'.[56]

Although the Mfengu on missions led in numbers, they were not alone; a vivid description exists of an early Ngqika experimenter with plough and irrigation. In 1835 (the diary of one C. L. Stretch informs us) a number of Ngqika led by chiefs Maqomo and Sandile visited Fort Cox, and one of the visiting group, Soga by name, attracted Stretch's attention: 'He began to work and produced peas, onions, barley, and potatoes, which he brought on horseback to Fort Cox, and for which

"Tommy", alias the Redjackets, gave him silver.' By June in the following year Stretch 'inspected a waterfurrow made by Soga' ('the first attempt of the kind by a Kafir' that he knew of) by which 'many acres' of land could be irrigated with water from the Tyhume river and cultivated.[57] Soga was the father of the missionary Tiyo Soga, although he is an early instance of a non-mission peasant.

At Pirie in the Ciskei, peasants on mission stations had been using the plough since 1836, and a few even before the 1835 war. The missionary there indicated in 1848 that plough cultivation beyond the mission was 'rare indeed', but that it did occur. On the station itself, he added, draught cattle were 'reared and purchased for the express purpose of tillage and transport'.[58] At nearby Burnshill, peasants had been growing wheat and barley since 1839.

East of the Kei river in the same decade, mission stations and traders worked their economic alchemy. A visitor to the Wesleyan mission in Butterworth in 1843 left this admiring description:

> The mission premises stood in a conspicuous position and presented a beautiful appearance. Close by was a row of English cottages, after the English style, erected by the natives for their own accommodation. It was gratifying to witness the life that pervaded the village. Some were digging in their gardens, others building habitations, and one man was occupied as a blacksmith at the forge.[59]

Similar accounts exist for the stations at Clarkebury, Wesleyville, Morley and Buntingville, all in the western Transkei.

A Transkei people who showed a willingness to alter the proportion of cultivation and pastoralism in their economy and who responded as the Cape's eastern frontier edged closer and closer to them in the mid-third of the century were the Thembu. Later in the century, some Thembu communities rivalled the Mfengu in the Transkei as farmers and buyers of land. When Sir Harry Smith called in 1848 upon missionaries to suggest methods of inspiring in 'the Bantu a desire to cultivate their lands by ploughing and to induce them to follow habits of industry', missionaries among the Thembu severally provided evidence of a vigorous peasant response by that date. Warner wrote from Shiloh (near Queenstown) of a chief who had bought a plough for seven pounds and who also thought nothing 'of spending to the amount of two or three oxen at once in the purchase of European clothing'. Other men in the community owned wagons which had cost from twenty to fifty pounds, and also ploughs which they were busy using in the cultivation of wheat. A Moravian missionary concurred; since he had arrived in 1832 the Thembu had become more industrious and desired better clothes and houses: 'To obtain these objects, they look out for to get money by the labour of their hands, and purchase clothes, spades, ploughs, wagons, and other useful articles.'[60]

The wars of 1846–7 and 1850–53 accelerated the loss by African polities of control over their destinies. New areas fell under direct British rule; the power of the chiefs was further curtailed; white settlement penetrated further into the Ciskei and 'Tambookieland' (Tembuland, later the districts of Wodehouse, Queenstown and Glen Grey). Crucially, the land available to the Cape Nguni peoples, especially the Ngqika, was greatly diminished: both wars saw the confiscation of fresh African territories. Macmillan and de Kiewiet have demonstrated the destructive impact of these new confiscations; they have illustrated how the power of the chief to allocate land – the basis of the precolonial economies – was curtailed by the loss of land as well as by restrictions on chiefly power. They have shown that numbers of Africans were forced to enter the Cape economy as wage labourers.[61]

Yet the wars of the forties and fifties had other economic consequences too: consequences sketched by Robertson in his pioneering articles of 1934–5. Xhosa and Thembu did their best, he pointed out, to conform to new economic circumstances: 'not only did they sell their labour to European farmers; they improved their agriculture, and indulged more and more in trade, by which they acquired European implements'. He quotes the Tenth Report of the Colonial Land and Immigration Commission, of 1850: 'In British Kaffraria, the Natives are reported to be actively engaged in agricultural pursuits, and to be displaying unexpected steadiness and perseverance, and they are said to be stimulated to these exertions by the presence of numerous traders.'[62]

If one pursues Robertson's theme a little further, it appears that the question of the economic impact of the wars is complex: the clashes conferred such different legacies to different individuals and communities. They widened further the gulf between the rough economic equity obtaining in the precolonial societies and the emerging stratification of the African population in the Ciskei. Most vividly, one might compare the fortunes of collaborators with those of defeated 'rebels'. The latter were deprived of their fertile lands, were forced to give up the bulk of their cattle, and were moved into inferior and more crowded areas.* At the other extreme, the 'loyal Fingoes' were the chief gainers (amongst Africans) from both wars. They were granted new locations, and they too were swift to turn to advantage the economic exigencies of war: 'They had been able to obtain advanced prices for their stock and wagons as a result of the war, and they added to their wealth afterwards by the purchase of captured cattle at low rates.'[63] The translation of political collaboration into economic gain

---

* For example, 'Sandile and his people were located on a long strip of unoccupied country. . . . The greatest part of it was absolutely bare, woodless, and unsheltered.' (C. Brownlee, *Reminiscences of Kafir Life and History and other Papers* (Lovedale, 1896), 341–2.)

was not confined to the Mfengu, nor to spoils of war. When stock recovered by mounted police from African raiders was sold at Fort Cox in 1849, 'many of the Kafir Police bought rather largely.'[64] A well documented individual case is that of the Ngqika John Go, a protégé of Charles Brownlee. Go finished the 1853 war with a reward for services rendered of 37 cattle, and an income of thirty shillings a month as a policeman. He borrowed a hundred sheep, and sold cattle to buy flocks of his own. By 1856 he was in a position to afford a farm costing £2,000, and he subsequently bought a second farm.[65] (Go's later career as a military collaborator and as an agriculturist on a considerable scale is detailed in Chapter 3, pp. 93–4.)

At the lower levels of Nguni society, too, the twin effects of the war – forced involvement in the cash economy, often at a disadvantage, and a positive response to whatever economic opportunities were available – are evident again and again. Both elements are fused in an experience that was reported by several visitors to the Ciskei in the late forties and early fifties: being stopped by groups of Africans who sought money, offering services or some meagre goods (firewood, eggs, poultry, tobacco). Thomas Baines, writing in 1848, described encounters with women importuning him for food, and also 'a group of Kaffir women crossing the drift with produce of their gardens for sale'.[66] Archdeacon Merriman, in 1850, encountered similar groups at Keiskammahoek, while near Whittlesea he 'saw Kaffirs trooping up, with baskets of gum and mimosa bark and bundles of skins on their heads, to trade for beads, tobacco, blankets, and money'.[67] Lieutenant Lumley Graham, on active service in 1853, reported widespread poverty in the Ciskei, and found 'the Kafirs everywhere very civil but most determined beggars'. He also described the 'other' side of the economic integration of the Xhosa: 'a good deal of cultivated land bearing oats' at the Fort Cox mission; the large number of inhabitants from neighbouring villages flocked to 'buy beads and brass ornaments and purchase powder of the Winkler [trader] Penn'. They presumably sold their own produce to Penn in order to do so; Graham does record that 'We bought some Kafir milk buckets and *zikali* of him.'[68]

Moving slightly up the economic scale, away from those fluctuating uneasily between mendicity and the sale of a tiny surplus, one meets peasants proper, faring relatively well in the midst of poverty, committed more fully to production for exchange. Still predominantly attached to mission stations, these peasants included an increasing number of non-mission members, and the scale and output of their farming activity were rising steadily. Seven hundred inhabitants of the Moravian mission at Shiloh (Mfengu and Thembu) greatly impressed Merriman in January 1850, when he saw them reaping a fine wheat harvest – a spectacle not matched elsewhere in Africa, he declared. H. H. Dugmore would probably have contested this claim: writing of his Methodist mission at D'Urban, in 1848, commented that:

The Fingoes are decidedly more of an agricultural people than the Kaffirs and ... they have already begun to adopt improvements from the Colony, both in respect of the grain grown and the method of cultivating it. For some years past wheat crops have been grown by Fingoes on this settlement, and the quantity sown is rapidly increasing every year. During the present season they are said to have reaped several hundred muids of this grain. There are several ploughs and wagons amongst them, possessed chiefly by individuals who have been connected with the Mission Station. The cultivation of wheat possesses to the Fingoes a powerful recommendation in its ripening some time before the kaffer corn, and therefore being available just when their garners are exhausted.[69]

Apart from wheat and vegetables, the adoption by Africans of sheep-raising and of wool production was an extremely significant development. John Go has already been mentioned; more modest, and more typical, was one Toise (mentioned by Baines), 'a civilized Kafir' and 'a bit of a sheep farmer, who wears European clothing, and ploughs his land instead of making the women "adze" it up with Kafir hoes'.[70] By 1849, 13,000 Africans on thirty-two mission stations were said to possess slightly fewer than 3,000 sheep between them, but this small beginning heralded an important peasant activity of later years (see Chapter 3).

These early peasants were experimenting with crops and products unknown to their parents; they had taken over ploughs, hoes, axes and harrows, as well as new building materials, irrigation and tilling methods; they no longer relied on muscle power alone, but employed draught oxen for ploughing as well as for the transport of goods. This last example, for instance, not only represented a major break with Nguni custom* but also demanded a sizeable investment. A plough cost several pounds, a second-hand wagon anywhere from £15 to £45, and new wagons from £50 to £70. To train and harness a span of eight oxen to pull the plough and/or wagon cost nearly three pounds and took three months.

In 1857 the cattle-killing of the Eastern Cape Xhosa assisted the attack by the administration on the cohesion of tribal authority, effectively ended the military threat of the Xhosa to the colony, and accelerated economic differentiation among Africans. Christopher Saunders has commented that 'If consequences explained causes, the theory that whites instigated the cattle killing ... would be difficult to disprove'[71] – and, by the same logic, one would expect to discover the culpability of the famous Governor Sir George Grey. Which is to say that the enforced participation in the money economy by pauperized survivors, the diminution of the power of the chiefs,

---

* A missionary noted that those who first used cattle for ploughing were 'calumniated as not properly caring for their cattle, and deteriorating them from the great national custom and pleasure of racing.' (A. E. Du Toit, *The Earliest South African Documents on the Education and Civilization of the Bantu* (London, 1963), 97.)

and the closer integration of frontier territories into the colonial orbit (which resulted from the cattle-killing) were precisely those aims Grey had pursued since taking up his residence in Cape Town in 1853.

Grey was outstanding among South African administrators in the clarity of his perception of ends and means, in the vigour with which he acted upon his beliefs, and in his personal capacity for administrative duties. He sought in South Africa to emulate his success in New Zealand at 'civilizing' rather than fighting the indigenous population – of establishing 'an enduring and peaceable master–servant relationship in a civilized context'.[72] To this end he encouraged education and built a hospital for Africans, as well as promoting commerce, permanent settlement and improved farming among Ciskeian peoples. These policies were informed by powerful political precepts: they would, Grey argued, confer social benefits to Africans as well as providing the colony with peace, labourers, tax-payers and customers. 'We should try,' he adjured the Cape legislature, to make 'the natives ... a part of ourselves, useful servants, consumers of our goods, contributors to our revenue'.[73]

Essential to the furtherance of his policies was an inhibition of the power and influence of those he called the 'haughty hereditary chiefs'. They were the major barrier to his intentions, 'administering such laws as they thought proper, each maintaining a large standing militia', and there was 'no bond of union between the Kafir chiefs and the Government'.[74] He detailed in 1856 a policy of undermining the chiefs by introducing white magistrates into their areas, by insisting that chiefs accept salaries from government instead of tributes and fines, and by the appointment of paid headmen to serve as a police force. These policies effectively curtailed the judicial, economic and political powers of the chief.

Grey's biographer has summarized his policy as follows:

> Grey's policy was to undermine the power of the chiefs, break up the larger tribes into smaller, more manageable units, overawe them by a show of military force, remove large numbers of natives out of the province altogether, concentrate the rest in village settlements under European officers, and convey large areas of the best land to European farmers. He announced in 1857 that the Kafirs must either be absorbed by the Europeans or succumb to them. He could even reach the startling conclusion that 'throughout British Kaffraria the native has no recognized right or interest in the soil.' On analysis, Grey's policy, notwithstanding his fluent expression of benevolence seems not very different in its purpose from that of General Michel, who would clear the Gaikas out of British Kaffraria in the next war, and push them and Kreli [Sarili] with them across the Bashee in the war after that – except that Grey hoped to do it without war.[75]

That this improbable design could become reality was due to the cattle-killing and famine. An estimated twenty to thirty thousand deaths took place, and perhaps forty thousand Xhosa-speakers migrated in search of food and employment. Some were scattered into other societies to north and east, while about thirty thousand moved into the colony to seek work. James Ayliff recollected in later life that 'thousands of them were drafted into the colony and entered the service of the farmers'; the process was accelerated by the creation of special courts to try 'vagrants': 'They were tried as fast as they came in and shipped off to Cape Town.'[76] Much of British Kaffraria and part of Tembuland fell into white hands. The remnants of Sarili's followers were rounded up and driven eastwards into an area beyond the Mbashe river. Grey sponsored white immigration to the Ciskei, and British influence was extended across the Kei in the form of magistrates appointed to control the resettled communities. Grey's policy involved the humiliation of 'supposedly "warlike and treacherous" chiefs', the dismemberment and dispersal of their societies, the confiscation of their land, 'and an almost Roman policy of colonisation'.[77] Although annexation only followed a few years later, British colonial sway in effect now extended to the Mbashe river.

Grey ('we can draw very great permanent advantages from the circumstance') pressed his advantage over the stricken chiefs by the wider use of magistrates and police, and he also redoubled his efforts to integrate Africans in the colonial economy. He envisioned the creation of a small class of settled, land-owning Africans who would be food producers with a stake in order and stability, and a much larger class of wage-earners ('useful servants'). White immigration would cast a beneficent civilizing aura over tribesmen in the propinquity of settlers, while permitting the colonist 'to draw supplies of labour from the location in his more immediate proximity'.[78]

The effect of the cattle-killing on African peasant production awaits detailed archival investigation. In broad terms, most of those already substantially involved in production for the market held aloof from the destruction. The Mfengu abstained almost *en masse*. The sales by the Mfengu of Fort Beaufort of grain to the government in 1857–8 have been mentioned: the same source gave these details of their prosperity and enterprise:

> Another manifest token of improvement in this people is their improved mode of cultivation and corresponding increase of grain they raise from the ground. At my first acquaintance with the Fingoes there [sic] only means of cultivation was a piece of iron about 2″ broad, sharpened and let into a knotty stick in the form of a hoe. This and a piece of hard wood pointed and flattened constituted their only means of cultivation. . . . Now the English or American plough is in constant use, increasingly so every year. This last ploughing season the demand for ploughs in Fort Beaufort was so great that almost every plough brought into the town by the traders was bought up at £6 cash.[79]

51

On the other hand, many Africans only marginally involved in production for the market, making hesitant or piecemeal experiments, lost their livelihood, if not their lives, and were 'shipped off to Cape Town' or other employment.

If communal ownership of land, and control over its allocation by the chief or headman was a defining characteristic of the precolonial economy, then the spread of individual land tenure amongst Africans was a measure of how deep-reaching a social change was under way. The earliest experiments in converting 'communal' ownership of land into individual tenure was undertaken amongst the Mfengu in the late 1840s. Lands attached to their settlements were divided into small allotments, which were distributed at £1 annual lease. A similar scheme was adopted in the Crown Forest Reserve, where Mfengu and other loyalists were allowed after 1853 to settle in return for an annual payment. This scheme was extended to a number of 'locations' in British Kaffraria, notably the 168 villages created at the missionary Impey's urgings in 1858. Administratively, these schemes were failures: surveyed allotments were not taken up, transfer fees were unpaid, lands were sub-divided so that a generation later few landholders could demonstrate legal title, even in surveyed locations.[80] Despite these limitations, such experiments were important in demonstrating alternative conceptions of rights in land.

George Grey used a slightly different approach, encouraging those peasants profiting from their participation in the cash economy to buy as much Crown Land as they could pay for. A proclamation in 1858 permitted Africans to buy Crown Land at £1 an acre: by 1864, 508 purchasers held 16,200 acres, while 106 lessees rented nearly 6,000 acres from the government.[81] Peasants also experienced rents and individual tenure on mission stations; this might be on a formal footing as at Farmerfield or Haslope Hills; or on a *de facto* basis with the mission station as landowner and the faithful as tenants, paying in cash or kind for the plots they farmed individually.

Another form of access to land was the leasing (for cash, kind or payment in labour service, or some combination of these) of a portion of a white landholder's farm by squatter-peasants. It is difficult to say just how early such arrangements were first entered into on the Eastern frontier, but 'squatting' was certainly taking place during the 1830s. In the vast majority of such cases the details of the agreements have long vanished, but in the 1840s, Baines observed an incident that must have been typical of many. Just south of Bedford a Mfengu requested permission to graze his two score cattle and 169 goats upon a white-owned farm in return for an agreed amount of labour. In this case, the colonist demurred: he felt that the labour of one man (who would necessarily be involved with his own herd) would not recompense him for the pasturage consumed.[82] Other farmers in the district were more willing than he to resort to this method of securing a labour supply or an income. By 1862, it was reported that some Bedford farmers were

> permitting large numbers of natives on their farms without any ostensible means of support. Most of these natives had certificates of citizenship, and hire small patches of ground from the farmers at an average rental of £3 p.a.... Farmers evade the law by contracting Kafir servants for whom they cannot find employment, so as to enable them (the Kafirs) also to hire ground.[83]

When the relationship entered into was strictly that of labour tenancy, the arrangement tended to favour the landholder; the amount of labour rendered left the squatter time enough only to keep himself and his family. In cases like those in the Bedford district just described – where 'squatting' (leasing) as distinct from labour tenancy prevailed – the squatter-peasant, for the payment of a fee, retained the free disposal of his labour power and its products. It was the presence of these squatter-peasants that provoked the wrath, throughout the period covered in this book, of would-be employers of cheap black labour. It was in the interest of such squatter-peasants to produce a surplus sufficient to enable them to preserve their 'independence', and this provided an incentive for them to innovate and diversify. A description of a community of just such squatter-peasants comes from an official on the frontier in 1863. Africans had moved into the Fort Beaufort district, he complained, who were averse to service for whites (more, they were 'therefore intractable, indolent and faithless') so that master-servant relations were 'anything but satisfactory'. It had been the practice, for some time past, for these newcomers 'to engage themselves as servants, to farmers, while in reality they became squatters, paying the farmer a certain sum annually, for the privilege of grazing their cattle, and cultivating a patch of land'. No sooner had the 'so-called servant become fixed, when a number of others were invited to assemble there, and in a short time villages were formed'.[84] Such peasants, in short, were 'unemployed and left to subsist themselves':[85] and this was the nub of the vast disapproval that they excited from employers, administrators and policy-makers. They were unemployed *because* they were capable of subsistence, even though that subsistence involved the payment of rent.

A recent survey of the economy of the Cape in the 1860s says of (white) agriculture that 'though still backward, with poor crop yields, poor land use, and an inefficient employment of the labour available, [farming] was in the sixties going through a period of experiment and diversification'.[86] Omitting the reference to the employment of labour, the assessment may be applied with equal force to African peasant agriculture in the same period.

In Peddie, the Mfengu heartland, the magistrate R. G. Tainton reported in 1860 that

The Fingoes ... have added considerably to their stock of cattle, sheep and goats and have begun to give some attention to breed – they have this year cultivated much more ground than formerly and many of them have land from farmers in this district at fair rates – they are gradually becoming better dressed and spend a good deal of money upon clothes.... A short time back the Revd. Mr. Davis Wesleyan Missionary and myself got a number of natives together to try and form an agricultural society – the attendance and subscriptions were even more than could be expected, amounting to nearly £40.[87]

His impressions were confirmed and his observations amplified in evidence to the 1865 *Commission on Native Affairs.** Both Christian and traditionalist peasants were 'making progress' in the possession of stock, wagons and ploughs and in the extent of land cultivated. Thirty Mfengu locally were 'landed proprietors' with 'farms varying from 500 to 1500 acres each, which they have purchased'. Other Mfengu were renting land from whites 'extensively', some cultivating as much as fifty or a hundred acres. Sheep-farming was also on the increase, as was the doubling up by peasants as 'transport riders' – wagoners conveying goods from one part of the colony to another. Forage, maize, and sorghum were being marketed.[88]

Mfengu members of the Agricultural Society competed against white farmers and won prizes; despite the drought prevailing (the Wesleyan Davis told the Commission) 'even this year I think their exhibition surpassed that of the Europeans. It was a universal remark in the district that the Fingo exhibition far excelled that of the Europeans both as to number and quality of the articles exhibited.'[89] Tainton added that 35,000 bushels of corn and 17,000 pounds of wool, as well as stock and poultry, had been sold by peasants in Peddie, and that the proceeds were being invested in land both within the district and in British Kaffraria.[90]

In another Mfengu settlement – Chumie (or more properly Tyhume), outside Alice – 900 men out of a total population of 4,600 grew maize, sorghum, wheat, oathay, pumpkins and other vegetables, and exported 5,000 bags of grain and a little wool each year. In the eight years previous, the number of ploughs and wagons in the location had trebled. From nearby Lovedale, apart from the purchase of land for themselves, Christian Mfengu there had enough cash to put £1,660 towards a church building.[91]

Moving farther from these Mfengu bases, the pattern is repeated. A white farmer in Bedford acknowledged that there were 'many respectable natives owning land' in the district; in Somerset district Sotho and Mfengu ('comparatively wealthy men') had bought land and houses.

---

* The Commission is a most valuable source for this period: its seven members included four missionaries, and the hearings relied more heavily on missionary evidence than did later enquiries. Amidst a wealth of detail, its pages convey a striking sense of the 'experiment and diversification' undertaken by black peasants during the 1860s.

From Tembuland, Warner said that the Thembu had taken 'very generally' to sheep, and that 'their wool trade has become very important, and the Queenstown merchants think it quite worth their while to attend to it'. Amongst the Ngqika at Umgwali, some 500 peasants marketed their wares in neighbouring villages, selling especially wheat, butter and maize, while the Stutterheim Ngqika, short of cattle, were relying increasingly on agriculture and were keen to invest in woolled sheep.[92] Near Kingwilliamstown over three hundred family heads had bought 1,675 acres of land from which they raised for sale as surplus 6,000 bags of grain and 2,000 bags of wool.

Finally, in written evidence to the Commission, two long-serving missionaries conveyed graphic impressions of the social distance travelled and the range of adaptations made by peasants. Laing, missionary at Burnshill, not far from Kingwilliamstown, wrote:

> When I came to this country, 34 years ago, the wooden spade was used in agriculture; now the hoe and the plough are used, and the wooden spade has disappeared. Then the chief agriculturists were the women, now a great part of the agricultural labour is performed by the men. Burdens were then borne on the heads of the women, now many of the people possess waggons for the transport of their goods. Then the hides of cattle and the hides of sheep were the clothing of the people; now the manufactures of the wool of the sheep and the cotton plant have been substituted. . . . Then scarcely any of them could read, now many of them – and their number is yearly increasing – can read both their own and the English language. No native in this quarter had then learned a trade, now a few, their number also on the increase, have proved themselves to be capable of learning trades as well as Europeans.

From Pirie, the Reverend Breece Ross corroborated:

> I am not a very old man, yet I remember the time when the gardens of the natives were much smaller than they now are. I can well recollect the time, when among the Kafirs, all field labour except fencing, was performed by the women. Now, however, the male part of the Kafir population, either universally or very generally, take a great share in such works. I can well call to mind the time when, with only one or two exceptions there were no waggons in Kaffraria, but those belonging to Europeans; now, however, native waggons are so plentiful as to be quite a nuisance. I have vividly before me the days when no Red Kafir would degrade his cattle by putting them under the yoke; now, however, the veriest calf is made to work for its grass by these painted gentlemen. Nor can I forget the year when almost all the natives of Kaffraria would not take money as pay; now, however, the love of money is fast becoming with them the 'root of all evil'. Once in my day the natives who could read existed only in units at the various mission stations, now they can be counted by tens and hundreds.[93]

Yet all this is only part of the social and economic landscape of the Ciskei. In the economic lowlands, the terrain was bleaker and harsher.

Metaphor and reality merge: many of the Ciskei's black inhabitants lived by the 1860s on lands that were too small, too infertile, to provide subsistence by farming. The 1865 Commission found that 'There can be little doubt that several, if not all, of the Fingo locations are greatly overcrowded, and very serious evils are arising from this fact.' The lengthy commendation by Ross quoted above went on to mention drunkenness, indebtedness, and a mood of resentment in the population.[94] The files of the Methodist Missionary Society archives for Grahamstown diocese (including nearly all the Ciskei stations) for the late sixties are dotted with references to the paucity of means available to the majority – what one missionary called the 'poverty and limited pecuniary means of the people'.[95]

In essence, the Nguni economy was being penetrated by market relations while the region was being incorporated within the emerging capitalist economy of the Cape (and hence within the ramifications of the nineteenth-century global capitalist system). These processes – taking place in a society where political power was vested in the hands of merchants and employers – were resulting *inter alios* in the Ciskei in the creation of differentiated classes in the African population. Some – the strategically well-placed, the collaborating, the enterprising – were relatively well-to-do in the upper strata, whether as skilled artisans or as peasant producers. Others were proletarianized – deprived of access to land, the basis of their means of production – and depended for a living upon the sale of their labour power to white employers. The majority of the Ciskei's population, in the year before the discovery of diamonds in South Africa, were marginal men. No longer precolonial cultivators, they were small peasants; they held precariously to the land (whether in Reserves, Locations, or on white-owned tracts), managing in good years to subsist, but in poor years having to seek work. As the Civil Commissioner for Bedford put in in 1868,

> the scarcity of labour ... has been to a great extent caused by the last two fruitful seasons, the abundance of food in Kaffraria having induced most of the natives to leave this district.... The wants of the natives in their present state are so few, that they are easily supplied, and like most men, white or black, they will not work when they have no want.[96]

If this survey of peasant activities in the 1860s moves across the Kei river, it will be discovered that trade and agricultural production, while rapidly increasing, were nowhere as firmly rooted or as widespread as in the Ciskei. In the virtual absence of white employers, and with lower rent and tax obligations, proletarianization was negligible. Peasant production was largely confined to mission stations and their immediate environs, with the exchange activities of the majority of the people limited to barter. Even in the Transkei, however, the decade was clearly one of change, and forces were already in progress that were to expand so vigorously in the last third of the century (see Chapters 3 and 4).

The most important impetus to economic change in the Transkei came in mid-decade, with the migration into land that had been occupied by Gcalekas of some 50,000 Mfengu and Thembu, including many thriving peasants. Thirty thousand Mfengu from Peddie, Victoria East, and Kingwilliamstown districts moved to 'Fingoland', where they rapidly demonstrated the same propensities for agricultural labour on their own behalf that they had in the colony. Two years after the move, a missionary reported that the land under cultivation at Butterworth was 'five times what it formerly was and is advancing from year to year'. In nearby Tsomo his colleague described how he had seen twenty-five preaching houses and twenty-eight chapels built – 'and this in a land where three years ago the Bushbuck and Hartebeast roamed unmolested'.[97] The Bishop of Grahamstown visited Fingoland in 1869 and pronounced that 'in all directions there are signs of prosperity not to be found among any of the natives within the colonial border', and that the Mfengu were 'cultivating the area with great success'.[98] Significantly, the Mfengu who settled here were by then a sheep-rearing peasant community, and their presence among other Transkei peoples was to have a direct effect in the spread of wool production. To the north of Fingoland, and south of Queenstown, lay the area into which some 20,000 Thembu migrated between 1864 and 1866 and which was named Emigrant Thembuland (what became the magisterial districts of St Marks and Xalanga).

Further east, at the Methodist station of Clarkebury, on the Tsomo river, the impact of the market economy was well defined, even before Mfengu and Thembu migrations had been completed. At this mission, reported William Shepstone in May 1865, there were three trading stores:

> A change has certainly come over the country since the first missionary wagons opened up the road. Previously there were *no* wagon trails to be seen. *We* had been the first to line the country with roads for vehicles ... these tracks are now the main arteries of the country; the well-traversed trails are now to be found diverging to the right and left in all directions ... this is the result of colonial trade.[99]

From information provided by one of the traders, he calculated that some seven and a half thousand blankets were sold every year: the cow-hide *kaross*, he reported, was almost completely replaced in the area by the Witney blanket.

The colonial trade that provided the Transkeians with blankets and other goods saw cattle, grain and animal products bulking larger in proportion to hunt products and locally garnered resources than in the earlier frontier period. At All Saints Mission, on a tributary of the

Mbashe, where a station had existed for seven years by 1866, a missionary observed 'large numbers of waggons and people from the colony, buying corn from the neighbourhood'.[100] The same reporter, Henry Waters, said of his own station, St Marks, that it might

> now be called an English village in the centre of a large population. The village consists of eight substantial buildings – a large stone chapel, a large brick schoolhouse, and another of wattle and daub, besides a few other houses of the latter material. Resident in the village are two well-to-do English traders, with stock worth respectively £2000 and £1000. A waggon-making establishment, employing four Europeans, an English carpenter, an English shoe-maker – three European farmers, besides several half-castes and Hottentots.

All the business concerns were profitable, and – felt Waters – they had a most beneficial influence 'on the native mind': they provided employment to some 'besides drawing a continual stream of natives from miles around to sell their produce – wool, straw, cattle, etc., for articles of European manufacture such as blankets, clothing, ploughs, spades, etc.'[101]

To dwell for a moment in the 'English village' of St Marks: its impact upon the 'large population' around it was a many-sided one. Apart from the pulls of trade and employment, there was also the dispersion amongst the outlying population of converts. By 1868, Waters had baptized about 800 people in twelve years, and he acknowledged that other denominations had been equally active, and that the Christians were now spread throughout the surrounding countryside. Civilization, measured in trinkets, trade goods and costume, thus spread rapidly beyond the spearheads of the stations. In *kraals* off the mission lands, Waters had 'often had dinner and tea served up, equal to an ordinary hotel on the frontier', and he attributed this to 'the quantity of European clothing and manufacture now sold in Kaffirland [that] amounts to thousands of pounds'. Almost anything could be had in the traders' stores, that could be found on the shelves of shops in Grahamstown.[102]

Pondoland, not to become part of the Cape until 1894, was still politically independent, and was habitually described in the nineteenth century as 'backward' and 'uncivilized'. Yet there too the lively trade between Mpondo and traders had considerably affected the economy by the 1860s. Traders, William Beinart has asserted recently, 'were the crucial factor in the economic changes taking place in Pondoland during the nineteenth century'.[103] According to the missionary Jenkins, by 1866 a single commercial firm had sold 20,000 hoes and picks to the Mpondo as well as many ploughs and a few wagons. 'Twenty-five years ago,' he went on, 'not a single cow or even a goat could be purchased at any price in all Pondoland. . . . Now thousands of cattle are bought and sent out of the country annually, and there are many successful traders established in the country.'[104]

This section has concentrated upon the effective and positive response by Southern Nguni agriculturists prior to 1870. It has detailed the adoption of new tools, new crops and new horizons, and chartered the emergence of a peasant class; it has examined the limited, but still significant, involvement of the Mpondo, Mpondomise, Thembu, Gcaleka, and Bhaca peoples of the Transkei in the colonial economy. Its findings underwrite de Kiewiet's assessment of the Transkei that 'by 1870 there was scarcely a man or woman who was not in some degree a consumer of manufactured goods.'[105] What de Kiewiet did not add (and the topic of peasant response is not one that he examined) was that, *ipso facto*, there can scarcely have been a man or woman in the Transkei who was not in some degree a producer of agricultural goods for exchange. Employment for wages to buy goods was the choice of a very tiny minority in the Transkei, and occurred predominantly in the immediate vicinity of mission stations or settlements, or amongst those few who journeyed to the colony. Far more Transkeians made their initial acquaintance with the cash economy at the counter of the trader's store, where they brought their baskets of grain, straw or tobacco, their hides, horns, milk and livestock.

In their turn, the trading stores in the Transkei were linked directly with the merchant houses in Cape Town, Port Elizabeth or Grahamstown, and thus ultimately with the accumulation of profit in the metropolis. Economic integration at the 'micro' frontier level did not take place independently of the broader processes of capitalist incorporation, or the expansion of the geographical boundaries of the capitalist global economic system. The Nguni coastal lands of the Cape underwent what Wallerstein calls 'peripheralization': their forcible involvement in core–periphery trade, the acceleration of the process of their political decline, and the re-organization of their class structure. Expressed another way, in terms of 'the development of underdevelopment', Leys has commented that the 'starting point of underdevelopment theory is the period in which any given region of today's "third world" began to be progressively incorporated into a permanent relationship with the expanding capitalist economy'.[106] What was happening in the Transkei was precisely the generation of that region's underdevelopment.

There are critics who feel that underdevelopment theory deals in broad and overly generalized concepts, and who profess uneasiness when confronted with terms like 'an expanding capitalist world-economy' or 'the incorporation of the periphery within the world economy'. The debate with those critics is not one that can be joined here, but mention of it provides the excuse to repeat a passing comment in a missionary's letter that initially caught my attention momentarily and has lain in my memory ever since. In 1869 a

Methodist missionary, Mr Davis, wrote to England from an eastern Cape station that he had collected from 'his' station people forty-six pounds in cash 'for the Lancashire Cotton Relief Fund'.[107] That the hard-won surplus of a Ciskei peasant community should have been channelled to the aid of Lancashire's mill-workers – and that the missionary who acted as conduit should have regarded it as an unremarkable and natural transaction – may serve for others (as it has for me) as an essay in miniature on the extent and implications of the incorporation of the periphery.

NOTES

1 S. D. Neumark, *Economic Influences on the South African Frontier, 1652–1836* (Stanford, 1957).
2 See S. Amin, *Accumulation of a World Scale: A Critique of the Theory of Underdevelopment*, 2 vols. (New York, 1974), 137–68.
3 M. Wilson, 'Co-operation and Conflict: The Eastern Cape Frontier', OHSA, I, 238.
4 ibid., 240.
5 For descriptions of Fort Willshire see S. Kay, *Travels and Researches in Caffraria* (London, 1833), 31, 64; A. Steedman, *Wanderings and Adventures in the Interior of Southern Africa*, 2 vols. (London, 1935), I, 7.
6 U. Long, *An Index to Authors of Unofficial, Privately Owned Manuscripts relating to the History of South Africa, 1812–1920* (London, 1947), 218.
7 Kay, *Travels and Researches*, 67.
8 Long, *An Index to Authors*, 258, 236, 237; S. Kay, *A Succinct Statement of the Kaffer's Case* (London, 1837), 9.
9 Kay, *Travels and Researches*, 454–5; *A Succinct Statement*, 81.
10 A. W. Burton, *Sparks from the Border Anvil* (Kingwilliamstown, 1950), 192.
11 See J. D. Omer-Cooper, *The Zulu Aftermath: A Nineteenth Century Revolution in Bantu Africa* (London, 1966).
12 H. M. Robertson, '150 Years of Economic Contact between Black and White: A Preliminary Survey', 2 parts, *South African Journal of Economics*, Vol. 2, No 4 (December 1934) and Vol. 3, No 1 (March 1935), 411.
13 C. W. de Kiewiet, *A History of South Africa: Social and Economic* (Oxford, 1941), 69–72; T. Kirk, 'Some Notes on the Financial State of the Eastern Cape, 1840–1850, and the fate of the Kat River Settlement', ICS, CSP, Vol. 3, 13–23, especially 18–21.
14 Annual exports of wool from the Cape were only 113,000 lb in 1833; had risen to 1,429,000 lb by 1842, to 3,195,000 by 1845, and to 5,447,000 by 1851 (Kirk, 'Some Notes on the Financial State', 14–15).
15 Especially the work of Richard Moyer to whom I am indebted for some of the information in this paragraph.
16 J. Ayliff and J. Whiteside, *History of the Abambo, Generally known as Fingos* (Butterworth, 1912), 17.
17 Cited ibid., 29–31.
18 R. Moyer, 'A History of the Mfengu, c. 1825–1860', unpublished seminar paper, ICS, University of London, 1970.

19 Robertson, '150 Years of Economic Contact', 411.

20 Ayliff and Whiteside, *History of the Abambo*, 17.

21 Omer-Cooper, *The Zulu Aftermath*, 167; Moyer, 'A History of the Mfengu'.

22 Long, *Index to Authors*, 212.

23 R. Moyer, 'The Mfengu, Self-defence, and the Cape Frontier Wars', in C. C. Saunders and R. Derricourt, *Beyond the Cape Frontier* (Longman, 1974), 101–26.

24 MMS Arch., Box XXIV SA, 'Kaffraria 1858–64', 1858–61 file, Ayliff, 18 March 1858.

25 J. Whiteside, *History of the Wesleyan Methodist Church in South Africa* (London, 1906), 196; W. Eveleigh, *The Settlers and Methodism, 1820–1920* (Cape Town, 1920), 154–5.

26 Wilson, 'The Growth of Peasant Communities', OHSA, II, 49.

27 Qualified invitations of the type described are mentioned, for instance, twice in Bishop Bramsby Key's Journal for 1875 (SPG Arch., E MSS). For an extended treatment of African response along lines indicated here see T. O. Ranger, 'African Attempts to Control Education in Central and East Africa', *Past and Present*, No. 32.

28 Wilson, OHSA, II, 50.

29 *The Kaffir Express*, V, 55 (April 1875); V, 53 (February 1875).

30 See: J. Du Plessis, *A History of Christian Missions in South Africa* (London, 1911); P. Hinchcliffe, *The Anglican Church in South Africa* (London, 1963); W. C. Holden, *A Brief History of Methodism and of Methodist Missions in South Africa* (London, 1877); J. Lennox, *The Story of Our Missions in South Africa* (Edinburgh, 1911); C. Lewis and G. E. Edwards (eds.), *Historical Records of the Church of the Province of South Africa* (London, 1934); D. Williams, 'The Missionary on the Eastern Frontier of the Cape Colony, 1799–1853' (Witwatersrand University, Ph.D. thesis, 1959).

31 A. F. A. Ajayi, *Christian Missions in Nigeria, 1841–1891* (London, 1965), 15.

32 J. Philip, *Researches in South Africa Illustrating the Civil, Moral, and Religious Condition of the Tribes*, 2 vols. (London, 1828), II, 72–3.

33 ibid., I, ix–x, 365, 386; II, 32–3.

34 Ajayi, op. cit., 17.

35 Philip, *Researches in South Africa*, II, 324, 329.

36 D. Williams, *When Races Meet (The Life and Times of W. R. Thomson, Missionary, Government Agent and Dutch Reformed Church Minister, 1794–1891)* (Johannesburg, 1967), 39.

37 W. B. Boyce, *Notes on South African Affairs from 1834 to 1838, with reference to the Civil, Political, and Religious Condition of the Colonists and Aborigines* (Grahamstown, 1838, reprinted Cape Town, 1971), 133, 134.

38 Williams, *When Races Meet*, 93–4 (and see 73–94 generally).

39 H. Calderwood, *Caffres and Caffre Missions* (London, 1858), 210.

40 B. Hutchinson, 'Some Social Consequences of Nineteenth Century Missionary Activity among the South African Bantu', *Africa*, XXVII (2) (April 1957), 169.

41 See N. Majeke, *The Role of the Missionaries in Conquest* (Johannesburg,

1952). For revealing examples of the sort of political intelligence missionaries could convey, see the confidential reports by N. G. B. Shepstone to Col. McLean, 21 June 1860, or the sequence of letters from J. Warner to Sir Philip Wodehouse, April 1864–June 1865, both in Cape Arch., G.H. 8/48, *Letters from Native Chiefs and others*.

42 SPG Arch., E MSS, E 39, 1884, D. Mzama, Springvale, 30 May 1884.
43 *The Mission Field* (October 1883), 329.
44 Hutchinson, 'Some Social Consequences', 164–6.
45 SPG Arch., E MSS, E 35, J. R. Ward, 31 December 1880.
46 MMS Arch., SA Box XVIII, Bechuanaland 1868–76, 1868 file, A. Brigg, 13 August 1868.
47 MMS Arch., Box Queenstown 1868–76, 1870–71 file, E. J. Barrett, 1 July 1870.
48 SPG Arch., E MSS, E 26, D. W. Dodd, St Albans, 31 December 1870.
49 MMS Arch., Queenstown 1868–76, 1870–71 file, E. J. Barrett, 10 August 1871.
50 MMS Arch., Queenstown 1868–76, 1868 file, *passim*.
51 A. Brigg, *'Sunny Fountains' and 'Golden Sands': Pictures of Missionary Life in the South of the Dark Continent* (London, 1888), 90.
52 Du Plessis, *History of Christian Missions*, 299; R. H. J. Shepherd (of Lovedale) cited by Majeke, *The Role of the Missionaries in Conquest*, 75.
53 Bishop Gray, cited in C. C. Saunders, 'The Annexation of the Transkeian Territories (1872–1895) with special reference to British and Cape policy' (Oxford University, D. Phil. thesis, 1972), 39.
54 T. Kirk, 'Progress and Decline in the Kat River Settlement 1829–1854', *Journal of African History*, XIV, 3 (1973), 411–28.
55 Ayliff and Whiteside, *History of the Abambo*, 46.
56 Whiteside, *Methodism in South Africa*, 215; W. Shaw, *The Story of My Mission in South-Eastern Africa* (London, 1860), 290–94; M. J. Merriman, *The Kaffir, the Hottentot, and the Frontier Farmer: Passages of Missionary Life from the Journals of the Venerable Archdeacon Merriman* (London, 1853), 68–9.
57 J. A. Chalmers, *Tiyo Soga: A Page of South African Mission Work* (London, 1860), 5–6, 7.
58 A. E. Du Toit, *The Earliest South African Documents on the Education and Civilization of the Bantu* (Pretoria, 1963), 43.
59 Whiteside, *Methodism in South Africa*, 212.
60 Du Toit, *Earliest Documents*, 17, 55, 64.
61 W. M. Macmillan, *Bantu, Boer and Briton: The Making of the South African Native Problem* (2nd rev. ed., Oxford, 1963, 1st ed. 1929); C. W. de Kiewiet, *A History of South Africa*, 56–87.
62 Robertson, '150 Years of Economic Contact', 417–18, 418, footnote 53.
63 ibid., citing MacLean's *Compendium of Kafir Laws and Customs*, 138–9.
64 T. Baines, *Journal of Residence in Africa, 1842–1853*, ed. R. F. Kennedy, 2 vols. (Cape Town, 1961), 143–4.
65 C. Brownlee, *Reminiscences of Kaffir Life and History* (Lovedale, 1896), 269–302.
66 Baines, *Journal of Residence in Africa*, 129 (footnote), 138–9.
67 Merriman, *Kaffir, Hottentot and Frontier Farmer*, 8, 15.
68 Rhodes House Library, MSS. Afr. r8, Lumley Graham and Alexander

Barclay, *Cape Journal*, Vol. III, entries for 20 March 1853, 2 July 1853. See also 7 June, 14 June and 16 July 1853 for other material relating to mission stations.
69 Merriman, *Kaffir, Hottentot and Frontier Farmer*, 18; Du Toit, *Earliest Documents*, 72–3.
70 Baines, *Journal of Residence in Africa*, 163 (footnote).
71 Saunders, 'The Annexation of the Transkeian Territories', 39.
72 D. H. Reader, *The Black Man's Portion: History, Demography, and Living Conditions in the Native Locations of East London, Cape Province*. For the Inst. of Soc. and Econ. Research of Rhodes University (Cape Town, 1961), 6.
73 Cited ibid., 7.
74 *Cape Monthly Magazine*, 1st series, II (October 1857).
75 J. Rutherford, *Sir George Grey* (London, 1961), 328–9.
76 James Ayliff, unpublished MSS. in possession of the Ayliff family, copy and permission to quote by courtesy of Richard Moyer.
77 Rutherford, *Sir George Grey*, 365.
78 Grey to Labouchere, cited by Rutherford, *Sir George Grey*, 355; S. H. Frankel and E. H. Brookes, 'Problems of Economic Inequality in South Africa', in E. H. Brookes *et al.*, *Coming of Age: Studies in South African Citizenship and Politics* (Cape Town, 1930), 137.
79 MMS Arch., SA Box XXIV (Kaffraria 1858–64), 1861 file, 18 March 1858.
80 For details of the various schemes, see CPP, G.4–'83, *1883 Commission on Native Laws and Customs*, app. X; A. E. Du Toit, *The Cape Frontier: A Study of Native Policy with Special Reference to the Years 1847–1866* (Archives Year Book for South African History, 1954, Vol. I, Pretoria, 1954), 259–84; J. S. Marais, 'The Imposition of European Control' in I. Schapera (ed.), *The Bantu-Speaking Tribes of South Africa* (London, 1937), 337–42.
81 Du Toit, *The Cape Frontier*, 278.
82 Baines, *Journal of Residence in Africa*, 120.
83 *Blue Book for the Cape Colony, 1863* (Cape Town, 1863), Report of the Civil Commissioner for Bedford, JJ23.
84 ibid., Report of the Civil Commissioner for Fort Beaufort, JJ26.
85 ibid., Report of the Civil Commissioner for Somerset, JJ28.
86 D. Hobart Houghton and J. Dagut (eds.), *Source Material on the South African Economy 1860–1970*, 3 vols. (Cape Town, 1972), I, 16.
87 Cape Arch., G.H. 8/48, *Letters from Native Chiefs and others*, Report on the State and Numbers of the Fingoes Location in the Division of Peddie, R. Tainton, 14 June 1860.
88 *1865 Commission on Native Affairs*, 23.
89 ibid., 24–5.
90 ibid., App. I, 89.
91 ibid., App. I, 102, 120.
92 ibid., 36, 48, 82, 141, 161.
93 ibid., App. I, 124, 143.
94 ibid., xxiv.
95 MMS Arch., SA XXV (Grahamstown 1868–76), J. H. Scott, 28 July 1869.
96 *Blue Book for the Cape Colony, 1868* (Cape Town, 1868), Appendix, JJ35.

97 MMS Arch., Queenstown 1868–76, 1868 file, J. Longden, 7 February 1868; W. B. Rayner, 5 June 1868.
98 SPG Arch., D MSS, D37, Grahamstown 1867–74, H. Cotteril, 14 December 1869.
99 *Wesleyan Missionary Notices*, 3rd Series, XII, Sept. 1865.
100 SPG Arch., E MSS, E20, H. Waters' Journal for 1866.
101 *Mission Field*, XI, 1866.
102 SPG Arch., E MSS, E24, 1868–9, H. Waters, 31 December 1868.
103 W. Beinart, 'Peasant Production, Underdevelopment, and the Traditionalist Response in Pondoland, c. 1880–1930' (University of London, M.A. thesis, September 1973), 8.
104 Cited in W. A. Campbell, *The South African Frontier, 1865–1885: A Study in Expansion*, Arch. Year Book for South African History, 1959, Vol. I (Pretoria, 1959), 35.
105 De Kiewiet, *A History of South Africa*, 81.
106 I. Wallerstein, 'The Three Stages of African Involvement in the World-Economy', in P. C. W. Gutkind and I. Wallerstein, *The Political Economy of Contemporary Africa* (London, 1976), esp. 32–9; C. Leys, *Underdevelopment in Kenya: The Political Economy of Neo-Colonialism* (London, 1975), 8.
107 MMS Arch., SA Box XXV, 1869 file, W. J. Davis, 12 March 1869.

3

Expansion of the Peasantry: 1870–90

All these people are in the strictest sense agriculturists; I believe there are but few heads of families in all this large population who are not cultivators of the soil; they are the largest producers of grain in the division; without them the trade of Queenstown would not be anything like what it is at present. It is an indisputable fact that comparing them with Europeans, taking man for man and acre for acre, the native produces from a smaller extent of ground, and with more primitive appliances, more than the Europeans.

Mr J. J. Hemming, letter in CPP, C.8–'81, *Correspondence on Encouragement to Natives to Engage in Agricultural and Other Labour.*

1 INTRODUCTION

'Trade is in a sound and healthy state,' exulted an Eastern Cape editor in 1871,

> the produce market is 'firm'; the money market is 'easy'; wool, feathers, hides, skins, and almost every description of produce are selling at high rates; the diamond-fields are yielding their treasures in finds of almost fabulous value; the seasons are propitious; crops have been good; food cheap and abundant; landed property is rising in value; commerce and agricultural prospects decidedly good.[1]

This panegyric must be read against the background of the middle and late 1860s, when the Cape – in common with the rest of Southern Africa – suffered an economic recession marked by an agricultural and commercial slump, insecurity of credit and rickety public finances.[2] With the discovery of diamonds, and especially with the boom started by the Kimberley Rush, the Cape economy received considerable infusions of capital and immigrants; there was increased investment and extended credit, a sharp rise in imports and exports, increased commercial activity internally and a surge of railway building and other transport activity. At the same time, international prices for certain export commodities, most particularly wool, rose sharply and conferred an independent stimulus to economic recovery. More detailed accounts of the 'mineral revolution' are available elsewhere;[3]

65

the brief statistics in Table 1 convey merely an impression of the magnitude and rapidity of the change.

TABLE 1

Impact of diamond discoveries on the Cape economy

	1865	1875
Imports through Cape ports	£2,111,000	£5,731,000
Exports through Cape ports	2,223,000	5,755,000
Annual expenditure	668,000	1,107,000
Annual revenue	537,000	1,672,000
Capital invested in railways	—	1,483,000

In 1872, on the eve of the grant of Responsible Government to the Cape, the Governor Sir Henry Barkly celebrated in a despatch to Lord Kimberley:

Probably no more prosperous year is noted in its annals. The seasons were in most districts favourable for agricultural and pastoral pursuits; the prices of produce ruled high both in Colonial and European markets; and trade, thus rendered brisk, attained an extraordinary development through the operations necessary for the supply of the wants of a large population suddenly congregated upon the Diamond Fields. The effects of the prosperity created by these combined causes are clearly perceptible throughout the returns.[4]

What Barkly was heralding (the economic historian can now see) was not merely an upsurge in economic activity, but the start of a qualitative change in the political economy and economic geography of Southern Africa. When major gold discoveries followed the diamond boom, South Africa ceased to be a meagre exporter of wine, wool and sugar, furnishing a limited market for British manufactures, and became a major supplier of the currency base of the international finance system. The economic focus swung inland, from Cape Town, Port Elizabeth and East London, to Kimberley and the Witwatersrand; new employers of labour competed with old; new political purposes were pursued via Confederation schemes, annexations, and finally a major war.

To remain for the moment, however, in the early 1870s: one feature of the altering economy which has won less attention than certain others was the manner in which Africans availed themselves of the new opportunities. Firstly, a growing number of Africans sought work in towns, as skilled and unskilled labour. They worked in the diamond mines, upon road, rail, and harbour projects, evincing a keen awareness of wage levels and employment conditions: as Sheila van der Horst has shown, 'where the natives who had been out to work reported favourably on the treatment and wages they had received ...

there was no difficulty in obtaining labour'.[5] Africans were employed in road transport as leaders and drivers, and they also succeeded as independent entrepreneurs in the transport trade, as contractors or 'transport riders'.

Farming – and in particular peasant production – was also affected by the economic conditions prevailing. Apart from the increased profits available after 1869 from wool production and ostrich breeding, new urban concentrations meant markets for pastoral and agricultural products. Although Goodfellow argues that it was not until after the discovery of gold that the first significant agricultural response to new opportunities took place,[6] the evidence suggests otherwise: prices of meat, draught animals, dairy products, grains, fruit and vegetables all rose sharply, and encouraged increased agricultural output.

Discussion of what response there was by agriculturists to the new economic circumstances has generally been limited to white farming, but two exceptions must be noted. Robertson, writing in 1935, observed how the volume of trade with Africans swelled in the 1870s; while van der Horst wrote that:

> The development of diamond production led to a rise in the demand for produce of Native as well as European farmers ... the prices of Native produce rose, that is, the terms on which Natives could sell their produce ... improved. ... There is fairly convincing evidence that the trade in Native produce increased in response to the more favourable terms on which they could dispose of their produce.

This picture is qualified: she adds that African efforts as individual producers were inhibited by 'the smallness of individual landholdings, the lack of capital, and the failure generally to adopt more productive techniques'.[7] It will be suggested elsewhere that differences in scale and technique did not necessarily mean that white owners of large tracts of land would 'outfarm' black peasants (pp. 112–13). In this chapter it will be argued that despite the restrictions van der Horst listed there was a virtual 'explosion' of peasant activity in the 1870s, which affected the lives of the great majority of the Cape's Africans, and that the rise in productivity most clearly observable before 1870 in the Ciskei was repeated in the Transkei. Moreover, for smaller numbers of Africans access to capital and to larger landholdings, and the successful adoption of new productive techniques, among other factors, created a class of small commercial farmers and large peasants who, by any index, responded vigorously and effectively to the new economic activities.

Indeed, in the period covered in this chapter, African peasants appear to have responded *more* effectively to economic change than white landowners. Many white 'farmers' found it more profitable to leave their lands or to trade in African-grown produce than to increase production of foodstuffs themselves. The fact that Goodfellow (and

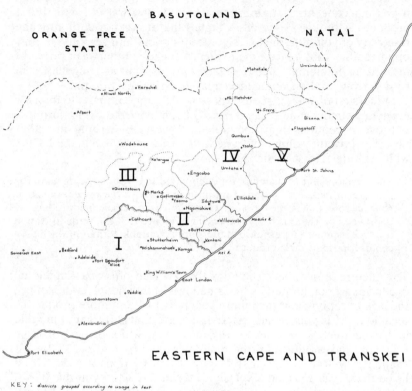

EASTERN CAPE AND TRANSKEI

KEY : *districts grouped according to usage in text*

I   Eastern Cape districts and Ciskei

II   Fingoland

III   Queenstown & Glen Grey districts and Emigrant Tembuland

IV   Gcalekaland, Bomvanaland, Tembuland and East Griqualand

V   Pondoland

others) have discerned no significant responses by agriculturists in this period may well be because their gaze was on white farmers only; they failed to observe that in this period 'African peasants were more efficient and productive than white farmers.'[8]

In this chapter and the next, the predominantly African areas of the Cape have been divided into five loose but convenient groupings (see map, p. 68). These are:

(i) the Ciskei and the eastern districts of the Cape;
(ii) Fingoland (Nqamakwe, Tsomo and Idutywa districts);
(iii) Queenstown district, Emigrant Tembuland, and Glen Grey (later Lady Frere) district;
(iv) the eastern Transkei (including Tembuland proper) and Griqualand East;*
(v) Pondoland.

The magisterial districts in each of these groups share not only geographical propinquity, but certain other distinctive characteristics: the length of time under imperial or colonial control, the extent of penetration by white landowners, and so on – consequently, as should become evident, the rate and extent of economic development differed from group to group.

2 OPPORTUNITIES AND ENTERPRISE

Prior to 1870, it was in the districts west of the Kei River that economic changes had progressed farthest (as shown in Chapter 2), so that in the Ciskei the developments of the early seventies were really only confirmation and reinforcement of trends already in existence. This was true of Victoria East, which was in many ways an archetypal Ciskei district: it had a large African population, a sizeable number of white farmers, storekeepers, and the like;† the local market at Alice was connected by road to Kingwilliamstown; and there was a well-established missionary and educational presence at Lovedale. Peasant agriculture was firmly established in and around Alice prior to 1870, and there was a history of tenurial experiments with surveyed plots and quit-rent holdings, as well as the purchase by a 'good number' of Africans in this district of 'considerable pieces' of land elsewhere in British Kaffraria. When just under 4,000 Mfengu from Victoria East joined the migration in 1867 to Fingoland, it seems that the emigrants were mainly well-to-do pastoralists who took with them large numbers of cattle, sheep and goats.[9]

* To express this fourth group in another way: it includes the people of Tembuland, and also the Bhaca, Mpondomise, Xesibe and smaller groups in Griqualand East, as well as the coastal strips of 'Galekaland' (Kentani and Willowvale districts) and 'Bomvanaland' (Elliotdale district).

† According to the 1875 Census (CPP, G.42–'76) the African population of Victoria East district in 1875 was 7,108 and the whites numbered 1,133.

Their departure meant that some grazing lands were made available to peasants who were predominantly agriculturists, and the rising prices for their produce spurred them to increased efforts. The Mfengu who remained 'set a high value on their lands', and appreciated their title deeds; in 1872–3, 188 American ploughs at an average price of £5 were sold in Alice; in all, concluded the magistrate, 'the Fingoes of this district are a thrifty and industrious people, and are increasing in wealth, prosperity, and civilisation every year'. The non-Mfengu population, Ngqika and Ndlambe, either worked for white farmers or held land as tenants on the farms of both white and Mfengu proprietors. A 'large number' of the Ngqika and Ndlambe peasants 'living on the immediate boundaries of this District' carried on 'a considerable trade' with the storekeepers in Alice. The Ngqika chief Oba and a few hundred of his followers had paid £2,000 for a farm on the banks of the Keiskamma river.[10]

By 1875, African peasants in the district sold to traders in Alice animal and grain products worth over £19,000: wool was the largest cash earner, worth £12,000, followed by grain at £4,275, skins at £1,093, and hides at £1,317. Percy Nightingale, the Civil Commissioner, argued cogently enough that

> it should be conceded that the people in this neighbourhood who have in one year raised 250,820 lbs of wool of a superior quality and excellent get up, besides 7,484 muids of corn, who attend to 77 wagons, which are mostly employed in the transport business, to say nothing of the labour they undertake ... cannot fairly be charged *en masse* with indolence.[11]

There was another side to the 'wealth, prosperity, and civilisation' Nightingale described – that is, that a number of peasants in the district were either marginally self-sufficient or already forced to depend upon labour rather than peasant cultivation. Elsewhere in his report, he mentioned 474 Africans who were farm labourers; he also distinguished between those on quit-rent grants, those on their own lands, and those who were tenants on the land of others. A report drawn up at the request of the Governor, Sir Bartle Frere, three years later underlines this impression of an increasingly differentiated African population in Victoria East: some Africans owned farms (of a fair size) outright; others leased farms or portions of farms; some peasants won a living from their quit-rent plots or rented plots; Mfengu and Ngqika were 'scattered' as tenants and farm labourers on white-owned land. Much of the population sought some wage labour each year: in the drought conditions of 1878 many had 'earned money on the roads and railways, generally in spells of three months at a time'.[12]

From other Ciskei districts came similar reports of peasant enterprise and trade. The Civil Commissioner of Peddie wrote in 1875 that 'many cattle are fattened here for the markets. ... Dealers and purchasers procure large quantities of slaughter animals from this district. The wheat and other cereals rendered excellent crops.' The peasants there were 'yearly becoming richer, and there is an increasing desire to obtain land'.[13] A statistician noted in 1870 that 'taking everything into consideration, the native district of Peddie surpasses the European district of Albany in its productive powers'.[14] In nearby Keiskammahoek, 'a large and increasing quantity of wool' was sold to traders in the vicinity or taken to Kingwilliamstown for sale; the district supported twenty trading stations.[15] In Kingwilliamstown district itself, a similar pattern was described. The 'more general use of the plough' was 'everywhere observable'; peasants were becoming 'comparatively wealthy from the high prices given for wool and every other product they [could] bring to market'. Those engaged in transport riding did so at rates which left a 'large margin for profit'. In the 'Gaika location' (Sandile's area and the Upper Kabousie Crown Reserve) there were by 1873–4 twenty-five stores doing 'fair business' where only five had stood in 1869. Increased cultivation, a greater reliance on the sales of wool and a growing desire to purchase land were mentioned in several reports during the early seventies.[16]

What of the land on the other side of the Kei river, in the Transkei? The Mfengu in 'Fingoland' set the pace in improvements, enterprise and prosperity. With encouragement from Matthew Blyth – an energetic, ambitious official, a disciplinarian and a proponent of the 'civilizing mission' – the Mfengu migrants built upon the platform of their substantial stock holdings and their agricultural experience. In 1872, reported Blyth, the Mfengu had taken at least 500 wagon-loads of corn into Gcaleka and Thembu districts, and sold it for cattle and sheep. The wool clip was valued at £60,000, and forage and potatoes were also being raised.[17] By 1873, the population of 44,000 owned some 440 wagons, and about 2,000 families (one in eight or nine) were using ploughs, while 182,000 sheep were grazed. An agricultural show was well attended, and the amount of wheat ànd forage grown increased, as did the total acreage under the plough. The forty-five trading stations in Fingoland did heavy business: 'At the lowest computation, the value of the import and export trade represents £150,000 p.a.,' wrote Blyth.[18]

An indication of the community's ability to generate a surplus, as well as of its capacity for social change, is the amount of money the Mfengu put into education and other benefits. In three years they raised £4,500 for the building of Blythswood, a sister school to Lovedale; they contributed £7,000 towards roads through the territory; and paid in addition church and school fees, as well as taxes and fees levied by the Cape Government.[19] The decision to pay a special road levy was agreed to at public meetings held by the Mfengu, and the opening of the bridge across the Kei was attended by headmen and other representatives of the community in demonstration of their appreciation of the advantages of improved transport facilities.

The third group of magisterial districts had an African population that was largely Thembu, with large concentrations of Mfengu in the Oxkraal and Kamastone locations near Queenstown. By 1872 the Agent with the Thembu was reporting improved agriculture, a wider use of the plough, the sale of 'a very large quantity of wool' and an increase in the numbers of wagons owned.[20] Two years later, these trends were seen to have accelerated; produce prices had reached new peaks. From Wodehouse district came word that the Thembu were buying more clothing and 'luxuries', and that the plough was almost universally used. In Queenstown district, 104 farms of from 1,500 to 2,000 morgen (1 morgen = 2·1 acres) had been allotted to various chiefs and headmen and their followers, and on these peasant agriculture flourished. Five times as many ploughs were sold as in 1870; much more soil was cultivated; indeed (wrote the magistrate) 'I believe that no part of this district is more cultivated than the Tambookie location, unless it be parts of the Kamastone location.'[21]

In 1876, John Hemming returned to Queenstown as Civil Commissioner after an absence of some years, and his first annual report is worth quoting. Having toured Oxkraal and Kamastone, he was

> struck with the very great advancement made by the Fingoes in a few years.... Wherever I went I found substantial huts and brick or stone tenements. In many cases, substantial brick houses had been erected, and strange in my experience of natives, fruit trees had been planted; wherever a stream of water could be made available it had been led out and the soil cultivated as far as it could be irrigated; the slopes of the hills and even the summits of the mountains were cultivated wherever a plough could be introduced. The extent of the land turned over surprised me; I have not seen such a large area of cultivated land for years.[22]

In Emigrant Tembuland, forty trading stores were supported by an (estimated) population of 50,000, while considerable trade from the area was also conducted through Queenstown. The estimated exports from the area for 1876 were: wool worth £50,000, hides and skins worth £4,000, grain and timber worth £3,000 each; and about £70,000 of merchandise was sold locally.[23] An agricultural show was held in 1876, and a Native Farmers Association formed. A missionary in their midst noted that 'the Tembus are on the whole much more advanced in civilization' than most other tribes; 'many of them have built good homes, made dams and water furrows, planted orchards, and plough and sow extensively'.[24]

African peasants in Emigrant Tembuland and in Glen Grey benefited from the presence of a market in Queenstown, and in the early seventies profited also by the departure of a large number of the economically vigorous colonists in the rush to the diamond fields: in

Queenstown a missionary recorded in August 1870 that 'the most active of our young men' had left the frontier for Kimberley. [25] Here, as they did in Fingoland, Africans may have nicknamed the mines 'the white man's Nonquase'* – and undoubtedly some of their number stepped forward to make use of the economic opportunities thus created. One field in which this did occur was transport-riding: much of this trade (which is described a little later) passed in the sixties and seventies from white into black hands.

In the fourth and fifth areas (the eastern Transkei and Griqualand East, and Pondoland) the tempo of economic activity was rather slower, but nevertheless the seventies brought changes there too. From Nomansland (Griqualand East) it was reported in mid-decade that Africans still farmed in a very rough manner, and that few enclosed or manured their lands, but that even a small minority did so indicates a propensity to experiment and adapt. Such propensity was borne out by the fact that wheat, barley and potatoes (all new crops) were being sown, trade was increasing, and ploughs being sold. In the Bhaca territory, peasants living at the large mission at Osborn brought in a large amount of maize and sorghum for sale and an increasing quantity of wool: that they were 'willing to cultivate and sell', added J. H. Garner, the Assistant Magistrate, was 'evinced by many of them complaining that they want[ed] more stores'.[26] The volume of trade was increasing in Pondoland, too: ploughs and wagons were being bought, in modest numbers, while wool and grain were 'hawked about for sale'. The Mpondo were so anxious to purchase woolled sheep that they were selling cattle for this purpose.[27] By 1876, there were between fifty and sixty traders settled in the area; as William Beinart has shown, they served as the chief agents of economic change.[28]

In sum, having reviewed all five areas and their economic relations with the rest of the Cape, it is clear that in the seventies a vigorous exchange had developed of manufactured goods on the one hand and pastoral and agricultural products on the other. For the simple reason that most of the available records were written from the 'white' side of the counter – from the point of view of the purveyors of blankets, iron-ware, and furniture – it is through the existence of this trade that peasant activity can best be illustrated. Writing in mid-decade, John Noble described the Ciskei's trade:

> The Border trade comprises a very extensive business with the native Kafirs, Fingoes and Basutos. King William's Town and Queen's Town are the centres where this branch of commerce is especially studied and developed, hundreds of shops and outstations having been established by them throughout the several locations, as far as St John's River and its

---

* Nonquase was the Xhosa prophetess who persuaded the cattle-killers of 1856–7: the soubriquet is recorded in SPG Arch., D MSS, D37 (Grahamstown 1867–74), H. Cotteril, 14 December 1869.

tributaries, and over the mountains into Basutoland, supplying native wants.

The chief trade item, he added, was the woollen blanket, of which 60,000 had been sold in Kingwilliamstown in a single year; the demand for clothing and for agricultural implements was greatly enhanced; and:

> The purchasing power of the natives for these and other articles is at present estimated at not less than £400,000 a year, and their productions – such as wool, Angora hair, hides, horns, goat and sheep skins, tobacco, and grain and cattle – are valued at three quarters of a million sterling per annum. The amount of native produce purchased by one firm alone in King William's Town we know to have been £58,000, from January to December 1873.[29]

A merchant house in Port Elizabeth boasted an annual turnover of goods for the African trade of £200,000[30] – and even allowing for proprietorial exaggeration, the figures from individual stores suggest that Noble's estimate of £400,000 as the sum of the Cape's Africans' purchasing power is too low. The merchant or wholesale house 'backed' the smaller traders who set up their stores in the countryside, supplying them with imported goods and accepting either cash or produce in return.[31] Many of these factors would have had links with Kingwilliamstown, by 1875 the fourth town by size in the colony and the focus for peasant trade. In successive issues of the local newspaper one can meet the wholesale merchants of the town advertising their latest importations to rural traders. Peacock, Weir and Co. had 600 American ploughs, hoes and picks, blankets, sheets, axes, iron pots, ring beads, clothing and grain bags; J. J. Irvine offered 1,000 ploughs, flour, sugar, wire, knives, ochre, buckets, chains, etc.; while Whitaker, Dyer & Dyer ('Our present stock will be found well assorted in Kafir stock . . . a splendid assortment for Native trade'), Boom & Co. ('Kafir truck of all kinds') and John McGregor ('Dealer in Colonial Produce and General Dealer') jostled for attention with large notices.[32]

That the trade was vigorous and of considerable importance to the mercantile interests of the Colony, is clear; and that its growth in volume was sustained largely by an increase in the production of saleable produce by the peasantry is also demonstrable. But it was not merely a question of *more* trade: the very great increase in the number of trading stores in the Transkei and the changing nature of the goods they sold, represented a major, qualitative shift in the consumption patterns of Africans. New 'permanent' wants were created: metal ware was preferred to traditionally crafted pots and baskets, the cow-hide *kaross* was replaced by the Witney blanket; the utility of tools and the value of ploughs all ensured that the coming of the commercial economy must restructure the peasant's perceptions of his own wants and needs. New wares, sampled at first as novelties and exotica, quickly became part of normal material requirements: African involvement in the money economy entailed what Arrighi has called a change from 'discretionary' to 'necessary' spending.[33] Implements, clothes, metal goods, fuels and new foodstuffs became items of subsistence.*

Two missionaries in Thembu areas provide a vivid picture of precisely this process from the 1870s:

This year I gladly notice that in the matter of civilization rapid strides have been made. Really good descriptions of clothing are more eagerly purchased, also articles of furniture, crockery, spades, and forks, etc. The good prices paid by traders for the wool of their sheep enables them to do this more easily than before; a much better style of English shopkeepers now occupy the trading stations in Kaffraria than were to be found a few years ago.[34]

These poor creatures, what steps Christianity and her handmaiden Civilization have taken amongst them since I first came. Twelve years ago – and to see a Kafir trader's shop with anything in the way of European clothing beyond blankets and handkerchiefs was a thing unheard of. *Red clay* to smear their bodies; *beads* and *wire* with which they used to manufacture native ornaments, *blankets* costing seldom more than 10/- or 12/- up here in Kafirland, and *common red handkerchiefs* for the head. Add to these a few *three-legged cooking pots, buckets* for drawing water, and *tin dishes* of different shapes and sizes and you have the complete requisites of the stock in trade of a Kafir trader's shop twelve years ago. No, I have forgotten to mention small circular *looking-glasses* set in metallic frames and *ear-rings, tobacco,* and *tinder-boxes* and *steels*. . . . In those days shops used to be far and few between. Now things are very different – shops are more numerous and every shop has some kind of European clothing. . . . Yes, and not only ordinary apparel such as *coats, trousers, boots,* stuff for making ordinary *dresses,* but often you will find a shop as well supplied in the heart of Kafirland as in many a shop in the Colony . . . *soap, candles, tea, coffee, cocoa,* and *sugar,* blue starch, ladies kid boots, ready made mantles, shawls, bonnets and hats (ready trimmed) all these sort of things are to be purchased in Kafir traders' shops. Also *scents, scented soaps, jewelry,* etc.[35]

Certain other features apparent in the 1870s occurred throughout the Cape. The first of these was the great rise of the part played by sheep and wool in the peasant economy. There were (mission figures of 1849 revealed) fewer than three thousand sheep on thirty-two mission stations, and Brookes suggests that this was probably the sum total of sheep owned by Africans in the Cape at that time.[36] Although this figure should be revised upwards (for there are several mentions in the 1840s of payment to non-mission Africans for service on farms being

---

* Several factors were at work in this shift, such as the psychological ones of habit and reliance, state or mission insistence on certain purchases (such as 'European' clothing), the decline of traditional crafts in the face of competition from manufactured goods, and so on. The topic awaits fuller exploration.

made in sheep), the enormous growth in African sheep ownership remains a striking feature of the sixties and seventies. While missionaries and administrators were pleased to encourage the raising of sheep by Africans,[37] the chief reason for the large-scale adoption of woolled sheep was the appreciation by peasants of wool as a cash crop. Wool provided most districts with the chief item for exchange or sale by the mid-seventies, and from district after district, evidence is found that the desire for sheep was keen and spreading.

For instance, the Ngqikas of Kingwilliamstown district (under powerful traditionalist leadership) had by 1874 doubled the production of wool in the decade, and such value did they attach to wool sales 'that a few of them in this district have hired sheep from Europeans, and many have exchanged their largest oxen, usually kept for show or for ox races, for sheep'. A year later in the same district came word that the acquisition of sheep by African peasants meant that 'gradually and by degrees they are entering into close competition with the regularly established sheep farmer'.[38] The same story was told throughout the Transkei: as early as 1871 it was commented that 'there are now tens of thousands of Sheep in the Transkei amongst the Fingoes and other native tribes – even the Pondas [sic] are getting sheep as fast as they can'.[39]

Another feature of the 1870s was the spread of ploughs and wagons. A discussion of the technological, social and economic impact of the plough upon Nguni society follows later in this chapter: for the moment, it is sufficient to note that the use of a plough represented the basic technological adaptation of the emergent peasant; it was the most effective means of increasing agricultural production, and by mid-decade it had been very widely adopted. The spread of wagons had two implications for the peasantry. In the first place, peasants deployed their wagons and carts in the absence of any more sophisticated transport system, to dispose of their own crops for sale.

Secondly, a recurring pattern of the period was the doubling-up of transport riding and peasant activities. What was a transport rider or kurveyor? With the new concentrations of population inland, and especially before the rail network was completed, the need for transport by road was greatly increased; the slow journeys of laden ox-wagons involved demanding but profitable work, and it was work which became the preserve of a flourishing group of African transport riders and drivers.* The essence of transport riding was that the possessor of wagon(s) and team(s) of trained oxen would contract with merchant, trader or farmer to deliver goods, at a price agreed per

---

* They are reminiscent of the wagoners and transporters who plied a similar trade in the American interior before the completion of the railway lines there. But while Wells Fargo and the Pony Express have become part of the popular image of the West, South Africa's transport riders with their wagons, Cape carts and Scotch carts, have been relegated to an almost total obscurity. They deserve a saga to themselves.

hundredweight. (A fully loaded buck wagon, with full team of eighteen oxen, would carry up to three tons of cargo.)

Many peasants resorted to transport riding once their own crops were harvested: typically, a Mfengu would make the trip from Tsomo or Nqamakwe to Queenstown or Kingwilliamstown to sell his own produce, and then return to Fingoland with a consignment of goods for local traders. Transport riding was also a convenient means of earning enough money to obtain land: many Africans at this time would pursue full-time occupations as teamsters or wagoners until they had accumulated sufficient wealth to purchase or hire lands and set up as farmers. A cross section of relatively successful Africans (whose biographical details were collected in 1887) illustrates these patterns. Of 926 ex-scholars of Lovedale, seventy were still full-time transport riders, almost as many were described as active in transport *and* in farming, while several of those successfully established as peasant farmers had acquired land after making money in transport enterprises.[40]

A third aspect of the period was the amount of diversification as well as the increased production of familiar crops resorted to in order to enlarge the saleable surplus. The adoption of wool on a large scale as a cash earner was the most obvious instance of this, but the tilling of larger areas and the raising of grains, vegetables and fruit specifically for marketing also took place. Africans around Kingwilliamstown profited from 'the high prices given for wool and every other product they can bring to market'. From Queenstown, it was reported that the quantities of maize and sorghum sown had actually diminished in favour of the more marketable wheat, barley and oats. An official from this latter district, writing in 1883, was explicit: 'it is noticeable that they are turning their attention to the growth of peas, beans, and fruit trees – in fact all that is saleable – these latter having a few years ago been quite unregarded by them'.[41] Just how willing to experiment and to diversify were the more enterprising among the Mfengu and Thembu peasants can be gathered from the records of two meetings. At an agriculture show held in Nqamakwe, Fingoland, in 1880, prizes were awarded for wheat, barley, oats, potatoes, sweet potatoes, forage, maize, sorghum, tobacco, cabbages, turnips, beetroot, wool, bread, butter, dried fruit, cheeses, bacon, ham and handicrafts.[42] Similarly, some of the hundred African farmers of Cofimvaba (Emigrant Tembuland) who met in 1876 reported their endeavours with wheat, oats, barley, fruit trees, potatoes, peas, melons, beet, radish, turnips and pumpkins.[43]

Such experiment and enterprise involved technological adaptations, too: the plough ceased to be the only 'European' agricultural implement used,[44] and enclosure and irrigation were increasingly resorted to. In Queenstown district, where plough and harrow had by 1883 'almost entirely' replaced pick and hoe, during a dry season the 'industry and intelligence of the natives in conserving water and excavating water furrows for irrigation' was remarked; while in Southeyville it was said that there was not a stream nor spring but was used for irrigation.[45]

None of the peasant advances of the 1870s thus far described took place in a social or political vacuum; indeed, the economic openings and opportunities so assiduously pursued were accompanied by legislative and administrative measures that in several instances might have been expected to stifle peasant enterprise, to prevent independent African economic activity and to channel black hands instead into areas of wage labour. Indeed, during the seventies two opposing and dialectically related sets of interests are plainly visible: the increased demands by white employers for black labour, and an increased attempt by Africans to find alternative forms of income than low-paid wage labour whereby to meet the demands of the state and their own steadily rising consumption needs.

That white employers – especially farmers – desired more labour is easily demonstrated: the editorials, correspondence columns and Assembly debates are replete with bitter complaints of 'labour shortage', especially from rural areas. White landowners found that Africans preferred the higher wages offered on public works, on the railways and the mines, and in domestic service in towns. As one writer put it, 'the only platform on which all stand agreed is this, that the prosperity of the country is retarded for a sufficient supply of labour and that something ought to be done to remedy the evil'.[46] Many were the prescriptions and nostrums devised to 'remedy the evil'. The Cape Assembly, enjoying Responsible Government after 1872, did its best to accelerate labour supplies to meet the new demands: revised tax laws, pass laws, location laws and vagrancy laws reflected the industry of the legislators and the interests of their constituents. A series of Location Acts (Nos. 2/1869, 6/1876, and 37/1884) were passed in the Cape with the aim of reducing the numbers of 'idle squatters' (i.e., rent-paying tenants economically active on their own behalf) on white-owned lands.* Another measure propounded in the Cape had the added attraction of being seen as 'progressive', and won considerable liberal and missionary support: namely, the granting of individual title deeds to Africans, and introducing surveys of communally owned lands. As de Kiewiet has pointed out, the collusion might have been unintentional but there was an overlap between 'a genuine

---

* Although, as Stanley Trapido has pointed out, there was no general anti-squatter act passed in the Cape until 1892 and thereafter (for which see pp. 135–7). The Cape Liberals managed to defeat a number of more swingeing anti-squatter bills that aimed to inhibit the growth of a market-oriented African peasantry: nos. 16/1859, 15/1871, 9/1875 all failed to become law. (S. Trapido, 'Cape Liberalism Revisited', *Coll. Sem. Papers*, Vol. 4, No. 17, University of London, Inst. Comm. Stud., 1973, pp. 55–6, and fn. 19.)

humanitarian desire to improve the condition of the natives and the selfish motive of exploitation'.[47] Desire and motive meshed neatly for J. X. Merriman, the Cape Liberal politician:

> The gradual introduction of individual tenure of land among the natives ...
> will ... deprive numbers of natives of the means of leading a lazy, lounging
> life, at the expense of their more industrious fellows, and will also form an
> inducement to others to endeavour to obtain the means of purchase....
> [T]housands of natives ... will be forced to enter the colonial labour market
> to supply the wants thus created.[48]

Despite these attentions, a very large number of Africans continued to pursue other livelihoods in expressed preference to working for low wages or upon poor terms for white landowners. Some chose wage labour at the more remunerative levels then obtaining elsewhere; others pursued trades, frequently but not exclusively transport riding, often linking this with peasant farming; the peasant majority relied upon wool and other products to meet hut-tax and rents or to buy trade goods.

Among this latter category were the Cape's squatter-peasants, including Africans living on unalienated Crown Land, as well as the larger proportion living upon white-owned land as labour-tenants, rent-tenants or as share-croppers. Statistics are almost totally absent: the Cape Census Report for 1875 complained that of the 'considerable class of bywoners' only seventy-seven were returned as such;[49] few farmers would ever admit officially to transgressing the various anti-squatter laws. In certain districts, however, it is clear that renting land in some form or other predominated as the *modus vivendi* for the African inhabitants, particularly where land ownership was concentrated and absentee landlordism common. This was true of several Eastern Cape districts, especially Albany (the land between Grahamstown and the coast, notably Alexandria and Bathurst) and the districts on either side of the Fish river (Somerset East, Bedford, Stutterheim, Fort Beaufort and Cathcart). From all of these districts there is evidence of wide-spread 'squatting'. From Fort Beaufort it was reported that 'vast numbers of Kafirs have been allowed by landed proprietors in this district to hire ground from them'; in Bedford the majority of Africans living in the district were share-croppers ('sowed on the halves'); and in Alexandria Africans could lease ground for agricultural purposes at very cheap rates, and grew enough grain for their own wants as well as 'a fair quantity' for the market.[50] The Cape *Commission on Laws and Customs* was told in 1883 that most Africans in Albany electoral division rented land from white farmers; an example was cited of an entire farm occupied by squatter-peasants who paid the not inconsiderable annual rent of £80. A more common rental in Albany was £5 to £10: the tenants lived by agriculture, doubling up as transport riders when opportunities offered. Apart from the maize and sorghum they raised for themselves, they sold wheat, barley and oats in local towns.[51] One can easily believe the description of the Albany district that appeared in an Eastern Province newspaper in 1887:

> Go where you will between Grahamstown and Bathurst, between Howison's Poort and Alexandria, and thence to the seaboard farms, and you may find at short intervals of distance Kafir huts. They have been erected by permission of the farmer whose ground they are on, in order that he may obtain a cheap supply of labour when he desires it.[52]

The Location Acts of 1876 and 1884, together with other expressions of anti-squatting pressure, sought to extirpate leasing by Africans on private lands by a system of fines, but excepting 'bona fide labourers'. While these acts might have been fairly strictly applied at times in some district or other, they were for the greater part evaded with impunity. In almost any area of the Eastern Cape, there would have lived whites who opposed, and others who favoured, leasing to Africans: the latter were often less vociferous for several reasons, not least among which was that advocacy of squatting was tantamount to public confession of the transgression of several statutes. But in every district there were farmers who sought through leases to squatter-peasants to assure a labour supply for periods like sowing and harvesting, and there were other landowners who simply sought the income from rents. When anti-squatting provisions were applied with any rigour, there were invariably some whites who suffered economically. In Fort Beaufort the application of the 1884 Act caused the exodus of 'a large number of natives who [had] been residing in the district a long time', and an annoyed (and anonymous) letter-writer reminded his readers that most of the large grain crops harvested in the district in the past had been thanks to the labour of African tenants. This was the case in neighbouring districts, too – he continued – and 'without the aid of the native squatters very many of our farmers would find their income from agricultural sources very much diminished'. Another correspondent to the same newspaper described the squatter-peasants who had been evicted as having become fairly well off in the possession of cattle, horses, sheep and goats.[53]

Thus far it has been argued that the development of a peasant class provided one of the ways in which Africans could seek alternative forms of existence within the colonial state and economy to that of wage labour on white farms. The successful peasant could grow enough crops or clip enough wool and sell enough hides to provide his family with trade goods and to pay the hut tax or road rate or rent levied upon him. For many, the involvement in the cash economy was not yet great; as the agent with the Gcalekas put it in 1875, few of that tribe worked upon the roads: 'The Galekas do not like hard work; their wants are so few that the money realized by the sale of wool and skins enables them to obtain all the clothing they require – blankets – and the produce of their gardens supplies the family with food, from year to year.'[54] More sophisticated consumers had also to become more sophisticated producers, and as we have seen this was precisely the response of the Oxkraal Mfengu, the Fingoland immigrants, the peasants of Emigrant Tembuland or the registered voters and landowners in Victoria East and other Ciskei divisions.

A further factor affecting the formation of a peasantry was the presence of those colonial interests – often strategically well placed to influence the Cape administration – which favoured the rise of a 'free' consumer-producer peasantry. Missionary support for the creation of a peasantry was discussed in the previous chapter; it remains to illustrate that important mercantile interests (the other wing of Cape Liberalism) also identified their self-interest with the development of an African peasantry.

At its ideologically broadest or vaguest, the creation of a peasantry was upheld as an economic good in that it expanded commerce, and as a social good in that it created class allies of blacks. Charles Levey, the magistrate at Cofimvaba (who encouraged the Native Farmers Association and the holding of agricultural shows, and who was later elected as a 'liberal' to represent the Tembuland division), explained why he was well pleased with the formation of the black farmers' body: it was 'creating a spirit of emulation amongst the native farmers, and forming a bond of association amongst the wealthiest classes; it does much to counteract the influences of the chiefs.'[55] He also mentioned that at the inception of the Association in question not only a hundred Africans of 'the wealthiest classes' were present, but also 'missionaries and merchants* interested in their welfare'.[56]

Why were merchants interested in the welfare of African peasants and farmers? An editorial in a pro-mercantile publication answered this question fairly explicitly in 1866:

> It is not only our interest to be at peace with them, but if they can be elevated in the scale of being, they may prove to be good customers. . . . But if these people can be taught to grow wheat and wool, and other commodities, like their European neighbours, their wants will increase as they rise in civilization, and they will take no mean share in the commercial success of the colony. In this direction Cape producers must look for a

* One wonders whether any of the merchants present in 1876 had earlier been among those Queenstown merchants and Glen Grey traders who worried (in 1864) about the impending exodus of Thembu from Glen Grey to Emigrant Tembuland. Warner, Agent with the Thembu, had warned Governor Wodehouse to 'strike while the iron is hot, and let [the Thembu] move at once, lest they should change their minds; for I fancy the traders, and some of the Queenstown store keepers also who fear their craft is in danger, are tampering with them, and trying to dissuade them from coming'. (Cape Arch., G. H. 8/48, Letters from Native Chiefs and Others, 1854–84, Warner, 8 April 1864.)

population of consumers, and not to emigration from Europe. So long as the Natives remain mere servants, it is not very likely that their wants will largely increase. But let them have farms and flocks of their own . . . let them have commerce, not only with their own tribe, but with the world – and we shall find the hut exchanged for the homestead, and the native districts become centres of commercial activity.[57]

This was couched in the future tense and conditional mood: to see prediction made real, one need travel forward in time a mere two decades, to Queenstown in 1885. It was proposed to evict several thousand African peasants from the Glen Grey district to facilitate the settlement of fewer than five hundred white farmers. The predominantly English-speaking merchant faction in the town opposed this as keenly as it was supported by the (largely Dutch) white farming population of the district. 'We admit to being selfish,' cried the editor of the *Queenstown Free Press*, himself a member of the Chamber of Commerce; the desirability of leaving the African inhabitants on the land was the value of the trade they represented.[58] A few weeks later he elaborated. The 31,000 Africans in Glen Grey produced at the very least £42,750 worth of produce, and bought a minimum of £35,000 worth of goods from the town – and the conclusion was hammered home: 'We believe the native population of six thousand families will be found far more profitable to Queenstown than European occupation of four hundred and fifty families.'[59]

The editor, a Mr Barrable, was also present at a public meeting held in the town shortly afterwards, where the nature of mercantile interests was made unselfconsciously plain. The wholesale merchant Mr A. Morum told the gathering that 'the natives cultivated ten times more than the farmers'; and his business rival T. W. Edkins concurred: 'Gentlemen not in business had no idea of the enormous trade that was done with these natives, nor the amount of grain produced by them in good seasons. If the removals took place, Queenstown would lose this trade.' The local Methodist minister, a Mr Lamplough, lent his support, urging Queenstown not to make the same error as other frontier communities: 'Look how Alice went down, and look at the depressed state of Fort Beaufort since the natives were cleared out.'[60]

When merchants and their publicists perceived their interests as accurately and explicitly as they did,[61] it comes as no surprise to find that they took active steps to encourage black peasants to sell their produce and to buy manufactured goods. They attended the Native Farmers Association meetings, and applauded Mr Levey's efforts; Peacock Bros of Queenstown offered £10 prizes to the three most extensive wheat growers in the district, and other firms followed suit with prizes at agricultural shows; Kingwilliamstown merchants wrote to Transkei magistrates pressing for increased and better quality wool production by African peasants.[62] J. J. Irvine of Kingwilliamstown, a wealthy merchant who took an active role in Cape politics, was a wholesale retailer 'more or less directly interested in as many as twenty large stores or trading establishments' in peasant areas,[63] and an articulate advocate of extended imperial control, of greater involvement of Africans in the commercial economy, and of the spread of a peasantry.

Merchants like these were the spokesmen for that group of interests that was served by the trade in frontier towns, especially Kingwilliamstown and Queenstown, but also smaller market centres like Alice, Komgha, Indwe, Wodehouse, and so on. The prosperity of Kingwilliamstown and Queenstown must have rested to a substantial degree upon trade with the peasantry; as J. X. Merriman noted in 1882, the wealth of Kingwilliamstown 'seems to have a solid basis in the increase of population and in the increased demand among the natives for manufactured articles'.[64]*

3 PROLETARIANS, PEASANTS AND 'PROGRESSIVE FARMERS': STRATIFICATION IN THE CAPE

What white landowners, farmers and their elected representatives had failed by legislation to bring about – the diminution of Africans' freedom of choice and their diversion into labour upon white farms – the droughts and wars of the years 1877 to 1881 were partially to achieve. Large numbers of 'marginal men' and small peasants in the Ciskei were proletarianized by the Cape–Xhosa war of 1877–8, as well as by the severe droughts which were its climatic backdrop. This war, and also the Mpondomise–Thembu uprising of 1881, was followed by further land expropriations and the enforced migrations of clans, and in several districts led directly to a reversal of peasant gains of previous years.

Even before war broke out, drought had bitten deeply into the resources of the Ciskei peasantry. Two-thirds of the crops failed; the number of men forced to seek work doubled in a single year; financial depression, scarcity, stagnating trade and want of food were the motifs in the dirge-like reports that preceded the war. The economic and social origins of the war were intermeshed with Gcaleka and Ngqika resentment of the Mfengu. Not only had Mfengu 'loyalists' been rewarded with tracts of Gcaleka and Ngqika territory, but they had also served the colonists as military allies and as an armed police force for several decades.[65] By 1877 Gcaleka hostility towards the economically favoured Mfengu reached uncontrollable proportions, and the fighting which began as a local skirmish spread to draw in imperial as well as colonial troops and their African allies to crush the Gcaleka and

* It would be extremely interesting – but is beyond the bounds of this book – to investigate the extent to which trade with the African peasantry contributed to the growth of these towns, to the rise of East London as a port, and to the economic development of the Border region as a whole.

Ngqika forces. (Ten years earlier, this sequence of events had been adumbrated by a colonial official who advised that the Cape government should 'keep up until a fitting time, without actually causing a rupture, the old animosity between Kafir and Fingoe, and this has effectively been done [by the Mfengu emigrations across the Kei].... For many years, the Kafirs will require a watchful policy, and if they are to fight, it is better that they should do so with the Fingoe first.')[66]

Detailed accounts exist of the military campaigns, of the clash between imperial command and colonial soldiery, and of the course of the war, seemingly over by December 1877, but flaring up again in the New Year and persisting until mid-June 1878, when the conclusion was hastened by the death of the Ngqika-Rarabe leader Sandile.[67] Here, discussion will be confined to the features of the 1877–8 war that affected the presence and condition of an African peasantry.

Especially in its prosecution by colonial troops and their black allies, the war was to a striking extent marked by plunder and looting of the meagre resources of the Ngqika and Gcaleka – that is, it was to a large degree warfare pursued by the destruction of the economic capacity of the enemy. It was not merely that the 'rebels' lost a vastly higher number of men than their mounted and better armed adversaries, that ensured their defeat, but in addition the capture of their cattle, sheep and corn stocks, and the destruction of their standing crops, reduced them to their piteous state in the Pirie forests by the first quarter of 1878. A few examples, selected virtually at random from the copious printed and manuscript sources for the war may serve to give something of its flavour.

In October 1877, the commander of a group of Mfengu soldiers reported that a patrol had resulted in 'the destruction of many huts, and capture of 150 head of cattle, 500 or 600 sheep, and forty of the enemy shot'; later in the same month, police, volunteers, and African levies 'went out ... [and] laid waste many miles of country'; by December, Commander Griffith was reporting as 'the result of the day's operations' the capture of 2,000 cattle and many more goats and sheep. A diary kept by a Captain Spalding applauded the Mfengu soldiers: 'blazing kraals as far as the eye could reach proclaimed the destructive activity of our native allies'. (Of his white – colonial – allies, the Frontier Armed Mounted Police, this regular soldier noted that their military conduct was 'apt to degenerate into desultory or promiscuous cattle lifting'.) By 27 November, General A. T. Cunynghame, the Commander-in-Chief, reported to Frere that 20,000 Gcaleka cattle – or half their total herds – had been captured by his forces.[68]

In January 1878, the post-war plans that Frere and Carnarvon were drawing up had to be shelved as full-scale rebellion in the Eastern Province broke out. It was essentially the rebellion of hungry and desperate men who attacked trading stores and food consignments guarded by police and soldiers on public roads.[69] The Ngqika were joined by some Thembu factions; the capture of livestock was renewed on a scale that outstripped even that of the previous year's engagements. Frere deprecated the 'misfortune' that in this 'present and all Colonial wars' local troops were paid not by salaries and rations, but by booty. Between eight and ten thousand cattle were taken in a single engagement near Komgha in January; by the end of that month it was reported that 'The Kafirs present the appearance of being in great want; all the mealie pits reported to be empty.' The Chichabes Valley clash – the heaviest fighting of the war – saw sixty rebels killed, and 12,000 cattle and 8,000 sheep captured.[70]

The manner of warfare was simple in the extreme, almost mundane. The magistrate J. Hemming exchanged his civil office for the rank of commandant during the hostilities, and described the progress of his detachment in typical language. He listed in detail the few thousand head of stock they had taken since his last report, and added: 'All the huts en route were destroyed, the kraals were also examined and only small quantities of grain found in some of the pits, and all found was taken out and given to our horses.' Eventually, by April 1878, the war was nearly over, limited by then to 'flushing out' Sarili and Sandile from the wooded strongholds in the Pirie forests and Buffalo Poort Valley. This operation was described by the 'War Horse', Sir Frederic Thesiger (who had replaced Cunynghame as Commander-in-Chief): 'All that could be done in the meantime was to keep the Kafirs in, and prevent their obtaining cattle and other supplies from the outside. To assist this, the Indian corn gardens in the vicinity of the forest were ... destroyed.'[71]

The defeated rebels, in short, lost not only the war, but also the bulk of their means of subsistence. By the end of April, 'the rebels in the Buffallo [sic] range were suffering from hunger',[72] and the devastated and depressed state of Africans in the Eastern Cape war zone was used by imperial and colonial authorities to serve the interests of would-be employers and settlers. Frere wrote that the Cape ministry was following the precedent of George Grey in 1857, distributing the survivors 'throughout the interior of the colony, where a large proportion settled down as a permanent addition to the labouring population'. They had 'taken steps to enable all who are ready for work to find it'.[73] The 'Gaika Locations' (land in the districts of Cathcart and Alice) were confiscated, and divided into white farms, and the shattered Ngqika were driven across the Kei to join a mainly Gcaleka population in the congested districts of Kentani and Willowvale. There they became in later years a byword for conservatism, for 'red' and 'heathenish' ways and for a resistance to any 'improvements' or experiments. Yet before the war and their spoliation, the Ngqika had demonstrated clearly their responsiveness to opportunity: evidence from the early 1870s has already been quoted which told of doubled wool production, the sale of cattle to buy sheep, a much greater volume of trade, and so on.[74] This is how these same peasants were described after defeat and removal to 'a very dry' area:

> The present position of the Gaikas who are forming their new home in the Transkei is not very favourable to agricultural development. The country to them is new; they have lost a great deal of stock during the war, and from want of pasturage. At present they are drawing mealies from the Government, and this will in all probability be continued until they have reaped their own crops.[75]

Not all the Ngqika supported Sandile's rebellion, and among those who remained loyal to the Cape Government were some who feared to lose the gains they had made as peasant producers. One of their number appealed to Charles Brownlee, in the year before war broke out: 'My father, I hear the rumours. . . . What is to become of me should war break out? I have hired land and have a large flock of sheep, and have waggons on the roads. I will lose all in the case of war.'[76] Yet the more enterprising of the Ngqika did not escape the fate of their rebel clansmen; a spokesman for the Aborigines Protection Society pointed out indignantly on their behalf that 'loyal Gaika' had been evacuated to the Transkei, including those whom Frere himself had described in a despatch of 9 January 1878 as 'the Gaika cultivators who are mixed up with the industrious and intelligent German settlers and are rapidly learning to cultivate almost as carefully and with as much industry as their European neighbours'.[77]

The Thembu and Mpondomise uprising of 1880–81 had very similar results for those involved, and the military operations followed the pattern of 1877–8, except that resistance was feebler, and the Cape's volunteer forces enjoyed an even more one-sided encounter. As early as February 1881, Commandant Frost telegraphed from the Transkei that 'The rebels are done; no fight left in them. It is now becoming a question of police.' (In a week's campaigning, Frost had taken 7,200 cattle.)[78] Francis Hall was a young Englishman who arrived in South Africa in 1880, and joined the Kingwilliamstown Volunteer Mounted Artillery; his account of service in the Transkei makes equally plain the lack of danger and the spur of booty. He took his place in a troop of 100 Khoisan, 150 whites, and 700 Mfengu, who 'marched on, burning all the kraals we came to. . . . On the last patrol we captured a tremendous lot of cattle and each man's share amounted to £25.'[79] After the uprising, African peasants lost further land in Tembuland, Emigrant Tembuland, and the Glen Grey location.

There were individual peasants and peasant communities which not only stayed afloat but actually prospered during the war. There were some who served in the Colonial forces, and won their share of military spoils, like those Mfengu who had 'become rich and independent from the spoils of the Galeka war',[80] or the Thembu who had 'gained considerably by the war, by the capture of large quantities of stock',[81] and others who were rewarded after the war by grants of land formerly belonging to insurgents.[82] Peasants also took advantage of the inflated demand and the higher prices for grain and stock occasioned by troop movements. In broad terms, however, the years 1877–81 saw a sharp reversal of peasant fortunes, a half in the response by peasants that had marked the early seventies. For many – but especially the Ngqika of the Ciskei – the process of proletarianization was speeded up. In the Ciskei and in 'Galekaland' (Willowvale and Kentani districts) one may accurately generalize that peasant production suffered a setback, that the standard of life deteriorated sharply, and that in those districts, henceforth, a much greater proportion than hitherto of the male population would find it necessary to seek wage employment. There were peasant farmers who continued to subsist, and even become moderately prosperous, but their survival was a concomitant of the stratification that was taking place in the Ciskei, and serves the more sharply to point up the poverty of the majority.

A glimpse of the holdings of some better-off Ciskei peasants is offered by a series of claims made for losses incurred during the 1877–8 war (and upheld by a Government Commission). From Komgha, Keiskammahoek, and Kingwilliamstown, from Queenstown, Middledrift, and Stutterheim, peasants filed claims. Their losses were mainly in livestock, but also in agricultural equipment, standing corn fields and harvested grains; they amounted to sums that ranged from a few pounds to several hundred pounds.[83] Throughout the eighties, there is evidence of continued enterprise and prosperity amongst some Eastern Province and Ciskei peasants. In Bedford, Africans raised for sale 'a considerable amount' of wheat and oathay; in Kingwilliamstown a wide range of crops was marketed, especially by peasants who sought to hold land on individual titles; the usual amount of land held on individual tenure in the district was from ten to eighty acres, but there were some peasants who owned from 200 to 400 acres;[84] in Stutterheim, lands once distributed to the German legionaries were purchased and occupied by a community of highly productive peasants.[85] The Peddie Mfengu continued to supply the markets of both Grahamstown and Kingwilliamstown with food; and in 1888 they were reported to have 'appreciated the advantage of machinery in agriculture, and have this year hired strippers to harvest their corn' and 'machinery to thrash and clean their wheat'.[86]

Yet the same area exhibited very clearly that such gains were not evenly distributed, and that the relative success of a minority was won while the majority experienced privation and poverty.[87] One of the most frequently sounded notes in official reports from the Ciskei during the eighties was the increasing level of proletarianization: from Victoria East, Peddie, Kingwilliamstown, Keiskammahoek, Stockenstroom, Komgha, and Middledrift came accounts of congestion, of the landlessness of younger men, and of the annual migrations of thousands in search of work.[88] Some reports specifically mentioned the disparity in wealth that characterized the Ciskei population at this time: from Tamacha, in the Kingwilliamstown district, one learns that some held large portions of arable land and others no land at all; from Keiskammahoek that the headmen and their relatives received the lion's share of the best farming ground; from Glen Grey that while 'a superior class of natives' owned 'substantial houses, dams, and enclosed gardens' the majority suffered 'a great deal of poverty'.[89]

East and north of the Kei river, the effects of the war were less heavily felt, and in both Fingoland and Emigrant Tembuland peasants managed to consolidate their earlier gains. In Fingoland, several of the most well-to-do Mfengu bought farms in the late 'Gaika locations': one man paid £520 and another £300 for his land. Even in a year of poor rains, the Mfengu in Tsomo had sufficient surplus grain (from their store-pits and from grain harvested more recently) to make good sales; a few years before, this district had been dubbed the 'granary of Fingoland'.[90]

In Emigrant Tembuland, peasants continued to bring a range of crops as well as wool to the markets in Indwe, Dordrecht, and Queenstown; they grew large quantities of wheat solely as a cash crop, they outbid whites for cattle and land at auctions, and they planted fruit trees more widely than any other peasant community in the Cape.[91] Let us look a little more closely at the peasant community in what became the districts of Cala and St Mark's, using evidence presented to a government enquiry in 1882. Specifically, we can examine 700 men and their families who qualified by previous residence and by loyalty during the 1880–81 uprising for small farms of from one to fifteen morgen (2·1 to 31·5 acres) of arable land plus some commonage for pasture, at a quit-rent of five shillings per morgen per annum. Their material circumstances were modest enough in absolute terms, but relative to those of their parents or grandparents, are a measure of the changes that had taken place in the Nguni economy. The 700 families were predominantly although not exclusively Christians; the size of their holdings conferred a rough equality of wealth among them, but permitted individual variations. At the upper reaches of the scale* were men like the Mfengu Danavu, who owned forty-two cattle, sixty sheep and goats, a wagon and two ploughs; or Nqueniso, who had twenty cattle, 100 sheep and goats, and also owned land in the Fort Beaufort district; or Kuse, with forty cattle and seventy sheep as well as a wagon and plough; or the father and son Mguli, with seventy cattle, nine horses, 200 sheep, three wagons and three ploughs between them – and so the list could be continued.[92]

* That is, the upper reaches of the 700 family heads: the wealthiest men in the district are *not* being discussed here, as they will be mentioned in another context – see p. 93 below.

In the fourth geographical grouping – the eastern Transkei and Griqualand East – the eighties saw the same sort of economic spurt that took place in Fingoland and Emigrant Tembuland a decade or so earlier. The by now familiar pattern of diversification, increased production and the search for forms of land tenure conferring security and individual control, repeated itself. A substantial amount of grain and wool was sold, more cash circulated, more land was bought, and much of the increased trade was borne by peasants doubling up as transport riders. In 1879 the magistrate of Umzimkulu in Griqualand East commented on the growth of trade, and on a 'growing desire on the part of the natives to become proprietors of land – they have purchased 38,000 acres, giving in one instance as much as £1,000 for a farm of £3,000 acres'. Only three years later the magistrate claimed that ownership of land by Africans was perhaps more conspicuous in Umzimkulu than in any other district, and that about 8,000 peasants dwelled on some 90,000 acres which they had purchased.[93]

The plateau of East Griqualand was excellently suited to grain crops, and a common feature of the reports from its districts in the 1880s was that of fairly large-scale grain exports. Gatberg (after the 1882 Tembuland Commission to be delimited as a white area, and renamed Maclear) supplied food to Dordrecht, Queenstown, Kamastone, Butterworth and Aliwal North in 1878. Tsomo, even in a year of comparatively poor harvest, 'sent out of the district for sale' a large quantity of grain. In Engcobo, it was specified, the cultivation of grain crops was being afforded close attention by black peasants who were irrigating the land and sowing more wheat.[94] The Bhaca clans in the Mount Frere district received a magistrate for the first time in 1876, and in 1880–81 they sided with the colonial authorities against the Mpondomise, their neighbours and traditional rivals. They reaped economic rewards from their alliance: 'the change that has come over the tribe in the last year is marvellous, ten years under ordinary circumstances would not have advanced them as much,' declared their magistrate.[95] Apart from earning £14,000 in wages with the military, the Bhaca were producing much more wool and were selling 10,000 hides a year to the colony. Nor were they backward as grain producers: in 1878 it had been remarked as 'unusual' that the Bhaca had exported grain to the Cape; by 1884, in contrast, the magistrate wrote that after ample provision for their domestic consumption the Bhaca 'always' had a 'considerable surplus' of grain to sell.[96] W. E. Stanford, then Resident Magistrate in Engcobo, summed up the changes taking place in the eastern Transkei: compared now

with what it was ten years ago ... marked progress will be found in many respects. Ten years ago Tembuland was in a most disturbed state.... In the Pondomisi country ... traffic was virtually at a standstill.... [Now]trade has been extensively developed. Traffic is open from the Kei drift to Kokstad

... and the ten years ago almost uninhabited plateau of Nomansland teems with population and bids fair to become a valuable grain producing district.[97]

Pondoland was also the scene of increased trading activity in the 1880s. Maize and sorghum were 'in large supply' in eastern Pondoland; cash transactions were 'largely on the increase', and the old system of barter found less favour daily: 'The thrifty native has learnt the advantage of a mode of dealing which gives him absolute control over the price paid him ... for his produce. ... There is a noticeable and increasing demand on the part of the natives for goods of a better class.'[98] The Mpondo did not only trade with Cape-based traders, but also with traders and merchants of Natal:[99] a Mr W. H. Griffin told a Natal Commission of Enquiry in 1885 that he was a merchant much involved with the Mpondo trade; that trade had 'much developed', and that the Mpondo traded 'backwards and forwards' with Natal, especially in the sale of their cattle. Hides, wool, maize and sorghum left Pondoland for various destinations – to Kingwilliamstown, East London or Natal; the maize was shipped 'to Natal or East London, just as the markets offer', as well as to Port Alfred and Port Elizabeth.[100]

By the middle or late eighties, then, the African peasantry was geographically much more widespread and numerically far greater than before 1870; in all the predominantly African areas of the Cape, as well as in those districts of the Transkei over which the Cape exerted influence but not yet formal rule, a peasant class had emerged. Peasants still included a core of mission-based or mission-oriented peasants, but they were by now greatly outnumbered by non-mission peasants. Even the supposed superiority on the part of mission-inspired peasants – taken for granted before 1870 – was no longer always the case. Archdeacon Waters, of the large St Mark's station in Emigrant Tembuland, recorded in 1880:

> The heathen Natives, seeing the result of industry on our mission lands, have followed the example; so that the possession of a plough or waggon is no longer the mark of a Christian owner. I have quite lately travelled through two districts, under notoriously heathen headmen, and yet the apparent cultivation in them is greater than in some professedly Christian locations.[101]

Many peasants farmed on lands still communally held – like those who lived under the 'notoriously heathen headmen' near St Mark's; others sought some form of individual or non-communal tenure. This might be through ownership by purchase or by quit-rent, or it might be in the form of a lease or 'squatting' arrangement with white landholders. Squatter-tenants might have paid in cash, kind or labour – or some combination thereof – for the right to farm a piece of land; they

90

might have farmed 'on the halves' with the land's proprietor (that is, as share-croppers); or they might have evaded all forms of rent by illegally occupying Crown or private lands. They all diversified their agricultural activities and participated in the accelerating economic processes of the Cape. In certain districts, the peasant response was more firmly delineated than in others: that is, the transition from precolonial cultivator to peasant occurred more rapidly and more fully in some areas. Often, this was due directly to market opportunities; sometimes it was aided by the modernizing 'push' from missionaries, administrators and merchants who desired the creation of an African peasantry. The timing of the transition was also affected by the leadership within the particular peasant community. The replacement of chiefs by headmen or others (who secured their position by collaborating with the colonial authorities) could weaken traditional restraints on innovation or individualism, as well as endow certain individuals with a head start in the matters of access to land and accumulation. Fingoland is one example of a community where this was the case, and Herschel (see Chapter 5) is another. Alternatively, peasant production – so far from being inhibited by the traditional leadership – could be accelerated or directed by those chiefs who thought that they could control the process (see pp. 97–8).[102]

A defining characteristic of a peasant is that he is subject to the economic demands of a political and social system outside his own immediate or traditional society. The involvement of the emergent Cape peasantry in the colonial economy is one of the most distinctive features of the period reviewed in this chapter. The development and ubiquity of trade has already been described; the other arm of the process was the collection of rents and taxes, and consequently the need for ways of raising the cash for the payment of such fees. Time and again, magistrates, missionaries and others described the disposal of agricultural surplus in order to pay taxes in terms that emphasize the ineluctability of the peasant's entanglement in the wider economic system. As the Resident Magistrate of Tsomo put it in the last year covered by this chapter:

> Now the price of grain is so very low, the native would be nowhere without his sheep, as he depends upon these . . . to get him out of what he is pleased to call his difficulties, i.e., the payment of his hut tax, school fees, and road rate. It is, I believe, generally admitted that in good sheep districts much less trouble is experienced in the collection of taxes.[103]

In addition to solving these 'difficulties' – that is, in addition to providing the African with a small cash income – peasant agriculture also conferred upon him a degree of economic 'independence': an ability to withhold, if he so preferred, his labour from white landowners or other employers. Bramsby Key, an Anglican cleric and a perceptive and sympathetic commentator on the Eastern Cape's African population, expressed this tellingly in 1890:

> They are peasant farmers. Why should they send their sons and daughters to work for wages amongst people of an alien race, who are not generally very fond of them, and who are often not very careful of their well-being? They prefer supplying their wants from the soil, as they can easily do.... So they stay at home, or if they are inclined to try their fortune in the great world outside their own valley, and have waggons and oxen, as is often the case, they 'ride transport'... for the neighbouring store-keeper.[104]

All peasants were food-producers, but not all food-producers were peasants. One is confronted with another class, much smaller in numbers, but individually more powerful; one meets with increasing frequency in the seventies and eighties African 'progressive farmers'* – men whose mode of production was more capitalist than peasant. They were men who had consolidated early peasant success or who invested income from other sources in agriculture; they were often conspicuously 'loyal' to the colonial government. Their farms – almost always on land they had purchased outright and held as individual proprietors – might be quite large, and were distinctive for the amount of re-investment of capital in the shape of fencing, walling, irrigation, improved stock breeds, and for the adoption of mixed farming. Progressive farmers adopted a way of life which in its material and ideological aspects closely resembled that of solvent and advancing farmers of other races in South Africa. 'Were it not for the colour of the occupants,' wrote the magistrate of Nqamakwe, 'I should have fancied myself in a European dwelling,[105] and remarks like this stud the sources of the late nineteenth century.

These small-scale commercial farmers built square houses, and stocked them with furniture, crockery, cutlery, stationery and the like; they bought the bulk of the food that they consumed, sent their children to boarding-schools, and were a mainstay of agricultural societies or associations.[106] Their responsibilities to the kinship group, and their observance of the distributive norms of Nguni society, tended to be replaced by more exploitative social relations and by individualistic and profit-maximizing motives. Progressive farmers employed wage

---

* Should one call them 'large peasants' or 'kulaks' or 'capitalist farmers'? I have adopted as an accurate, if clumsy, designation, 'small-scale commercial farmers'; and have also used as synonomous the usual contemporary description: 'progressive [Native] farmers'. This convenient shorthand term distinguishes its bearers from peasants on several counts: (i) that of scale: they were wealthier, and held larger units of land; (ii) that of social relations: they extracted surplus from tenants and wage labourers outside the extended family; (iii) that of market relations: they were predominantly cash farmers, not subsistence farmers who sold a small surplus; (iv) that of cultural or ideological identity: they had broken more decisively with traditional Nguni culture, and identified far more keenly with 'European' ways (or with the 'high' culture).

labourers and leased portions of their land to tenants, labour-tenants and share-croppers, and they were indistinguishable from their white neighbours in their voicing of those prejudices which accompanied the private ownership of landed property. A Mfengu farmer named Hlombeni (who owned 500 cattle) discussed 'the servant problem' with a Commission on Labour Supply, and criticized 'school natives' as unsuitable tenants: 'The educated man wants high wages; I endeavour to get the cheapest labour.' A Thembu farmer from Xalanga would 'not allow squatters unless they work or are a profit to him'.[107] E. Makholiso, a farmer from Cala, also inveighed against squatters and called for sterner penalties against them: 'We would like to have a severe law to deal with them. Because we are black you may perhaps think that we have sympathy with other black fellows who go to gaol, but as a fact we are just as great enemies of bad black people as white people are.'[108] His language illustrated to a nicety one of the basic arguments of the missionary-mercantile spokesmen who asserted that 'civilization' would forge bonds of class solidarity across the colour line.

In some cases, the circumstances and careers of individual small-scale commercial farmers can be traced in the Cape records. At the inaugural meeting of the Cofimvaba Native Farmers Association in 1876, forty-four of the farmers handed in lists of the improvements that they had carried out. Headman Ncamiso Kalipa (the Kalipas were a wealthy family who crop up in several sources) had sown ten bags of wheat, as well as oats, barley, potatoes, beet, cabbage, pumpkins and maize; Paulus Madhliwa had erected a stone kraal and fenced his fields, and sown thirty-six acres of wheat; Jonas Tyuluta owned two houses, irrigated his lands with three water courses, had an orchard of fruit trees, and had sown wheat.[109] In 1882, the Tembuland Commissioners, in their report, left further details of the Cofimvaba-Xalanga community and its stratum of progressive farmers. They described the substantial farms of thirty-eight Thembu and Mfengu proprietors, farms which ranged from 250 to 1,710 morgen; on his farm, Sol Kalipa owned 120 cattle, 20 horses, 500 sheep and goats, two wagons and three ploughs; Mayongo ran 220 cattle, 44 horses, and 350 small stock, rode transport on his two wagons and employed no fewer than five ploughs on his lands. These prosperous farmers surface again, several of them, in a report by P. Mtyoba, Secretary of the Native Farmers Association, of a meeting held in 1884: once again, against the names of individuals are listed an imposing array of agricultural improvements and achievements.[110]

For a few individuals, the details of their careers are even fuller. John Go's passage from being a policeman and government agent into sheep-farming has already been described (p. 48). He then made enough money from wool and from a poultry venture to buy a farm for the considerable sum of £2,000 near the Impetu river and to buy other land elsewhere: even after these purchases, commented Brownlee in 1866, 'he is still a wealthy man'. Indeed he was: the Commission that adjudicated claims for losses in the 1877–8 war upheld his claim for 200 cattle, 300 sheep and a house, and in his evidence Go admitted that he had been fortunate, for besides the flock that he had lost, 'the greater part' of his sheep were safe upon another farm![111]

A most illuminating account of the genesis of a progressive farmer and a precise statement of his economic aims and outlook is provided by Stephen F. Sonjica, a Mfengu and 'a man of substance'. He addressed a meeting of African peasants in Middledrift, near Alice, in 1911 or 1912, calling his talk 'How I Became a Successful Farmer'. His own parents had 'loved stock-raising to a fault, and on the contrary had a laissez-faire attitude towards soil-tillage'. Despite them, he had clearly foreseen (he told his audience) the benefits of the proper cultivation of the soil and expressed to his father the desire to buy land. 'Buy land,' expostulated his father, 'How can you want to buy land? Don't you know that all land is God's, and he gave it to the chiefs only?' In the face of this 'short shrift', Sonjica

> planned to buy myself land of my own to plough elsewhere. . . . I was adamant and determined to go to seek work. Thus I left home for Kingwilliamstown and served as a mounted policeman during the War of 1877. . . . While ostensibly sending home my month's earnings to my father in the usual Native custom, I cunningly opened a private bank account into which I diverted a portion of my savings without the knowledge of my father. This went only until I had saved eighty pounds. . . . [I bought] a span of oxen with yokes, gear, plough, and the rest of agricultural paraphernalia.

He resigned his position in Kingwilliamstown and staked his all upon the land. The first year brought him only seven bags of grain, but by the fifth year he was reaping 125 bags. He had made good. He bought a wagon, and within a short time had accumulated £1,000 in savings through his farming.

> I now purchased a small farm . . . and plots of land at various places at what was considered high prices in those days. . . . I cannot too strongly recommend [farming] as a profession to my fellow men. . . . They should however adopt modern methods of profit making. . . . No native farmer is worth calling a farmer who has no agent in a big town through whom he may dispose of his produce at market prices.[112]

There were never, in the late nineteenth century, very many Sonjicas, Kalipas or Gos; one has direct evidence of some several hundred, and by inference and indirect evidence could safely estimate that there were in the Cape by 1890 somewhere between one and two thousand small-scale commercial farmers in the African population. More important than their numbers is their existence as a social group, the manner in which they highlight the response by Africans to economic opportunities, and the way in which their emergence illustrates the extent of social stratification amongst Africans.

4 SOCIAL CHANGE IN NGUNI SOCIETY

The basic technological bridge from precolonial cultivator to peasant was undoubtedly the adoption of the ox-drawn plough; not all the ramifications of that change have been fully recognized in the histories that allude to it. In districts where the plough was widely used, the balance shifted from pastoralism to cultivation as the basis of subsistence; decreasing reliance on the herds, the use of animals in drawing the plough and the necessity of raising a cash income all had the effect of making southern Nguni settlements more permanent. (That this in turn had a deleterious effect upon the land and its crop-bearing capabilities will be shown in Chapter 4.) Crucially, the plough greatly increased the area open to cultivation by a family unit or household in any year, and thus made the deliberate production of an agricultural crop for sale a feasible enterprise, as opposed to the more adventitious ability to dispose of a surplus only in better-than-average years. Directly related to the deliberate raising of saleable crops was diversification, especially the sowing of wheat, vegetables and fruit.

It has been widely observed that the animal-drawn plough altered the basic sexual division of labour within Nguni societies: the use of animals was the male preserve, hence ox-drawn ploughs ensured that men would become more active in tillage. Other aspects of the change are also apparent. The widespread use of the plough meant that the economic basis of polygamy – the need of the head of a large household to have more than one (food-producing) wife – was greatly diminished. A thoughtful civil servant commented in the 1870s that:

> The more general use of the plough for gardening and other purposes, by performing work which in former years was done solely by women, is everywhere observable, and may in my opinion, be regarded as a powerful ally in restricting the extension of polygamy, and obstructing, if not entirely stopping, its progress and advance. In former times when gardening and planting of all kinds was imposed upon women, the necessity of having more than one wife, if only for gardening purposes, was at once felt, but the introduction of the plough has tended to remove this necessity.[113]

Nor were African women blind to the advantages implicit in this change: the Chief Magistrate of the Transkei wrote in the 1890s that 'Few girls will consent to marry a man who does not possess a plough, knowing that if her husband is without one, her life must be one of severe toil.'[114]

How many ploughs were acquired in these decades? De Kiewiet suggested that

the relatively expensive ploughs and wagons were not, as settlers and
magistrates were prone to believe, a reliable indication of any really general
increase in wealth. Fingoland was by all odds the most prosperous of the
native districts, yet its magistrate calculated in 1874 that there was but one
wagon to every hundred of population ...

and he proceeded to argue from this that poverty, by the seventies, was
the general condition of the Cape's Africans.[115] One is not at odds with
de Kiewiet in his survey of the shortage of land and resources imposed
upon African societies in the conquest and expropriation of their
territory, but it does appear that the actual economic topography
differed from that which he sketched. De Kiewiet seems to have relied
throughout upon the abstraction of 'the average native'; he does
mention in passing that 'possessions in cattle were not equally distributed,' but nowhere gives any indication of just how stratified African
societies were becoming. Thus he asserts that the 'moderately prosperous native was then no better off than a mediaeval serf who was
very well to do with a two wheeled wagon and a harness of thongs'.[116]
Enough evidence has been led in this chapter to demonstrate that there
were African farmers and peasants who made even 'very well to do'
serfs look decidedly impoverished. There were men whose material
possessions, as well as the income that those possessions generated, far
outstripped not only their mediaeval forebears, but also their poorer
black contemporaries.

Using only the example of Fingoland cited by de Kiewiet,
'one wagon to every hundred of population' meant (accepting the
customary contemporary estimated average family of five) that one
householder in twenty owned a wagon – and as these represented
an estimated total investment of £8,780 (or twenty pounds each), this
statistic alone might suggest inferences other than that drawn by de
Kiewiet. The number of ploughs in Fingoland (according to the same
report) was just under two thousand, so that every fourth household
used a plough, and, of course, the existence of wagons and ploughs also
meant, *a priori*, a substantial degree of concentration of the ownership
of cattle in Fingoland (just under 40,000 in 1875). That sheep were
also concentrated in Fingoland is demonstrated by a report of a generation later: in a population of 25,000 people, over 40,000 sheep were
held in about 1,500 flocks.[117]

A second set of reverberations within Nguni society caused by the
spread of peasant activity might be designated the socio-political
results. Traditional political leadership was overtly opposed and
restricted by the imperial, colonial and missionary interests, and there
were also forces within the changing society that threatened the
authority and power of the chiefs. Foremost amongst these was the
altered concept of land tenure that accompanied the emergence of
large peasants and progressive farmers: individual Africans not only

sought land within an overall situation of land shortage, but they did so within new contexts in which land could be granted by authorities other than the chief. They might still look to the chief for land allocation, but they increasingly demanded some form of security of tenure over their lands, some certainty that they could rely upon an arable plot to provide the new necessary cash income each year. A single, unusually full, source – the 1883 *Commission on Laws and Customs* – gives an indication of how widespread the hire and purchase of land on an individual basis was by the early eighties.[118]

Time and again, the authority of chiefs was challenged by the decision of peasants to look elsewhere for their rights in the land they sought. As the pressure on land increased, the chiefs became in any case less able to provide for the younger men who in turn clamoured for holdings of their own. Men who already had secured some form of individual tenure had a powerful vested interest in preserving the arrangement, so as to prevent the diminution of their own plots by overcrowding. A typical instance of this conflict between chiefs and their followers occurred amongst the Ngqikas moved to Kentani after the 1877–8 War, when the district was surveyed and divided into ten-acre lots. 'Some of the chiefs and headmen objected, but most of the people were pleased' – and, Matthew Blyth added sapiently,'the chiefs see that the granting of individual titles will destroy their influence among the headmen'.[119]

There were several ways in which traditional leaders might respond to this crucial challenge to their authority. Outright hostility to any form of individual tenure or even to steps that might suggest a desire for individual tenure, was a short-term solution: it was frequently reported that chiefs regarded with disfavour any 'improvements' upon arable lands, tending to 'regard them as an individual claim to land'.[120] Alternatively, chiefs accepted that their own powers over land had been curtailed by colonial conquest, and that they could only exercise land allocation rights over land secured in the first instance from the government; there were several instances in the seventies in the Ciskei of the purchase of farms by chiefs (usually by a form of 'communal subscription' in which followers were called upon to donate cattle towards the ultimate purchase price).[121] In these cases, land once secured was allocated by the chiefs on the 'traditional' basis. Rather different in their approach were those chiefs who accepted as inevitable the desire by their followers for individual tenure, and who operated within this novel context, still rewarding their followers with grants of land, but on a permanent and individual basis. A Methodist missionary wrote in 1871 that:

> One of the petty chiefs who governs the country towards our Xalanga station has so little faith in the stability of his power as a chief that he is endeavouring to provide for himself by disposing of his land to those who

will buy of him among the civilized natives, thus the principle of personal ownership of land is acknowledged.[122]

Equally flexible and ingenious were the Thembu chiefs who moved into Emigrant Tembuland, Matanzima, Gecelo and Darala. They awarded to some of their wealthiest subjects (usually Christians) large tracts of land, and then lobbied to have these awards upheld by the colonial authorities, which in its turn reinforced their standing amongst the Thembu. In the case of Matanzima, a particularly sophisticated approach was essayed in which personal economic advantage, the recognition of social change and a desire to retain the maximum political leverage were nicely blended: he awarded farms to 'advanced' followers, applied to have individual and inalienable title to his own extensive holdings, but requested that he retain the authority to allocate land to the majority of his (poorer) subjects, who should continue to hold land on a traditional or communal basis![123]*

It was not only over the issue of land tenure that the emergence of peasants created strains in African societies. Traditional customs and authorities were menaced in a variety of other ways. To take a simple example, the cultivation of wheat was often adopted by peasants, as the grain was readily saleable; moreover, as it was a winter crop, it could be grown after food demands had been satisfied by the maize and sorghum harvests. But, because it was a winter crop, its cultivation meant that the custom of allowing cattle to graze over stubble fields must be abrogated; the successful raising of wheat not only usually needed irrigation, but also an enclosure of some sort so as to keep the cattle out. This was the very type of 'improvement' that the chiefs were wont to contest. (An early – and obvious – response by chiefs and other traditional figures of authority (priests) was to prohibit any adoption of 'European' ways: new crops or tools or trade items were all banned by various leaders.)[124] In a discussion of economic and social changes in Pondoland, William Beinart has suggested that the rising importance during the 1880s of the production and sale of grain was one of the factors weakening the Mpondo paramount chief's control over outgoing and incoming trade in the territory. Grain production was localized in each household, tribute in grain was difficult to levy, and paramount control of surplus was further weakened. 'Local chiefs rather than the paramounts were likely to have benefited from the increase in grain production.' Similarly, at the level of the local chief,

* In the Transkei today – which was proclaimed an independent state in October 1976 in accordance with the South African government's Bantustan policy – the Chief Minister and his foremost deputy (the brothers Kaiser and George Matanzima) are descended from the Thembu chief described above. Reports of their expropriation of choice land as their own, as well as the agricultural policy which seeks to consolidate a class of well-to-do agriculturists while completing the proletarianization of the majority, call so strongly for a comparison – perhaps in a footnote – that it is with the utmost difficulty that I have resisted making it.

the same 'atomization' of productive activities to the household level was increased by a rise in cultivation, and perhaps 'even the local chiefs were displaced in some of their crucial economic activities by the traders'.[125]

Most dramatically, social antagonisms generated by the uneven spread of peasant practices could take violent forms. The 1880–81 uprisings saw a high incidence of attacks by rebels upon mission peasants and other innovators. In Xalanga, of thirty-five progressive farmers, all bar two remained loyal to the Cape Government, and their farms were all devastated by the rebels.[126] In Mpondomise territory, at the station of St Paul's, at Xokonga, the rebels

chased all the black English – i.e., Native Christians especially. . . . All were included by the name of Fingoes, although not Fingoes all, but of different clans; their places burnt down, stock taken away – cattle, horses, sheep, goats, pigs and fowls – with the exception of those who called themselves rebels.[127]

The rebel Thembu at Gwaytu 'first commenced the disturbances by plundering all the native Christians',[128] and this pattern was widely reported.

Another feature related to the emergence of a peasantry concerns the geographical mobility and dispersion of individuals and communities, and particularly the colonizing role played by Mfengu peasants. Much has been written about the conservatism of tribesmen, of their adherence to ancestral lands, and of their unwillingness to move – and South African history has cases illustrating all these. Yet there was also, in the period under discussion, a considerable amount of migration by peasants in pursuit of economic gains. Mobility tended to increase *pari passu* with the amount of skill and enterprise displayed by the individuals; the short biographies in *Lovedale: Past and Present* convey a vivid sense of the willingness of Africans to move from one district to another in search of opportunity or gain. A notable spur, sharpened by the land expropriations of mid-century, was the desire to secure land on some sort of favourable tenure: one finds individual peasants who leased land in one district, bought a plot in another, and who would then trek off into a third district when Crown Land was being sold or their own area becoming overcrowded. Districts being 'opened up', like Nomansland in the early seventies, attracted Africans from all over the rest of the Cape.

This was most sharply evidenced amongst the Mfengu, a people whose recorded history begins with a major migration and whom we have already observed moving in large numbers from the Ciskei into Fingoland and Griqualand East. During the years covered in this chapter, Mfengu migrations – either as individuals or as communities – were continuous; by the time of the 1894 Census, no district in the Cape was without a quota of Mfengu. Alan Gibson, who served as a missionary near Qumbu in Griqualand East wrote in 1885 that 'Fingo members of the church continue to pour into this district from all quarters' and that 'Fingo are trekking in large numbers, owing to the drought and overpopulation farther south.'[129] Bramsby Key commented two years later of the Mfengu that 'these people are always on the move, and will go anywhere that they can get a place to set their ploughs going'.[130]

As far as the inhabitants of a district were concerned, the ingress of Mfengu often represented more than mere immigration: in a real sense, the Mfengu came as colonizers of Transkei districts. Not only did they arrive and establish settlements that were often technologically or economically in advance of their new neighbours, but they tended to have favoured treatment in access to land and to enjoy the backing or support of the government, the ultimate wielder of political power. Governor D'Urban's vision of the Mfengu as a human buffer enjoyed a long lease; as late as the middle eighties Bishop Key described the 'fine basin of very fertile land' in the Cala district where there were 'three of the late Archdeacon's most promising colonies of Fingoes . . . they are placed most judiciously by the magistrate to act as a buffer between the colonial farmer and the raw, heathen Tembus'.[131] A magistrate of the period characterized the 'Fingo' as an 'experienced colonizer' who knew how 'to take root to the ground', who appeared 'naturally more adapted to business than his native allies', who was rich in stock, who built a superior dwelling, and was 'pushing and inclined to improve'.[132] These characteristics were resented by weaker, poorer peasants in the Transkei. A missionary who admired the Mfengu admitted that they tended to make mission stations unpopular; another that they were 'very grasping'.[133] Gibson explained the Mpondomise rebellion primarily in terms of local hostility to Mfengu settlers: 'as far as Umditshwa's tribe was concerned, the quarrel was much more bitter against the Fingo than it was against the white people'; and the assertion by an African present at the time (quoted in another context) was that all the 'black English', whether Mfengu or not, were called Fingoes and attacked.[134]

It seems that the Mfengu viewed themselves, and were viewed by other African peoples as well as by white administrators, as constituting a separate interest, exemplified by their colonizing behaviour in the Transkei. Not all peasants were migrant Mfengu, but the great majority of migrant Mfengu were peasants; as peasants, they were also subordinate political allies and military collaborators with the government, they were economic innovators and important transmitters of social change. A contemporary described the Mfengu in these words:

> Naturally as sturdy and conservative as the Kaffir, they have transferred their allegiance to us. Their chiefs have been changed to a sort of titled landowner, much as the Highland chieftains have, highly respected but

without political power, and the clansman has risen in proportion. No longer afraid of the jealousy of the chief or of the deadly weapon ... the witchdoctor, which strikes down the wealthy cattle-owner, the able counsellor, the introducer of novel customs, and skilful agriculturist, reducing them all to the uniform level of mediocrity – no longer apprehensive of this, the Fingo clansman ... is a progressive man. Still remaining a peasant farmer, for that is the only line he has yet taken to, he owns wagons and ploughs; he opens water furrows for irrigation; he is the owner of a flock of sheep, and in the interests of his agricultural pursuits he acts as carrier to the European trader.[135]

This quotation – and particularly its final sentence – recapitulates many of the features of peasant activity that this chapter has surveyed: it might be applied not only to the Mfengu but to other African peasants whom it describes equally accurately. Used thus, it serves as summary or epitome to this chapter, which has sought to narrate and to account for the large-scale emergence and establishment of the 'peasant farmer' in the two decades following the discovery of diamonds.

NOTES

1 *Eastern Province Herald*, 5 September 1871.
2 See C. G. W. Schumann, *Structural Change and Business Cycles in South Africa* (London, 1938), 75–80; D. Hobart Houghton and J. Dagut (eds.), *Source Material on the South African Economy 1860–1970*, 3 vols., (Cape Town, 1972), I, 18–19, 25, 28, 75–6, 127, 230.
3 Hobart Houghton and Dagut (eds.), op. cit., I, 222–331; D. Hobart Houghton, 'Economic Development 1865–1965', OHSA, II, 10–22; S. H. Frankel, *Capital Investment in Africa* (London, 1938), 52–74.
4 PRO, Col. Off. Papers, Series 48, Vol. 460, esp. No. 54, 27 May 1872.
5 S. T. van der Horst, *Native Labour in South Africa* (London, 1942), 89. Further interesting details about the sensitivity of the East Cape's Africans to wage levels and work conditions, and about their strikes and other strategies during the 1870s in resistance to the efforts by the Cape Government and employers to depress wages, are in an unpublished paper by A. J. Purkiss, 'The Terms of Labour on the Cape Railways, 1871–1885', delivered at the Workshop on the Social and Economic History of Southern Africa, Oxford, Inst. Comm. Stud., September 1974.
6 D. M. Goodfellow, *A Modern Economic History of South Africa* (London, 1931), 136; but see Hobart and Dagut (eds.), op. cit., 224, 228, 231; Van der Horst, op. cit., 99; J. Noble, *Descriptive Handbook of the Cape Colony* (Cape Town, 1875), 261, 273, 275.
7 H. M. Robertson, '150 Years of Economic Contact between Black and White: A Preliminary Survey', 2 parts, *S. A. Jnl. Econ.*, Vol. 2, No. 4 (December 1934), and Vol. 3, No. 1 (March 1935), p. 422; Van der Horst, op. cit., 102, 104.
8 D. J. N. Denoon (with B. Nyeko), *Southern Africa since 1800* (London, 1972), 61.

9 CPP, G. 27–'74, BBNA for 1874, 3–4; *Blue Book for the Cape Colony for 1875*, Report of Civil Commissioner for Victoria East, p. JJ16.

10 CPP, G.27–'74, BBNA, 4, 5. (According to PRO, CO 879/13, Conf. Print Afr. No. 154, p. 191, by 1877 Oba and his followers had paid off £3,300 of a total of £5,300.)

11 CPP, G.16–'76, p. 74.

12 PRO, CO 879/13, 3259, Conf. Print Afr. No. 154, p. 191 (Frere to Hicks Beach, 4 June 1878).

13 CPP, G.16–'76, BBNA, 72.

14 W. L. Blore, *Statistics of the Cape Colony* (Cape Town, 1871), 137.

15 CPP, G.16–'76, BBNA, 64.

16 *Blue Book for the Cape Colony, 1875*, pp. JJ30–31; *Blue Book for the Cape Colony , 1874*, p. JJ35; CPP, G.27–'84, BBNA, 12–13; G.21–'75, BBNA, 58; G.16–'76, 64–5.

17 CPP, G.34–'73, *Report on the Political and Social Condition of the Transkei*, 4.

18 CPP, G.27–'74, BBNA, 40–41; G.21–'75, BBNA, 33.

19 *Kaffir Express*, III, 36, 6 September 1873; J. Ayliff and J. Whiteside, *History of the Abambo, Generally known as Fingos* (Butterworth, 1912, reprinted Cape Town, 1962), 57–8; Board of Missions of the Scottish Episcopal Church, *Occasional Paper No. 2* (October 1873), 3 (report by G. Callaway).

20 CPP, G.35–'73, *Report on the Political and Social Condition of the Tambookies*, 1.

21 CPP, G.27–'74, BBNA, 59–63.

22 CPP, G.16–'76, BBNA, 85.

23 CPP, G.12–'77, BBNA, 100–101.

24 MMS Arch., SA Box XVI, Queenstown 1877–85, E. J. Warner, 17 April 1885.

25 MMS Arch., SA Box XV, Queenstown 1868–76, H. H. Dugmore to Wm. Boyce, 2 August 1870.

26 CPP, G.12–'77, BBNA, 55–7.

27 CPP, G.16–'76, BBNA, 27; G.12–'77, BBNA, 58.

28 W. Beinart, 'Peasant Production, Underdevelopment, and the Traditionalist Response in Pondoland, c. 1880–1930' (University of London, M.A. thesis, September 1973), 11–12.

29 Noble, *Descriptive Handbook*, 230–31; cf. 'The Material Advantages of Christianity', *Christian Express*, VII, 85 (1 October 1877).

30 BPP, C. 2000, Frere to Carnarvon, 13 November 1877.

31 See Frances MacNab, *On Veldt and Farm: In Bechuanaland, Cape Colony, The Transvaal and Natal* (London, 1897), 17–19.

32 *Cape Mercury*, advertisements in Vol. I, Nos. 4–6, May–June 1875.

33 G. Arrighi, 'Labor Supplies in Historical Perspective: A Study of the Proletarianization of the African Peasantry in Rhodesia', in G. Arrighi and J. Saul, *Essays on the Political Economy of Africa* (New York, 1973), 192–3.

34 SPG Arch., E. MSS, E27, J. Gordon, St Mark's, Report for quarter ending 30 September 1872.

35 SPG Arch., EMM, E29, E. Patten, Bolotwa, Report for quarter ending 30 June 1874 (emphasis in original).

36 E. H. Brookes, *The History of Native Policy in South Africa* (2nd edn., Pretoria, 1927), 392–3.

37 C. Brownlee, *Reminiscences of Kafir Life and History* (Lovedale, 1896), 10: he favoured sheep-rearing because 'the care of sheep would induce them to lead a more sheltered life' and thus help prevent fresh wars.

38 CPP, G.27–'74, 15; G.21–'75, 58. See also SPG Arch., D MSS, D37, Grahamstown 1867–74, Journal of Bishop Merriman for 1871, p. 1289, for evidence that the Gcaleka under Sarile were exchanging cattle for woolled sheep; and CPP, G.27–'74, BBNA, 61, for details of Thembu in Queenstown district who 'thoroughly under[stood] the value of woolled sheep' which were 'gradually superseding their fancy for cattle'.

39 *Eastern Province Herald*, 22 August 1871.

40 *Lovedale: Past and Present, A Register of Two Thousand Names* (Lovedale, 1887). The total of transport riders is taken from the table at the back of this book. For those active in transport and agriculture, see entries for: G. and J. Jacob (né Mqandi), I. Mahlutshana, A. Makabeni, J. Makalima, K. Mbulunga, W. I. Nonimba, T. Ntloko, N. Ntloko, P. Menzi, *et al.* For those investing in agricultural land after making money in transport, see J. Dlanga, A. Fadanu, S. Makiwane, H. Maquebela, Myoli, *et al.*

41 *Blue Book for the Cape Colony, 1875*, p. JJ35; CPP, G. 12–'77, BBNA, 135; G.8–'83, BBNA, 13.

42 CPP, C.8–'81, *Correspondence on Natives in Agricultural and Other Labour*, 22–7.

43 CPP, G.12–'77, BBNA, 101. The meeting was held to launch the Native Farmers Association in the district. For another account of it, see SPG Arch., D MSS, D44, 1876, H. Waters, St Mark's, 30 June 1876: 'The varieties of grain, vegetables, fine flour and meal surprised everyone, as they were all *bona fide* native produce.' And see *Christian Express*, 1 June 1879, for a report of the April 1879 meeting of the Association.

44 *Blue Book for the Cape Colony, 1875*, JJ39.

45 CPP, G.8–'83, BBNA, 13, 169. And cf. accounts of irrigation in Cofimvaba: in 1876 (G.12–'77, 101) among lists of 'improvements' were several water courses and dams; in 1879 the *Christian Express* (1 June) reported that in three years the number of water courses had risen from 30 to 200 (and that twice as much ground was cultivated and ten times as much wheat sown).

46 Quoted by van der Horst, op. cit., 100, fn. 3.

47 C. W. de Kiewiet, *The Imperial Factor in South Africa: A Study in Politics and Economics* (Cambridge, 1937), 159, 177. Cf. van der Horst, op. cit., 117: this 'reform' was often advocated by those who saw as its chief good that it would 'force lazy Natives to earn their keep ... [and] bring about an increase in the supply of labourers'.

48 CPP, G.8–'76, *Report on Immigration and Labour Supply for 1875*, memorandum by J. X. Merriman, 3.

49 CPP, G.42–'76, *Cape of Good Hope Census for 1875*, 20. (*Bywoner* was the Dutch term used to describe those who did not own land but farmed on small areas made available to them by others.)

50 CPP, G.17–'78, BBNA, 50; G.12–'77, BBNA, 131; G.33–'82, BBNA, 133.

51 CPP, G.4–'183, *Report and Proceedings of the Government Commission on Native Laws and Customs*, 127–8.
52 *Fort Beaufort Advocate and Adelaide Opinion*, 19 August 1887. (For some interesting details of stock, ploughs, etc., held by individual squatter-peasants, see reports for Stockenstroom and Stutterheim in CPP, A.16–'81, *Reports and Returns of Inspectors of Native Locations in the Colony.*)
53 *Fort Beaufort Advocate and Adelaide Opinion*, 13 March 1885, and 8 May 1885.
54 CPP, G.16–'76, BBNA, 44.
55 CPP, G.17–'78, BBNA, 42.
56 CPP, G.12–'77, BBNA, 103.
57 *Cape and Natal News*, VII, 152, 7 September 1866.
58 *Queenstown Free Press*, 2 October 1885.
59 ibid., 27 October 1885.
60 ibid., 30 October 1885. It is worth recalling here a citation used earlier in this chapter: six months before Mr Lamplough spoke, a writer from Fort Beaufort had warned that 'without the aid of the native squatters very many of our farmers would find their income from agricultural sources very much diminished'. (See note 53 above.)
61 See S. Trapido, 'Cape Liberalism Revisited', ICS, CSP, Vol. 4, No. 17 (London, 1973), 53–66, for further examples – especially notes 21 and 55.
62 CPP, G.12–'77, BBNA, 106; G.3–'84, BBNA, 112.
63 See, e.g., Irvine's memos in PRO, CO 879/12, Conf. Print Afr. No. 142, encl. in Frere to Carnarvon, 14 November 1877; the quoted comment on Irvine's interests comes from Frere.
64 *Selections from the Correspondence of J. X. Merriman*, 4 vols., ed. P. Lewson (Cape Town, 1960), I, 112, Merriman to Capt. C. Mills, 9 September 1882.
65 See R. Moyer, 'The Mfengu, Self-defence, and the Cape Frontier Wars', in C. C. Saunders and R. Derricourt, *Beyond the Cape Frontier* (Longman, 1974), 101–26, esp. 120–22.
66 A. Bissett to Colonial Secretary, 23 October 1867, quoted by C. C. Saunders, 'The Annexation of the Transkei Territories, 1872–1895' (Oxford D. Phil. thesis, 1972).
67 De Kiewiet, *The Imperial Factor*, 142–80; Saunders, 'The Annexation of the Transkei', chapter 3; G. Tylden, 'The South African War of 1877–78', *Journal of the Society for Army Historical Research*, 1941.
68 PRO, CO 879/12, Conf. Print Afr. 142, desp. No. 134, 18 October 1877 and 23 October 1877; desp. No. 157, encl. No. 3, 5 November 1877; desp. No. 163, sub-encl. No. 3, encl. No. 1, 29 December 1877, and desp. No. 163, encl. No. 2.
69 PRO, CO 48/485, Frere to Carnarvon, 1 January 1878.
70 PRO, CO 879/13, Conf. Print Afr. No. 150, desp. No. 4; ibid., desp. No. 45, report by Col. Bellairs.
71 ibid., desp. No. 63, encls. 3 and 4 (report by J. Hemming); CO 879/13, Conf. Print Afr. No. 151, desp. No. 46, Thesiger to Secty for War.
72 PRO CO 879/13, Conf. Print Afr. 151, desp. No. 70, Thesiger to Secty for War, 5 May 1878.

73 ibid., desp. No. 47, Frere to Hicks-Beach, 30 April 1878; desp. No. 34, Frere to Hicks-Beach, 16 April 1878.

74 See notes 15 and 16 above.

75 PRO, CO 48/486, 15245, Frere to Hicks-Beach, 23 October 1878.

76 CPP, G.12–'77, BBNA, 152.

77 PRO, CO 879/14, Conf. Print Afr. 162, desp. No. 312, A.P.S. to Hicks-Beach.

78 PRO, CO 48/499, 61, H. Robinson to Kimberley, 15 February 1881.

79 Rhodes House Library, Mss. Afr. s54, Coll. letters of Francis George Hall, 1880–92, 19 December 1880.

80 PRO, CO 879/13, 151, desp. No. 46, Thesiger to Secty for War, 10 April 1878.

81 CPP, G.43–'78, *Appendix* to BBNA, Report by Secty of Native Affairs, W. Ayliff, p. 1.

82 ibid., 2–3; G.66–'83, *Report and Proceedings of the Tembuland Commission, passim.*

83 CPP, G.76–'181, *Report of the Commission to Enquire and Report upon the Losses sustained by farmers and other residents upon the Eastern Frontier of the Colony during the late war and rebellion of 1877–78.* (For examples of peasants with large claims, see Vol. II, pp. liv, civ, cxxxii, clxxviii (Malagras, Mene, 'Mboxa, Nosimama, respectively), etc. The details of the holdings of several hundred peasants, and in some cases verbatim transcripts of interviews with some of the larger claimants, make this a fascinating source, and one which has apparently not been used by any of the historians of the Cape frontier.)

84 CPP, G.8–'83, BBNA, 106, 87–8; G.4–'183, *Commission on Native Laws and Customs*, 174–5.

85 CPP, G.4–'83, *Commission on Native Laws and Customs*, 245, App. E, 348.

86 CPP, G.4–'83, *Commission on Native Laws and Customs*, App. E, 333; G.3–'89, BBNA, 20–21.

87 De Kiewiet, *The Imperial Factor*, 150–68, contains a powerfully written and fairly well-known description of the slump in the fortunes of the Africans in the Ciskei, and because of this it has been decided to keep the evidence for this aspect of the 1880s limited to the brief items cited immediately below.

88 See CPP, G.20–'81, G.33–'82, G.8–'83, G.3–'84, G.2–'85, and G.5–'86 (all BBNAs), reports for districts cited.

89 CPP, G.3–'84, BBNA, 31, 37; G.2–'85, BBNA, 23.

90 CPP, G.20–1881, BBNA, 46; G.8–'87, BBNA, 134; G.33–'79, BBNA, 100. And for Fingoland in the eighties, see especially C.8–'81, *Correspondence ... on Natives ... in agricultural and other labour*, 22–7; G.4–'83, *Commission on Laws and Customs*, App. D, 265–70.

91 CPP, G.8–'83, BBNA, 169; G.2–'85, BBNA, 127–8. For Emigrant Tembuland in the eighties see esp. G.4–'83, *Commission on Laws and Customs*, 373–81, App. D. 286–96.

92 CPP, G.66–'83, *Report and Proceedings of the Tembuland Commission of 1882*, 71–3, 81–4, App. C, C1–C168.

93 CPP, G.3–'79, BBNA, 38; G.33–'82, BBNA, 108. In SPG Arch., E MSS,

E39, T. Button reported for the quarter ending 30 June 1884 that Africans in the Umzimkulu district owned 100,000 acres.

94 CPP, G.33–'79, BBNA, 41, 55; G.3–'84, BBNA, 125.
95 CPP, G.33–'82, BBNA, 80–81.
96 CPP, G.33–'79, BBNA, 59; G.2–'85, BBNA, 103.
97 CPP, G.3–'84, BBNA, 128.
98 ibid., 149. W. Beinart describes the early 1880s as a second 'phase' of increased production and the adoption of new technology (mainly ploughs): the first was during the early 1860s. (In 'Economic Change in Pondoland in the Nineteenth Century', ICS, CSP, No. 21, Vol. 7, London, 1977, 26–40, esp. 32.)
99 Beinart, 'Peasant Production, Underdevelopment, and the Traditionalist Response', 16–17; D. G. L. Craggs, 'The Relations of the Amapondo and the Colonial Authorities (1830–1866) with special reference to the role of the Wesleyan Missionaries' (University of Oxford, D. Phil. thesis, 1959), 18–19 *et passim*; CPP, G.22–1905, *Report on Trade with the Native Territories*, 3–8.
100 *Report of the Trade Commission 1885–6* (Pietermaritzburg, 1886), 69, 71, 74.
101 SPG Arch., *St Mark's Mission, Report for Quarter Ending 31 Sept. 1880* (St Mark's, 1880).
102 For a discussion of this pattern in Pondoland, see Beinart, 'Peasant Production, Underdevelopment, and the Traditionalist Response', 26–31.
103 CPP, G.3–'89, BBNA, 33; and cf. G.6–'88, BBNA, 41 ('The natives depend chiefly upon the wool and grain for the payment of their taxes'); G.3–'84, BBNA, 102; etc.
104 B. Key, 'Our Converts: Are they better for their Christianity?' *The Church Chronicle* (Diocese of Grahamstown), XI, 1 (January 1890).
105 CPP, G.4–'83, *Commission on Laws and Customs*, App. D, 287. An archetypal description of 'progressive native farmers' ran like this: 'they have advanced in wealth, and material prosperity ... they are patterns of industry; they are loyal in the true sense of the term; they are better clothed, better fed and better housed than any of the surrounding natives. They live in decent square houses ... have orchards, and have irrigated and cultivated widely.' (CPP, G.33–'79, BBNA, 91, report for Xalanga.)
106 *Mission Field*, Vol. 1877, Archdeacon Waters: 'how much latent desire for progress has been evolved by the mere formulation of this [native farmers] society. I was present at the preliminary meeting and saw how anxious the progressive party were for the best means of farming.'
107 CPP, G.3–'94, *Report of the Commission on the Labour Supply*, II, 21; G.9–'94, BBNA, 63.
108 CPP, G.3–'94, *Commission on Labour Supply,* III, 84. (In App. D of the 1883 *Commission on Laws and Customs*, G.4–'83, magistrates from Lady Frere, Xalanga, and Southeyville submitted written evidence that black employers had taken action against defaulting black employees under the Cape's Masters and Servants legislation.)
109 CPP, G.12–'77, BBNA, 103–6. (Cf. G.13–'80, BBNA, 136: thirty-five

African farmers on holdings of 500 to 1,000 acres cultivated widely, ran transport and timber businesses, and had built houses 'superior to the dwellings generally occupied by labourers in England'.)

110 CPP, G.66–'83, *Tembuland Commission*, 127–9; G.2–'85, BBNA, 127–8.

111 Brownlee, *Reminiscences*, 269–302, quotation on p. 301; CPP, G.76–'81, *Report on . . . losses sustained . . . during the late war*, pp. 304–5, cxxvii.

112 D. D. T. Jabavu, *The Black Problem* (Lovedale, n.d.), 113–15. Sonjica later taught agriculture at the University College of Fort Hare; the Sonjicas are today still a well-to-do Ciskei family.

113 *Blue Book for the Cape Colony, 1875*, JJ30–31.

114 R. W. Rose-Innes, *The Glen Grey Act and the Native Question* (Lovedale, 1903), 14, quoting Sir Henry Elliot, Chief Magistrate of the Transkei.

115 De Kiewiet, *Imperial Factor*, 152.

116 ibid., 153.

117 CPP, G.27–'74, BBNA, 40–41; G.35–'98, *Report of Chief Inspector of Sheep and Superintendent Sheep Inspector in Transkei for 1897.*

118 For evidence of land being held variously on quit-rent, on purchase, or rented from private landholders in Keiskammahoek, Albany, Kingwilliamstown, Pirie, Stutterheim, Kamastone, Glen Grey, Southeyville, Griqualand East, etc., see CPP, G.4–'83, *Commission on Native Laws and Customs*, 121, 127, 157, 174–5, 213, 224–5, 228, 233, 245, 267, 333–6, 374, 513 *et passim*; and App. F, Surveyor-General's Report on Individual Land Tenure System.

119 PRO, CO 879/16, Conf. Print Afr. 204, encl. in No. 228, Frere to Hicks-Beach, 18 October 1879, report of M. Blyth, Chief Mag. of Transkei.

120 Rose-Innes, *Glen Grey Act*, 14.

121 *Blue Book for the Cape Colony, 1874*, JJ34: 'The purchase and leasing of farms by native chiefs is a new feature in frontier affairs.' And cf. CPP, G.17–'78, BBNA, 126.

122 MMS Arch., SA Box XV, Queenstown 1868–76, Barrett, Wodehouse Forests, 10 August 1871.

123 CPP, G.4–83, *Commission on Native Laws and Customs*, 356. Chiefs could also play a powerful role in innovating and encouraging others to do so. For examples of traditional leaders who spearheaded and promoted peasant responsivity to market opportunities, see T. D. M. Skota, *The African Yearly Register* (Johannesburg, 1932), 13, 64, 169, for biographies of Chiefs Dalindyebo, Moroka and Scanlen Lehana ('farmer-chief').

124 As, e.g., SPG Arch., E MSS, E44, H. T. A. Thompson, Springvale, 31 December 1889: 'Their witch-doctors also discourage the cultivation of European eatables, as tending towards the adoption of European customs and habits.'

125 Beinart, 'Economic Change in Pondoland', 35–6.

126 CPP, G.33–'82, BBNA, 50.

127 P. M. Lokwe, 'The Experience of the Catechist and Christians at St Paul's' in A. S. Gibson (ed.), *Reminiscences of the Pondomisi War of 1880* (Edinburgh, 1890), 25–6.

128 SPG Arch., E MSS, E33 (1878), A. J. Newton, report for quarter ending 31 December 1878, and see E33 *passim*.
129 SPG Arch., E MSS, E40 (1885) Report for quarter ending 31 March 1885.
130 *Mission Field*, 1887, 14.
131 ibid., 1885, 114.
132 CPP, G.3–'84, BBNA, 104.
133 *Mission Field*, 1887, 14; ibid., 1883, 329.
134 Gibson, *Reminiscences of the Pondomisi War*, 16, 26.
135 SPG Arch., CLR Series, Kaffraria 1827–1927, Vol. I, Bishop Key, 26 November 1884.

4

The Crucial Years: The Cape, 1890–1913

1 INTRODUCTION

A. H. B. Stanford, Chief Magistrate of Transkei: [Population pressure and competition for land are acute] and we are getting to the end of our tether in some parts....

W. P. Schreiner, member of Select Committee: Of course, the natural economic result would be, after giving out your allotments, that the surplus population would turn to handiwork and labour throughout South Africa; they would go abroad, so to speak?

Stanford: They will have to develop other avocations besides agriculture.

Schreiner: And make their living by honest toil somewhere?

Stanford: That seems to me to be the only solution.

Schreiner: And a very good solution too, is it not?

Select Committee of Native Affairs, A2/1909, 97–8.

This chapter discusses certain features of the economy of the rural Cape and (particularly) the Transkei in the quarter-century after the discovery of gold on the Witwatersrand. The period must loom large in any history of South Africa: the Raid, Rhodes, railways, the influx of capital and consolidation of the mining companies, Kruger, Milner, war, reconstruction, convention and Union – the barest recital reminds one how momentous were these years, pivoting neatly about the turn of the century. Less spectacularly, the same period was a crucial one in the history of the black peasantry in the Eastern Cape and the Transkei. Between about 1890 and 1913, limits were prescribed for the growth and development of that peasantry within the emerging capitalist economy; the peasant's relations *vis-à-vis* the wielders of political and economic power were restructured, and his role in the political economy was defined.

In the pages that follow, some of the changing conditions of life in the peasant areas of the Cape will be outlined, and an attempt made to relate these to certain specific features of the South African economy as a whole. It will be proposed that:

109

(i) Between the discovery of gold and the First World War, the quickening economic pace and modernization of South Africa produced qualitative changes in the rural economy of the Cape.

(ii) Some peasants were able to consolidate, and others to enjoy for the first time, modest economic success, as they grasped opportunities for profit, improved their agricultural techniques, and produced a surplus for sale.

(iii) At the same time, there was a sharp rise in social and economic pressures upon the peasantry. These had their origins in physical/demographic/natural causes; in aspects of the 'internal economy' of peasant areas – especially peasant/trader relations, debt and stratification; and in aspects of the 'external' Southern African economy – market prices, transport costs, the commercialization of white farming, the increased demand for labour and the legislative and recruiting practices this gave rise to.

(iv) Substantial numbers of Cape and Transkei peasants lost the measure of economic independence they had enjoyed at the beginning of the period under review – that is, they lost the ability to meet their subsistence requirements through pastoral and agricultural pursuits as they became separated from the means of production (although without experiencing the full geographical and social departure that this 'normally' entails).

(v) By 1914, a growing number of individual peasants had become proletarianized, most commonly as migrant labourers; the peasant community as a whole was less economically resilient and increasingly less self-sufficient; the peasant sector was in the process of becoming underdeveloped. The Ciskei and Transkei had become structurally underdeveloped regions within the developing economic system of Southern Africa.

2 THE CHANGING ECONOMY

In 1885, the purse-strings of colonies and republics in Southern Africa were drawn tight: the growth generated by the diamond discoveries had momentarily spent itself, and acute commercial recession set in. An over-subscribed stock market and expensive credit system both underwent sharp contraction, leading to a banking crisis. The Transvaal was barely solvent, the Cape and Natal loaded with debts for their rails and roads. In 1886 the flagging pulse of economic activity was administered a potent restorative – the discovery of the Witwatersrand gold reefs. Extraction and crushing began amazingly rapidly; so did consolidation and control of the industry by relatively few powerful companies. These technological and organizational triumphs have been described elsewhere,[1] and so have their major economic conse-

110

quences which, of greater relevance to this chapter, may be briefly summarized.

The economic changes engendered by the discovery and exploitation of gold may be said to have continued, intensified and multiplied the processes initiated by the diamond boom (pp. 65–7). By any indices – population, immigration, trade, banking, construction, transport and other service industries – the economic life of South Africa spurted forward. Republican and colonial revenues increased even more startlingly than they had in the 1870s: in the Transvaal from £178,000 in 1885/6 to £638,000 in 1887 and almost £1,500,000 two years later. In the Cape, where revenue stood at £1·9 million in 1886/7, it touched £2·5 million in 1889/90. Trade increased more abruptly than revenue in the Cape, reflecting the colony's role as an entrepot district and provider of goods and services to the dynamic market in the interior (see Table 2).

TABLE 2

Cape imports and exports (excluding specie)
after the discovery of gold

Year	Imports	Exports
1885	£4,772,904	£5,811,444
1890	9,366,446	9,837,796
1895	13,612,405	16,798,137
1899	15,370,971	23,247,258

Space precludes a full discussion of industrialization and modernization in South Africa; for the moment the focus is on two specific and interlocking features of the altering political economy: the commercialization of agriculture and the changed nature of the demand by employers for African labour. These were the features that most acutely affected the peasants who are the subject of this book.

Although some white farmers in South Africa had responded to market opportunities created by the diamond boom (especially those near new rail lines and towns), and although the production of wool as a major export was established, the development of a capitalist agriculture in South Africa had not proceeded very far by the mid-eighties. Even more striking is the hiatus after 1886, after the creation of major new markets and transport opportunities. A response there was – as will be demonstrated – but what demands attention is the limited and tardy nature of that response. It was not really until after the South African War that South Africa's larger cultivators displayed the technological and managerial adaptations that might have been expected earlier, given the stimulus of the mines.

The reasons for this lag are manifold and complex, but the more important can be identified. First, the period 1873 to 1896 was that of

111

the 'great depression', a trough of economic recession that affected adversely the economies of the advanced capitalist countries in Europe and North America as well as those of the farther-flung participants in the western economic system. South African farmers, like their counterparts in the American south and west, suffered from a steady fall in the prices they commanded for agricultural products; unlike the farmers of the mid-West, they did not attract substantial capital from industrial areas. The highly capitalized agriculture of the American mid-West, in fact, played a role in the underdevelopment of South Africa's agriculture in this period; for so cheaply were maize and wheat produced in the prairies that they could be imported and consumed in South Africa at a lower cost than grain from South Africa's own hinterlands. This undercutting of home-grown wheat and maize was central to the process whereby South Africa became a net importer of foodstuffs in the 1890s.

Further brakes on the development of a dynamic commercial agriculture derived from the internal economy of South Africa: in particular, the retention of large amounts of land in relatively few hands, the establishment of quasi-feudal relations on these lands and their occupation by squatter-peasants and *bywoners*,* and the continued ability of large numbers of African peasants to produce an agricultural surplus large enough to pay taxes and satisfy consumer wants. This last had a double impact on white farmers: it meant that they remained 'victims' of a labour 'shortage' at the very low wages they offered, and it meant that they encountered effective competition from African farmers. There were other factors in operation: the low level of existing technology and productivity meant a dearth of capital; the unyielding soils and climatic vagaries and natural pests discouraged enterprise; the control of credit and banking by mercantile interests also prevented farmers' access to capital.[2]

To return to the double-edged barrier to white commercial agriculture posed by the emerging African peasantry: it might at the outset be objected that Africans possessed even less capital, less scientific background, less defence against international or natural pressures on an agricultural community – all of which is valid – and deduced therefrom that they were in no position to compete with the more powerful white community. This is a false deduction. Despite the limited land available to peasants, and despite the low levels of accumulation and technology prevailing there, certain social and economic circumstances enabled African peasants to participate in the produce and labour markets on terms not wholly unfavourable. Apart from his specialized knowledge of local conditions and methods, the peasant tended to cultivate more intensively because of the growing scarcity of land. His lower consumption costs and his use of pre-capitalist forms of

* The term applied to landless white tenants or share-croppers.

labour meant that production of a modest surplus – the sale of a few bags of grain or a bale of wool – enabled him to participate in the exchange economy largely on the terms of his own choosing and without the surrender of his land, security or cultural identity.

Often the peasant could produce a surplus for sale when the white agriculturist could not. As J. W. Sauer, the Cape politician, put it in 1903:

> I am inclined to think that the Natives make rather more out of [the land than do whites] – though perhaps that is not a popular thing to say – if for no other reasons than that the land is divided up into small allotments and a man can easily cultivate the whole of his allotment and it is in his interest to do so, and so the whole becomes cultivated.[3]

A similar conclusion is reached by Denoon, who wrcte of the nineteenth century that 'African peasants were more efficient and productive than white farmers.' Until agricultural technology and other aid were made widely available to white agriculturists in the twentieth century the 'African communities ... devoted a far greater proportion of time and land to agricultural purposes'; although both white and black agriculture adapted to the demanding environment, 'the African adaptation and the African agricultural traditions enabled them to sustain a massively greater rural population than their white competitors'. The editors of a recent collection of historical research in the agricultural sectors of Central and Southern Africa make the same point more generally: 'it is now generally conceded that in unit terms peasants were more productive farmers than settlers: large ploughed fields had a lower unit yield than careful hoe cultivation of selected soils'.[4]

These factors might operate at one end of the peasant continuum in favour of the large peasant or small-scale commercial farmer, enabling him to diversify and improve his agriculture and to compete success-fully with white agriculturists. At the other end, the same factors could just tilt the balance for the small or marginal peasant, permitting him to retain access to the means of production – his plot of land and livestock – and to withstand the demands being made for his labour power by white employers.

In other words, a large number of peasants – certainly a majority of the Cape's African peoples – retained at the beginning of the gold-mining era a measure of economic independence. There is consider-able evidence, often provided by would-be employers, that white colonists were aware of this at the time. The Cape Labour Commission of 1893–4 was told by several witnesses of the difficulty in obtaining sufficient agricultural labour at the low wages being offered; when asked 'Is there any reason you can give for this want of labour with such a labour supply as we have in this colony?' one George Warren replied succinctly that 'the natives are independent. They have land and grow what they choose, and their wants are extremely small.' In Alice, a white farmer said that Africans 'seem to be able to raise sheep here, the Europeans not'. In Komgha district, said another, white farmers had 'no means of cultivating the ground themselves, so it is cultivated by the natives'. In Alexandria and Stutterheim districts, 'the native can live by agriculture, but not the white man', it was explained; while W. P. Keeton of Port Alfred said simply: 'Europeans cannot compete with the natives. The labour kills them.'[5]

The commissioners themselves were obviously impressed with the evidence on this topic, for they concluded that the shortfall of labour arose from the living conditions of the Africans:

> The mere necessities of life are few, and are obtainable with little effort. These people do not therefore feel impelled to work.... A cause of the insufficiency may also be found in the fact that some natives are in some sense land or rather lease-holders ... on shares as it is called.... The natives are also in another sense landholders, where they cultivate their own fields in the parts of the country called Native Locations or Reserves, in what was known as the Eastern Province and in what may be called generally the Transkeian Territories.[6]

The gold era introduced a new problem for white farmers: sharp competition from other employers for such African labour as was forthcoming. The rise of the gold-mining industry (and also transport, construction and service industries) created a qualitative increase in the need for a class of permanent wage-earners. In the case of the mines, the major potential employer, a specific cost structure, determined by certain geological and economic factors, ensured that profits could be ensured only through cost-minimization of labour costs.[7] Mine-owners on the Rand knew that 'sufficient' labour at the rates they offered would not be forthcoming while the black peasant enjoyed access to his lands and the ability to produce enough agricultural surplus to meet his cash requirements. The President of the Chamber of Mines explained:

> The tendency of the native is to be an agriculturist, who reluctantly offers himself or one of his family as an industrial worker for just so long as the hut tax can be earned, and expects the industrial demand to expand to give him work when his crops are bad. He cares nothing if industries pine for want of labour when his crops and home-brewed drink are plentiful.

He called for a policy that would ensure 'that the surplus of young men, instead of squatting on the land in idleness ... must earn their living by working for a wage' and to this end urged the government to 'do everything to encourage the native to be a wage-earner by extending the policy of splitting into family holdings land now held in the native reserves under tribal tenure'.[8]

Both the farmer and the mine-owner perceived in the late nineteenth century the need to apply extra-economic pressures to the African peasantry; to break down the peasant's 'independence', increase his wants, and to induce him to part more abundantly with his labour, but at no increased price. Implicit in their demands was the assumption that Africans had no right to continue as self-sufficient and independent farmers if this conflicted with white interests. Their coincident needs and perceived solutions provided the basic terms of settlement between the partners-to-be, gold and maize;* political consummation was effectively celebrated in the first three years of Union government.

While it was not until after the war of 1899–1902 and especially after 1907 that the speed and scope of white farming were great enough to affect adversely large numbers of peasants, a certain amount of commercialization did precede 1899, and introduced for African peasant communities new pressures and problems, most acutely in the case of squatter-peasants. Increased awareness by white farmers of market opportunities, increased diversification and re-investment, more intensive and more scientific farming all raised the value of the land they owned. The enhanced value of the land, and its productive capacities, led to a reversion of the quasi-feudal practices described in earlier chapters. In Section 3, examination will be made of the effects of anti-squatter legislation; for the moment, attention is on the purely economic compulsion on squatter-peasants.

Once again, the most precise and pithy descriptions of some of the processes involved are provided by participants in them. A Komgha farmer said in 1914 that many whites who had previously been happy to permit Africans on their lands in quasi-feudal relations (paying rent in cash or kind) 'are beginning to realize now that such farming does not pay – that they can get more out of the land themselves'. From Stutterheim, another witness observed that the tide had turned in a district where Africans had been cultivating more and more land: 'Now there is a tendency for the European to buy out the native.' Across in Umzimkulu, the influential and observant Donald Strachan was most explicit. In that district, he said, Africans had bought perhaps 100,000 acres of land from Griqua burghers and from whites. In the 1870s and 1880s, whites had found the cost of farming there too great, while Africans had lived off the land. These peasants, however, had suffered two major epidemics and lost most of their stock, were deep in debt, and their lands were heavily mortgaged to whites. 'Owing to the opening of the new railways, land here is now in demand by Europeans

---

* 'The well-known [German] "marriage of iron and rye", an alliance which succeeded in suppressing political freedom in its own economic interests, has its South African counterpart in the uneasy union of "gold and maize".' (S. Trapido, 'South Africa in a Comparative Study of Industrialization', *Journal of Development Studies*, 7, 3 (April 1973), 311.)

and the price of these farms is and has been rising during the last year or two.'[9]

There were other ways in which the turn-of-the-century transition from pastoral and quasi-feudal occupation to commercial agriculture and more intensive stock-raising affected Africans. In small-stock areas the spread of fencing before 1910 was enormous, usually greatly diminishing the farmer's demand for *bywoners* or African squatter-peasants.[10] As sheep-farming became more capitalized, many Africans who had gained access to land in exchange for limited shepherding duties (duties often performed by the young sons of the squatter-peasants) were now told to leave. Irrigation also led to a decrease in the numbers of leases on farms: 'Where a man irrigates,' a farmer told a Select Committee, 'he does not want labour tenants; he has constant crops, which he can depend on, and he can employ monthly servants.'[11] In many cases the white-owned land was put to agricultural instead of pastoral use, and the black tenant was offered the choice between departure or selling his stock.

All these effects were to be intensified by the ability of white commercial farmers to secure favourable legislation from colonial, republican and later Union governments. The commercialization of white agriculture was aided by a massive programme of subsidies, grants and other aid. Assistance to farmers came forth in the shape of fencing, dams, houses, veterinary and horticultural advice; farmers were cushioned by generous rail rates, by special credit facilities and by bountiful tax relief. As early as 1908, with the floodgates of interest politics not yet fully raised, it was remarked that 'it is probable that during the last twenty years more money per head of the rural population has been devoted to the relief of farmers in South Africa than in any country in the world',[12] mainly through the diversion by the state of the surplus from gold mining. This beneficence to white commercial agriculture had profound implications for black peasant agriculture (and for white *bywoners:* legislative supports for farmers did not help the small tenant farmer, nor were they intended to). In the first place, almost all of the legislation was racially discriminative, and blessed only modernizing white farmers, which of itself conferred important competitive advantages on that class. These were buttressed in the second place by legislation (most particularly the 1913 Natives Land Act) aimed at curtailing the possibilities open to peasant production, at preventing the accumulation of capital by Africans and at translating independent squatter-peasants into wage-labourers.

3 'PASSING THROUGH A PERIOD OF STRESS'

During the decade between the gold discoveries and the outbreak of war there were peasants in the Ciskei and Eastern Province who prospered in their response to opportunities inherent in the economic quickening. In Herschel, for instance, the demand for transport to the gold fields had boosted cattle and grain prices by 100 per cent, which together with a rise in the price of wool circulated a large amount of money in the district.[13] In 1891, a year of uniformly good crops, the benefits were fairly widely spread. In many districts magistrates attested to the difficulty white farmers were encountering in attracting any labour. As Fleischer of East London put it, 'the native will not work so long as he has sufficient grain on hand to supply his moderate wants'.[14] More frequently, however, the profits or improvements reported were the advances of only one stratum in the Ciskei peasantry, those who had already emerged with more land, more resources and more skills. By the 1890s stratification in the Ciskei and Eastern Province was already well advanced, and it became even more pronounced during that decade. A sizeable landless group – a rural proletariat – was already in existence in the Ciskei, and this class increased dramatically during the lean years in the mid-nineties.

In the absence of first-hand accounts, one has only an impressionistic idea of the personal and human experiences of the process of pro-letarianization, of how tenaciously it was resisted, and how impossible it was to withstand. It bore most heavily on the young men coming of age, who could appeal neither to family nor to clan for the traditional plots of grazing and arable land. All sorts of expedients were resorted to. Land was divided and sub-divided within the family far past the point of declining returns for all involved. Marginally productive and hitherto undesired land was ploughed and reploughed, until it was leached of its limited fertility; hillsides, ridges, dry and stony patches were sought out; reports are replete with phrases like 'every available inch of land is being cultivated.' Commonage was encroached upon by men anxious to sow and reap a modicum of grain, often provoking bitter feuds between those who sought to diminish the grazing area and those who owned stock they wanted to provide for; these latter were usually better off. Landless men sought to use any and all of the feeble political devices which they might have at their call, both of traditional and colonial varieties: they besought headmen, chiefs, magistrates and missionaries; they pleaded their cases to civil servants and commissioners; and they embarked on litigation, all too frequently at great cost. Others turned to stock theft or vagrancy; many entered wage labour with the express intention of accumulating enough cash to buy or lease land a little later. With the twin pressures of increasing population and rising land prices, fewer and fewer were able to achieve this aim.

It is unnecessary to cite detailed evidence for this process. The printed official sources teem with corroborating details for the districts concerned, and a tiny selection conveys their essence:

117

they are beginning to recognise the necessity of labour more than hitherto, and for that purpose go out in larger numbers and to greater distances. (Middledrift, 1889)

every available inch of ground in each location is cultivated ... [there is] a steady and increasing exodus of young native men in search of employment. (Middledrift, 1892)

[Of 18,500 total population] four thousand men and women were absent at work on the gold-fields, railway works, reaping, and in seivice. (Peddie, 1890)

now they are in a perfectly congested state. They have no sufficient grazing lands, and the arable lands are becoming more insufficient every year. (Keiskammahoek, 1893)

In many parts of the locations, very little if any arable land remains available for cultivation, while generally the limits to which cultivation can be carried have been reached. (Kingwilliamstown, 1894)

The greater part of the young men of the location have been away at work. (Queenstown, 1895)[15]

Across the Kei river, the four magisterial districts of Fingoland had been among the foremost areas of African response and prosperity during the 1870s and 1880s. Travellers, magistrates, and missionaries penned encomiums upon the hard-headed, hard-working Mfengu peasantry who had subscribed thousands of pounds to the building of roads and schools, raising much of the money through their transport riding and sales of wool, grains and vegetables. Another area singled out for especial mention in Chapter 3 was Emigrant Tembuland, where similar reports of industry and progress were the rule rather than the exception in the twenty years prior to 1890. The prosperity experienced by the substantial peasants in these districts was in some respects more firmly based than that of their counterparts in the Ciskei. The Transkei was far less penetrated by white settlers, so better land and more land was available; the region was better watered, and the population density lower.

As these factors would suggest, the 1890s saw continued instances of enterprise and economic reward in Fingoland and Emigrant Tembuland. African peasants still disposed of surplus grain and wool; there was 'an enormously increased trade' in the Territories, wrote the Chief Magistrate after the good harvests of 1892.[16] African farmers near the Mbashe river experimented with coffee; in Emigrant Tembuland thousands of fruit trees were planted in a cash venture; in Xalanga 4,000 bags of wheat were threshed by machinery and 'the prize wheats of the last show were pronounced by competent judges to have been equal to the best grown in the colony'. In the same district, 125 houses valued at from £20 to £600 were built by African farmers, and the Cala and Indwe markets were supplied with the vegetables they grew.[17]

Yet at the same time, and from the same districts, another note was being sounded. In tones varying from puzzled regret to impatient scorn, magistrates and others remarked upon arrested progress and signs of economic hardship. Agriculture, they noticed, showed seemingly contradictory features of advance and degeneration; class formation and stratification were permitting simultaneous gains and losses by different individuals. In the context of what has been said of these areas during the phase of prosperity engendered by the diamond boom it is noteworthy that several officials described what was taking place specifically in terms of a comparison with the recent past. Thus, graphically, the magistrate of Tsomo recounted that:

> There are headmen and others who fifteen years ago had fine square houses, fine enclosed gardens with fruit trees.... Today ... you will find the square houses dilapidated and the roofs falling in. You will find the men living in the huts, the garden wall has fallen down, and the trees eaten down by the goats. Fingoland has gone back tremendously in the last four or five years. It is not in the progressive state in which it was fifteen or twenty years ago.

In neighbouring Nqamakwe, the magistrate noted that the agricultural shows once held there had fallen away; some years earlier

> the enthusiasm of the Fingoes was more easily aroused than at present ... agriculture and stock farming have attained to no higher order of merit now than they possessed then.

Another long-serving magistrate was equally gloomy about Fingoland. Once, he said, the inhabitants had prospered and built Blythswood, but 'at the present moment these men are far worse off and not so loyal as they were twenty years ago'. In Emigrant Tembuland, the Municipal Chairman of Cala told the Labour Commission in 1893 that 'there is no question about it. In this district they are becoming poorer than they were.'[18] In Xalanga the magistrate said: 'During the past twenty-five years I think degeneration has taken place.... The natives as a body are growing poorer.'[19] In sum, although it was obviously exaggeration for a magistrate to speak of 'indications of retrogression and a rapid relapse into barbarism', there is no denying the worried conclusion of the missionary who wrote in the same year that 'just now we are passing through a period of stress'.[20]

In the late 1890s, the peasant economy of the Transkei, in common with all South Africa's rural areas, was jolted by a sudden and severe setback in the shape of the rinderpest epidemic. The political and social consequences of the disease have been well described by Charles van Onselen;[21] those that affect the analysis to follow are recapitulated

here. For countless South African peasants, the disease which destroyed 80 to 90 per cent of the cattle in the Transkei and nearly as many
in the Ciskei was an economic disaster: it liquidated much of the
peasant's capital, adversely affected his credit-worthiness, made
ploughing more difficult and transport facilities rarer and dearer. The
immediate effect was to impoverish thousands of peasants and to force
Africans onto the wage labour market in considerably greater numbers
than before (see Table 3). Rumours circulated amongst the peasantry
that rinderpest was deliberately spread by whites to induce poverty and
compel Africans 'to work for very low wages'.[22] Such tales had no
factual basis, but possessed a symbolic truth; the cattle scourge brought
about several results long advocated by the stern logic of nineteenth-
century liberalism; the rumours accurately reflected motives, if not
means. Missionary reports of 1898–9 contained several accounts like
that of Charles Taberer, who felt the disease was 'not altogether an
unmixed evil' as

> with the natives, the possession of great numbers of cattle is as a rule
> conducive to idleness. After the fields are planted, they have little to do
> until harvest time if they have plenty of milk and a supply of grain on hand
> from the previous season's crops. Now however, we have them going off in
> all directions to earn money to provide for their families.[23]

With uncomplicated satisfaction the magistrate of Kentani observed
that the peasants no longer held cattle like 'fixed deposits', and
concluded that the loss of this security had 'left the native less
independent, more inclined to work, less impudent, and generally
better in every way than he was before'.[24]

The impoverishment of the peasants was not necessarily long-term;
numbers of them demonstrated that they had accumulated sufficient
resources to begin rebuilding their herds almost at once, and even
greater numbers took to labour with the immediate and limited objective of replacing their cattle. The disease was a far more serious blow to
the small or marginal peasant than it was to the relatively well-off
peasant; the former was less resilient, possessed fewer resources, and
would find it more difficult to produce a surplus through extra exertion
on his own land. Put simply, the wealthy peasant who lost – say – forty
of his fifty beasts could employ the remainder to plough his lands (of
which more had been released from grazing needs) and sow a larger
crop than usual with the grain fetching enhanced prices because of the
demand. The small peasant, with a proportionate loss of four out of five
cattle, could look to the survivor neither for ploughing nor for reproduction.

No totting up of profit and loss to individual peasants can convey the
overall impact of rinderpest upon the peasant economy; the topic is
one that awaits detailed economic analysis. Tentatively, it will be
suggested here that one result was to promote differentiation and the

unequal distribution of resources, and that another was to intensify the structural inferiority of the peasant economy *vis-à-vis* the capitalist sector. Bishop Bramsby Key suggested one element in this – the dilution of the peasant community's social and cultural integrity:

> The rinderpest has done a great deal to wean the people from their old traditions of heathenism, as cattle have always been the foundation of their whole system, social, political, and to a great extent religious; and although they are rapidly collecting cattle again ... they will never be to them what they were in the past.[25]

Bley, in a comment upon the impact of rinderpest upon South West Africa, provides a different emphasis. He indicates the manner in which the epidemic sapped the economic base of the peasantry while at the same time offering certain advantages to the wielders of social and economic power:

TABLE 3

Patterns of labour migration from Transkei, 1893–1916

Year	Total leaving Transkei	Number going to Transvaal/mines	Number leaving 7 Pondoland districts
1893	27,511	8,500 (T'vaal)	
1894	38,582	16,800 (T'vaal)	
1895	40,000*	18,000* (T'vaal)	
1896	38,400	15,491 (T'vaal)	
1897	45,000*	22,120 (T'vaal)	
1898	61,033	18,302 (T'vaal)	
1899	45,000*	7,105 (T'vaal)	
1900			3,473
1901	50,000		5,388
1903	76,556	14,806 (mines)	12,000
1905	48,000		
1906	56,066		
1907	63,149		
1908	67,825	25,000* (mines)	6,000*
1909	63,802		
1910	79,377	50,866 (mines)	
1911	79,839	51,000 (mines)	
1912	96,667	63,000 (mines)	
1916	90,000*	50,000* (mines)	8,000*

Note: In the third column I have indicated whether the total is for *all* employment in the Transvaal, or merely for gold-mining. Indications are that during the 1890s the proportion of those working in the Transvaal actually on the gold-mines was quite low – perhaps about half the total.

* These are estimated figures based on incomplete statistics (not all districts giving figures in annual reports, etc.) and educated guesses: they serve as a crude guide.

In rebuilding the herds, European agricultural superiority was more widely accepted, because for the first time European cattle breeders found a large enough market. If it was true that the Hereros' large cattle herds had previously acted as a sufficient counter-balance to European industriousness, then it was now true that every European thrust forward – for instance, in the sphere of trade on credit – threatened the economic base of the tribe.[26]

The impact of the South African War on peasant agriculture in the Cape was more ambiguous. In certain districts it led to confiscation and destruction of stock and crops; peasants were looted, harried, dispersed and plunged into abject pauperism. The loss of wages on the gold mines must have thwarted the aspirations of many who were still seeking to recover from the rinderpest reversal; we learn that 'many of the few cattle that survived ... found their way into the hands of the traders in exchange for grain'.[27] In some districts large sections of the population were forced into desperate straits and had to live on roots.

Yet other peasants were able to turn to gain the exigencies of war. Wherever troops were quartered and fed, prices for agricultural produce and stock rose sharply. Peasants in the vicinity of troop concentrations (as in Tembuland and East Griqualand) as well as those who could arrange or afford the transport farther afield prospered in consequence. Once again, this was a circumstance that favoured the peasant already relatively well off; the reports from the Albany districts, for instance, make this plain.[28] Peasants produced surpluses for grain and meat 'at prices never attained before' and (in the Transkei) 'at remunerative prices', while thousands of horses were sold to the remount officers.[29] Some years later a commission discovered that one of the factors behind the purchase of a lot of land in the Komgha district by Africans had been that 'the largely increased scope afforded the industrious Natives during the war to amass wealth enabled a number of them to acquire land in exchange for their savings'.[30] After the war was over, Transkei peasants sold 24,000 sheep at profitable rates in the administration's efforts to restock the ex-Boer republics.[31] These, and similar instances of agricultural enterprise, as well as the wages that could be earned in military employ, undoubtedly played a part in enabling Africans to withhold their labour at the end of the war, despite the shrill demand for their services.[32]

In the decade between the end of the war and the passage of the 1913 Land Act, African peasant agriculture in the Eastern Cape and Ciskei deteriorated further. Overcrowding and an annual deficiency in subsistence requirements had become the chronic, debilitating marks of the region's underdevelopment: the difficulties chronicled in this chapter and in the previous one became even more widely reported than before.[33] Within the overall pattern of decline and proletarianization, there persists the phenomenon of a small stratum of successful and moderately well-to-do peasant farmers: the 'enlightened people' who 'tended to grab as much land as they [could] get'.[34] The Inspector of Native Locations at Barkly West, W. H. Hall, identified the 'wealthiest natives' in the district: they were 'interlopers, having obtained a foothold in the Reserves some fifteen or sixteen years ago, and are now monopolizing the best grazing grounds, and waxing fat at the expense of the poorer natives'.[35] Members of this class created quite a stir in several districts by buying extra land in these years; one witness cited cases of individuals known to him who could afford to pay sums of £2,000, £1,600 and £750 for farms. Around Kingwilliamstown the three hundred or so owners of small farms continued to profit and to 'support the produce market' of that centre.[36]

One of the questions that was asked of those who submitted written evidence to the 1903–5 Commission on Native Affairs was how the economic and social conditions of the Africans compared with the 1880s. From Eastern Province and Ciskei districts, the answers – although not unanimous – strongly suggested that growing impoverishment was apparent. Some replies mentioned the differing fortunes of 'the enlightened people' and 'the poorer natives', and said there was a 'widening of the gulf between the poor and the well to do'.[37]

Thus far, the chronological outline has concentrated upon those nine or ten of the Transkei's two dozen magisterial districts that contemporaries would have called the 'most advanced'. Mention must now be made of the extent to which different districts displayed levels of development/underdevelopment. This was particularly evident in the decade after the war. In Pondoland, 1894–1910 has been described as 'the high point in the peasant response';[38] with annexation and the imposition of taxes, the Mpondo invested in agricultural implements and sheep, and stepped up the sales of wool, grain, cattle and tobacco. There were indications, wrote a magistrate early in the century, that 'Western Pondoland will soon vie with many of the older districts in these territories,' and he added significantly that the labour recruiters could attract hardly any migrant workmen from the district. 'Why should we work?' asked the Mpondo peasants. 'Is not the country ours, and have we not lots of land and many women and children to cultivate it? We prefer to remain as we are.'[39] To remain as they were, however, meant that they had to change, to adapt, and this they did. There had been only six trading stores in Bizana at the time of annexation, but ten years later there were fifteen,

> and the largest shop among these fifteen does, I should estimate [wrote the magistrate] far more business than the whole six did [in 1894]. . . . In the old days there was not much encouragement to grow much more grain than they required for their own use, as there were no regular markets, and the producer usually obtained about half a crown a bag. Now there is a steady demand and prices range . . . from 5/- to 15/- . . . there is quite three times as much ground cultivated as there was ten years ago.[40]

Beinart has calculated that Pondoland was producing a larger per capita amount of grain than the rest of the Transkei at this time; apart from a surplus of grain, the Mpondo also marketed cattle, tobacco and vegetables. An Umtata trader asked whence the Mpondo derived their purchasing power answered that it was 'principally from the proceeds of their gardens, tobacco and mealies ... then they have surplus stock, and down there there is almost nothing in the way of labour'.[41]

In other similarly 'red' or 'traditionalist' (or 'less civilized') districts, peasant agriculture continued to respond dynamically, while labour agents made thin pickings.[42] The 1893–4 Labour Commission commented on this phenomenon: 'These [Transkeian]territories appear to provide labour for work outside them somewhat in proportion to the length of time their inhabitants have enjoyed good government.'[43] The commissioners' findings might be rephrased thus: that the territories produced wage labourers somewhat in proportion to the extent that structural underdevelopment had been induced by the penetration of colonial rule and capitalist economic relations. The more it was integrated into the advanced economy, the greater tended to be social stratification and proletarianization within a region.

If one's gaze shifts from Pondoland after the South African War to Fingoland, Emigrant Tembuland, Gcalekaland, and northern Griqualand East (Umzimkulu and Matatiele districts) a different picture is revealed. These ten (out of twenty-seven) magistracies, although they contained less than 40 per cent of the total population of the Territories, continued to supply the majority of migrant labourers (63 per cent in 1894, perhaps 66 per cent in 1905). The total number of wage labourers who left the Transkei continued to rise year by year, with an exceptional exodus in 1903, a year of drought and crop failures. It reached about 80,000 in 1910 and 1911, and then increased by over 20 per cent as a consequence of East Coast Fever.

This disease, like rinderpest, decimated herds and pauperized families, and its effects seem not to have been as rapidly offset as were those of the earlier epidemic. In part, this was due to the lingering nature of the disease, and the manner in which it could reinfect a 'clean' district; but there were also certain long-term economic aspects.[44] One was that the increased incidence of debt amongst the peasantry by 1910 made the repurchase of cattle very difficult; it meant that recourse to wage labour was necessary for greater numbers for longer periods. Secondly, the regulations imposed for the control of East Coast Fever made it almost impossible for an African peasant to sell his cattle to any purchaser other than the local trader, whose response to this monopoly was to offer the peasant very low prices.* This

---

* Walter Stanford reported that the regulations had 'been so framed that only the European trader or speculator can make use of them.... Consequently ... I know of oxen being bought from natives lately at £2 each ... [which]I was assured by a competent

contributed directly to the overstocking deplored by so many observers, as well as to the 'irrational' and 'uneconomic' attitudes that Africans were said to have in relation to their stock. Not until 1930, during the Depression, was there a relaxation of the regulations, when (commented a senior civil servant) 'Quite a number of Native stockowners took advantage of this opportunity to dispose of some of their surplus stock.... [Since the imposition of the restrictions] there had been no outlet ... for Natives to get rid of their surplus stock.'[45]

The number of labourers who registered for passes from the Transkei was just under 100,000. The 1911 Census gave the total of males between the ages of twenty and seventy, plus two-fifths of those between fifteen and nineteen (a formula used to calculate the potential labour force) as 172,562. The chief magistrate, in his report for 1912, while expressing reservations about the accuracy of the pass statistics, wrote that it was becoming 'usual rather than rare' for men to 'go out regularly each year' and that thousands went twice a year.[46] In particular, Transkei migrants became a regular and major supply of labour on the gold mines (an account of links between mine recruiting and the plight of the peasantry follows later). From having supplied less than 10 per cent of the total workforce on the Rand in 1896, the Cape's share rose to 13·7 per cent in 1906, and swelled to nearly 40 per cent in 1912, levelling out at 33 per cent in 1916. It was to remain a more or less steady supply after 1912; fifty or sixty thousand Transkei peasants turned gold-miner each year – an enormous rural-based workforce composed of individuals with no land, or too little land, or insufficiently productive land, who could not subsist without wage labour. It was moreover a stream of labour that was forthcoming despite 'a massive drop in the real value of wages of African mine workers in this [1911–1919] period'[47] – a phenomenon in contradistinction to the sensitivity of response to wage rates demonstrated by Transkei workers in the 1890s and immediately after the South African war.

Another indication of the intensified agricultural degeneration of the Transkei between about 1900 and 1914 was the increasing inability of the Territories – and especially of some districts – to produce enough grain to feed their population. Grain was imported, either from other parts of South Africa, or from the American prairies, into some districts in almost every year between 1902 and 1914; in a year of poor harvests like 1903, the Transkei as a whole depended on imported food. The next section will show how in the same period the pressure upon the competition for available land intensified; it is during these years that Transkei magistrates (notably from the districts where Glen Grey surveys and titles were introduced) came increasingly to sound

---

authority would on removal from the location ... readily fetch £10 to £12.' (Jagger Library, Univ. of Cape Town, Walter Stanford Papers, F (mm) 3.)

like their fellow-officers in the acutely crowded African areas of the Ciskei, with refrains of 'the rising generation will have no land for allotment' and 'the land is already becoming exhausted.'

4 UNDERDEVELOPMENT AND STRATIFICATION

The system of social-economic relations existing among the peasantry shows us the presence of all those contradictions which are inherent in every commodity economy ... competition, the struggle for economic independence, the grabbing of land (purchasable and rentable), the concentration of production into the hands of a minority, the forcing of the majority into the ranks of the proletariat ...

(V. I. Lenin, *The Development of Capitalism in Russia*)

In the chronological sketch above, it has been asserted that peasant production in parts of the Transkei showed signs of strain and weakness in the 1890s; and that these grew more pronounced after 1900, causing increasing numbers of peasants to accept wage labour, even when the rise in supply was not matched by any rise in attractiveness of employment. Some peasants left the land completely, taking their families with them or founding new ones; they settled in the 'locations' of Johannesburg, Port Elizabeth or East London, or they entered domestic or agricultural service in the villages and towns of the Transkei (there were 17,000 whites in the Transkei by 1911). The majority of the wage labourers retained their foothold in the 'reserves', a tendency reinforced both by post-Union policy and by the preference of peasant-migrants for the world they knew best.

They lived in underdeveloped rural regions and migrated to their places of employment; and this obviated the need for employers to pay individual 'units of labour' the wages necessary to support a family. It meant that the state need not house nor police a large urban population, nor be menaced by the unrestricted growth of an organized urban proletariat. They lived, explained Howard Pim, in a reserve which was 'a sanatorium where they can recuperate; if they are disabled they remain there. Their own tribal system keeps them under discipline, and if they become criminals there is not the slightest difficulty in bringing them to justice. All this absolutely without expense to the white community.'[48] A more explicit statement of the benefits to the developed economy of its relation with an underdeveloped region could scarcely be wished for: it remains to explain how the symptoms of underdevelopment came to be imbedded in the Cape's peasant regions after 1890.

One set of factors operating to make more costly a continued existence within a peasant mode of production was the toll wrought by
geophysical, demographic and natural phenomena. It is impossible to
provide precise population statistics for the Transkei territories, but
the following figures provide a rough guide: 1891, 640,000; 1898,
770,000; 1904, 800,000; 1911, 870,000.[49] Natural population
increase in the Transkei was augmented by the influx of peasants
pushed off the land elsewhere in the Cape, especially by the Location
Acts of 1892, 1899 and 1909, and more generally by the propensity of
commercializing white farmers to dispense with the quasi-feudal relations that had previously afforded thousands of Africans access to land
owned but not occupied by whites. In 1893 (several magistrates were
startled by the 1891 Census figures) the Chief Magistrate of the
Transkei posed the problem in simple terms: 'Year by year the territories are becoming more thickly populated, and the question arises,
what is to be done with a population that promises to be too numerous
to be supported on the land under the existing conditions?'[50]

Population increase was closely related to the physical deterioration
of the land; the available area was required to bear more people and
more stock than it had hitherto been accustomed. The accumulation of
cattle, as well as the major technological adaptations of the nineteenth
century – the use of the ox-drawn plough – were both forms of surplus
absorption, Arrighi has argued, with a 'land-consuming bias': that is,
they tended to eliminate the 'traditional' abundance of land and to
promote an actual shortage of land.[51] Additional garden plots were
hacked out of fallow bush that was undergoing natural regeneration;
trees and shrubs were cleared to create more grazing or sowing space,
loosening the sandy topsoil and baring it to erosion by wind and water;
the sharp rise in the number of sheep owned by Transkei peasants
represented another potent agency for the destruction of natural flora.
Peasants were compelled to exist on a smaller total arable area, so that
despite adaptations such as irrigation or fertilizing that might stabilize
or increase production in individual peasant holdings, in overall terms
normal rotation was disrupted, fertility lessened, erosion hastened and
returns diminished. 'Compared with 25 or 30 years ago,' wrote an
administrator who had lived all his life in the Transkei, 'the desiccation
of the country in many parts is clearly apparent'.[52]

The role played by droughts and animal diseases in weakening the
peasant's ability to produce an agricultural surplus needs no further
stress. The situation of increasing land scarcity and of falling returns
bred competition for resources. Within the traditional redistributive
tenets of Nguni society, such competition might have been cushioned
or contained; in conditions of increasing stratification its effects were
given freer rein. Resources were not only becoming scarcer, they were
also becoming more unevenly distributed. Scully wrote in 1894 from
Nqamakwe that

127

there is far more poverty among the Natives than is generally supposed, or would be inferred from the amount of live stock that one sees in passing through the country. The property is very unevenly distributed. Some natives own thousands of sheep and hundreds of cattle ... while others – and these forming far the larger proportion – own very little, if any, stock. A large number of men are absent at work in the different mines.

From Griqualand East came equally pointed evidence:

In marked contrast with the farm servants or squatters, or inhabitants of the locations are the few natives who own land. There are about a dozen in that happy position. They are well housed, well clad, well fed, in fact they have become a sort of aristocracy among the other natives.[53]

In Emigrant Tembuland some members of this 'aristocracy' gave notice of their intention to defend their elevation against 'commoners'. Sixty-two land-owning Africans petitioned the magistrate in these words:

When we were allowed to come and take possession of these morgen we were strictly told that the Government wanted only civilized natives. Now some of these natives who were dressed up have pulled off their breeches and turned out to be Red Kaffirs.[54]

The General Council and District Council administrative system introduced by the Glen Grey Act of 1894 gave the upper stratum of peasants institutional form: in its membership one finds a class of headman-bureaucrat-farmers keenly aware of their place in a stratified society. When a credit system on the lines of a Land Bank was discussed during the 1909 session of the Transkeian Territories General Council, one Councillor Nkala

quite approved of the introduction of the land bank system because it appeared it would not help every one. Poor people would not reap any advantage from it. It would only raise those who already had property. ... It was good that men who desired to improve their position should be given the opportunity to do so.[55]

A generation later, a survey of the Transkei found that about 33 per cent of all the cattle were in the hands of 5 per cent of the people, including many of the Bunga (General Council) members. In one location, three out of a thousand stock holders held 70 per cent of the sheep and 50 per cent of the cattle there. Some of the councillors had as many as three thousand sheep, and most had two hundred sheep and fifty cattle.[56] Stratification is not peculiar to underdeveloped regions, but it does have the characteristic of bearing particularly heavily upon the have-nots where the general level of economic activity is low. Each stock disease or drought could have provided the Ciskeian or Transkeian missionary with a sermon on the text that ends 'But from him that hath not shall be taken away even that which he hath.'

Another set of factors that raised the cost of peasant subsistence, and that derived directly from the penetration of predominantly African areas by market relations, was the whole complex of peasant/trader dealings. The traders, backed by merchants in the Cape and Natal, who entered the region, built their stores and plied their business, were the most important single agents of economic change, the influential envoys of the advanced economy.* The relationship was, from the outset, a major means of the appropriation of the peasant community's surplus. In exchanges between peasant and trader, the terms of trade were against the contractually inferior peasant producer-consumer. In the trader's hands were concentrated the several economic functions of purchaser of agricultural produce, purveyor of manufactured goods, and supplier of credit. The trader's control of these functions meant that agricultural surpluses tended to be absorbed in the form of his profits rather than made available for re-investment by the peasantry.[57] Trader and peasant enacted in microcosm the adverse terms of trade of a colonial relationship.

The African peasant was disadvantaged as a consumer in several respects. He could do little more to affect the prices of the manufactured articles that the trader sold than to travel to more than one trading store, and it is clear that, buttressed as they were against untoward competition by the five-mile law, there was little tendency amongst traders to undercut one another's prices.[58] The goods that passed from trader to peasant were not only retailed at a profitable margin over their wholesale price, but also tended to carry substantial duties; 'loading' articles that were clearly destined for 'native trade' was a popular resort of politicians. A magistrate calculated in 1906 that a Transkei peasant paid an average 20 per cent customs duty on all the goods he purchased.[59]

He suffered as a producer inasmuch as the trader was able to buy his grain and animal products cheaply, precisely because of the 'lack of development of the market – the inability of the producers to effect an exchange on any more than a parochial scale'.[60] The peasant in need of cash for taxes, debts or consumption wants, had little bargaining power, and had to accept depressed prices for his products, especially when good seasons meant that he had more to sell. The adverse trade terms encountered by the peasant as consumer and producer were summed up by the 1932 Economic Commission: 'The Native, particularly in the rural areas, has to pay more for the same article than would

* Their counters (commented a missionary author) were 'more than anything else the medium by which Kafir thought and life become penetrated with European ideas.' (G. Callaway, *Sketches from Kafir Life* (London, 1905), 7.)

a European, while for the same class of goods of the same quality he would receive less than a European.'[61]

It was, however, in the system of credit that the trader/peasant relationship was most heavily slanted against the petty consumer-producer. The extension of credit involved peasants in costly repayments, and the spread of debt in the peasant economy was one of the most striking features of the post-1890 years. The trader advanced goods on credit, commonly on the security of stock possessed by the buyer. If payment was not forthcoming, the sheep or cow would be forfeited, and in these cases (one learns without great surprise) the trader made 'a huge profit'.[62] When the peasant did manage to pay his debts, the trader still fared handsomely; goods sold on credit were far more expensive than the same items in a cash transaction. This feature prevailed throughout the period under review, and twenty years later a study of Transkei trading practices found that goods were sold on credit for double the market price (and that this was especially the case in the sale of grain).[63] A second form of credit extended by the trader was the cash advance: apart from the cash that flowed back to the trader in purchases, these debts commonly bore punitive interest rates.*

The practice of cash advances and the provision of commodities on credit both developed enormously in the 1890s as a result of the recruiting procedures adopted by the gold mining companies, procedures that amounted to systematic debt inducement. Labour agents received a capitation fee per every recruit that they 'signed up', and the majority of traders took out licences as agents. Labour agents were empowered to make a cash advance – commonly five pounds – to the labourer, to be repaid either by remittance or upon return from the mines.[64] Indebtedness – either as 'instant debt' on receipt of the agent's advance, or in long-term endemic form – became the crucial device in separating Transkeian peasants from the means of production.[65] Quite apart from the fees that he received for migrants formally recruited, it was in general terms in the trader's interest to offer credit on a scale which was likely to be recoverable only through wage labour. As A. W. G. Champion told the Mining Industry Board in 1912:

> The native is induced and encouraged to take as much in the way of goods as he likes although he has no cash to pay for them. Then his crop fails and he finds that he cannot pay, and the trader comes along and says 'If you do not join I will run you in, and you will have to pay all the costs. I will take out a civil action and annex your cattle.'[66]

Indebtedness spread enormously in Ciskei and Transkei. By 1904, it

---

* Interest rates varied enormously, especially before the Cape's Usury Act (1908). A common rate of interest in the Transkei was a shilling per pound per month – or 60 per cent a year.

was estimated that the sixty-four traders in Glen Grey district were owed about £100,000; the Umtata magistrate wrote two years later that he was convinced 'that a large proportion of the Natives in this and other districts are virtually insolvent'.[67] Two of the traders who showed Haines their account books had, respectively, made cash advances of £10,500 in eight years and sold goods on credit worth over £18,000 in a nine-year span.[68] Debts became most burdensome at those times when the peasants were least well off; the growing integration of the Transkei's economy in the national (and international) economy was clearly demonstrated in times of recession. As in the depression of 1908, traders would refuse to allow the normal terms, would press for payment or foreclose on outstanding accounts, while such crop surpluses that were raised realized only depressed prices.[69]

A further aspect of the peasant/trader nexus emerged in the 1890s: an increasing reluctance by traders to buy African-grown grain or an insistence on paying for it in kind, not cash. Behind this lay the trader's growing difficulty in disposing of grain profitably at market towns like Queenstown, Kingwilliamstown or East London. In the 1870s and 1880s the grain he transported there competed with maize or wheat grown elsewhere in the hinterland, also transported by ox-wagon. Now it would suffer in competition with cereals brought to the towns by rail – or even by steamship and rail from the American mid-west.

For this reason, the reports of the period are dotted with comments on the new reluctance of Africans to raise grain (that they would not be able to sell); in a confidential report for the Cape government in 1905, it was stated that between the Kei and Umtata rivers underproduction for want of access to markets was the great drawback.[70] As Stanford, the Chief Magistrate, put it in 1908: 'The easy access to the labour market . . . contrasts with the difficulty or absolute lack of transport for agricultural produce.'[71] The 'difficulty' of transport costs was spelled out by the magistrate of Umtata; the prevailing transport system, he said, operated

> very unfavourably on the price of mealies. In fruitful years when growers wish to sell, it does not pay to export, the cost of transport being too great. In seasons of scarcity, when consumers wish to buy, the cost of transport again enhances the price of grain; a few months ago when mealies were selling at Butterworth at 12/6 per muid, they were selling here at 18–20s, the difference being due to the fact that, at Butterworth, dealers were able to import from the Free State, by rail, while at Umtata they had to depend on local supplies or to import by wagon.[72]

Perhaps the most important variable introduced into structural relations between the white agricultural sector and the black peasantry after the mineral discoveries was the relative ease of access to markets for farmers in each sector. Macmillan has pointed out that 'to locate the native reserves it is no bad rule . . . to look for the areas circumvented or entirely missed, by even branch railway lines'.[73]

While the 'difficulty of transport' cut down the amount of grain that the trader would purchase, it certainly did not abolish trade in crops, for the good reason that a limited local trade in grain was one of the largest sources of the trader's annual income. Grain was sold by peasants immediately after harvest, to be resold later in the season by the trader at considerable profits.[74] Probably no other item of African economic behaviour elicited the scorn of white observers as regularly as this 'fecklessness', 'improvidence' or 'childishness'. Yet examination shows that the seemingly irrational behaviour was in itself an indication of the pressures to which the peasants were subjected. The sales after harvest took place because cash or goods were needed – to pay debts, to meet tax obligations or simply to provide consumer demands that had become imperative. Storage facilities were inadequate to allow 'banking' the grain until it could be off-loaded at more favourable rates, and more sophisticated storage or marketing devices were ruled out even for substantial peasants by the dearth of private or public investment in the region and the growing inability of peasants to accumulate capital.[75]

For one must bear in mind that ultimately any production of agricultural surplus by the peasantry would involve competition with white agriculturists; at the same time that changes in the internal economy of the Eastern Province and Transkei were restricting the surplus-generating capacity of African peasants, the commercialization of white agriculture was being facilitated by the programme of subsidies mentioned earlier. The peasant's ability to participate in the produce market was being weakened at the same time that the competitive position of white farmers was being shored up by state aid and by modernization 'from above'. Once capitalist agriculture 'has overcome the initial difficulties related to its competitive weakness in the produce market . . . market forces themselves tend to widen the gap between productivities in peasant and capitalist agriculture'.[76] Between 1929 and 1939, the production of maize and sorghum in the Transkei declined by about 25 per cent, while that of white farmers rose by over 40 per cent.[77]

This section has described some of the day-to-day disabilities against which the peasant tried to contend; the effects of each operated not in isolation, but in cumulative and interacting fashion. Taken together, they were the symptoms and agents of underdevelopment in the peasant regions. It must be mentioned that the picture of a Transkei economy already underdeveloped before 1914 is somewhat at variance with other historical assessments. The broadly current version was stated most strongly by Brookes, who fifty years ago celebrated the Transkei peasant as 'the most prosperous, the most advanced, and (with the exception of the Natal tribal native) the most contented

Native in South Africa today'. This was so because of a 'unique progressive policy', a 'coherent, intelligible, progressive and conscious evolution' from Blyth through Rhodes to the workings of the Transkeian Territories General Council (TTGC) under the paternal eyes of white magistrates. The Transkei entered the twentieth century 'in a state of great tranquillity and prosperity' and under the Glen Grey system it 'stood alone' in its 'remarkable progress'. De Kiewiet also stressed the 1894 Act, and said that the Transkei thereafter showed 'distinct elements of success'. More recently (and in the context of the chapter in which it appears, more surprisingly) Monica Wilson has written that agriculture declined in the Transkei only 'after 1930'.[78]

These favourable judgements seem to have arisen in large part because the historians concerned have taken the proceedings of the General Council of the territories (with their expenditure on agricultural schools and improvements, their debates on stock breeding and soil conservation) as evidence of agricultural innovation and material well-being. And so they are – but, crucially, the enterprise and well-being that they reflect belong to a specific class that had emerged and was even then consolidating its position in the society. The Glen Grey Act contributed to the definition of that class: to the overlapping of the categories of bureaucrat and well-to-do peasant, to the enjoyment by the headmen and their favourites of the choice land, to the circulation of funds and skills at the upper strata, and to the heightened pressure on the young and landless to sell their labour. (Symbolically, the General Council's first agricultural school, in Tsomo, stood alongside the educational institution for chiefs' sons!) Like the kulaks in the Russian countryside, who had the 'great advantage of being members, very important members of the village commune', the most prosperous peasants in the Transkei were also able to 'use political power' in their own interests.[79] As has already been argued, the success of a stratum of large peasants is not only compatible with but is a predictable feature of the underdevelopment of a peasant community as a whole.

Viewed structurally, the workings of the internal economy of the Transkei, as well as the subordination of the regional economy to the capitalist economy make it clear that underdevelopment and not progress was the distinctive feature of peasant production in the period reviewed in this chapter. The daily existence of the peasant was increasingly influenced by economic disabilities beyond his control; their effects were mutually reinforcing. From the rising cost of a peasant mode of production there stemmed the distinctive form of proletarianization in the Cape's African regions: the creation of proletarians who retained the semblance of access to the means of production, but who had to sell their labour power in order to subsist.

133

5 LEGISLATION AND LIBERALISM

Chairman: If I understand you correctly, this [Glen Grey] Act creates, as one side of it, a large number of black peasant proprietors upon entailed estates, and the remaining natives become either workers or vagabonds...?

J. Liefeldt (Magistrate of Willowvale): It would make a certain proportion of them small agriculturists, and they would advance accordingly.... It forces out labour, because the ground is limited, and those who are unable to obtain land must go into the labour market.

(*Transvaal Labour Commission*, 1904, Minutes of Evidence, 257)

A process that paralleled and contributed towards the debilitation of peasant agriculture between 1890 and 1913 was the movement in the Cape during those years to undermine the class of squatter-peasants. In South Africa at large, the various legislative and administrative pressures upon 'independent' black peasants immediately before and for a decade after the South African War amount in sum to what may be termed an employers' offensive.* In the Cape, the move against squatter-peasants was the major element in that offensive. Pressure against squatter-peasants arose directly from the commercialization of white agriculture (and was reproduced, of course, against *bywoners* – white squatters – too: thousands of indigent whites were pushed out of the countryside into the towns in the early twentieth century). Apart from the desire by commercializing farmers to maximize the returns from their land, and their impatience with the quasi-feudal relations existing, white farmers were also sensitive to the threat of competition from black squatters, and resentful of the ability of that class to limit the amount of labour forthcoming. There is abundant evidence in the printed sources of the continuing benefits available to squatter-peasants and share-croppers, as well as of the rising animus against this class. The 'wealthy native' who 'looks upon himself as an independent farmer' was the target of a typical complaint.[80]

Legislators in the Cape thus sought a means of discouraging potential labourers from making a living as peasants. However, they did not seek to abolish entirely the system of black dwellers on white-owned lands, for this would have meant expelling the very hands whose labour was sought. Legislation was pursued that would retain potential labourers, but so circumscribe their status as to transform them from 'independent' squatters, lessees, or sharers to dependent, wage-earning servants. Social engineering on this scale took time and effort,

---

* Details of such legislative devices in Natal, the Transvaal and Orange Free State will be found in Chapters 6 and 7.

but the incentives were powerful. Act 33/1892 created a system of 'private locations' in the Cape: the onus was put on the white farmer to register the black population on his farm as a location, and he would be liable to a cash penalty for the residence there of more than the permitted number of Africans not earning a wage. This Act led, in some districts, to evictions: in Uitenhage, Alexandria and Bathurst, reported the Chief Inspector of Locations, many Africans were turned off farms; they suffered a great loss of stock, and much land was 'thrown out of cultivation'.[81] In other instances, the Act succeeded in forcing tenants to become labourers. Generally, however, the Act was evaded or simply not applied; only £1,500 a year was collected in licence fees.

In 1894 the Glen Grey Act – the great contribution by Cecil Rhodes to employers' efforts – became law. It was not confined to the question of squatters, but sought more ambitiously to proletarianize large numbers of Africans on 'tribal' as well as on 'white' lands. The Act was eagerly welcomed by many who discerned a precise coincidence of interests in its workings: the institution of individual tenure would offer to 'barbarians' those very habits of industry and civilization long praised by the liberal tradition; sober and energetic blacks would be the agents of their own uplifting; at the same time, their less hard-working or talented kinsmen would be emitted from the locations, in accordance with impersonal economic laws, in gratifyingly large numbers as wage labourers. The *Queenstown Free Press* (a self-styled Cape liberal publication) proselytized for just such an act before its details were published: the institution of 'landed property' on individual tenure would benefit the African while also being 'distinctly in our own interest', as 'the only labour supply that can be counted upon with anything of reliance is obtained from the locations'. If such locations were kept and fostered there would 'always be a nucleus of labour'. The land in the possession of one holder would 'in most cases be insufficient to provide a living for the whole family' and so some males from each family would have to seek work. The locations would 'become a source of wealth to the country in supplying a continual stream of labour'.[82]

The Act is noteworthy in several other respects. In its provision for local councils, as well as in its concern for fixity of tenure, it sought to perpetuate a 'producing class' in African areas; it sought to keep the reserves self-supporting; they would continue to feed the black population and thus free the capitalist sector from that responsibility.[83] Yet at the same time the sanctity of private property was qualified: the nature and capacity of the members of the producing class was held to certain acceptable bounds. The proposed size of agricultural holdings – five morgen (just over ten acres) – as well as the principle of 'one man one lot' seems designed to prevent the emergence of black farmers so successful that they might compete with white farmers. (It was largely this aspect of the Act that was objected to by the very group of African producers – the small-scale commercial farmers – that it threatened. They protested that their 'rights and property' were prejudiced by the measure; and a letter from one of the most influential African spokesmen in the Eastern Province, Charles Pamla, elaborated: 'No man is allowed to occupy more than *one* lot. This shuts out all improvements and industry of some individuals who may work and buy. . . . Surely Mr. Rhodes can't expect that all the Natives will be equal. He himself is richer than others; even trees differ in height.')[84]

From Rhodes's wide vision we return to the more narrowly focused squatting legislation. The ineffectual 1892 Act was buttressed by Act 30/1899: this permitted white farmers to keep on their lands any number of Africans in continuous employment, and also permitted leases for which £36 or more per annum was paid. This Act was more widely applied than its predecessor, and in 1905 its execution was transferred to the Cape Mounted Police. In 1906, however, a Select Committee concluded that further legislation was necessary, as existing statutes had not checked 'the evil of squatting' nor the 'invasion of private lands'.[85] (Marais is undoubtedly correct in suggesting that the estimated population in 'private locations' in the Eastern Cape of 37,500 is too low: there is no little evidence to suggest that farmers were continuing, illegally, to offer land to squatters in return for a limited amount of labour.)[86] In 1908, a Commission investigated the problem in detail. In forceful and unequivocal terms its report stated that

> these native lessees are now forming a distinct and very numerous class, an appreciable proportion of which is composed of men who have holdings in Crown locations, but who, dissatisfied with the congested condition of those locations, have left their holdings in charge of relations or friends and migrated to where they may be able to secure the hire of a piece of arable land and some pasturage, and combine with these advantages the comparative liberty attaching to life in a Native community.

This system made it

> increasingly difficult for young Europeans to secure the hire of ground, and a desirable class of farmer is thus displaced. . . . It is the opinion of the Commission that the existence of the Native lessee system must considerably enhance any inadequacy of labour demand. The ease and liberty of the situation appeals to the ordinary Native peasant . . . and he will usually prefer it to daily toil at the mines or ports or in towns or on farms. If the system were placed under greater restriction a large number of these Natives would be compelled to go out to labour.[87]

From the recommendations of this report there came forth the Location Act 32/1909. This raised the licence fees, tightened the definitions of *bona fide* labourers (exempt from the fee), and was fairly stringently applied, notably in districts where its provisions were welcomed by commercializing farmers. By the following year, there were reports of evictions, with squatter-peasants being driven off their plots for refusing to pay the higher fees. (Although formally levied on the landlord, the general practice was for the fees to be 'passed on' in the form of higher rents or a straight levy.) As an official in East London district put it, squatting was being 'closely dealt with by the South African Police'. This was 'causing numbers of Natives with their families to be rendered homeless'.[88]

In other words, by the time of the Natives Land Act of 1913 (fuller discussion of which is reserved for another chapter) the Cape already possessed and employed a formidable battery of anti-squatter laws, and had already done much to undermine the position of the squatter-peasant in the Eastern Province. The 1913 Act's provisions were declared inapplicable in the Cape by the Court in 1917, and although its anti-squatter provisions had been applied in that province during 1913 and 1914, it was relatively unimportant there. Even without it, a squatter population of at least 40,000 (and probably much more) was reduced by the 1909 Act to 7,000 by 1931; a Union report in 1930 indicated that of 2,000 farms owned but not occupied by whites in South Africa, only seventy-four were in the Cape.

The anti-squatting laws and practices in the Cape had as their most obvious effects first, the evictions of share-croppers and lessees, and secondly, the surrender by thousands of these of their relative independence in the form of their altered status, as they became wage labourers or labour-tenants. Many opted for the change rather than leave the only agricultural land they knew. Its effects were also registered in the Transkei, whither numbers of those evicted moved with their families and their animals. This increased the competition for land; those who already possessed land pressed for the survey provisions of the Glen Grey Act in order to secure their titles against others less fortunate.

It has been argued in earlier chapters that the political tradition known as Cape liberalism included a commitment to or belief in the creation of an African peasantry as a social and economic good: land-owning and food-producing peasants would make good citizens, customers and Christians; the 'native' areas would be integrated into the import–export sector of the colonial economy. Characteristically mid-Victorian articles of faith in 'civilization' and 'progress' served as points of reference in a schema whereby prosperity, property, the Anglican Church, the Colony and the Empire would all wax strong. By the late nineteenth century Cape liberalism had divested itself of some of its ideological baggage; its spokesmen were by then more cautious, less optimistic.

At the broadest level, this change was merely a reflection or a component of the one that took place in metropolitan Britain. After the outbreak of the New Imperialism in the final quarter of the nineteenth century, there was a widespread shift in European attitudes towards Africa. The official mind as well as the public imagination settled upon a stereotype of the African as half-child, half-savage; the claims and aims of the civilizing mission became more modest; Kipling's *Recessional* put into words what already existed in thought. 'The mid-Victorian objective of turning Africans into black Englishmen had long been given up.... The tendency was ... towards segregation rather than assimilation.'[89] The adjusted attitudes were particularly evident in missionary circles, in South Africa as elsewhere. Etherington makes the point that the dousing of missionary optimism was due in part to the resistance that they encountered in Nguni society, and their limited success in effecting conversions. Missionaries lost confidence in their own ability to succeed in areas still ruled or heavily influenced by traditionalist elements, and came increasingly to support the 'civilizing' content of imperial conquest and rule.[90] Missionary thought also moved away from its original conception of the social objectives of conversions and mission stations; the desire of the mid-nineteenth century for an African middle class was diluted or set aside, and in its stead there rose an interest in industrial education and a concern for establishing 'habits of industry'. In an editorial in 1902 the leading missionary publication in South Africa said that not only the mines, but manufacturers, farmers and housewives were short of black labour and that 'for his own sake, the native must be weaned from his capricious and spasmodic habit of work'.[91]

At a local level, the changing conceptions of Cape liberalism derived from the completion of conquest and from the demands of modernization. Simons has demonstrated how the policy towards tribalism shifted in the late nineteenth and early twentieth centuries. The 1883 *Commission on Laws and Customs* saw the first slackening of the root-and-branch hostility to tribal laws and institutions. With the assertion of control over Bechuanaland and the whole of the Transkei, the spectre of frontier warfare finally evaporated, and the earlier desire for a 'buffer class' diminished in proportion. By 1910, 'tribalism was a spent force. It no longer menaced settler communities, or kept men off the labour market.'[92] A spent force, but not a vanished one; its surviving forms could be manipulated and usefully preserved to provide certain advantages. It began to be realized by the end of the nineteenth century that in the traditional leadership existed a ready-made source of social control, and Cape officials came increasingly to search for a collaborating class in chiefs and headmen. They explored Glen Grey and General Council channels instead of the older reliance on a propertied, Christian, progressive and secular leadership.

Cape liberals also responded to the demands by mines and farms for African labour, and amended their ideas of the future of the African reserves accordingly.* Their acceptance of the tenure provisions of Glen Grey meant that Cape practice meshed neatly with that of the rest of the Union in pursuing a policy for the next sixty years that 'consistently refused to allow any accumulation of land by individual Africans, and wherever it had control ... it had insisted on the principle of "one man one lot".'[93] Cape liberals saw the solution of the 'labour question' to lie not in the 'coercive' means of Rhodes's labour tax or of the Transvaal's 'apprentice' system, but in the measure of controlled proletarianization that was to take place in the reserves. As J. X. Merriman phrased it, in discussion with the 1903–5 Commissioners:

Q: I wish to ask you what, in your opinion, should be done with those people for whom no land can be provided?

J.X.M.: What is done with any European for whom no land is provided? He has got to go and work....

Q: Can I get from you an answer as to what you think should be done with the surplus population of natives ...?

J.X.M.: There is a general demand for agricultural labour ... at present there is a cry for agricultural labour everywhere; why do they not fill that up?

Q: Would you drive them out to the farms, for instance?

J.X.M.: I would not drive them, but they will drive themselves when they get congested in land held under individual tenure. And that is just the point. I do not want to drive the natives at all. It is the gradual process of civilization that will force them to work, and is forcing them every day.[94]

Trapido argues that by about 1900 Cape liberalism had accepted the need for the creation of a mass labour force[95] and it seems that the altered vision of the peasant sector was one of the clearest ways in which that acceptance manifested itself. As the peasant sector became 'modernized' (through the introduction of surveys and titles), while it continued to raise enough food to keep the workers' dependants alive, ineluctable forces would provide employers with the labour they needed, and all these desirable ends could still be loosely construed within a (slightly thinned) Cape Tradition. The authentic voice of turn-of-century liberalism in the Cape can be heard (appropriately enough, in a passage critical of the labour tax provisions of the Glen

* Martin Legassick has examined liberalism in South Africa in the early twentieth century in a series of pioneering and stimulating seminar papers. In particular, he demonstrates that between 1903 and 1923 many South African liberals identified in 'segregation' (the creation of Reserves) a Native Policy which would serve several ends, including the promotion of capitalist economic growth in the specific conditions existing in South Africa. These papers have been extended and developed for a book entitled *Capitalism and Segregation in South Africa* (Macmillan, forthcoming).

139

Grey Act): 'We must have patience and be tolerant and allow the natural forces of supply and demand to improve the position gradually.'[96]

Even a successful peasant – one, say, who had been an adept farmer, who had ploughed, irrigated, sheared, threshed and marketed with skill and reward for many years – even he would have been keenly aware by the first years of this century of the rising social costs involved in extracting a living from the land in an underdeveloped region. He might well have become dissuaded from investing further in agriculture; other forms of saving or re-investment might offer more return. His hard-won property itself would seem to him an equivocal legacy to his children.

This hypothesis seems quite clearly to have been the case: even in a society where continuity and ancestral lands had been greatly valued, one is aware of a search for alternatives. Many prosperous peasants sought investment not in agricultural improvements, but in education and the acquisition of skills for the younger generation. The mayor of Lady Frere wrote to the 1903–5 Commission that many of the young educated Africans were becoming clerks, teachers, law agents and the like: 'their fathers', he added, were 'generally respectable peasant proprietors, making a decent living, keeping a few head of stock, and raising kaffir corn, mealies, wheat, beans and forage, which is sold in all the large centres'.[97]

There is a danger in generalizing from particular cases, and it is not maintained that the instance of R. Joseph, a Mfengu farmer of the Komgha district, is 'typical'. Yet his evidence to a Select Committee[98] in 1909 illustrates very accurately the perception by a well-off peasant of the rising social cost of agriculture. More than this, in the family history of three generations that emerges, one has a thumbnail sketch – almost a metaphor – of the history of the Eastern Cape peasantry. Joseph's father had been a 'red' peasant, 'an uneducated man' of a Mfengu clan in the Alice district, who had seized his opportunity in the 1870s. Through farming (and his son spoke admiringly of his skill at agriculture) and transport riding, he accumulated enough capital to provide his son with the rudiments of an education *and* with a portion of land and a transport team of his own. On this favourable foundation, Joseph had built well; by 1909 he farmed on a substantial scale, cultivating a hundred acres, employing wage labourers and leasing part of his property to tenants. For his own children, however, he was investing not in land purchases and survey fees, but in education: one son was in the final year at Lovedale, and the other engaged in medical training in Canada.

NOTES

1 On early gold-mining see: S. H. Frankel, *Capital Investment in Africa* (Oxford, 1938); I. Katzen, *Gold and the South African Economy, 1886–1961* (Cape Town, 1964); E. B. Jeppe, *Gold Mining on the Witwatersrand* (Johannesburg, 1946); F. Wilson, *Labour in the South African Gold Mines* (Cambridge, 1972).

2 See F. Wilson, 'Farming, 1866–1966', OHSA, II, 104–71.

3 SANAC, IV, 935.

4 D. J. N. Denoon (with B. Nyeko), *Southern Africa since 1800* (London, 1972), 61, 128, 129; R. Palmer and N. Parsons (eds.), *The Roots of Rural Poverty* (London, 1977), 8.

5 CPP, G.3–'94, *Report of Commission on Labour Supply* (cited hereafter as *Labour Commission*), 3 vols, III, 57, 174, 136; II, 525, 561.

6 ibid., III, 5.

7 F. A. Johnstone, *Class, Race and Gold* (London, 1976), Chapter 1, especially 17–21.

8 Speech by President of Chamber of Mines, 1911, quoted by Johnstone, op. cit., 27.

9 *Report of the Natives Land Commission, 1916*, 2 vols., Vol. II, U.G. 22–1914, Minutes of Evidence (cited hereafter as the *Beaumont Commission*), 162, 175, 206.

10 J. F. W. Grosskopf, 'Rural Impoverishment and Rural Exodus', Vol. I of *The Poor White Problem in South Africa* (The Carnegie Commission, Stellenbosch, 1932), 8.

11 CPP, A.2–'09, *Select Committee on Native Affairs*, 184.

12 F. B. Smith, *Some Observations upon the Probable Effect of the Closer Union of South Africa upon Agriculture* (Pretoria, 1908), cited by M. Legassick, 'Gold, Agriculture, and Secondary Industry in South Africa, 1885–1970', in Palmer and Parsons (eds.), op. cit.

13 CPP, G.4–'90, BBNA, 112 (and see Chapter 5 for a detailed study of Herschel district).

14 CPP, G.7–'92, BBNA, 9–10, and see generally 1–21.

15 CPP, G.4–'90, BBNA, 15; G.4–'93, BBNA, 20; G.4–'91, BBNA, 20; G.3–'94, *Labour Commission*, III, 168; G.9–'94, BBNA, 27; G.5–'96, BBNA, 49.

16 CPP, G.7–'92, BBNA, 31.

17 CPP, G.4–'93, BBNA, 61, 63; G.8–'95, BBNA, 81; G.19–'97, BBNA, 108.

18 G.3–'94, *Labour Commission*, II, 110, 54, 76, 71.

19 CPP, G.9–'94, BBNA, 63.

20 SPG, E MSS, 1894, II, E. Coakes, St Mark's Mission Station, 30 September 1894.

21 C. van Onselen, 'Reactions to Rinderpest in Southern Africa, 1896–97', *Journal of African History*, 13, 1972, 473–88.

22 CPP, G.42–'98, BBNA, 76; and see van Onselen, op. cit., 477, for prevalence of this belief and other examples.

23 SPG E MSS, 1898, II, St Matthew's Mission, Keiskammahoek, 31 December 1898. Cf. van Onselen, op. cit., 487.
24 CPP, G.31–'99, BBNA, 81.
25 SPG, C.L.R. Series, Kaffraria 1874–1927, vol. 2, 20 January 1900.
26 H. Bley, 'Social Discord in South West Africa 1894–1904', in P. Gifford and W. R. Louis (eds.) Britain and Germany in Africa (New Haven, 1967), 627–8.
27 CPP, G.25–'02, BBNA, 8.
28 ibid., 6–8.
29 ibid., 8.
30 CPP, G.46–1908, Report of a Departmental Commission on the Occupation of Land by Natives in Unreserved Areas, 13.
31 CPP, G.37–'03, Sheep Inspector's Report for 1903, 44–5.
32 See D. Denoon, 'The Transvaal Labour Crisis, 1901–06', Journal of African History, VII, 3 (1967) 481–94.
33 Apart from the annual reports from the relevant districts in the Blue Books, the evidence to SANAC is particularly informative on the Ciskei: see II, 424–840.
34 SANAC, II, 593.
35 CPP, G.12*–1904, BBNA, 5.
36 SANAC, II, 622, 565.
37 SANAC, V: see replies from W. G. Bennie, C. J. Dovey, H. Briscoe, C. A. Lloyd, J. S. Moffat, C. Orpen, 8, 15, 53, 62, 70, 94.
38 W. Beinart, 'Peasant Production, Underdevelopment, and the Traditionalist Response in Pondoland, c. 1880–1930' (University of London, M.A. thesis, September 1973), 11.
39 CPP, G.25–1902, BBNA, 37; G.42–'98, BBNA, 111.
40 CPP, G.12*–1904, BBNA, 57.
41 Beinart, op. cit., 19; SANAC, II, 1088.
42 See e.g. Tembuland proper, the districts north of Umtata, widely described at the time as 'less advanced' or 'more tribal' than Fingoland or Emigrant Tembuland: especially reports for Qumbu (G.9–'94, G.52–'01, G.25–'02, G.29–'03), Mt. Fletcher (G.36–'07, G.24–'08, G.28–1910), and Tsomo (G.24–'08, G.28–1910) (all BBNAs).
43 CPP, G.3–'94, Labour Commission, III, 5.
44 There is an excellent contemporary description and analysis of the effects of the disease in J. R. L. Kingon, 'The Economic Consequences of East Coast Fever', Christian Express, XLV, Nos. 539, 540, 541, and XLVI, 542 (October 1915–January 1916).
45 J. T. Kenyon, An Address on the General Council System of the Transkeian Territories (Umtata, 1932), 64.
46 U.G. 33–1913, Native Affairs Departmental Report for 1912, 14.
47 Johnstone, Class, Race and Gold, 181. The average earnings per shift for African workers barely fluctuated between 1911 and 1919; yet between 1910 and 1920 the price index rose from 1,000 to 2,512.
48 Royal Commission on the Natural Resources, Trade, and Legislation in Certain of His Majesty's Dominions, Minutes of evidence taken in South Africa, 1914, 2 vols., (Cd. 7706–7), Vol. 2, 111 (Evidence of Howard Pim).
49 Figures are for the African population of the Transkei. They are based on

the census reports of 1891, 1904 and 1911, with considerable reliance on informed guesswork to supplement the 1891 figures which do not include Pondoland.

50 CPP, G.9–'94, BBNA, 52.

51 G. Arrighi, 'Labour Supplies in Historical Perspective: The Proletarianization of the African Peasantry in Rhodesia', *Journal of Development Studies*, 6, iii (April 1970), 214.

52 CPP, G.12*–1904, BBNA, 40. The administrator was A. H. B. Stanford, Chief Magistrate in 1904.

53 CPP, G.5–'96, BBNA, 92; G.19–'97, BBNA, 141.

54 CPP, G.25–'02, BBNA, 31.

55 Transkeian Territories General Council, *Proceedings and Reports*, 1909 Session, lxiii.

56 E. Jokl, *A Labour and Manpower Survey of the Transkeian Territories*, cited by P. G. J. Koornhof, 'The Drift from the Reserves among the South African Bantu' (Oxford University, D.Phil. thesis, 1953).

57 A. Pearse, 'Peasant and Metropolis', in T. Shanin (ed.), *Peasants and Peasant Societies* (Harmondsworth, 1971), 73.

58 E. S. Haines, 'The Transkei Trader', *South African Journal of Economics*, I, 1933, 203. Licences for new stores were only granted if they were at least five miles away from existing stores.

59 CPP, G.46–'06, BBNA, 48.

60 M. Dobb, *Studies in the Development of Capitalism* (London, 1946), 89, quoted by I. R. Phimister, 'Peasant Production and Underdevelopment in Southern Rhodesia, 1890–1914', *African Affairs*, 73 (1974), 217–28.

61 U.G. 22–1932, *Report of the Native Economic Commission*, para. 946; cf. Phimister's suggestion (op. cit., 225), that in many respects 'traders represented institutionalized "raiding" of the peasant produce surplus for the ultimate benefit of the capitalist sector'.

62 U.G. 17–1911, Dept. Nat. Aff., BBNA, 180.

63 Haines, 'The Transkei Trader', 208.

64 CPP, G.46–1906, BBNA, 63.

65 Cf. the situation in nineteenth-century Russia where poorer peasants 'tended to sink progressively into dependence, until burdened by debt and taxation and no longer able to maintain themselves on their meagre holdings, as whole families they joined the ranks of the rural proletariat or at least supplied part of the family as semi-proletarians to eke out the income from the family holding by wage-employment in ... mines or factory towns'. Dobb, *Studies*, 253.

66 Cited in Johnstone, *Class, Race and Gold*, 28.

67 CPP, G.12*–1904, BBNA, 14; G.46–1906, BBNA, 63. For prevalence of debt in Ciskei and Transkei, see also SANAC, II, paragraphs 6311, 11773, 11800, 11824, 12053, 12119, 12299, 12581, 12958, 13448, 13501, 13638, 14554, 14574, 14582, 14589.

68 Haines, 'The Transkei Trader', 206.

69 CPP, A.2–'09, *Select Committee on Native Affairs*, 233.

70 CPP, G.22–1905, *Report on Trade with Native Territories*, 7–8.

71 CPP, G.24–'08, 24.

72 U.G. 17–1911, Dept. Nat. Aff., BBNA for 1910, 142. (One Cape muid was the equivalent of three bushels or about 109 litres. In late nineteenth-

century South Africa, the average bag of maize was reckoned as a three-bushel bag.)
73 W. M. Macmillan, *Complex South Africa* (London, 1930), 212.
74 Haines, 'The Transkei Trader', 206: 'As a general rule it is probably safe to reckon the trader's purchase price is about 50% of his (cash) selling price in the following summer.'
75 Transkeian Territories General Council, *Proceedings and Reports*, 1909 Session, xxxvii. A co-operative storage and marketing scheme was proposed but fell away because it would have been too expensive to institute.
76 Arrighi, 'Labour Supplies', 224.
77 Koornhof, 'Drift from the Reserves', 233.
78 E. H. Brookes, *A History of the Native Policy of South Africa* (Pretoria, 1923), 108, 115, 386; C. W. de Kiewiet, *A History of South Africa: Social and Economic* (London, 1941), 199; Wilson, 'The Growth of Peasant Communities', OHSA, II, 56.
79 S. Stepniak, *The Russian Peasantry* (London, 1888), 55. Cited in Dobb, *Studies*, 252.
80 CPP. G.12*–1904, BBNA, 5. Cf. ibid., 23, 43; G.46–1906, BBNA, 18–19; G.24–1908, BBNA, 12–13; and especially G.46–1908, *Departmental Commission on Occupation by Natives*, 1–15, et passim.
81 Cited in J. S. Marais, 'African Squatters on European Farms in South Africa, 1892–1913', unpublished seminar paper, Institute of Commonwealth Studies, University of London, 1967. Much of the detail on anti-squatting legislation in this section is based on this valuable paper.
82 *Queenstown Free Press*, 11 October 1892.
83 D. M. Goodfellow, *A Modern Economic History of South Africa* (London, 1931), 136–7. A most interesting assessment of the workings of the Act by the early 1930s is contained in S. H. Fazan, 'Report of a Visit made to the Union of South Africa for the Purpose of Comparing the methods of land tenure in the native Reserves there with the systems obtaining in Kikuyu Province', typescript, Rhodes House Library. Fazan noted that by the late nineteenth century 'a gradual process of differentiation of [land] rights between clans, families, and individuals would have begun to appear' but that the process was 'put in a straight jacket, in the shape of Glen Grey and in the name of efficiency'. In a telling understatement he pointed out that Cecil Rhodes's 'agrarian views were not untinged by his appreciation of the need of labour for the mines', and argued that the 'particular system of peasant-proprietorship which the Glen Grey Act introduced was considered best calculated to produce as great a density of population as would be consistent with physical fitness from the labour field'. (See esp. pp. 11–32; quotations from pp. 18, 29.)
84 PRO, CO 48/524 contains many items relating to protests by Africans over the Glen Grey Act. Pamla's letter (first printed in *Imvo*, 5 September 1894) is enclosed in CO 48/524, No. 17284.
85 CPP, A.20–1906, *Report of the Select Committee on the Location Act*, iii.
86 Marais, loc. cit. And cf. CPP, C.2–1907, *Report of the Select Committee on Farm Labour*, 49 (evidence of A. J. Fuller, MLA and formerly Secretary for Agriculture in the Cape): 'In the Eastern Province ... the farmer today is finding very great difficulty in getting anything like a continuity of labour,

except he is prepared to offer big inducements to the Natives in the shape of squatting rights.'
87 G.46–1908, *Report of Departmental Commission on Occupation by Natives*, 9, 10.
88 U.G. 22–1914, *Beaumont Commission*, App. XI, 11.
89 R. Hyam, *Elgin and Churchill at the Colonial Office, 1905–1908: The Watershed of Empire* (London, 1968), 539.
90 Cf. J. F. A. Ajayi, *Christian Missions in Nigeria, 1841–1891* (London, 1965), 255–64; N. A. Etherington, 'The Rise of the Kholwa in Southeast Africa: African Christian Communities in Natal, Pondoland, and Zululand, 1835–1880' (Yale, D. Phil. thesis, 1971), 85–7.
91 *Christian Express*, XXXII, 377 (February 1902).
92 H. J. Simons, *African Women: Their Legal Status in South Africa* (London, 1968), 45.
93 M. Wilson, 'Effects on the Xhosa and Nyakusa of Scarcity of Land', in D. Biebuyck (ed.), *African Agrarian Systems* (London, 1963), 386.
94 SANAC, II, 395–7.
95 S. Trapido, 'Liberalism in the Cape in the Nineteenth and Twentieth Centuries', ICS, CSP, Vol. 4 (London, 1973), 57.
96 R. W. Rose-Innes, *The Glen Grey Act and the Native Question* (Lovedale, 1903), 32.
97 SANAC, V, 35.
98 CPP, A.2–1909, *Select Committee on Native Affairs*, 243–58.

5

The Herschel Peasantry: A Case Study

Ill fares the land, to hastening ills a prey,
Where wealth accumulates, and men decay:
Princes and lords may flourish, or may fade;
A breath can make them, as a breath has made:
But a bold peasantry, their country's pride,
When once destroyed, can never be supplied.

Oliver Goldsmith, *The Deserted Village*

This chapter provides, in a sense, a conducted tour. Our starting point is an agricultural community in a district that, although distant from major economic centres, impresses observers both with its evident fertility and with the enterprise and exertions of its inhabitants. After moving through successively less attractive vistas, the tour ends up in a forlorn and desolate district: it is one of the most badly eroded areas in all South Africa; its population suffers visibly from malnutrition and want, and exudes a sort of mute apathy; economically it 'survives' because of the annual exodus of contract and seasonal migrant workers to mines and factories and to farms. Its cruel overcrowding is so dire as to have been scarcely relieved by the haemorrhage of the few thousand people who left the district rather than become inhabitants of an 'independent' Transkei Bantustan.[1]

The distance between the start and finish of the tour is a large one – yet it is no distance. In both cases the territory surveyed is the same one: the journey is through time, not space, and lasts about a century. The changing and deteriorating landscape is at the same time a description of the actual economic geography and a metaphor for the rise and fall of a peasantry in a single South African district. Preceding chapters have provided an overall, general account of the emergence of an African peasantry in the Cape, of what characterized such a class, and of the pressures sustained by that peasantry. A single district is now subjected to considerably closer, more extended examination: the examination should serve both as a case study and as representative of the process as it was experienced in the Eastern Cape.

The district selected is Herschel, a triangle of high-lying land in the north-eastern corner of the Cape, bordering on the Orange Free State and Lesotho. For over twenty years before it became the magisterial district of Herschel it existed as the Wittebergen Native Reserve.

146

A specific incentive to study its social and economic history in some detail is that it was visited in the late 1920s by the late W. M. Macmillan, who painstakingly assembled a set of valuable data[2] – data which provide a comparative framework against which to assess earlier evidence. Apart from this particular suitability, it should be noted that what took place in Herschel has a more general explanatory value. While minor variations are visible from place to place, the broad pattern of the process being described in Herschel holds true for the eastern portions of the Cape; the district was (commented Macmillan) typical of, although probably better off than most, other Ciskei areas in the 1920s. (In one way, the Herschel case might be regarded as more relevantly an 'ideal type' for the Transkei than for the rest of the eastern Cape, in that the peasant community there was almost wholly African: the 1891 Census Report remarked that in the Colony proper Herschel had the lowest proportion of whites in any district, 'and 99·23 blacks in every hundred of the population'.)[3]

Herschel also provides an illustration of another aspect of the history of the Cape's African peasantry: the political 'alliance' between peasants (more especially, those wealthy enough to register as voters) and the mercantile-liberal interest.* Herschel fell in the political constituency of Aliwal North which was one of the Eastern Cape districts – others were Kingwilliamstown, Fort Beaufort, Victoria East, Wodehouse and Uitenhage – where non-white voters played a significant role. In Aliwal North, the vote of Africans who met the property qualifications for the franchise (almost all of whom were wealthy peasants in Herschel) was almost sufficient on its own to return a member.[4] Aliwal North consistently returned one member – successively J. W. Sauer, J. M. Orpen, E. G. Orsmond, and W. J. Orsmond – identifiable as a Cape liberal; it was represented, that is, by men who recognized that the prosperity of trade in the district was bound up with the marketing of a surplus by African cultivators.†

This chapter will argue that Herschel evinced very clearly the phenomenon of a 'period of early prosperity', and that its people responded far more positively to market opportunities than has commonly been suggested of South African cultivators by historians. For Herschel, as for the rest of the Cape (see Chapters 2, 3 and 4) it is maintained that the subsequent checking of the peasant response and the reduction of the peasantry cannot be explained in terms of the failure by Africans to adapt their tribal economy, nor simply in terms of population pressure on land. The manner in which the peasantry of

* See pp. 81–3.

† In August 1893, W. J. Orsmond addressed a meeting of African voters: they needed more than ever, he told them, a member who would devote himself to protecting their interests. The government needed reminding that the Colony's prosperity depended upon the black population; few whites realized the importance of Africans as producers of grain, wool, hides and skins. He also attacked the pass laws as an obstacle to trade (*Cape Times*, 5 August 1893).

Herschel was integrated into the developing capitalist economy of South Africa was affected by policies pursued by those (whites) who had access to political and economic power, and by changes in the economy of Southern Africa. These influences reinforced and perpetuated the impact of other factors – droughts, diseases, population increase and the like – that tended to threaten peasant production.

The Herschel peasant's capacity to produce an agricultural surplus was diminished, and his control over the disposal of that surplus was weakened; and even while the possibilities for the most modest accumulation of wealth were being restricted, the penetration of the capitalist economy into the peasant sector was raising the demands for a cash income. Then, especially in the years after Union, when the agriculture of white South Africans was being commercialized and directed towards export through incentives and protection, Herschel – like other African areas – was starved of such aid, support or encouragement. At the time when the capacity of whites to produce for cash and to bid for labour was being enhanced, the peasants' ability to produce on their own account was being reduced, and increasing numbers of them were forced into the labour market.

An explanation of peasant difficulties simply in terms of 'land shortage' or 'population pressure' on its own is incomplete. That Africans were forced to find subsistence on a sharply reduced land surface is patent; what has not been fully recognized is the extent to which competition for the land available was heightened by certain linked consequences of the impact upon African societies of colonial rule and capitalist relations. That is, while the shortage of land was 'the key to the status of inferiority, exploitation, poverty, lack of culture, in a word the status of underdevelopment ... of those who participate all too fully in the social process of capitalist development'[5] that shortage was exacerbated by other features. These included a disruption of the existing mechanisms for maintaining roughly equal allocation of resources, a division of peasant society into distinct strata, and the pursuit of new economic interests by methods (such as collaboration, litigation, wage employment) that widened the gap between peasant 'haves' and 'have-nots'. The narrative account of social and economic change in Wittebergen-Herschel will illustrate these points.

Herschel appears to have received a settled African population for the first time in the 1830s, when refugees from the *mfecane* and from the frontier wars peopled this rugged and remote area, although it had been a San stronghold before that. In the late 1840s, the Wesleyan Methodist Missionary Society was permitted by Moshweshwe to set up stations on either side of the Orange river, and one of these was established at Wittebergen,[6] in the south-western area of the eventual Herschel district. In July 1850, under promptings by William Shaw of the same missionary society, an area of about 150 square miles was promulgated as the Wittebergen Native Reserve, for inhabitation by 'aboriginals' only.[7] Further land was added during the 1850s, as the population swelled, and in 1870 the Wittebergen reserve area became the magisterial district of Herschel, with an area of 684 square miles.

The population was built up by successive infusions of refugees: a group of Thembu, several thousand strong, entered in 1852, and numbers of Southern Sotho (perhaps some 4,000) moved south from the Free State–Basutoland hostilities in the later 1850s.[8] There were smaller groups of other Southern Sotho peoples (Phuthis, Tlokwas) and a band of 'bruinmenschen' (variously described as Hottentots, Bastards, descendants of slaves) under their own *kaptein*. The largest single group of the population was Mfengu (of the Hlubi, Zizi and Bhele tribes).[9] Missionary estimates put the total population during the late 1860s as between 17,000 and 20,000; the magistrate in 1878 adjudged the total to have reached 24,500, of which he designated 12,500 as 'Fingoes'.

An important feature of this heterogeneous and largely refugee population was the absence of any powerful traditional leadership, and hence an absence of opposition by chiefs to agricultural and other innovations. Macmillan noted that the district had 'no big chiefs and no cohesion',[10] and this was an aspect that had been remarked as early as 1850: 'we have got quite a mixed population,' wrote the missionary J. Bertram, adding that the number of different clans and their refugee origins meant that the people were 'thus not so bound under the influence of heathen authority'.[11] Again, a report drawn up for Sir Bartle Frere in 1878 described the population – which possessed 'no principal chief' – as grouped into 'locations' or 'villages', each a few hundred strong, under some sixty headmen, some of whom were 'under government pay at from £5 to £10 per annum'.[12] These headmen had established their standing and authority in the eyes of the officials in the Cape by their loyalty to Austen (Superintendent of the then Wittebergen Reserve) during his clash with Moorosi in 1858.[13]

This absence of powerful traditional authority in the Wittebergen Reserve was one of the factors, particularly during the fifties and sixties, that attracted enterprising peasants from elsewhere in the Cape. Writing in 1868 from Wittebergen-Herschel, a missionary spoke of Africans who had 'accumulated a little flock of sheep or a few cattle. They will not take their hardly earned property into the Independent Native States, from which they first came, for fear of its being "eaten up" by their greedy relatives or envious chiefs.'[14] The Wittebergen Reserve, in other words, was in some degree free of the traditional sanctions against the accumulation of wealth by individuals (or of the mechanisms to 'insure' individuals against need) that existed in Nguni societies. It is interesting, in this respect, to observe that alternative, non-traditional social and political pressures and axes of conflict could – and did – rapidly emerge. In 1869, and again in 1870, groups of

Africans associated with Arthur Brigg's Methodist mission station at Wittebergen petitioned the Cape Parliament in protest against the illegal activities (including summary justice, 'eating up' and destruction of property) of headmen, African 'Reserve Constables' and the Frontier Mounted Armed Police. The Governor, Sir Philip Wodehouse, viewed these opportunistic and heavy-handed allies of the Reserve Superintendent with polite distaste. The administration of the Reserve, he commented, had been carried out 'on a mixed principle' that would not 'bear the test of strict legal enquiry'. The petitioners requested that they be brought under 'British law', and the upshot was the incorporation of the Reserve as a magisterial district of the Cape.

Given the favourable social climate for enterprise and accumulation, and given the fairly fertile and well-watered nature of the terrain, as well as the proximity of the Southern Sotho grain trading activities, one would expect that conditions favoured the appearance in the district of an African peasantry, of agricultural and trading activities, and the establishment of a cash economy. The evidence for the decade of the 1860s bears out this supposition convincingly.

In 1862, the Civil Commissioner for Aliwal North congratulated the Wittebergen Reserve:

> At present, the inhabitants raise large quantities of grain, kafir corn, maize and wheat; and are fast becoming stock farmers also. From being ten years ago a source of perpetual annoyance to the farmers of Albert and Aliwal North, owing to their thieving habits, they are now one of the best-regulated native communities on the frontier.[15]

Three years later, a Commission on Native Affairs was told by the Superintendent Austen that 'very large quantities of all kinds of grain are sold annually' out of the Reserve. In his written evidence, the Superintendent added that there were 'many' Africans in the Reserve who could qualify for the property franchise; that the majority of the population wore European clothing; and that he had observed 'a very considerable advancement in the social position of the people generally. Many wagons are bought annually, and also many ploughs. The old Kafir picks have fallen much into disuse.'[16] His comments were confirmed in the following year (1866) by Brigg, a Methodist missionary who spent fifteen years in Herschel. All classes were 'making marked advances in civilization'; the adoption of the plough was widespread (with the result that men were doing the bulk of the tilling), square houses were being put up, and merchandise was being transported within the territory and exported from it upon the wagons of African peasants.[17]

In 1868, Brigg indicated that considerable crop diversification had taken place: while maize and sorghum were the principal crops and staple foods, 'many cultivate in addition wheat, oats, beans and potatoes, for which they find a ready sale'. Mfengu, Sotho and 'Hotten-tot' peasants were active in transport riding: 'they own wagons and spans of oxen, with which they convey merchandise between the various towns of the colony. . . . By these earnings they gradually rise to a condition of considerable respectability. A good wagon, such as some of them possess, is worth £100 or upwards, and a full span of oxen not less than £70.'[18] After 1866, the amount of wheat exported to the Orange Free State from Basutoland declined, providing an opportunity for the peasants of Wittebergen-Herschel to extend their markets into the republic. The following description of peasant activity and prosperity comes from the pen of H. H. Dugmore, one of the most senior and most experienced missionaries in South Africa at the time, who visited Wittebergen in 1869, and whose other correspondence proves that he was not lightly impressed:

> The extent of cultivation carried on is something surprising. *Ploughs* were at work in all directions, and kaffir picks where ploughs could not work. Wagons and even horse carts were to be seen at several of the native establishments. The quantity of wheat, mealies, and kaffir corn raised is such as to bring buyers from among the farmers on all sides, and even as far as Colesberg. Indeed, the 'Reserve' since the Basuto war has been the granary of both the [Cape's] northern districts and the Free State too.[19]

In addition, Herschel peasants were able to take advantage of the spurt in trade and the rising demand for foodstuffs occasioned by the discovery of diamonds, not only on the Fields but also along the routes between the ports and the mines.

These favourable conditions remain clearly apparent during the first half of the 1870s. The existence of a healthy peasant economy in the district – that is, of a peasant economy offering not only subsistence from agricultural effort but also the opportunity to meet the demands of the state and the attractions of the store-keeper by the disposal of an agricultural surplus – is confirmed by the magistrate's report for 1873. In that year, when 1,400 cattle and (significantly) 14,000 sheep were brought into the district by migrant peasants who had received them as wages, the district produced 'about 1,000 bales of wool, 6,000 bags of wheat, and 30,000 bags of kafir corn and mealies *more than was required for consumption*, and these, with a large number of slaughter and draught oxen, were, owing to the diamond fields demand, sold at unprecedentedly high rates'.[20] A good year, indeed: so much so that in 1875, Africans in the district offered to spend £2,000 for the building of school premises if the government would assist.[21] John Noble was vigorous in his admiration for the level of production in Herschel, and wrote in mid-decade that Africans there raised 'immense quantities of maize, wheat, etc., and like the farmers of the ward of New England, which they adjoin, supply the country for a considerable distance, as far as the diamond fields. About 35,000 sacks of grain is estimated to be the annual amount raised.' He described Herschel as an area 'to which natives retire after a time of successful service down in the colony'.[22]

In Herschel, as elsewhere, rising peasant market production and trade did not confer equal gains on the entire community. Instead, one finds as early as the 1870s that Herschel was beginning to exhibit the symptoms of greater pressure on the land available, of stratification of the population, and of migratory responses to economic and social pressures. It has been observed that Herschel attracted peasants who had already accumulated a certain amount of wealth, and that the absence of powerful traditional political structures facilitated further accumulation. Social stratification proceeded apace in what was an almost purely African district. Apart from those peasant farmers who could afford the considerable outlay of £170 for a wagon and the requisite span of oxen, it was reported that other 'native men are becoming adepts as brickmakers, builders, thatchers, blacksmiths, roadmenders, basket makers, and tanners; and many more find employment as farm servants among the Boers; or as wool-washers, warehousemen, constables, grooms, and waiters in the towns'.[23]

Emigration from the reserve was of two kinds. First, as the letter just quoted indicates, there was a growing need for *some* of the population to work as labourers. A proportion of these, certainly, may have done so in preference to living by peasant agriculture, or as a means to the accumulation of capital whereby the more effectively to farm: the presence of semi-skilled trades as well as of relatively well-paid seasonal labour (wool-washing) fits this hypothesis. On the other hand, service as 'roadmenders' and as farm labourers was usually indication of proletarianization, of the pursuit of labour through necessity rather than through choice. In 1875, about two and a half thousand left the area in search of work of various kinds.

Secondly, there was permanent emigration out of the district by peasants who had accumulated considerable herds and/or flocks, but who found access to additional land blocked by the increasing competition within the peasant economy for available land. From about 1870 to at least 1910, there appears to have been conflict between Herschel peasants who were primarily agriculturists and those who were primarily pastoralists, over the most desirable use of land. Several reports by civil servants alluded to dissension over the extension of arable land: would-be farmers sought new ploughing 'gardens', and the headmen – whose authority derived from their land allocation powers (which evolved under Austen and continued under the magistrates) – were keen to grant these even at the cost of encroaching on commonage.[24] This incurred the antagonism of those who were predominantly stock farmers, and also of the more successful peasants who already had sufficient arable land and opposed any diminution of grazing

* The *Queenstown Free Press* carried a report on 2 September 1892 of a meeting of

lands.* In moves reminiscent of the migrations by similarly circumstanced Mfengu and Thembu in the mid-sixties (see pp. 57 and 69) sizeable groups of peasants left Herschel in search of greater opportunities and fresh land, particularly to 'Nomansland' (East Griqualand). Those migrating included some of the 'most wealthy' stock owners, who took with them 'large numbers of cattle, sheep and horses'. Their places, predicted the magistrate in 1875, would 'soon be filled up by those with less stock, who will depend more upon agriculture'.[25]

The difficulties of a section of the peasantry were heightened by the droughts and the depression of the late seventies. In 1878, it was reported that 'bad seasons have brought much poverty among them', although – significantly, in the light of what has been said of the growing discrepancy between haves and have-nots – the same informant noticed that 'the occupations of the people are agricultural. There is a very extensive cereal trade with the Colony, and they are rich in flocks and herds.'[26] Worse years followed. In 1883, a great number of passes were issued to those seeking wage employment, and in the following year not only was the drought very severe, but money was scarce: the 'natives generally barter in cattle and sheep for grain instead of paying in cash'.[27]

There is continual evidence of the difficulty encountered by a (growing) number of peasants in obtaining enough land to farm at a subsistence level. In a single report, a magistrate mentioned land disputes, over-stocking, over-grazing, and the creation of *dongas* (gully or ravine) by erosion.[28] The quit-rent plots granted in the 1850s and 1860s had fallen into administrative confusion; these areas jostled others held on communal tenure; boundaries, obligations, and ownership were all sources of friction; land matters bred 'continual disputes, jealousy and wrangling'.[29] Many peasants asked for permission to move to Griqualand East or the Transkei, 'complaining they had insufficient land to cultivate', and others simply found subsistence from peasant agriculture no longer possible: 'the labour market was well supplied'.[30]

Yet, during this same depressed period, there were among the Herschel peasants those who continued to export a surplus, to acquire cash and to spend it on a range of consumer goods eloquent of their relative affluence. The magistrate told a government enquiry that Africans were selling wool, wheat and other grains, and he said of certain mission-based peasants that 'their children are sent to Heald Town for instruction, and they have fruit gardens, decent houses, tables, chairs, stools, plates, cups, saucers, knives and forks, wagons,

---

over 500 Africans in Herschel with their new Resident Magistrate over this issue. The headmen – charged the magistrate – were permitting new land (including commonage) to be ploughed without first getting permission as laid down in the Circular 1/1890. The veldt, said the reporter, was being rapidly 'eaten up'.

153

ploughs, clocks, and some iron bedsteads'. Some had houses on surveyed plots of land. A local merchant testified on the same day that
goods sold locally were 'approximating more and more to those sold in
European towns.... [Africans] bought articles previously not known
amongst them – e.g., blacking, sponges, concertinas, chairs, trunks,
lace, ribbons, pomatum, scents, almanacs, date cases, clocks, watches,
dictionaries, ready reckoners, etc'.[31] A further indication of
stratification was the emergence of employer–employee divisions
among the African population of the area. In 1883 the magistrate told
the Laws and Customs Commission that 'The Fingoes are now trying to
engage refugee Tambookies from Basutoland as servants as they pass
through the district in search of work,' and another witness stated that
Herschel Africans 'frequently' employed servants, who came
'generally from an inferior tribe or from very poor families'.[32]

Although Herschel was geographically remote, its economic health
remained intimately bound up with that of the South African economy
as a whole. The economic recovery attendant on the Witwatersrand
gold discoveries was reflected, in parochial image, in Herschel. The
price of oxen and grain had by 1889

> advanced at least one hundred per cent during the past year, in consequence
> of the demand for transport to the gold fields, and the drought. A consider-
> able number of trek oxen have been purchased at these advanced rates, as
> also large quantities of grain and this together with the substantial rise in the
> price of wool has been the means of circulating a large amount of money in
> the district.[33]

Enough cash was available for the peasant community to pay off
£3,500 owed in tax arrears.

Similarly, the Census Report for 1891 indicates that a considerable
amount of oats, wheat, maize, sorghum, barley, oathay, pumpkins and
beans, as well as small crops of tobacco, lucerne and sweet potatoes,
were raised in the district. There is no information as to what proportions of the produce were exported, and what consumed within
Herschel, but certain pointers suggest that a considerable amount
would have been disposed of as surplus. Apart from the magistrate's
report that quantities of wool, grain and stock were sold that year, it is
noteworthy that more wheat was grown than either maize or sorghum,
the staple foods; in the same manner, oats, barley and oathay were
predominantly products raised for marketing, as was, of course, the
451,000 pounds of wool and the hides, skins and horns.[34]

Between 1895 and 1899, peasant production in this district was
disrupted by droughts, locusts and rinderpest. Here as elsewhere,
numerous Africans were reduced to the most severe poverty;
thousands left the district in search of employment, while others
stayed, living on edible weeds. The rinderpest bacillus recognized no
social gradations, but attacked the herds of all; certainly, there were

154

peasants in Herschel who experienced for the first time in the late nineties the failure of their farming activities to provide sustenance: an Anglican missionary wrote in the aftermath of the cattle disease that many were compelled to leave the district in search of work, including 'men who other years stayed home'.[35]

Certain factors aided the partial recovery from the slough of the late nineties, foremost among them the return of good seasons, abundant harvests, and the proximity of troops during the South African War. Africans from Herschel were in great demand for military labour at what were relatively high wages: almost £7,000 was paid to those who served in a single capacity, as mounted Police during the war.[36] The army also paid inflated prices for remount ponies and grain, and for draught oxen. While the resilience of cattle-keeping economic systems was once again demonstrated, it was plain that it was much easier to recover from locusts, rinderpest and war for those peasants who had already accumulated some reserve capital, or whose capacity to generate a surplus was great enough to withstand natural and man-made disasters. These men could recoup; and the corollary was that marginal peasants were forced below the subsistence level, either to become fully extruded from the land and permanently proletarianized, or to become regular migrant labourers. The records for Herschel in the early twentieth century confirm that this was the case, and they suggest that the stratification noted in the 1870s and 1880s increased substantially in the 1890s and early 1900s.

In this context, the magistrate's report for 1895 is of interest: a total of 24,000 peasants possessed 44,000 cattle and 89,000 sheep, with 236 wagons and 1,348 ploughs.[37] The relatively small number of wagons and ploughs suggests a concentration of wealthier peasants at the top of the spectrum. Nor can one assume that the stock was evenly distributed; quite apart from other evidence that it tended to be concentrated, the 236 wagons would account for something like two and a half thousand cattle, while the possession of ploughs also predicated the ownership of a number of cattle. In 1898, it was reported that 105,000 sheep in Herschel were held in only 1,465 flocks.[38] A newspaper account of a meeting between magistrate and peasants said that the varying sizes of land allotments in Herschel were 'a standing example of unfairness', and bluntly accused the headmen there of 'feathering their own nests'.[39] Contemporary accounts are littered with signs that the limits of arable land had been reached, that endemic squabbles and litigation about land rights persisted, and that the magistrate spent much of his time trying to 'quiet the clamour of those who have no garden lands'.[40]

The gulf that had opened by the nineties between moderately well-off peasants and the inhabitants at the bottom of the heap is graphically illustrated by the evidence of one A. E. Fowler, the local gaoler, to the 1893–4 Labour Commission. That functionary explained that not only white landowners but also wealthy African farmers in the district complained (in good seasons) of a want of labour, and that twenty or thirty of these prosperous black farmers had applied to him for the use of prison labour, employing batches of eight to ten convicts at a time (for ninepence a day) to do their reaping.[41] The facts of stratification were clearly enunciated by two other officials in 1904. The magistrate, D. Eadie, wrote that the position then was 'that many men set up the right to 10, 15, and in some cases as many as 20 lands of varying extent, while, on the other hand, there are a large number of persons in the District paying precisely the same hut-tax, with only one or two lands, and in some instances no lands at all'.[42] H. G. Turner, the Inspector of Locations, corroborated: 'The Headman and his particular friends have large lands and all the good ground, whilst others have either small lands or none at all.... I have almost daily complaints of the well-to-do men (who are the headman's friends) having been given or taken land which they have no claim to.' Some individuals, he continued, owned and grazed over a thousand head of small stock in addition to cattle and horses: 'These men, owing to their wealth, ride roughshod over their poorer brethren, and I regret to say it appears to have been the tendency to encourage and assist these men to the detriment and starving of the poorer and struggling class.'[43]

So there were peasants in the early years of this century who were relatively well off: the 'headman and his particular friends', those with wagons and large herds or flocks, and those who possessed sufficient capital to be able to counter competition for land by purchasing plots in other districts.[44] These are the large peasants, familiar from previous chapters. Another group of peasants (of what numbers it is impossible to say, but apparently not large) in Herschel and neighbouring districts found that by entering quasi-feudal relations of mutual assistance with white proprietors – especially share-cropping – they could protect their access to land and derive a fair subsistence income.[45] But for a majority of the peasant population of the district, for the 'poorer and struggling class', fortunes were in sharp decline by the early 1900s. Their situation was sketched in the matter-of-fact language of the local Inspector of Locations who gave evidence to the 1903–4 Commission on Native Affairs: 'They cannot be compared with those of twenty years ago. This, I take it, is because they have acquired more European habits, which is detrimental to their health. Their present resources are not as good as in former years.... So far as I can see, the cost of living is increasing every year.'[46] Following the punitive drought of 1903, the magistrate managed to extract a consoling moral from the distress he described:

Natives have been compelled to barter away a lot of stock in return for grain. The Natives are very averse to parting with their stock, being their capital, but I think this compulsory alienation of their capital in order to

156

obtain food supplies will do good, in that it will bring home to them . . . the advantage of going out to work.[47]

The reports of the next few years attested further to the facts of decreasing resources and a higher cost of existence. In poor seasons, Africans sold off their grain as soon as they had reaped, and then later had to buy it back at prices of about 50 per cent more. This was a far cry from the grain-exporting peasantry of thirty and forty years before, and indicative of the demand upon individuals for ready cash. Large quantities of grain and sorghum were imported into Herschel in 1909 from the Orange Free State.* Roles had been reversed: 'granary' had become hungry customer.

The details cited so far have brought this survey of Herschel to about 1910, the year of Union; but the decline of peasant agriculture and the intensification of impoverishment did not end then, and was not a temporary phenomenon. The dwindling wealth and failing social health of the district, the fall in resources, in earning capacity and in economic resilience, and the mounting pressures of population growth (sharpened by unequal distribution) all persisted over the next two decades, until in the late twenties Professor Macmillan conducted his on-the-spot investigation into Herschel's economic well-being.

He discovered that about 40,000 Africans lived in the 684 square miles of the district, an area easily distinguished from its 'white' neighbours because it had 'obviously received no tangible or visible benefit from public expenditure on its needs', and lacked attention to the simplest material wants like bridges, roads and public buildings.[48] Despite being 'relatively well-suited to the production of the two great staples, wheat and wool' (p. 161) Herschel was desperately impoverished. All the available data indicated that 'the district is barely self-supporting even with regard to foodstuffs' (p. 160). '*In a good year* it may have produced enough grain to last perhaps as much as six months' (p. 160, emphasis added). In broad terms, Macmillan indicated that there was an annual shortfall of expenditure over income of £35,000 to £50,000. This deficit was made up (a) by large credit advances and the accretion of indebtedness, and (b) by the sale of labour, mainly as migrant labour. Overall, conditions in the district were worse than they had been ten years earlier (p. 184), and Macmillan came to the measured and sombre conclusion that 'a large proportion of the community here depicted exists almost on the very lowest level of bare subsistence' (p. 185).

His argument is underpinned by a series of statistical findings. Details are drawn from official statistics, adjusted in accordance with local observation and information. He aimed at drawing up an economic balance-sheet for an average or fair year in the 1920s, and

* For an account of the commercialization of maize farming by Free State whites at this time, see Chapter 7, pp. 214–15.

TABLE 4

Amount and value of peasant production in Herschel for selected years

Products exported:	1873		1891		1921–9 (average)	
Wheat	6,000 bags	£12,000[a]	45,000 bushels	£13,500[g]	15,000 bags	£15,000
Maize and sorghum	30,000 bags	15,000[b]	nil[h]		15,000 bags	10,000
Wool	1,000 bales	12,500[c]	450,000 lb[i]	8,500	250,000 lb	10,000
Mohair	no information		33,500 lb[j]	850	60,000 lb	3,000
Hides and skins	estimate[d]		2,000 & 7,800[k]	1,750	4,000 & 10,000	2,000
Stock	'large number'[e]	13,750	no data[l]	2,700	(stock, barley,	5,000
Barley, oats,	no information		no data[m]	2,150	oat-hay, etc.)	
Horns, misc.						
TOTAL VALUE		£54,475		£29,400		£35,000
African population	23,000[f]		25,000		40,000[n]	
Income from sales per capita	£2/7/4d		£1/4/0		17/6d	

158

Notes to Table 4: Amount and value of peasant production

a 6,000 bags=18,000 bushels, at 12/8d per bushel, rather lower than Aliwal North price of 17/6d.

b 30,000 bags seems high (although partly corroborated by contemporary evidence): it would come to 90,000 bushels at 7/6d a bushel or £30,000 – I have halved this figure.

c At 435 lb per (unwashed wool) bale, 435,000 lb; at 8d per lb for unwashed wool (lower than average for eastern districts in 1873) it would be £14/10s a bale; I have lowered a bale's value even more, to £12/10s.

d No figures exist for such sales, but as more stock must die every year, it is safe to assume some sales. I have halved the 1891 figures for hides and skins sold, at slightly lower than prevailing 1873 prices: 1,000 hides at 17/6d and 3,750 skins at 2/-.

e An estimate of 500 cattle and 1,000 sheep seems conservative in the light of what the magistrate deemed 'a large number': one remembers that inflated prices were obtaining for stock on the diamond fields. Cattle and sheep have both been assigned slightly lower than average prevailing prices: £10 and 10/- each respectively.

f Without explanation, the 1875 Census omits a population figure for Herschel; this estimate is derived from missionary assessments of late 1860s and magistrate's tally in 1878.

g Of the 50,000 bushels raised, I have allowed 10 per cent to be locally consumed, although contemporary sources stress that wheat was raised for sale.

h Taking the same dietary needs as Macmillan uses a population of 25,000 would need over 40,000 bags of grain. Only 82,000 bushels (or 28,000 bags) was raised, according to the Census. It seems that contemporary references to sales of these grains (and there is no evidence that any were being imported to Herschel) probably refer solely to sales within the district, from 'big' to 'small' peasants, etc.' and it is reasonable to suppose for the Table that none was exported.

i At 4½d per lb.

j At 6d per lb.

k Hides at 10/-, skins at 2/9d.

l Impossible to estimate with any precision: we know that in 1889 'large numbers' of stock were sold; so say that (only) 400 cattle at £5–10 and 1,000 sheep at 10/- were sold in 1891.

m 1605 bushels of oats at 5/-=£400; 500 bushels of barley at 3/-=£750; also horns, rye, oat-hay, peas, beans, potatoes, tobacco, sold – say a total from these sources of £1,000.

n Macmillan revised the census figure for 1921 of just over 39,000 to an estimated figure for the late twenties of 40,000.

collated the figures for about a decade to arrive at his table. Figures for production *consumed* locally, he pointed out, were extremely difficult to obtain, but he concluded that not even in a good year was enough maize and sorghum grown to meet an (estimated) need of 67,500 bags. The valuation of produce *exported* from Herschel district was 'more measurable and perhaps more significant' (p. 157) and it is to these figures that we turn.

Macmillan found that about £35,000 worth of wheat, wool, mohair, stock, animal products and miscellaneous items were exported in a fair year, i.e., produce worth 17/6d per capita of the peasant population.

The total might be raised as high as £50,000 with 'a singularly favourable combination of high yield and good prices' (p. 168).

Using data for the years 1873 and 1891 (two years for which the available evidence is fairly detailed) it has been possible to draw up some figures (Table 4) comparing the peasant production and income for those years with Macmillan's figures for a (notional) 1920s year. The basis for the calculations of 1873 and 1891 are, respectively, the magistrate's report for 1873 and the Census Report of 1891,[49] amplified, modified and interpreted in the light of other evidence where this is available. The prices obtaining in 1873 and 1891 for agricultural produce have been taken from the *Bluebook for the Cape Colony 1873* and the *Statistical Register* of 1891. All values are expressed in current prices. Wherever there was room for doubt or for informed speculation, estimates for the 1873 and 1891 data have deliberately been kept to the *lowest* probable figure. In particular, it will be observed that in most instances the prices obtained for produce have been estimated at less than the prevailing quotations for Aliwal North and/or the Eastern Province markets; it seems fair to assume that African peasants might have had to sell at reduced rates.

How informative is Table 4 and its implications? While making due allowance for the uncertain nature of many of the figures, and accepting a generous margin of error, the broad outline of the story that they tell seems firm enough to confirm that the exercise possesses some value. In Herschel, the African peasantry over the period 1870 to 1920 became both relatively and absolutely less well off. Overall production fell, per capita income fell, the number of 'independent' peasants fell correspondingly. The total income from agricultural sales in 1873 was in the region of £54,000, or £2/7/4 per capita, and might (Table 4, notes *a* to *e*) have been considerably higher: say £70,000 plus, or over £3 per capita. In 1891, the total income from exports was about £30,000 (and again this estimate errs deliberately in favour of too low a sum) and the per capita figure £1/4/0.

In addition to the cash differential for the per capita figures in each case, it will be appreciated that – with higher rents and taxation levels, as well as greater demands for education and goods – the diminished purchasing power of the income for the 1920s is even more marked than the sums suggest.

If the 1873 figure seems high, compared with Macmillan's totals, there are nevertheless substantial grounds for accepting it. The relative wealth that the figure indicates is consistent with the descriptions of the peasant community of Herschel that were made at the time. It is consistent too with estimates of other successful African peasant communities at the same time.[50] Finally, the figures appear to be consistent with the nature of social and economic change described in this chapter. By the 1870s, the peasant community of Herschel had responded to economic opportunities and changes; individuals and adapted and diversified the traditional agricultural economy, accepting innovations in their social organization as well as in their economic life. Fifty years later, the population was in almost every respect economically worse off than it had been.

Compared with the community Macmillan investigated, the Herschel peasantry in the 1870s was more productive, more self-sufficient, and more prosperous; it was less crowded, less indebted, and less dependent upon migratory labour. About one hundred years ago, this area was called 'a beautiful settlement of well-watered fertile hill and dale', and its population described as 'loyal, peaceful, and contented'.[51] Fifty years later, the same area had become congested, eroded, overstocked, suffering from 'thoroughly unsound economic conditions' and 'general depression', while the population was 'seething with discontent', 'poor in production and very low in consumption'.[52] The concept of underdevelopment, at its simplest, is the difference between these two sets of descriptions, viewed against the backdrop of the developing capitalist economy of Southern Africa at the time. (For it should be remembered that the same years, 1870–1918, have been described in summary as a period when 'population, wealth, and living standards increased greatly'.)[53]

Like the imaginary tour mentioned at the beginning of this chapter, this history of the Herschel peasantry concludes in the recent past. Forty years after Macmillan's visit to Herschel, the Franciscan priest Cosmas Desmond toured the district on his fact-finding journeys in areas affected by the South African government's 'resettlement' policies. Desmond's account makes plain that the poverty and dependence of Herschel measured by Macmillan have not improved, but have deepened and ramified. Part of Desmond's description of the district's hastening ills, its decaying men and its destroyed peasantry, is reproduced here:

> The whole of the magisterial district of Herschel, apart from the two villages of Herschel and Sterkspruit, and a few Mission stations, is an African Reserve, which is obvious enough when you drive through it. It is approximately 514 square miles in area and has an estimated population of 75,000. A lot of the area is mountainous and most of the rest is badly eroded, so there is not much left for cultivation.... According to the Tomlinson Report, the Herschel area is one of the most badly eroded in the whole country, yet at the time of its study had a population density as high as a hundred per square mile ...

> The grazing and arable land is allocated by the headmen and councillors: the amount of arable land per family varies from nothing to six acres. The people complain that the headmen and councillors keep the biggest and best portions for themselves and that they have much less land than they had before. This is particularly true of the old and widows. In some villages the land is divided only into grazing camps, with no arable land available ...

161

There is virtually no work in the whole area. Herschel Reserve is merely a labour-pool for contract and seasonal workers, since only headmen and councillors can possibly make a living from the land. As in other Reserves, white farmers come from miles away to collect labourers for the harvesting season ... in Herschel they come from as far as Bethal and Standerton, a distance of about three hundred miles. I saw hundreds of people standing waiting in the village of Herschel for the lorries to arrive ...

Many of the men work on the diamond mines on the South-West African coast, or in Cape Town, Johannesburg and other cities, returning home only once a year. The local clergy say this has caused many broken marriages and other problems ...

All forms of malnutrition are obviously a problem throughout the Reserve.[54]

NOTES

1 See *A Survey of Race Relations in South Africa 1976* (South African Institute of Race Relations, Johannesburg, 1977), 245–6, and see various reports in the South African press, October and November 1976.

2 W. M. Macmillan, *Complex South Africa* (London, 1930), 144–86.

3 CPP, G.6–'92, *Cape Colony Census of 1891*, xix.

4 S. Trapido, 'White Conflict and Non-White Participation in the Politics of the Cape of Good Hope 1853–1910' (University of London, Ph.D. thesis, 1970), 131.

5 A. G. Frank, *Capitalism and Underdevelopment in Latin America* (New York, 1969), 136.

6 William Shepstone, the missionary concerned, took occupation 'by consent of the colonial and the nearest native authorities'. (MMS Arch., S.A. Box XVII (Bechuanaland 1838–57), File 1850, J. Bertram to Wes. Meth. Soc., 5 July 1850.)

7 BPP, 1851, xxxvii (1360), Sir H. Smith to Lord Grey, desp. 120, 12 May 1850 and enclosure, for annexation of Wittebergen.

8 PRO, C.O. 879/13, Conf. Print Afr. No. 154, 192.

9 A. Brigg, *'Sunny Fountains' and 'Golden Sands': Missionary Adventures in the South of the Dark Continent* (London, 1888), 106–7, 134–6. See also CPP, G.5–'86, BBNA, 23.

10 Macmillan, *Complex South Africa*, 147.

11 MMS Arch., S.A. Box XVII (Bech. 1838–57), File 1850, J. Bertram, 5 July 1850.

12 PRO, C.O. 879/13, Conf. Print Afr. 154, 192.

13 Moorosi, the Phuthi chief, and a neighbour and ally of Mosheshwe, claimed a tract of land within the Reserve in 1858. Austen, who exercised his authority through the headmen, ordered Moorosi out of the Reserve area, and Moorosi retaliated by attacking and raiding the disputed area, carrying off a number of horses with him. A lengthy sequence of accusation and counter-charge ensued, with competing versions of events drawn up by Austen and by a law agent employed by Moorosi; the upshot was that

Austen's authority over the land was upheld, while Moorosi and his followers kept some of the horses. (See A. E. Du Toit, 'The Cape Frontier: A Study of Native Policy with Special Reference to the Years 1847–1866', *Archives Year Book for South African History*, 1954, Vol. I (Pretoria, 1954) 128, 202; and Cape Archives, G.H. 8/48, *Letters from Native Chiefs ... 1854–1884*, correspondence for 1858 and 1859, for the petitions and letters to the Lieutenant-Governor on this matter.)

14 CPP, *Votes and Proceedings*, 1870, App. I, Vol. 2, Message from Governor to House of Assembly, 16 April 1870 (Minute xxx 1870). And for the petitions (signed by Brigg and 125 others) see CPP C.2–'69, *A Petition From Certain Inhabitants of the 'Wittebergen Native Reserve'* and A.9–'70, *Petition of the Inhabitants of the Wittebergen Native Reserve.*

15 *Bluebook for the Cape Colony for 1862*, JJ39.

16 CPP, *Report of the 1865 Commission on Native Affairs*, App. I, 105.

17 *Wesleyan Missionary Notices*, 3rd Series, Vol. XIV, January 1867, A. Brigg, 20 July 1866.

18 MMS Arch., S.A. Box XVIII (Bech. 1868–76), 1868 File, Brigg to Wes. Meth. Soc., 13 August 1868.

19 MMS Arch., S.A. Box XV (Queenstown 1868–76), 1869 file, H. H. Dugmore to Secty, Wes. Meth. Soc., 1 November 1869 (emphasis in original).

20 CPP, G.27–'74, BBNA, 10 (emphasis added).

21 PRO, C.O. 879/13, Conf. Print Afr. 154, 193.

22 J. Noble, *Descriptive Handbook of the Cape Colony* (Cape Town, 1875), 224.

23 MMS Arch., S.A. Box XVIII (Bech. 1868–76), 1868 file, Brigg, 13 August 1868.

24 See *inter alia* CPP, G.9–'94, BBNA, 22; G.42–'98, BBNA, 33; G.31–'99, BBNA, 28.

25 CPP, G.21–'75, BBNA, 64.

26 PRO, C.O. 879/13, Conf. Print Afr. 154, 192.

27 CPP, G.2–'85, BBNA, 188.

28 CPP, G.13–'80, BBNA, 188.

29 CPP, G.5–'86, BBNA, 24.

30 CPP, G.2–'85, BBNA, 27.

31 CPP, G.4–'83, *Commission on Native Laws and Customs*, App. D, Part II, 317, evidence of Capt. Hook, and ibid., 319, evidence of Mr O. Brigg.

32 ibid., 317, 319.

33 CPP, G.4–'90, BBNA, 12.

34 CPP, G.6–'92, *Census Report for the Cape Colony for 1891*, 448–9.

35 SPG Arch., E MSS, E1898, Vol. 2, J. H. Bone, 31 December 1898.

36 CPP, G.25–1902, BBNA, 21–2; G.12–1904, BBNA, 13.

37 CPP, G.5–'96, BBNA, 32.

38 CPP, G.35–'98, *Report of the Inspector of Sheep*.

39 *Queenstown Free Press*, 2 September 1892.

40 See BBNAs for almost every year of the 1890s; the quotation is from G.5–'96, 28.

41 CPP, G.3–'94, *Labour Commission 1893–4*, vol. III, 277–8.

42 CPP, G.12*–1904, BBNA, 19.

43 ibid., 23–4.

44 For mention of the last category, see U. G. 17–1911, Dept. Nat. Aff. *Bluebook for 1910,* 258.

45 See U.G. 22–'14, *Report of the Native Land Commission* (Beaumont Commission), II, 121 (evidence of W. C. Orsmond).

46 South African Native Affairs Commission 1903–5 (SANAC), V, 26.

47 CPP, G.12*–1904, BBNA, 18.

48 Macmillan, *Complex South Africa,* 147. All the quotations that follow are from the same source, and pagination is indicated in the text for easier reference.

49 CPP, G.27–'74, 10 and G.6–'93, 448–9.

50 Thus, in Fingoland (population 44,000) we are told in 1874 that at the lowest computation 'the value of the import and export trade represents £150,000 p.a.' (CPP, G.21–'75, BBNA, report for Fingoland). And in Basutoland, close by Herschel, in 1873 2,000 bales of wool – worth, say, £25,000 – and upwards of 100,000 muids of grain – say £75,000 – and also 'much stock', were exported. The previous year had seen merchandise worth £150,000 imported into Basutoland (CPP, G.27–'74, report for Basutoland).

51 *Bluebook for the Cape Colony 1862,* Civil Commissioner for Aliwal North, JJ39; CPP, G.12–'77, BBNA, 144.

52 Macmillan, *Complex South Africa,* 150, 185, *et passim.*

53 D. Hobart Houghton, 'Economic Development, 1865–1965', OHSA, II, 22.

54 C. Desmond, *The Discarded People* (Penguin Africa Library, Harmonds-worth, 1971), 98–101.

6

Natal: Variations Upon A Theme

There is something about Natal in the past one hundred and fifty years, that is difficult to define or give a name to, but that colours the region's history throughout that time: it is a febrile quality in the public temperament, particularly of white Natalians. That temperament – at least in its observable moods – is frequently hysteric and delusive, occasionally laughable and sometimes vicious; in a multi-ethnic society, it manifests itself particularly in exaggerated and morbid forms of racially defined conflicts and fears. An abiding feature of politically charged moments in Natal's past is dissonance between rhetoric and reality, a gulf between announced objectives and existing capabilities. Can not one discern some taxonomic similarity in a series of events, from the trekkers' 1841 decision to expel the 'surplus' black population (and then including reactions to Langalibalele and Bambatha, the perfervid Britishness of the Dominion Party, the anti-Indian Pegging Act) to the fantasies of secession at the time of referendum and republic in 1961?

Such speculative generalities aside, it is useful before commencing upon an outline of the peasant response in Natal and implicitly comparing that with the pattern already established for the Cape, to make the point that Natal was in several significant respects a very different British colony. The settler population in the Cape was much larger and more firmly established; the Cape's economy throughout the nineteenth century was more vigorous; Africans within the Cape's borders had lost a larger proportion of ancestral lands to colonists; the mercantile-missionary-liberal influence in Cape politics was older and sturdier; while several factors – including demography, land allocation and the ideology loosely summed up as 'Shepstonism' – meant that for the majority of Natal's Africans the cultural pressures of white rule were less sharply experienced than in the Cape. A priori, each of these factors might be supposed to have been reflected in slight adjustments to the model elaborated for the Cape. Thus, with the white colonist interest weaker, effective retention by African agriculturists of the means of production would be greater for longer; with the commercialization of agriculture even more laggard than in the Cape, the dependence of a proportion of whites on African-grown produce would be correspondingly greater; with the advocacy of a modernizing stratum of African producers more muted, the breaks with traditional methods would be fewer and more noticeable (the *kolwa* converts being even

165

more differentiated from 'traditionalists' than 'school' from 'red' in the Cape). Moreover, the part played by large-scale absentee land proprietors in Natal would mean that when the state fell into the political control of white colonists, the use of political methods to enforce economic ends (in this case including the proletarianization of the peasantry) would be more transparent, the employers' offensive shriller, than in the Cape, but also far less capable of translating aims into action; that is, that quasi-feudal relations would remain imbedded in the rural economy of Natal for longer, and that effective pursuit by commercializing white farmers of their interests conflicted with the aims of those who preferred to extract a surplus through a system of labour-tenancy. Each of these suppositions, it will be argued in the rest of this chapter, was borne out, and can be empirically demonstrated.[1]

1 THE RURAL ECONOMY TO THE EVE OF MINERAL DISCOVERIES: *C.* 1835–70[2]

Owing to the limited number of Europeans, and the many obstacles arising from inexperience, want of suitable implements, deficiency of capital, and consequent difficulty of commanding labour, for the proper and extended cultivation of the soil, cotton has not yet been produced in a quantity sufficiently large. . . . Perhaps in no British colony do the elements for cheap production, i.e. cheap land, cheap labour, and cheap food, exist in a greater degree than Natal. . . . It is computed that there are 100,000 native inhabitants scattered over the country; they are now simple and harmless barbarians who might be trained by a vigorous and enlightened exercise of authority, into habits of industry and peace. Like all barbarians, they are constitutionally indolent and averse to labour.

(From an address to Pietermaritzburg's Chamber of Commerce, 1848, quoted in J. S. Christopher, *Natal* (London, 1850), 45)

The *de jure* existence of the Voortrekker Republic of Natalia may still provide constitutional lawyers with grounds for disagreement over details, but its brief *de facto* existence in the latter 1830s and early 1840s provides our starting point. Some six thousand trekkers by 1838 were occupied in 're-establishing themselves as pastoral farmers [while] the ambitious and public-spirited were also laying the foundations of a government'.[3] Their settlement of the area, and their appropriation of farms on the traditional 6,000-acre scale was made possible by the substantially underpopulated state of Natal at the time the Voortrekkers traversed the Drakensberg.

During and following the rise of the Zulu state system, and under the impact of regular Zulu raids, large numbers of Africans had migrated from Natal into neighbouring territories. The Voortrekkers had moved into this relatively depopulated land – recent research has suggested that it was never as empty as Voortrekkers then and their historians subsequently claimed – occupied some of it, and laid claim to vast areas besides. The settler republic lacked, however, the administrative machinery or effective means of coercion to exercise any significant authority over the area it nominally ruled; desperately short of funds, of experience, of unity, the Voortrekker state fell far short of its constitutional aspirations.

The demands made by the trek community on its leaders were limited and simple enough: they called for plenty of land, for security and for labour. All three of these depended ultimately upon the relations of the settlers with the indigenous African population of Natal. The initial underpopulation of the region seemed to solve the call for land; the Blood River campaign and the vassalage of Mpande instead of the enmity of Dingane went some way to establishing security; and the expropriation of 'apprentices' (African children captured on raiding expeditions and impressed into service until adulthood) helped slake the demand for labour on lands and in homes. But these were all secured only fragilely, and did not add up to a satisfactory control by the trekkers of population movements, military or labour relations.

After the defeat of Dingane, Africans returned in large numbers to the lands claimed, but not occupied, by the Dutch republicans. These latter were wholly unable to stem this influx, or reflux, although their disapproval of it and desire to 'deal with' the 'squatters' were patent. The well-known proposal to shift 'surplus' Africans into the area between the Mzimkulu and Nmtavuna rivers serves to highlight the discrepancy between the government's aims and its effective executive authority: 'More and more Africans,' concludes Thompson, 'lived in the Republic without being controlled'.[4]

The absence of control over the swelling African population (from 10,000 in 1838 to 50,000 in 1843) was not merely a question of effective police powers or social control, but also of an inability to impose economic control over the tribesmen. The Voortrekker state could not effectively levy taxes, nor could individual *trekboers* control the labour power of Africans sufficiently to expropriate from the indigenous population the means of subsistence or to render untenable their accustomed modes of production and levels of consumption. The Voortrekker economy itself, it must be emphasized, was when it entered Natal characterized by low productivity and unsophisticated means of accumulation. The diaries of Erasmus Smit make plain the extent to which the *trekboers* depended either upon barter or raiding of African produce for their subsistence. Military attacks upon African villages enabled the Dutch emigrants ('through God's guidance') to 'harvest and eat what others have planted'. The trekkers sought to use not only their own military superiority over small groups of Natal

Africans, but also that of the Zulu Kingdom: there were such rich pickings for a Dutch patrol 'harvesting in the gardens of the Kafirs destroyed by Dingaan' that additional wagons had to be called for. Eventually, a hundred full wagon loads of maize, sorghum, pumpkins and other produce were driven off: 'through God's care came a great blessing for these poor emigrants', observed the pious Smit.[5]

The Voortrekkers, their capital depleted by barter, unable to press their claims to the land or to force 'unapprenticed' Africans to labour (it has been pointed out recently)

> proved unable to develop and maintain regular patterns of colonial exploi-
> tation of Natal's indigenous population.... The attempts of individual
> trekker families to enforce rights of ownership over land claims by personal
> settlements, by the removal of the earlier occupants, by placing agents on
> the claim, or by extracting rent in the form of labour or produce, all met with
> determined resistance and rarely proved successful. In consequence, the
> trekkers did little farming; most remained concentrated in groups, subsist-
> ing on hunting and African produce, which they bartered for livestock.[6]

British annexation of Natal was announced in December 1842, given legal form in 1843, and commenced in practical terms in December 1845 with Lieutenant-Governor West's arrival. About half of the Voortrekkers left the colony, and they were replaced between 1849 and 1851 by some 5,000 men, women and children from England and Scotland – a demographic shift that saw the white population become predominantly English-speaking, unfamiliar with the country, in-experienced at farming, and short of capital. These circumstances are relevant in understanding their ineffectuality in the political economy for the period prior to and immediately after the mineral discoveries in the Cape and Transvaal.

The immigrant settlers found themselves, contrary to expectations raised by the brochures, short of both land and labour – and this in a colony that seemed to promise both farm-lands and potential black hands in abundance. Slater – like de Kiewiet before him[7] – has drawn attention to the concentration of land ownership in Natal; the Natal Land and Colonization Company, with nearly a million acres, was the largest but by no means the only absentee landlord responsible for the ownership of huge areas of Natal. These proprietors, large and small, individuals and companies, comprised in the 1850s and 1860s the most influential of several groups of whites who laid claim to control of the land resources of Natal. Over five million of the six million acres of land owned by whites were in the hands of absentee proprietors, and occupied, as will be seen, by African peasants. Other white groups before 1870 included the small farmers, Dutch and English, practising the typical pastoral-mixed subsistence farming, and a numerically smaller group of larger farmers and planters, experimenting with

168

various cash crops, such as sugar and wool. Shortly after mid-century, a sizeable amount of land – just under 175,000 acres – had been granted to various mission societies, while the Government retained the rights of disposal of unalienated Crown Lands. (Of a total of 12,000,000 acres, over 3,000,000 remained unalienated by 1870.)

Mention must be made of a further category of land: the Reserves or Locations. The Locations Commission (1846–7) which first delimited the wholly African areas (which comprised by 1870 a total of over two million acres) appeared to countenance the development of an independent African peasantry. It spoke of African cultivators reaching 'a different description of agriculture to that which now obtains among them, both to the manner of cultivating and the articles cultivated'. It drew vague plans of cultivating cash crops and of the emergence of a class of African producers with a stake in the land; Theophilus Shepstone, a member of the Commission, expressly precluded measures aimed at 'so crowding the Kaffirs as to compel them to leave their location and seek work'.[8] This outlook – clearly analogous with the liberalism discussed in reference to the Cape (pp. 81–3 and 137) – was never the dominant ideology in Natal, did not remain Shepstone's own, and certainly was never translated into effective policy.

A competing ideology was that of the colonial farmers, and especially those who sought to put their farming operations on a commercial footing. Their chief concern was for a 'native policy' that would deprive Africans of their access to land which they farmed for themselves; this included opposition to the 'locations system', demands for more stringent policing of the Crown Lands, and above all opposition to 'squatting' on the lands of absentee proprietors. They pressed for measures designed to force the African population into labour tenancies, or so to increase their cost of living as to impel a reliance on wage labour.

A third standpoint was that which had clearly evolved by the 1850s, when

> many landowners in the face of African resistance to white labour demands, had concluded that the key to wealth lay in exploiting Natal's existing rural economy based on African producers rather than in awaiting a transformation of the colonial sector which showed little sign of coming about through the free play of market forces. For these men . . . the extraction of rent in the form of produce or cash from the Africans on the land constituted the most attractive form of 'farming'. They were thus unlikely to fully support measures designed to reduce the capacity of their 'tenants' to earn an independent income and to force them into labour relationships.[9]

This circumstance had important implications for the development of an African peasantry: such an outlook and the economic interests it represented were likely to persist for as long as certain aspects of land tenure prevailed in Natal. With land ownership concentrated in the hands of merchants, land companies and other speculators, and at the same time with the market in land static and prices very low, the tendency to rely upon rent as the most convenient way of extracting profit from the land was reinforced. The stagnation of the colonial agricultural sector – which was a major factor in keeping the value of land low – was in turn perpetuated by the relative cheapness of African production of foodstuffs for the local market.

The 1846–7 Commission intended to set aside two million acres for African occupation: this was pruned back to one and a quarter million acres of conspicuously inferior farming lands (dubbed by the American missionary Grout, in a well-known phrase, as 'fit only for the eagle and baboon') and increased by later grants of equally unattractive tracts to some two and a half million acres. It was of course Theophilus Shepstone who was the driving force in the Commission, and he also who persuaded large numbers of Natal Africans to remove and live in the designated locations. Large numbers, but by no means a majority of the African population: in 1851 Shepstone estimated that two-thirds of the Africans still lived outside the locations on Crown and private lands; in 1882, there were 169,000 living on reserved lands (locations *and* mission reserve glebe lands), 162,000 were renting privately owned land, and some 43,000 lived on Crown Lands.*

Such figures amplify what has already been said about the leasing of land by absentee proprietors; it also illustrates that in the middle third of the nineteenth century Africans in Natal, to a greater extent than was the case for the Cape's black population, retained access to various types of land on terms which allowed them to exercise a degree of choice. Slater has suggested that the nett effect of immigration, land speculation, concentration of ownership, and the grants to missions, was 'to make land a more scarce and differentiated resource', but that despite this it remained before 1870 'fairly easy [for Africans] to gain access to it'.[10] African cultivators could choose between occupation of Crown Lands, or land owned by absentee landlords, or mission lands, or land provided in return for labour services or rent by white farmers or graziers, or they could reside in the locations. The choice would naturally be affected in every part of Natal by local circumstances: by the prevailing rent levels, population density, soil fertility, market facilities, and so on; but in each case the obligations entered into (rents in cash or kind, labour service, observance of missionary standards and the abandonment of certain practices, and so on) could be balanced against the prospects of producing an agricultural surplus sufficient to

* Or, to express this in another way, those living on location lands occupied just over 2,000,000 acres; those on mission lands 174,000 acres; and it was estimated that no fewer than 5,000,000 acres of Natal land owned by colonists or companies was occupied by Africans in the 1870s. (PRO, CO 179/116, Shepstone to Carnarvon, 22 September 1874.)

meet the demands of state and/or landlord, and to permit the acquisition of trade goods.

As will become clear, in the last quarter of the nineteenth century the ability of Natal Africans to exercise this choice in relation to their access to land decreased. For the 1850s and 1860s, however, the choice was one open to the majority of the African population, and this meant that 'in the 1860s the majority of Africans had been able to withstand the pressures on them to work for the white man and had been able to pay their taxes by selling off their surplus grain or cattle'.[11] That which offered to the African a measure of economic independence, to the white colonist represented the cause of the 'uniformly insufficient supply of labour'.[12] The labour 'shortage' – massively and repetitiously attested to in the colonial records and newspapers – is most simply illustrated by the decision to import indentured Indian labourers to Natal, from 1860 onwards.

Africans were withholding labour from white employers (or, very often, they chose carefully for whom to work, and for how long) but they were doing so within the context of a colonial administration that bore as heavily as it thought it could upon the African population for revenue, in the shape of rents on Crown Lands, taxes, excise duties and other fees; and in the context of a number of other demands for cash or kind: rents to private landlords, trade goods, clothing, and so on. This meant that access to the means of subsistence, in the form of the occupancy of one of the various types of land described already, was not in itself a guarantee of economic independence. African cultivators had also to produce an agricultural surplus.

A not insubstantial trading system through Natal and Zululand already existed when the Dutch and English communities established themselves in Natal in the early nineteenth century.[13] The raiding and bartering activities of the Voortrekkers have been noted; but in comparison with the systematic depredations instituted by the Zulu state, these represented a relaxation of the pressures upon Natal's African cultivators, permitting greater control over the disposal of the surpluses they produced. The participation of Africans in the colonial economy intensified after the British occupation and immigration into Pietermaritzburg and other inland towns and villages. In 1849, it was reported that large quantities of maize grown by Africans were exported to Cape Town, and African peasants also sold wool on the Natal market. A letter from the American missionary, Grout, specified in November 1848 maize, oats, barley, beans, peas, potatoes, sweet potatoes, onions, beets, carrots, cabbages and pumpkins raised by peasants upon the garden plots attached to his mission station. Certainly, by 1853 African peasant production was well enough established to cause the Native Affairs Commission (1852–3) to grumble that 'the Kafirs are now much more insubordinate and impatient of control; they are rapidly becoming rich and independent'.[14]

171

The evidence for the 1850s and 1860s points to certain tendencies of African agricultural production. One was the concentration of agricultural enterprise and innovation upon mission stations, and the pursuit by *kolwas* (African Christians) of profits through cash crops and trade. Secondly, it is also clear that non-Christian individuals and communities also stepped up production and sales – this to such an extent that in many areas the local African population produced sufficient surplus grain to support white villages (as well as many individual white graziers).

Natal had perhaps more Christian missionaries than any other area of Southern Africa. A combination of factors meant that some of the earliest evangelical endeavours met with the greatest success: the recent exactions of the Zulu kingdom, curiosity about the newcomers, and the various advantages that missionaries could represent to chiefs all led to a relatively enthusiastic response to missionaries in the 1840s, when attendance figures reached levels not equalled until forty and fifty years later.[15] In Natal, as in the Cape, the secular attractions of life on the mission stations were clearly uppermost in attracting converts. Arable land, in particular, was a lure; an Anglican missionary explained the correlation between soil fertility and evangelical growth thus:

> The natives may be *converted* in any place, but they know the country too well to *settle* where they cannot have good pasture and where they cannot at the same time carry out agricultural pursuits with profit. Where that is not the case they will leave and go to other places (generally to other Mission Stations).[16]

Alvin Grout reported cheerfully from the Mvoti mission in 1861 that religious interest was always accompanied by an increase in civilization, although the year's events that he described attested more to secular than to spiritual initiatives: 'Every man now desires to own a plot of ground, and there is a rush for wagons, oxen and plows, and many are laying plans for upright houses.' Three years later there were forty-eight 'upright houses' on the same mission station; two members of Grout's congregation held property estimated (perhaps over generously) at £1,000 each, while twenty others owned a span of oxen and ploughs, and fourteen possessed wagons. Analogous concentrations of wealth existed on other mission stations, at Amanzimtoti, Edendale, Driefontein, and Verulam.[17] Henry Callaway recorded in his journal for 1861 that he had become accustomed to requests for demonstrations of ploughing, while one of his junior colleagues reported of Emwabi mission (in Umlazi district) that 'the newly-tilled land might give one the idea that our station is that of a farmer-immigrant!'[18]

Writing in 1867, Robert Mann (Superintendent of Education in Natal) stressed the role of the missions in stimulating agricultural production and trade:

Wherever townships, or fairly prosperous settlements, of white people have grown up in the close neighbourhood, so that there is transport work to be performed by waggons and oxen, and a ready market for such articles as the Kaffir can make, or such produce as the Kaffir can rear, or where there is a sugar-mill at hand to manufacture such cane as he may be able to grow, there the native Christian communities thrive and enlarge quickly.

The same writer gave an interesting example of the spread of economic and technological adaptations to non-Christians, independent of missionary or other white intervention. Travelling in the area of Natal where he knew no white settlers lived, he was puzzled to observe 'land broken with the familiar furrow of the ploughshare', but

> At the end of the day he found the solution of the enigma by learning that the wild Kaffirs of the district were in the habit of sending twenty miles to a settlement of their more advanced brethren who possessed draft oxen and ploughs, to get one of the fraternity to bring up the magic implements and break up the ground for their grain-crops.[19]

Langalibalele's Hlubi were another non-Christian community to adopt the plough and increase food production. By the late 1860s, it seems clear, numbers of Africans living in Natal were capable of producing an agricultural surplus for trade, and of withholding their labour, at least upon the unattractive terms offered by white farmers and planters. Taxes and rents were met out of the sales of foodstuffs. Forty years later an early settler reminisced of the 1860s that 'in the early days ... if we wanted supplies we would take a wagon and oxen and go into the location, or into the district where the Kafirs were, and used to buy corn for our supplies from the Natives'.[20]

Lieutenant-Governor Keate summarized changes taking place in African agriculture in an official report on the year 1869. He commented upon the 'very considerable improvement in the methods of husbandry adopted' by Africans, and the way in which 'where the nature of the land is more favourable, and its surface more even, ploughs, harrows, and other such-like agricultural implements' were being introduced in 'great quantities'. Even in a 'less advanced' district like Newcastle, the magistrate reported that 'the natives on all sides are anxious to have [ploughs]'.[21] Keate also mentioned that (in locations alone) the acreage under cultivation had risen from 103,500 acres in 1868 to 127,124 acres at the end of 1869. While the reliability of Natal's statistics for this period prompts no great confidence (particularly in cases of spuriously precise totals), if one accepts merely the tendency being described it is of an increase of about 25 per cent in just over a year. Keate offers no explanation of this advance; it seems probable that it was in part due to increased opportunities for sales when the level of production by whites fell even lower with the exodus of young men to the diamond fields in 1868 and 1869. Colonists' farms stood 'empty and unattended',[22] and there was an increase in transport riding and farming activities by Africans in those years.

The relative success of the African peasantry in the sixties was firmly enough stated by the *Natal Witness:*

> Perhaps the most striking feature in the Kafir character is his energy and industry as a farmer. Wherever he has lived beside a farmer, who is industrious, and has shown how, by use of the plough, he can raise large quantities of produce, and that he can find a market for them, the Kafir has eagerly imitated him, has bought a plough and a wagon, and has discovered that he also can obtain a large return in this way. The thousands of acres that have been ploughed up by Kafirs, and the hundreds of wagons they possess, are conclusive proof of their readiness and fitness to become agriculturists.[23]

To sum up. By 1870, the basic patterns of land usage in Natal had been established, and the involvement by a black peasantry in the wider economy was well under way. Numbers of mission-based and peri-urban peasants, and very many more small peasants and squatter-peasants on locations and privately owned lands, were cultivating more widely and seeking to dispose of a surplus. The colonial sector of Natal's rural economy continued to stagnate, especially during the commercial depression of the mid-1860s. Local farmers complained long and loud about the shortage of labour and the 'independence' of Africans living about them. That independence, the ability (already under attack) to exercise choice as to which lands proffered the best balance between agricultural opportunities and the demands of the exchange economy, derived from an interlocking set of factors specific to the political economy of Natal between (about) 1845 and 1870. These included: the conflict of interest between absentee proprietors and colonial farmers; the decision of the former that their economic interests were best met by the extraction of rent from African peasants on their lands; the resultant inability of the colonial farmers to make the state compel Africans to become labourers; the absence of a commercialized food-producing agricultural sector, which meant that many white settlers looked to Africans for grain production; and the retention by the African population (in addition to access to various types of land) of sufficient cattle and family labour to enable the prevailing socio-economic system to produce an agricultural surplus for sale.

2 'TAKING ADVANTAGE OF ANY FAVOURABLE OPPORTUNITY': 1870–93

It must be remembered that most of the land in the colony is farmed by the Kafirs ... who form the bulk of our farmers.

(*Natal Witness,* 4 June 1872)

Henry Slater has argued that the debate in Natal between various colonial and metropolitan interests on 'native policy' was fundamentally concerned with the precise manner in which surplus was to be extracted from the African population. His formulation merits quotation:

> In the event a compromise was evolved which took account of most of the interests within the ranks of the colonizers. The state ... defended the rights of white landlords to extract rents from Africans living on land which the colonizers now claimed as their own, but Africans could accumulate the necessary surplus through production for the market, transport operations, trade, or whatever. Labour for the colonists was not insisted upon. If landlords chose to offer only a labour tenancy arrangement, the state did not interfere to prevent Africans from migrating into the locations or onto other private lands where the terms were more favourable. At the same time, the embryo capitalist agricultural sector was not allowed to suffer. With the support of most of the absentee landlords, the farmers successfully campaigned for the introduction of indentured labour from India. Begun in 1860, the system of indentured labour, which was originally envisaged as a stop-gap until local Africans were forced onto the labour market, came instead to be a permanent feature of the economy.... It was not until the end of the century that the balance of social and political forces altered in such a way that the state finally closed the African alternatives to labouring for white employers.[24]

Accepting this as a highly compressed description of the constellation of social and political forces for the quarter century reviewed in this section, it remains to add a few comments referring more directly to African peasant agriculture. The period saw an intensification of peasant production, characterized by diversification and sensitivity to market opportunities; white farmers found it difficult during these years to compete with African peasants in the production of food for the market. The wealthier peasants – largely but not exclusively *kolwas* – included some who became in this period small-scale commercial farmers and planters. The increasing incidence of land purchases by Africans in these years was a sign not only of successful accumulation by some peasants and small farmers, but also of the rising competition for available land. The mounting scarcity of land as a resource, together with a rising population, higher rents and a greater demand for labour than ever before, combined to promote social stratification amongst the peasantry.

As in the Cape, the economic opportunities introduced by the diamond rush spurred an increase in peasant production in response to the needs of the suddenly concentrated population in Griqualand West, and also a response to changes in the local economy. As an example of the former, W. A. Illing (missionary on a large station near Ladysmith) recounted in 1872 that 'the merchants buy all the mealies in from the Kafirs to the end that they may convey it to the Diamond

Fields where they get a high price for it'.[25] From a dozen districts, magistrates and others reported in the seventies and early eighties that more land was being cultivated, more implements used, more crops raised, and more sold. From Umgeni (which included the Pieter-maritzburg market) the use of ploughs and harrows meant that 'very many Natives endeavour, besides an abundance for home consumption, to contribute to the supply of local markets'. From Umlazi, with Durban in its bounds, came report that 'the high wages the Natives now obtain, together with the profitable sale of their superfluous crops', as well as the increase in their flocks and herds, had tended 'rapidly to enrich them'. In Umkomaas, which abutted the two districts already mentioned, the magistrate noted that high prices and transport rates were benefiting industrious whites and blacks alike. Of the latter he commented: 'They are a race who are eminently fitted for taking advantage of any favourable opportunity for sale or barter. In favourite localities they frequently pay as high a rental as £5 per hut per annum.' They had increased the land under cultivation, he added, and some now had 'a very large acreage under maize; the possession of wagons, which was a short time since exclusively in the hands of Europeans and Kafirs on mission stations, has now extended to outside natives, many of whom are largely engaged in transport'. Farther to the north, in Weenen district, African peasants had 'considerable quantities of grain to dispose of' and were plying their wagons so as to profit from the presence of troops and the consequent enhanced demand for foodstuffs.[26]

Another motif that appeared several times during the early 1880s was an observed relationship between a rise in peasant production and a reduction in the flow of labour. From Ixopo, Umgeni, and Newcastle respectively magistrates discussed this:

It has been seldom that Natives here have been at all dependent on wages, earned by entering the service of the whiteman. Nay! All, or nearly so, have ploughs, which are worked by the younger male branches of the family, enabling them to dispose of produce on a much larger scale than formerly when they used the land-hoe only – their thriving stock of cattle gives them all they stand in need of ... [and consequently very few from the district entered service].

[The labour supply] has year by year become more inadequate as the Natives become richer, and yearly cultivate a large acreage with the plough, besides engaging in transport riding on their own account.

It is this desire on the part of the Natives to supply their own wants by the productions of the soil that has to a considerable extent interfered with the labour market.[27]

Two features of the seventies and eighties were closely linked: that white farmers found it difficult or impossible to compete with African agriculturists in the production of foodstuffs for the market, and that the bulk of foodstuffs consumed by white Natalians was produced by the colony's peasants. The competitiveness of grains and vegetables raised by African peasants derived in part from the relatively low level of consumption of manufactured goods and from the use of family labour in the production of crops; with grain prices kept fairly low in Natal by the ability of Africans to produce for the market, this further inhibited white farmers from competing.

The *Natal Witness* surveyed the rising competition from black farmers in 1871: whereas in the early days African women had grown maize by the pick, African men were now using the plough, utilizing new techniques, and so 'found little difficulty in entering into competition with their instructors'. The growth of a farming and tenant class among Africans, the writer continued, meant that there was now a glut of maize, so that white farmers were unable to compete. The theme was taken further a year later. Speaking of the tract of relatively unworked land in the belt between Pinetown and Pietermaritzburg (between the coastal sugar belt and the grazing lands of the midland plateau) the editor noted that little was produced there except maize:

> It must not, however, be supposed that, though the agriculture of this particular zone of the colony may not be visible to the traveller on the high road – it is not as a rule carried on by Europeans, and its returns do not figure to any great extent among the exports – it is therefore of small importance ... the quantity of the cereal grown in the locality by Kafirs is considerable, and not only supplies the deficiencies which occasionally occur in the crops of those natives who live in less favoured localities, but also, furnishes large quantities to the planters for their native labourers.[28]

As a direct result, the colonist found it difficult – the editor concluded – to compete in raising maize.

Colonists themselves commented upon the difficulties involved: Thomas Phipson wrote that the African's polygamous and low-consuming life-style gave him the competitive edge over whites; and a correspondent complained to the *Natal Herald* that 'so long as the native finds a ready sale for all his produce ... so long as shopkeepers and others buy of the native's produce' then so long would 'the struggling white farmer' be 'cheerless and comfortless'. An immigrant settler summed it up thus, in 1875:

> It seems impossible for anything to be done in Natal while everything is managed so badly; there's no labour to be got and there is no competing with the natives as they are all large growers, all have wagons and oxen, and having so few wants can afford to sell and treck at a much cheaper rate than the English.[29]

When an 'Old Colonist' advised 'New Settlers' the book he edited contained notes on farming in different areas of the colony, and several of these bore eloquent and aggrieved witness to what white colonists perceived as their own competitive weakness. The editor himself commented upon the low prices for grain, and the production of maize by Africans: 'their herds are so numerous, their own fields so prolific,' he complained, that they did not readily enter service. From Ladysmith came a long grumble by a farmer who explained why colonists there could not raise any crops: he blamed foreign competition, inadequate transport facilities and the climate, but the district was one in which Africans on missions, on white-owned farms and on farms purchased by 'syndicates' of peasants raised foodstuffs, and this was obviously an important factor. In Newcastle district, too, white colonists found that 'stock-breeding is more easy and more certain in its results than agriculture': and this in a district where many 'white' farms were entirely occupied by African producers. Moreover, explained Mr J. Scoble (who wrote the Newcastle section), 'Whereas the average produce of mealies per acre under white management is but five muids, the kafirs absolutely obtained six muids to the acre!'[30] Detailed statistics for production per acre are lacking for Natal in this period, but it seems likely that Scoble accurately described a reality of the rural economy.* A further fragment of evidence from the same district, Newcastle, suggests another way in which African agriculture was more competitive than that of the colonists: that it was more responsive to opportunity. The magistrate from the district noted that 'the extremely good market' prevailing in the area because of the proximity of troops (in the war between Britain and the Transvaal, 1881) had probably 'induced the increased cultivation'. His figures showed that whites in the district had increased the area under maize and sorghum from 932 acres in 1880 to 1,525 in 1881 (a rise of 65 per cent), and that Africans had sown respectively 2,545 and 7,980 acres in 1880 and 1881 – a rise of over 210 per cent.[31]

In his recent study David Welsh rather depreciates the extent to which African agriculture ever competed with white agriculture: 'Competition between white and African producers in Natal was never ... [a] major political issue.... The records reveal only occasional references to it.' The labour question, he continues, was 'incomparably more important to the colonists than the question of competition'.[32] This assessment fails to take sufficient account of the difficulty colonists experienced in growing foodstuffs for sale in the face of peasant production; it also loses sight of the very direct relationship between 'the labour question' and the ability of African producers to compete effectively with white farmers, a relationship not overlooked by contemporary observers.

The other feature mentioned was that African peasants produced the

* See Chapter 4, pp. 112–13.

bulk of the maize crop raised in Natal – and on this the evidence is clear. From Ixopo in 1879 one learns that 'At present, the natives grow most of the mealies consumed;' from Newcastle in 1882 that the 'principal crop-producing people are as yet Natives'. In the same year, it was reported that whites in Umsinga district did not grow much maize, and that they depended on Africans for it. Agriculture was neglected by whites in Alfred County 'and nearly all the produce of the country [was] grown by Natives'. The same story, in a different tense, comes from Impendhle in 1902: 'Till lately, many of the farmers relied more upon the natives. They could buy mealies cheaper from them than grow them themselves.'[33]

In a process very similar to that described in the Cape, there emerged among the peasantry a small elite of proprietor-farmers, most of them mission-educated, distinguishable from the broad mass of the peasantry both in material standards of life and in their cultural and ideological distance from traditional African society.[34] Archtypical of this stratum in Natal were the Africans who settled in 1851 and thereafter in Edendale (an area in the Umsindusi river valley, a few miles south-west of Pietermaritzburg). The original six hundred inhabitants – allotted portions of a 6,000-acre farm, paid off over four years – were a multi-ethnic band who had thrown in their lot with the Methodist missionary James Allison. Some based themselves in trades or crafts in the township (builders, masons, carpenters, hedgers, thatchers and brickmakers); others accumulated wealth through farming the well-watered land and supplying the Pietermaritzburg market with vegetables, grain, and meal. By 1860, a thousand acres were under cultivation: the chief crops were maize, oats, beans and melons; the most successful farmers re-invested their profits in further land, and there was a concentration of ownership. The community (says the *Natal Regional Survey*) enjoyed a 'golden age' between its inception and 1891. One admiring contemporary spoke of

> this beautiful dale ... with ... a good mill for grinding the millions of bushels of maize they grow on their little farms, their neat village of a thousand population, with nearly all the space along the sides of the streets and front and rear of their little homes, covered with fruit trees.[35]

Those who made money through farming, and who sought extra land, spearheaded the 'colonizing' movement out of Edendale in the 1860s and 1870s – the purchase of land and the establishment of communities elsewhere in Natal. In 1867, between thirty and forty Edendale families paid £1,100 for the farm Driefontein, near Ladysmith; nearby Kleinfontein was bought in 1870. Two further offshoots from Edendale – on the upper Mzimkulu valley, and in the north of the Klip river district – were established in the following decade. These colonists – reminiscent of the Mfengu migrant communities of the Cape (see pages 99–100) – became well known in Natal for their prosperity and respectability; members of their communities appeared as witnesses before all the major commissions of enquiry into African affairs.[36]

Another group of well-to-do Africans were those who turned to sugar production. On the American Board Station at Mvoti, Grout encouraged the planting of sugar-cane; by 1871 the community by then known as Groutville (the mission station lands as well as the village that had grown there) boasted a flourishing small-scale sugar industry. There were forty-seven African planters (of whom one in seven was not a Christian convert) who cultivated 300 acres of cane, and milled 140 tons of sugar that year. There was another mill on the Amanzimtoti mission, instituted on the initiative of a convert named Nembulo; he had raised some of the capital, successfully lobbied the Lieutenant-Governor for more and hired an English engineer so as to acquire the necessary technical skills.[37] Sugar was also grown at Ifumi, a third American station, while at Verulam, Methodist converts emulated the Amanzimtoti experiment in instigating sugar planting independently of missionary initiative. The resident missionary wrote in 1870:

> The Natives are becoming large cultivators of sugar cane. The success of a native last year has made its cultivation quite a mania and there is little else thought of and talked of besides sugar cane. Land is in great demand near the Station and all the available Station land is absorbed.... My men say sugar is their diamonds.[38]

Etherington points out that African planters were handicapped in competition with the large plantations: as J. Matiwane told the 1881–2 Commission on Native Affairs, Africans were 'afraid of sugar growing because it takes so much capital'.[39] Etherington is incorrect, however, in suggesting that African sugar production effectively came to an end by the 1880s (he seems to be generalizing from the decline of production on the Mvoti station). A group of African planters (including members of such politically active families as Gumede and Lutuli) remained in sugar production, especially in Umzinto, Umlazi, Stanger, and Mtunzini.*

A third identifiable group of *kolwa* individuals whose success and enterprise won them repeated mention are those ex-servants (or ex-slaves) of Transvaal *trekboers,* who had immigrated into Natal in the 1840s. A missionary described this group ('a more prosperous and civilized community') in these terms: 'By their own steadiness and perseverance [they] gradually raised themselves into a position considerably above the majority of the Natal natives. They each live in

---

* Sugar cultivation was still the source of income for some African farmers in the 1930s – indeed, Chief Albert Lutuli began his political career by organizing Natal's African sugar farmers.

their own farms, occupying well-built houses, and aim at giving their children a better occupation.'[40]

It is not clear when the first land in Natal was bought by an African or Africans, although a few such purchases took place during the sixties and seventies. In 1880, however, new regulations were promulgated for the sale of rural lands, and from that date on, land sales to Africans who could afford it became increasingly widely reported. The Surveyor-General commented in 1881 that of the applications for land in freehold,

> a considerable number were received from Natives who appeared to put forward much solicitude in the frequent enquiries they were making with regard to forms of tenure, and other conditions of occupation and payments.... In the few sales that were held, a good beginning was made by some of the Natives who were able to attend personally and enter into a spirited rivalry with other persons (Europeans) who desired to secure some portions of the land then offered.

In 1882, the Native Affairs Commission gave cautious approval to the purchases that were taking place: they promised to give Africans a stake in the country, to extinguish eviction complaints, and to introduce better methods of cultivation.[41]

It was in districts like Ixopo where for years previously magistrates had reported on thriving peasant agriculture that land sales to Africans were briskest: in that district 'very extensive sales' of Crown Land to whites and blacks were reported. From Richmond, in Upper Umkomaas, a missionary indicated the link between agricultural enterprise and land purchases:

> Civilisation is advancing among the Kafirs in every direction around us. Transport riding or working bullock wagons for hire is the order of the day. And ploughing with oxen instead of women working with hoes is greatly resorted to. On the hills round here natives have *purchased* from white men plots of land from 50 to 200 or more acres, on which they build a house and fence a large extent for cultivation.[42]

In the first decade governed by the 1880 regulations, Africans in Natal bought 67,077 acres for £36,412 (white colonists bought over half a million acres for £275,000 in the same period); between January 1890 and July 1891, Africans bought a further 56,000 acres for £34,000.

Land purchases were not unaccompanied by difficulties. In some areas, especially in northern Natal, Africans encountered white opposition to their even taking up their lands: in Newcastle division, for instance, some thirty-two plots of Crown Land were bought by Africans, but (wrote the magistrate) 'European farmers, especially the Dutch, are, as a rule, very much opposed to the Natives being allowed to acquire land in any form; and it is easy enough for Europeans to

181

throw obstacles in the way of Natives.' In particular, white farmers objected to the sub-leasing of land by African purchasers: this practice (which offered access to the means of subsistence to a number of squatter-peasants besides the buyer) the colonists deplored 'because it is considered that the system interferes with the supply and control of labour'. The other difficulty encountered in the depression of 1883–6 was simply that of keeping up with payments: by 1884, Africans owed £9,000 in arrears on land purchases.[43]

This debt on land purchases was one among several ways in which the instances of peasant enterprise and prosperity between 1870 and 1893 must be qualified: setbacks and hardships were experienced too. This was the case most particularly during the middle years of the 1880s, when from many districts came evidence of a cycle of depressed prices, falling production, food shortages, and greater numbers of peasants seeking work.[44] Access to various types of land was becoming more difficult in the 1880s than in the 1870s and earlier: rents had averaged five shillings per year in 1860, while by 1886 the return of rents of the Natal Land and Colonisation Company reveals an average as high as twenty-eight shillings a year.[45] During the 1880s, there is evidence that congestion in the locations was becoming a serious problem, that sales of Crown Land were causing evictions of African tenants, and also that evictions were taking place in cases of incipient commercialization of agriculture.[46]

It is part of the argument of this chapter that each of these pressures – land prices, rents, overcrowding, evictions and commercialization – was considerably greater in the period 1893 to 1913, and so fuller discussion of them has been held over to the next section. One additional source of pressure upon Natal's African peasants should be mentioned: the competition they encountered from Indian peasant farmers in Natal. As Indian immigrant labourers completed their five-year indentures, they became involved in the Natal economy in a wide range of capacities: as labourers, skilled and semi-skilled artisans, shopkeepers and traders, and as agriculturists. Indian participation in food-production took two forms: as specialist market-gardeners in and near the large towns, and as small-scale farmers elsewhere. They 'captured practically the whole of the fruit and vegetable trade in the peri-urban areas of Durban' as well as that of Pietermaritzburg and the coastal areas of Natal. In addition, they settled and bought small farms 'wherever fertile land [could] be obtained not too far from a market'. In certain districts Indian farmers became the main producers of various crops: of maize in Inanda, of tobacco in Alexandria. Their agricultural prowess won encomiums like the following, by the magistrate of Umlazi: 'It behoves me to speak in eulogistic terms of the Indian agriculturists ... thrifty, steady, and hard-working. ... They are rapidly enriching themselves, and excel in the cultivation of crops.'[47]

Individual Indian peasants and small farmers came to agriculture from a different social and ideological setting to that of the majority of Natal's African peasants, and this conferred upon them certain competitive advantages. They came largely (from India) from urban or semi-urban backgrounds, while their years as indentured labourers introduced them thoroughly to the money economy. A large number of them had been agricultural labourers, and many had begun to cultivate plots while still indentured. They were more mobile, less tied to particular areas by considerations of kinship or ancestry than were African peasants. They did not become pastoralists (the Hindu, of course, could not), and their horticultural and agricultural enterprises were from the outset geared to winning a market. It also seems probable that many small farmers were able to rely upon the relatively wealthy Indian merchants and shopkeepers for favourable credit terms.[48] All of these factors seem to have played a part in fostering the emergence and consolidation of Indian agriculture in the seventies and eighties, and thereby to have introduced an additional source of competition for resources and for markets to Natal's African peasantry.

3 'BY THE HEAD AND BY THE LEGS': 1893–1913

Twenty years ago there was not a European farmer in the [Ixopo] district who grew mealies; they relied upon the natives, and the natives had a surplus to sell, but now the scale has been turned.

(Col. W. Arnott, to the Beaumont Commission (1914), 510)

It is maintained in this section that the political economy of Natal underwent far-reaching changes after (about) 1890, and especially after 1893. Multiple and complex alterations took places, but these can be reduced to two fundamental changes, two processes that took place at roughly the same time, that interacted upon and affected one another, and that may be broadly characterized as 'economic' and 'political' features. They were:

(i) the development of the mining industry (on the Rand and in Natal itself), of the rail system, of entrepot and other mercantile activity, created a qualitatively different market for the agricultural produce of Natal and spurred the commercialization of the (white) colonial agricultural sector;

(ii) the granting by Britain of 'responsible government' to the colony in 1893 meant a change in the locus and composition of power in the state: Natal was under the rule of the elected representatives of its white colonists, with an electoral system that greatly favoured the rural areas.

The conjunction of these two broad tendencies was to shift the ultimate control of the political economy of Natal out of the hands of those local and British interests 'with a stake in the continued capacity of Natal Africans to earn an independent income' – the rentiers – and into the hands of 'the burgeoning class of commercial farmers and its allies'.[49]

That is to say, those interests which gained politically by the grant of responsible government stood to gain economically by a rise in the value of land, the commercialization of agriculture, and a diminution in the competitiveness of a (culturally and ethnically distinct) rival agricultural class, the black peasantry. The union of these political and economic interests is clearly visible in the pattern of legislation and in the echoing rhetoric of the years 1893 to 1910: colonists invoked the state on the side of white agriculture and instituted state pressure upon African peasants. Although the existence of the locations and the retention of access to other forms of land continued to benefit some of Natal's peasants and to increase their bargaining power, and although the persistence in Natal of various quasi-feudal relationships (especially labour-tenancy) significantly impeded the process of proletarianizing Natal Africans, it nevertheless became suddenly much more difficult for numbers of peasants to find land to live on, and more costly to live as peasant farmers.

The overall effect as far as the African population was concerned of this conjunction of economic and political factors (as well as of other important reinforcing factors like rinderpest, East Coast Fever, population increase, and so on) was that it became possible for a diminishing proportion of Africans to pursue a relatively independent existence as petty agricultural producers instead of as wage labourers. Peasants in this period were under pressure to alter their status from rent-paying tenants to labour tenants, to give up their occupancies of certain classes of land, to contribute to the state and to landholders increased taxes, rents and fees. Consequently, they were squeezed off certain lands, they were forced onto the labour market in substantially greater numbers, and even those who continued as peasants and squatter-peasants were less able to compete with white food-growers.

All the major indices of economic growth exhibit steep rises in Natal between 1890 and 1910. Roads, rails and harbours were built; agriculture, commerce and banking literally doubled their wealth. The major impetus came from the mineral discoveries: the growth of the Transvaal's gold fields meant that Natal's entrepot role and transit trade were greatly enhanced. Of great significance too was the development of coal mining in the colony: production of coal in Natal rose from a scant 8,000 tons in 1888 to 80,000 by 1890. The extension of the railway line in the latter year to the Newcastle fields made large-scale extraction possible, and by 1905 production exceeded a million tons a year. The use of local coal at ten shillings a ton, instead of imported fuel at four times the cost, benefited rail construction, while trains carrying goods to the northern hinterland could carry coal on their return to the Natal coast.[50]

No sector of the economy was more strikingly transformed than agriculture. The total area under cultivation increased between 1870 and 1890 from 182,000 acres to 391,000 acres; between 1891 and 1908–9, it rose to 993,000 acres. The overall figures are even more remarkable when it is realized to which extent they reflect an increase in *white* agriculture: whereas perhaps two thousand colonists were engaged in agriculture by 1875, by 1895 there were over three thousand. In the whole period 1870–1913, there was an increase in the per capita average cultivated by whites from 2·08 acres to 4·88 acres, while the per capita average cultivated by Africans actually fell from fractionally over half an acre to just under half an acre. The area cultivated by white farmers rose between 1891 and 1908–9 from 85,000 acres to 541,000 acres, or, to express this growth in another way, in 1893 the colonists' combined agricultural output stood at 129,925 tons, but by 1904 had risen to over 850,000 tons.[51]

The transition of white agriculture from a pattern of pastoral subsistence farming with a fringe of planting activity along the coast to one of a rapidly developing commercial venture is really the story of the transformation of the Natal midlands. A vastly increased market for food was created; Natal's own increasingly urbanized white population rose from 46,000 in 1891 to 97,000 in 1904, and there was also the non-agricultural population of the Witwatersrand to be fed. Meat, dairy products, maize and vegetables were all put on a commercial footing in response to opportunities, particularly in the agricultural zone along the main rail line north, past Lion's River, Estcourt, Klip River and Newcastle. Wattle and eucalyptus gum plantations had become widely established in the grasslands of the interior: wattle bark for tanning was sold within southern Africa and a quarter of a million pounds worth a year exported, and the plantations also provided timber for rail sleepers and mine props. As land value and commercial opportunity rose, there was a substantial shift away from absentee proprietorship towards active exploitation of agricultural land in the Midlands.

Another vital change was the harnessing of the expanding transport system to the needs of agriculture.

> In the nineteenth century Natal railways were built mainly with a view to providing the shortest route to the North ... insofar as the main line touched agriculturally important areas, farming became more intensified and diversified.... During the first years of the twentieth century, agricultural development became a conscious aim of railway policy. In order to serve agricultural areas ... costly branch lines were undertaken.[52]

Rail construction was by no means the only way in which the Natal legislature exerted itself 'within the limits of its powers' on behalf of its most influential constituency, the farming community. It provided a range of agricultural extension services, government backing for food freezing and processing, the Agricultural Development Act of 1904 and the Land and Agricultural Development Act of 1907 (promoting occupation, cultivation and improvement of rural land, with favourable credit terms).[53]

Although they were almost entirely excluded from the assistance won by white agriculturists, there were some African farmers and peasants for whom the economic changes of these years represented opportunity. Some were geographically favoured: when the railway arrived in Umlazi district, those Africans previously engaged as carriers 'sold their wagons and oxen and settled down ... as market gardeners' using the railway to transport their produce. In Dundee, also served by rail, Africans renting private land were still able to 'pay rent out of crops instead of going out to work'; and (it was reported in 1905) it 'was a common sight last winter to see waggons standing in the Dundee streets loaded with mealies and kaffir corn while the owners went from one produce store to another, ascertaining prices'. Similarly, the Chairman of the Pietermaritzburg Chamber of Commerce pointed out that 'at the present time, within twenty miles of Maritzburg, there will be, I suppose, quite 50,000 bags of mealies coming in this year, grown by natives'. There were others who had carried out successful strokes of enterprise or speculation: the 'native mealie traders' of Newcastle district travelled south to Umsinga to exchange grain for cattle, as the latter district had suffered poor harvests; William Africa rented one of his farms to a coal company for 'a big rent'; and so on.[54]

Most commonly, it was those few (and only 1,500 Natal Africans were registered individual landowners by 1907 – others bought and held land collectively) who already owned enough land or had accumulated sufficient wealth to capitalize on new opportunities. This category was represented predominantly by *kolwa* peasants and farmers. The wealthier peasants in Ixopo drained and irrigated their lands, used fertilizers and practised crop rotation: techniques which demanded capital, and which rewarded the practitioners with increased profits. In Estcourt, a few peasants (again, only a few could have afforded it) were reported to have hired suitable land in some quantity for the purpose of going in for agriculture on an extensive scale. During a period of competition for land, another source of profit to those who already owned land was through rents, and there were several accounts of wealthier Africans leasing portions of their lands to others less well off.[55] Johannes Kumalo, one of the Driefontein syndicate (who farmed between thirty and forty thousand acres of land by the first decade of the new century) gave evidence to the South African Native Affairs Commission (1903–5) that included this exchange:

186

Are all those living on this farm proprietors or shareholders of this property? – No.

Do the others living around pay rent? – Yes. . . .

What rent do they pay? – Some pay two pounds and others three pounds.

Have you any that work for you in lieu of rent? – Yes.

You have virtually the same system as the white man has? – Yes.[56]

Ten years later, another Driefontein proprietor, Simeon Kambule, told the Beaumont Commission that he owned 796 acres of land himself:

> Some of our people live there as tenants and pay rent. I cultivate a lot of land myself. Some of the others have only five acres. I expect to reap this season on my land about 250 bags, which was about the number I reaped last season, which was a good season however. I have some stock also. . . . I bought another farm near Newcastle on the twenty year purchase scheme.[57]

These instances of peasants or farmers staying afloat or even improving their buoyancy stand out somewhat in the twenty years under discussion as exceptions to a general pattern. There is a volume of evidence after 1890 that agriculture in African-owned or -occupied land was (so far from prospering) stagnating, falling back or suffering from 'growing neglect'.[58] Pointed testimony on this score came from a number of individuals. J. W. Mackenzie, a farmer and contractor from near Richmond, surveyed the African's position thus:

> That native's earning power is not sufficient to enable him to pay his way . . . to pay his debts and his taxes. A man cannot live on nothing. When a man had cattle and land, like they had years ago, he could sell a beast and pay his rent; now they have no cattle and the land has practically run out; their cultivation has got worse and worse – where they used to grow mealies years ago, you cannot get a sack now. . . . Before they could exist on cattle. . . . wages have risen, and other things have risen in comparison; he is worse off now because he has no cattle, and the land he cultivates does not produce nearly as much as it used to do, therefore his position is worse than it was before, and it is getting worse.[59]

From Dundee, in 1908, the magistrate wrote gloomily that 'year by year, everything seems against them'; from Ixopo (for so long a source of optimistic reports) there were fears that 'in a few years we shall have a large pauper population'. An Impendhle farmer estimated that 90 per cent of the local Africans were indebted to storekeepers or money-lenders; and in Ladysmith a merchant told the Natal Native Affairs Commission (1906–7) that peasants 'were not doing as much cultivation now as years ago'; that formerly he had bought as many as twelve thousand bags of maize in a season, but did not at the present buy twelve hundred.[60]

To explain the phenomenon, widely noted at the time, of a degeneration in peasant agriculture after 1890, a number of factors must be taken into account. As in the Cape, the nineties saw several years of poor rains and reduced harvests cruelly compounded by rinderpest, which reached Natal in 1897. Six-sevenths of the cattle owned by Africans in the colony (it is estimated) died, and African peasants found it far harder to rebuild herds afterwards than did whites. Catastrophe struck again in the shape of East Coast Fever, not as devastating as rinderpest, but lingering much longer. First reported in northerly districts in 1904, the fever spread south and west, reaching the Transkei boundary by 1910. Cattle losses incurred in both diseases not only depleted the wealth of individual peasants, but also made it impossible for many to plough: this led directly to the 'growing neglect of cultivation' discerned by the 1906–7 Commission, and presumably forced a reversion to hoe culture in a number of instances.[61]

A further cluster of causes of agricultural degeneration amongst black peasants are those that arose out of the rise in land values, in the profitability of farming and in the demand for labour. Maurice Evans (a member of the Legislative Assembly and leading spokesman on 'native affairs' in the colony) made a shrewd summary of the process:

> What happened was that white men increased in the land; the apostles of progress demanded that fuller use should be made of the fertile land, that ground simply used for grazing should be broken up and cultivated and varied crops grown for market.... Land-hunger swept the country, and Government was pressed to throw open the Crown lands to survey and allotment for whites, and charge a rent to natives remaining on the unappropriated balance, the demand being that, finally, all should pass into the private possession of the white man, and the native lands confined to those already allotted as locations. The men who lived in the old way were denounced as being backward and unprogressive ... the new ideas prevailed, fences enclosed the wide open country, grazing areas came under the plough, many new crops demanding much labour, such as wattles, were planted, improved stock was imported, and the Crown lands given out as private farms, all profoundly altering the position of the native on the land.[62]

White landowners, in short, had come to a simple conclusion: 'It pays me better to work a farm myself,' said one R. W. Comins, 'than rent it out to natives.' Africans paying rent and farming on 'white' land were 'driven off ... because white men found they could make a better use of the land than allow it to be occupied by the natives,' said a Swedish missionary. The value of land was rising, explained the wealthy George Hulett of Eshowe, 'and people are coming into the country and the natives get notice to quit because of the stock and agricultural operations'.[63]

Evictions took place in a number of different ways. First, the sale of previously unalienated Crown Lands (and much land was snapped up even at the rising prices) often saw the new owner take steps to remove any Africans 'squatting' on it, other than those he could persuade to enter into labour tenancy relationships with him.[64] Identical in effect – for the tenants – was the situation that prevailed when privately owned land changed hands from absentee landlord to commercializing farmer: not very much board-room wisdom was necessary to prompt such sales – the Natal Land and Colonisation Company was selling off its rural lands 'wherever possible' at this time.[65] Thirdly, evictions took place where no title-deeds but merely the intentions of the proprietor were changed: wherever an individual landowner decided that dairying or wattles was more lucrative than 'kaffir-farming'. F. E, Foxon, the magistrate of Ixopo, told the 1906–7 Commission how he had recently ordered ejectments of sixty-six *kraals* of two or three huts each: 'In almost every case the reason given was that the Europeans required the land for themselves.' Even where evictions did not take place, knowledge of their imminence and the general uncertainty of tenure for so many Africans in these years led to hesitancy about improvements and to the further decay of peasant farming: 'even the "childish" native,' said Harriet Colenso sharply, 'would not go and manure his lands against next year under these conditions. He would not plant wattles because they take several years to mature. What was the use of his troubling about the succession of crops or leading water?'[66]

Evictions apart, there was another set of pressures that bore very heavily upon rent-paying squatter-peasants. Most simply, there was a ubiquitous rise in rents commensurate with the rise in the value of land. There was in addition a multi-pronged drive upon rent tenancies that attempted to redefine their status in terms of labour tenancies. Just how important some of Natal's white farmers felt this objective to be may be gauged from the incidence and vehemence of their complaints against absentee landlords and rent-paying tenants.[67] The squeeze did not end there. A process of tightening up existing labour tenancies all over Natal took place early in the century; its main forms included demands by landowners for written contracts, or demands for rent in cash instead of in produce (and whenever the money was hard to come by, the insistence was that it be replaced by a labour agreement).[68] Another device was to inhibit the possibilities for accumulation open to a tenant, by limiting the amount of stock he might run, or by dictating (instead of permitting choice as previously) where the squatter-peasant's garden plots should be. Peasants in Polela were 'always getting into trouble about their cattle and horses and goats with the farmers', wrote a missionary, and also about whether they might 'plant their gardens where they lived'.[69] All these pressures upon rent-paying peasants reached a logical extension in the operation of the 1913 Natives' Land Act in Natal. As A. T. Bryant told the Beaumont Commission, white farmers used the Act not to evict tenants who were potential labourers, but to transform them, to force them to render service: 'the idea is to turn them off and get them back under the Act, and thereby to get more power over them'.[70] It is difficult to think of a more concise statement of 'the idea'.

One response to these pressures – the prevention of access to certain categories of land and the imposition of disabilities on rent tenants – was for Africans to buy extra land. Two difficulties presented themselves here. Repayment costs proved a great burden in the years following rinderpest and East Coast Fever. Secondly, the government actually prevented sales of Crown Lands to Africans after 1903, in which year an order to the Lands Department prohibited such sales.[71] Another factor pushing up the cost of living for peasants and making land purchase, land hire or any form of improvements more difficult to afford, was the increased demand by the state upon their cash resources. A number of new levies and fees were imposed upon Africans between 1903 and 1905, the most onerous of which was the Poll Tax of August 1905;[72] imposing as it did an extra toll of over £76,000 on Natal's African population out of a direct contribution by them to the Colony's revenue in 1905 of £306,484. Konczacki comments upon the fact that Africans 'were forced to pay a higher percentage of their income in taxes' than whites, and adds that 'in the last years of colonial rule it [the burden of taxation] tended to grow heavier'.[73]

Clearly, the pressures detailed thus far in this section did not affect all peasants in Natal equally. That perhaps half a million acres of land came under the ploughs of commercializing white farmers between 1893 and 1913 must not mask the fact that on a much larger extent of land, other white proprietors – companies and individuals – continued to rely on rents from peasants. In areas like Dundee and Newcastle, squatter-peasants also found refuge on the farms of a 'large number' of African landowners. It was still possible for some squatter-peasants, pressed by farmers to become labour tenants, to remove to the 'private locations' on an adjoining company farm: a spokesman for the Klip River Agricultural Society complained that 'So long as they had these big unoccupied farms with nothing on them but native tenants, they would never get the natives to turn out to work for the small farmer.' An English-speaking farmer, who said he represented 'progressive farmers', was aggrieved that Afrikaner farmers in the Ingogo district (impoverished during the South African War) had 'opened up their farms as private locations' to take on tenants 'who paid rent pure and simple'.[74]

In the broadest terms, it must be remembered that over half of Natal's African population continued to live after 1913 upon 'white' lands: the major change that had been effected there was undoubtedly the growth of labour tenancy at the expense of 'rent pure and simple'. The Act brought about a substantial increase of labour tenancies[75] – all over Natal, but particularly in the midlands, peasants became serfs.

Nevertheless, when allowance has been made for those peasants who escaped the constellation of pressures that threatened their access to land on favourable terms, and when the persistence of quasi-feudal relationships has been acknowledged as a major braking factor upon commercializing practices, the sum effect of the processes described in this section upon the lives of Natal's peasants is plain enough.

The owners of land and the wielders of political power, after the desperate Bambatha rebellion (1906) as they had before it, 'continued to tighten the conditions under which Africans could gain access to land'.[76] Any peasant who could not or would not 'give up his independence' (wrote a missionary), who did not wish to pay rent in labour, was adjudged 'an objectionable tenant'.[77] During earlier years, Africans had been able to withhold their labour and to pay taxes by sales of agricultural produce; by the turn of the century they could no longer do so. There was a steady increase after the mid-eighties in the number of migrant labourers in Natal: in 1897 F. R. Moor asserted in the Legislative Assembly that 'there is a very small percentage of natives who are at the working age who do not turn out to work during some time of the year', and in 1903 it was estimated that approximately 25 per cent of the total African population took paid employment each year.[78] The ceaseless complaints by farmers of labour shortage were in part a reflection of the growing number of alternative sources of wage labour, on rails, in mines, in construction work and in towns. Over 200,000 Africans a year sought employment in Natal after the South African War, and about 25,000 left the area each year for work in the Transvaal.

A corollary of this was that the generally prevailing advantages that black producers had once enjoyed over white, and the reliance on African grown foodstuffs by many whites, were rapidly reversed. From many districts, there was evidence that Africans were 'more dependent upon their wages for food and the food of their families', and that while once they 'used to supply themselves with corn' they now (1903) had to 'buy a large portion of their supplies of corn from the European traders'.[79] As Colonel Arnott (describing the same phenomenon and quoted in the superscription to this section) had it, 'but now the scale has been turned'. These pages have tried to show how that shift in balance was achieved; how the weights of economic and extra-economic coercion were piled up in the scale-pan until the beam swung irreversibly against the interests of the African peasantry, hastening their impoverishment and proletarianization.

Such details as we possess of these latter processes came usually from colonial civil servants, from white farmers, or from missionaries: they range in tone from perfunctory comment to self-commendation or mild surprise. By contrast, one Nkantolo, a peasant who fought for the Natal government against Bambatha, summed up the distress of his generation in a speech whose simple eloquence is clearly transmitted even through the interpreter and stenographer of the 1906–7 Commission:

> The money they paid was thrown into a big tank which never seemed to fill.
> What surprised them was that whilst on the one hand they were heavily
> taxed by government, on the other hand they were called upon to pay high
> rentals by private land-owners. The Government had them by the head, and
> the farmers by the legs.... They were extremely poor. How much ...
> remained of their earnings after they had paid their taxes and their rents and
> bought food for their children?... The land that was given them was
> circumscribed.... The Europeans had taken up every available bit of good
> ground. The Natives had no means of making wealth.[80]

NOTES

1 By 'Natal' this chapter refers to the colonial area before 1897: it does not
deal with Zululand. Zululand is in certain important respects an exceptional case in late nineteenth-century southern Africa; the particularity of
the Zululand case may be summarized thus: the Zulu kingdom remained
until the outbreak of the Zulu War (1879) economically independent of
colonial society, its social structure intact. Even the forms of economic
involvement that did exist between the Zulu kingdom and its neighbouring
'white' states exerted no pressure on the structural relationships of Zulu
society. The hides and cattle that flowed from Zulus to white traders
represented the surplus Zulu society could produce without consequent
alterations in productive relations or techniques; the trade with white
traders was assimilated into existing patterns of Zulu economic activity.
Trade goods obtained in South Zululand were transferred northwards,
where they were exchanged for African products from Zululand's northern neighbours. The Zulu War itself, but more precisely the decade of civil
war in Zululand that followed it, destroyed the economic bases of Zulu
society. Competition for arable and grazing land, a series of alliances with
different settler communities, and the eventual alienation by the settlers of
the choicest areas of the lands in question, saw Zululand pitchforked into a
relationship with 'white' Natal that other Africans societies had entered
more gradually and over a longer period. The formation of a peasantry in
Zululand took place, but rather later than the events discussed in this
chapter: that is, the nature and timing of Zululand's underdevelopment
differed significantly from those of the Ciskei and Transkei, as well as from
those of Natal's African communities. My decision not to consider Zululand in this book was confirmed by discussions with Jeff Guy whose own
major study of the crucial period in Zulu history has been completed (J. J.
Guy, 'The Destruction of the Zulu Kingdom: The Civil War in Zululand,
1879–1884', Ph.D. thesis, London, 1975). This footnote is a brutally
compressed statement of some of his findings: I am grateful to him for his
communications on the whole topic of Zulu particularity and the relative
absence there of a peasant class in the years 1870 to 1913.
2 The outline of Natal's history in this chapter is necessarily of drastic
brevity, conveying only the minimum amount of information consonant

with a comprehension of the changes taking place in the rural economy. For a general history of Natal, see E. H. Brookes and C. de B. Webb, *A History of Natal* (Pietermaritzburg, 1965); or, briefer and more incisive, OHSA, I, 334–90; for the Voortrekker period see J. A. A. I. Agar-Hamilton, *The Native Policy of the Voortrekkers* (Cape Town, 1928); A. J. du Plessis, *Die Republiek Natalia*, Arch. Year Book, 1942, i (Cape Town, 1942); for the colonial period see A. F. Hattersley, *The British Settlement of Natal* (Cambridge, 1950) and *Portrait of a Colony* (Cambridge, 1940). Two recent monographs have important background sections: S. Marks, *Reluctant Rebellion: the 1906–8 Disturbances in Natal* (Oxford, 1970), and D. Welsh, *The Roots of Segregation: Native Policy in Colonial Natal, 1845–1910* (Cape Town, 1971).

3 L. Thompson, OHSA, I, 364.

4 ibid., 368.

5 *The Diary of Erasmus Smit*, ed. H. F. Schoon (Cape Town, 1972), entries for 30 January 1838, 9 July 1838, 10 July 1838. (For other examples of raiding see entries 24 March, 9 April, 23 June and 23 July (all 1838). For examples of barter see especially entries for 18 October 1837 and 13 December 1837.)

6 Henry Slater, 'Land, Labour and Capitalism in Natal: The Natal Land and Colonisation Company, 1860–1948', *Journal of African History*, XVI, 2 (1975) 257–8.

7 Slater, op. cit., and his 'The Changing Pattern of Economic Relationships in Rural Natal, 1838–1914' ICS, CSP, Vol. 3, No. 16 (London, 1973), 38–52; C. W. de Kiewiet, *The Imperial Factor in South Africa: A Study in Politics and Economics* (Cambridge, 1937) 191–206.

8 Cited by Welsh, *Roots of Segregation*, 177.

9 Slater, 'Land, Labour and Capitalism', 263.

10 Slater, 'Changing Pattern of Economic Relationships', 42–3.

11 Marks, *Reluctant Rebellion*, 119. Cf. F. Wilson, OHSA, II, 118: 'In Natal ... there was still sufficient land available to Africans for them to support themselves independently.'

12 Report of Natal Native Affairs Commission, 1852–3, quoted by H. M. Robertson, '150 Years of Economic Contact between Black and White: A Preliminary Survey', 2 parts, *SA Jnl Econs*, Vol. 2, No. 4 (December 1934) and Vol. 3, No. 1 (March 1935), Vol. 2, 413.

13 See A. Smith, 'The Trade of Delagoa Bay as a factor in Nguni Politics', in L. Thompson (ed.) *African Societies in Southern Africa* (London, 1969), 171–89; and for a tentative discussion of the pre-colonial forms of economic activity in Natal see H. Slater, 'Peasantries and Primitive Accumulation in Southern Africa', *Southern African Research in Progress: Collected Papers: 2* (Centre for SA Studies, University of York, 1977) especially 88–90.

14 Welsh, *Roots of Segregation*, 187; J. S. Christopher, *Natal, Cape of Good Hope, a Grazing, Agricultural, and Cotton-growing Country* (London, 1850), 38–9; Robertson, loc. cit.

15 N. A. Etherington, 'The Rise of the Kholwa in Southeast Africa: African Christian Communities in Natal, Pondoland, and Zululand, 1835–1880' (Yale, D.Phil. thesis, 1971), 7, 137–40. Dr Etherington's thesis contains a wealth of information on the early African Christian communities of Natal;

even though not all the conclusions he draws from the evidence are equally convincing – for instance, he creates an unreal distinction between economic activities of Christian and non-Christian peasants (253 and *passim*) – his abundance of data more than offsets this.

16 SPG Arch., E MSS, E 13, Quarterly Report by A. Tönneson, 31 March 1863 (emphasis in original).

17 Etherington, op. cit., 244, 246, 248, 249, 253–5. From Edendale in the 1860s (a witness told the 1882 Commission on Native Affairs) 'big waggon trains of 13 or 14 waggons set off for the interior at regular intervals', and there is evidence of Natal *kolwas* selling produce in Zululand as early as 1853 (ibid., 263–4).

18 C. Lewis and G. E. Edwards (eds.), *Historical Records of the Church of the Province of South Africa* (London, 1934), 375.

19 R. J. Mann, 'The Black Population of the British Colony of Natal', *The Intellectual Observer, Review of Natural History*, Vol. X (London, 1867), 437, 439.

20 SANAC, III, 153 (evidence of Sir Jas L. Hulett).

21 BPP, C.334, *Reports on the State of Her Majesty's Colonial Possessions . . . for the year 1869* (London, 1871), Keate to Granville, 8 August 1870.

22 N. Hurwitz, 'Agriculture in Natal', *Natal Regional Survey*, Vol. 12, p. 8. See also *Report of the Trade Commission 1885–6* (Pietermaritzburg, 1886), 43, 55, for details of white Natalians giving up farming at the time of diamond discoveries.

23 *Natal Witness*, 1 April 1870.

24 Slater, 'Land, Labour and Capitalism', 264–5.

25 SPG Arch., E MSS, E 27 (1871–2), 4 March 1872.

26 *Natal Blue Book for 1877* (Magistrates' Reports) JJ2, JJ4; *Natal Blue Book for 1878* (Magistrates' Reports) JJ16, JJ14.

27 *Natal Blue Book for 1879*, JJ18; *Natal Blue Book for 1880*, JJ89; *Natal Blue Book for 1882*, GG10.

28 *Natal Witness*, 21 March 1871; 30 April 1872.

29 *Letters and Other Writings of a Natal Sheriff (Thomas Phipson, 1815–1876)*, ed. R. N. Currey (Cape Town, 1968), 131; Welsh, *Roots of Segregation*, 183; R. E. Gordon (ed.), *Dear Louisa: History of a Pioneer Family in Natal, 1850–1888* (Cape Town, 1970), 188–9.

30 J. Robinson (ed.), *Notes on Natal: An Old Colonist's Book for New Settlers* (London, 1872), xvi, xxvi, 153–5, 161, 171, 179.

31 *Natal Blue Book for 1881*, GG41. And cf. the report from Upper Umkomaas (*Natal Blue Book 1878*, JJ16): agricultural prices had risen, and the 'area of ground under cultivation has increased very considerably during the last season, more especially on the land held by natives'.

32 Welsh, *Roots of Segregation*, 182.

33 *Natal Blue Book for 1879*, JJ18; *Natal Blue Book for 1882*, GG10; ibid., GG62; *Natal Blue Book for 1887*, B21; *Report of Natal Lands Committee, February 1902* (Pietermaritzburg, n.d.), 190.

34 For discussion of the amaKolwa, see Etherington, op. cit.; Marks, *Reluctant Rebellion*, Chapter 3, and 'The Ambiguities of Dependence: John L. Dube of Natal', *Jnl. SA Stud.*, Vol. 1, No. 2 (April 1975), 162–80; and Welsh, *Roots of Segregation*, Chapters 3 and 4.

35 The description of Edendale is based upon: *Natal Regional Survey*,

Additional Report No. 1, 'Experiment at Edendale' (Pietermaritzburg, 1951), 1–8; Etherington, op. cit., 242–5; the quotation is from W. Taylor, *Christian Adventures in South Africa* (London, n.d.), 468 (internal evidence suggests that Taylor visited Edendale in 1867).

36 For details of the Driefontein Syndicate, see G. G. Findlay and W. W. Holdsworth, *The History of the Wesleyan Methodist Missionary Society*, 5 vols. (London, 1921), Vol. 4, 297; Etherington, op. cit., 244–5, 249–50, 257; SANAC, III, 455–61, 486–8; PRO CO 181, 62(17), *Report of the (Natal) Native Affairs Commission, 1906–1907*, Minutes of Evidence, 2 vols., 910–31 (cited hereafter as NNAC, 1906–7).

37 Robinson, *Notes on Natal*, 46, 97; Mann, 'The Black Population of Natal', 437, 438.

38 Quoted by Etherington, op. cit., 255–6.

39 ibid., 256.

40 SPG Arch., E MSS, 1896, Vol. 2, A. P. Troughton, Enhlonhlweni (near Colenso), June 1896. And cf. NNAC, 1906–7, 247: 'They lived very much like the old Dutchmen whom they copied ... respectable houses, well furnished ... the cultivation of their gardens was very good,' and ibid., 307.

41 *Blue Book for Natal for 1881*, Report of the Surveyor General, FF117; *Natal Native Affairs Commission, 1882* (Pietermaritzburg, 1882), 9.

42 *Blue Book for Natal for 1884*, B16; SPG Arch., E MSS, E30, E. Baugh, 30 September 1875 (emphasis in the original).

43 *Natal Blue Book for 1884*, BB34, H2.

44 The magistrates' reports for the years 1884 to 1887 contain many references to the depression: the *Report of the Trade Commission* (Pietermaritzburg, 1886), 105, has further details about the deleterious effect of commercial depression upon peasant subsistence.

45 A. F. Hattersley, *Later Annals of Natal* (London, 1938), 215, and see Slater, 'Land, Labour and Capitalism', 273–4.

46 *Report of the Native Affairs Commission, 1882*, 7–8; ibid., 2; *Blue Book for Natal for 1885*, B51; SPG Arch., E MSS, E41 (1886), B. Markham, Polela, 21 March 1886.

47 *Blue Book for Natal for 1885*, B51; Hurwitz, 'Agriculture in Natal', 6; M. S. Evans, *The Problem of Production in Natal* (Durban, 1905), 15; Hurwitz, op. cit., 6–7; *Blue Book for Natal for 1879*, JJ14.

48 The ideas in this paragraph are derived very largely from an important recent study of Indians in Natal: F. Ginwala, 'Class, Consciousness and Control: Indian South Africans 1860–1946' (University of Oxford, D.Phil. thesis, 1974). See 66–131, especially, for a discussion of entry by ex-indentured labourers into agriculture and other enterprises.

49 Slater, 'Land, Labour and Capitalism', 272, 276.

50 Z. A. Konczacki, *Public Finance and Economic Development of Natal, 1893–1910* (Durham, N.C., 1967), esp. 10, 22.

51 Hurwitz, op. cit., 10, 25; Konczacki, op. cit., 8; Marks, *Reluctant Rebellion*, 6–7.

52 Konczacki, op. cit., 23.

53 ibid., 168–9.

54 *Blue Book for Natal for 1881*, GG19; *Natal Annual Reports (1905)*, 42; SANAC, III, 435; *Supplement to Natal Blue Book for 1889*, Magistrates' Reports, B51; NNAC 1906–7, 247.

55 NNAC 1906–7, 384; *Natal Annual Reports (1908)*, Dept. Native Affairs Report, 18, 21; NNAC 1906–7, 237, 242, 353.
56 SANAC, III, 486. (For details of similarly prosperous peasants and farmers, see ibid., 455–61, 492–4, 859–60, 936, 966; NNAC 1906–7, 353, 384, 928.)
57 *Report of the Native Land Commission* (U.G. 22–'16), 587 (hereafter cited as *Beaumont Commission*).
58 For general indications of this trend, see Blue Books, Annual Reports, Departmental Reports, of the period – e.g., *Dept. Nat. Aff. Report, 1905*, v, 6, 25, 27; or U.G. 17–1911 *(Dept. Nat. Aff. Bluebook)* 143–7.
59 SANAC, III, 547; cf. ibid., 559, 576, 895.
60 *Annual Reports, 1908*, Dept. Nat. Aff., 18, 28; NNAC 1906–7, 22, 237.
61 NNAC, 1906–7, 2.
62 M. S. Evans, *Black and White in South-East Africa* (London, 1916), 128.
63 *Beaumont Commission*, 517; NNAC, 1906–7, 436 (evidence of K. V. Karlson); *Beaumont Commission*, 483–4.
64 Instances are described in SPG Arch., E MSS, E41, by B. Markham, writing from Polela, 31 March 1894; and see also NNAC, 1906–7, 154, 436.
65 Slater, 'Land, Labour and Capitalism', 277. See NNAC, 1906–7, 252, for the case of a farmer who bought land from the Company, found it 'simply swarming' with tenants, some 120 of whom he drove off when they refused to become labourers for him, and fifty of whom he retained as labourers.
66 NNAC, 1906–7, 363, 122.
67 ibid., 34, 104, 197, 206, 236, 251–2, 309, 328, 330 *et passim*.
68 *Natal Annual Reports, 1908*, Dept. Nat. Aff., 15–17.
69 SPG Arch., E MSS 1894, Vol. 2, Markham, 31 March 1894.
70 *Beaumont Commission*, 442.
71 See NNAC, 1906–7, 179, 652.
72 For details of the new financial obligations see Marks, *Reluctant Rebellion*, 139–41. This work considers in detail the immediate relation of the Poll Tax to the 1906 Rebellion.
73 Konczacki, 155–6.
74 SANAC, III, 390–1; NNAC, 1906–7, 252, 259.
75 See Hurwitz, op. cit., 28–9, and R. H. Smith, *Labour Resources of Natal* (Cape Town, 1950), 41.
76 Slater, 'Land, Labour and Capitalism', 279.
77 SPG Arch., E MSS, 1894, Vol. 2, Markham, 31 March 1894.
78 Welsh, *Roots of Segregation*, 193.
79 SANAC, III, 152–3. And cf. *Beaumont Commission*, 510, 518 *et passim*; NNAC 1906–7, 33, 237; *Blue Book for Natal for 1895* (report of magistrate for Lion's River); *Blue Book for Natal for 1897* (reports of magistrates of Lion's River and Umvoti).
80 NNAC 1906–7, 711.

7

The Transvaal and Orange Free State

The history of the northern republics (anachronistically but conveniently referred to as the Transvaal and Orange Free State throughout this chapter) from the 1830s to 1870 is a complicated saga of relations between African and Afrikaner communities, whose nomadic fringes, skirmishes, migrations and internal political rivalries – turbulent and intricate – make brief summary virtually impossible. Some of the older Afrikaner histories were at pains to ascribe to the recently arrived trekkers a sense of unity and purpose, and a capacity to translate this into effective control over their new territory; they explicitly or implicitly compare the cultural, technological, economic, military and political attributes of Africans in the area unfavourably with those of the trekkers. Such interpretations derive not only from a quest for the roots of Afrikaner nationalism, but also serve as a retrospective legitimation of the seizure of the High Veld.

Recent evaluations of the Boer Republics during the middle third of the nineteenth century provide a striking contrast. Leonard Thompson characterized the Orange Free State at mid-century as 'an imbroglio, containing elements of every type of society that existed in Southern Africa – hunters, pastoralists, and husbandmen; San, Khoikhoi, Sotho, Afrikaner and British' and as 'a scene of anarchy', while the 'poor, scattered, disunited, politically inexperienced' burghers of the four republics that finally accepted constitutional union as the South African Republic (Transvaal) in 1860 promptly fell apart again in civil warfare.[1] Shula Marks pointed out significant similarities between African and Afrikaner societies during and immediately after the Greak Trek: both were 'small-scale, closely-knit communities, based on subsistence agriculture, with wealth and prestige concentrated on cattle'; state formation was a key political process – as was a propensity to fission and fragmentation – in both sets of societies.[2]

Now Philip Bonner has drawn attention to the failure of the Transvaal's whites to create an effective state, and accounts for it in terms that explain the initial military advances – like the defeat of Mzilikazi's Ndebele in 1837 – as well as the fragility of subsequent political control. He argues that when trekker parties first moved across the Vaal river they travelled in compact bodies whose mobility and fire-power made them almost impossible to withstand. 'That initial tactical and technological superiority was made all the more pronounced by the recent ravages of the *difaqane*. Many chiefdoms had been

197

shattered, many others displaced and they could be expropriated relatively easily of their labour and their land.' Once the trekker parties began to spread over the Transvaal plateau, one of the prices that the burghers paid for their expansive individual holdings was the loss of the collective security, co-ordinated mobility and concentrated fire-power: the military and political balance was, to some extent, reversed. 'Now it was the trekkers who were thinly spread over the land and African chiefdoms who began concentrating in more consolidated blocs. The situation would not have been so serious had the trekkers been able more effectively to combine, but this proved beyond their capabilities.' Bonner concludes that the trekker communities showed little of the political and military predominance sometimes claimed for them, and that their weakness and dependence were particularly marked in the late 1840s and early 1850s, and again in the mid-1860s.[3] This aspect of the period before 1870 – the exiguous nature of trekker political and military authority, and the sharp limits to their control over Africans in the Transvaal – is directly relevant to this chapter.

By 1870, the white population of the two republics was fairly widely distributed, totalling perhaps a meagre 45,000 with three-quarters of those in the Transvaal. Although the white population was still relatively homogeneous, the process of land accumulation and its concentration into fewer hands was already under way. The tempo of economic life lagged considerably behind that of the Cape and Natal, with the Orange Free State the more monetized and market-oriented of the two. In 1870, the exchange economy was still rudimentary in the Transvaal; although itinerant pedlars were being replaced by traders in the *dorps*, exchange was still predominantly of the 'frontier' variety, with ivory and other hunt products, ostrich feathers, hides and cattle being traded for simple household needs and gunpowder. Almost all Afrikaners were engaged in petty subsistence agriculture on large farms upon which they grazed cattle and other stock.

As far as relations with the indigenous population were concerned, Thompson has commented that the growth of the Afrikaner settlement, following upon the wars and the enforced removals of the 1820s – the *difaqane* – 'presented the African inhabitants of the high veld with their second massive challenge in a generation'.[4] Where depopulation had aided the process, the territorial rights of the tribes were most brusquely ignored: the incoming trekkers announced ownership over virtually all land within the new states' boundaries. In the Transvaal, the burgher councils set aside 280,000 morgen (the treaty areas) plus 580,000 morgen (the government locations) for African occupation – out of a total of 71,000,000 morgen!

On the face of it, *refoulement* so vigorous, and a land allocation so lop-sidedly in favour of the dispossessors made impossible the creation of a peasantry. In fact, the republics' coercive equipment was so lacking, their rule so tenuous, the value of land so low for so long, and the forms of African resistance so varied, that Africans occupied, tilled and grazed nominally white lands in enormous numbers; their ability to subsist was for a considerable period not dramatically altered, and their involvement in the exchange economy was largely discretionary. There were areas where the kingdoms and chiefdoms continued to defend an autonomy and practical independence; although by 1870 all of these were subjected to manifold pressures and forms of penetration. Some – like the South Sotho kingdom and the Tswana peoples – eventually saw their resistance constitutionally recognized in the form of British protectorate status. Others were forced to yield their independence, either gradually – in the form of treaties, concessions and dynastic changes – or convulsively, as the burghers 'mopped up' those chiefs who continued to resist white control after 1870,[5] a process not concluded until the victory over Mphephu in the Soutpansberg in 1898.

The main features of the 'peasant response' in the northern republics between 1870 and 1913 may be summarized before their fuller discussion:

(i) Throughout the period, Africans remained in occupation of state and private lands, for which they paid rent or other forms of tribute when they had to, and evaded these when they could.

(ii) For other peasants (particularly where access to white-owned lands was difficult or threatened) the response was different, and the social transformation more far-reaching: they stepped up production, disposed of their surplus, and 'adopted the only method open to them, and proceeded to buy back when possible the land of which they had been deprived'.[6]

(iii) African peasant agriculture in the Transvaal seems to have been in certain important respects more effective than white agriculture in responding to economic changes; production and sale of food by black peasants was a feature of the Transvaal's political economy both before and after the South African War (and after gold-mining had greatly increased the demand for foodstuffs).

(iv) During the years of Milner's 'reconstruction' some of the circumstances attending the defeat of the Boer state (the prevalence of absentee landlordism, certain administrative decisions that favoured both land companies and peasants at the expense of Boer producers, and the enterprise of large numbers of peasants) meant that African peasants continued to subsist, to trade, to buy land and to accentuate the 'poor white problem'.

(v) In the Orange Free State, a characteristic form of squatter-peasant emerged (the share-cropper or farmer-on-the-halves) which was one of the most distinctive features of the rural economy of that province in the 1902–13 period.

(vi) The political victory of *Het Volk* in the Transvaal, and of the South African party in the Union, gave Transvaal and Orange Free State white farmers – but particularly those who were keen to commercialize their farming in response to a series of incentives – the opportunity to move against various 'offending' categories of peasants. Overriding all other aspects of the 'employers' offensive' in the northern provinces was the 1913 Natives Land Act. In the Cape and Natal, as has been argued, the state had been used to supplement economic forces in restoring white agricultural capitalist production. The 1913 Act illustrates the manner in which 'the state continued to be so used after the establishment of Union, to subsidise white agricultural development, to freeze possibilities of peasant production, and to transform from above feudal into capitalistic production relations'.[7]

1 BEFORE GOLD: 1870–86

In the Transvaal before 1876, state expenditure and revenue were minimal: 'the administrative machinery of the embryonic state was incapable of collecting sufficient revenue to finance both military expenditure and the barest essentials of civil administration, including the collection of taxes' – a situation which led to the widespread use of land to pay salaries and to secure debts.[8] The Republic's precarious solvency had slithered into bankruptcy when that country was annexed by Shepstone and his two dozen policemen in 1877. Only £3,000 in taxes was collected from three-quarters of a million Africans; and – sniffed a British official after the annexation – 'I can come to no other conclusion but that the late government did not attempt to collect from any of the strong and powerful tribes.'[9]*

The 'strong and powerful tribes' included the Tswana peoples Kwena, Ngwaketse, and Ngwato, in the west, and the North Sotho peoples of the north (Venda and Tsonga) and east (Pedi). The western groups in particular continued during the seventies to trade in hunt products (with large amounts of ivory) and hides. A missionary described Zeerust (in the western Transvaal) in 1874 as lying athwart 'the great native trading road to Secheli's country ... and many other northern and western tribes' all of whom dealt in 'ivory and ostrich feathers'.[10] The tribes continued to practise traditional agricultural methods, and attained self-sufficiency in so doing. The sale of agricultural produce tended to be sporadic and of marginal importance to the economies of these kingdoms, although where opportunities

---

* Or see an outraged Anglican missionary's description of the Soutpansberg district – especially the area occupied by the followers of Maxato and Malitsi: 'The Boers themselves live in the district on sufferance. Instead of the Kafirs paying taxes, the farmers pay blackmail to them. The Government is powerless to help them. If they complain at Pretoria of thefts of stock they are told to go to the native chiefs. In cases of outrageous behaviour on the part of the Kafirs, the Government, through the Marabastad magistrate, mildly remonstrates.' (*Mission Field*, 1876, 242–3.)

offered a vigorous trade in foodstuffs indicated their ability to increase agricultural production. Sekhukhune's Pedi people were conducting a sizeable trade in maize which they exchanged for cattle and diamonds, in the 1870s.[11]

The picture was rather different in the areas of the Transvaal where white settlement was more firmly established, and where African involvement in the exchange economy took different forms. One of these was an active participation in the produce market of established urban centres, like Pretoria and Potchefstroom. In the year before gold was discovered on the Witwatersrand, a missionary wrote to London:

> I will try and describe a scene which is as common in the streets of Pretoria as is the presence of a horse and cart in an English town. Early in the morning, a party of native women numbering about ten may be seen coming in from the kraal carrying baskets on their heads containing fruit and vegetables for sale.[12]

From Potchefstroom another missionary described the 'trading and carrying' that his congregation undertook, journeying as far afield as Natal with their produce. He indicated, too, that the circulation of currency in the district was largely due to agricultural production by black peasants; the 1884 drought, which had so adversely affected peasant crops, was largely responsible for the 'terrible depression' and shortage of cash: 'The trade in native crops is a *cash* trade – and hence the scarcity of money.'[13] Emil Holub, a German traveller who spent seven years in Southern Africa, visited Potchefstroom in 1873, and described its vigorous trade activities. Maize (whole and milled), meat and tobacco went to the diamond fields, while cattle, hides, animal skins and small amounts of ivory and ostrich feathers went on wagons to Natal.[14]

Some interesting glimpses of agricultural production and trade involvement by Africans in the Transvaal are contained in the account of Mrs Heckford (an astute and forceful Irish settler who tried her hand at both farming and trading). She describes barter with Africans who had been very little affected in cultural or social aspects by white settlement in the Transvaal, and also indicates the greater level of trading activity in the vicinity of towns and mission stations. One incident that she recounts illustrates an economic consequence of the annexation: with the Shepstone administration calling for taxes, and showing every intention of collecting these more assiduously than the Raad had been able to, her African customers were swift to appreciate the increased need for surplus cash. They did not want to have to part with cattle in tax payments; and thus Mrs Heckford let it be known that she would commence a cash trade in maize and sorghum (instead of barter, as previously): 'When I made this intention known, the Kaffirs came in swarms.'[15]

Another feature of this period was the extent to which peasants made exertions to rent and to buy land, especially in areas where very little or no African ownership of land was recognized. Land purchases by Africans became more frequent in the years after 1886, but there were reports in the late seventies like that of S. J. V. K. du Toit, a 'General Agent' who made representations to the British Government in 1878 on behalf of African clients (who were complaining about their statutory inability to buy land and about the consequent hardships of having to have land purchased by missionaries): 'Not only the chiefs but individual Kafirs in the district of Rustenburg are anxious to acquire landed property.... In several instances the blacks are paying high rents to acquire irrigated lands.' He added that Africans had already acquired by purchase some forty freehold farms in the district, although not in their own names.[16]

They could not buy land in their own names because the Raad did not recognize land sales to Africans, and so various ruses were adopted to foil this ban. 'Leases' which were *de facto* sales were one method; the more common procedure was the use of a missionary as 'dummy' purchaser: the price, in typical cases, would be 'collected by each native chief from his tribe principally in cattle, and the missionary arranged the transaction'.[17] There were cases in which this procedure worked to the mutual satisfaction of missionary and peasant community concerned. George Weavind, a Methodist missionary based near Potchefstroom, bought several farms which he leased to African communicants, and he described the inhabitants of one of these farms as 'an industrious tribe, who made considerable money out of the surplus crops which they did not need for themselves'. Another missionary described a farm which lay within access of the markets at Ventersdorp and Potchefstroom:

> About in the centre of it there is a small native town built around the house of the old chief, Petros. The chief, and several of his people, have large, well-built square houses ... the Natives who live on the farm support themselves by raising cattle and cultivating mealies and ... kaffir corn.[18]

They had recently built a dam on the farm for irrigation purposes, he added.

The relationships between missionary purchaser and peasant user were not always as cordial. There were cases in which tensions and discord arose between them, and often these resulted in the loss by peasants of land for which they had paid.[19] Often – but not always. In one unusually well-documented instance, it is possible to trace the history of bargain struck, transaction executed, amity eroded and missionary discomfited. In 1883, Charles Clulee of the USPG first proposed buying a mission farm for Africans near Potchefstroom; he spoke indignantly of how heavily taxed were 'squatters' on Boer farms, and how difficult it was for them to prosper.[20] The initiative had in fact been taken by the chief of the 'Manakhotla', one Ratheo (known to the Boers as September) who was living with his followers in the Orange Free State. He wrote to Clulee saying that he had heard that the farm of Ed Bosman was for sale, and that certain other chiefs were interested in buying it. The land had belonged to his tribe before the *difaqane*; he would welcome a missionary among his people – if the missionary would help him buy the farm. Clulee met Ratheo, and then arranged a meeting between the two of them and the Bishop of Pretoria. At this meeting, episcopal approval was won for the purchase; it was agreed that Clulee would live on the farm as resident missionary-teacher, and that his authority on religious matters would be recognized; other Africans might live on the farm for the payment of rent.[21] Ratheo and his followers paid for the farm in part by the sale of stock, and in part from the earnings of some fifty men in the diamond fields. Clulee reported to London in June 1886 that he had bought 'a large farm' at the request of 'a Caffre chief'.[22]

One wonders if the recipients of Clulee's reports thought of the fears of another missionary in the Society, who confided in 1890 that he was anxious about 'the large mission farms belonging to the Church' where 'many of the tenants have settled on the land, rather ... for the temporal privileges ... than for their spiritual good'.[23] In the five or six years following upon his purchase, relations between missionary and peasants deteriorated. By Christmas 1892, Clulee's successor on the farm 'Molote', Archdeacon Temple, was complaining that he had suffered 'the persistent persecution of the chief and his lawless followers' who had 'made a stand against the Church and her minister' and had resorted to 'every expediency imaginable to get rid of them both'. The trouble had arisen over the question of the actual ownership of the land. The wrangle over the title to the farm was still being waged a few months later, and Temple laid a fresh objection against the farm's occupants, who were obviously active agriculturists as well as litigants: class and school work had been disrupted, wrote the missionary, by 'the rush to market with fruit and all recently won produce'. By the following year, Ratheo was in complete command; Temple's disgruntled report came from Krugersdorp, and not from Molote, which he had departed, leaving it to 'that old heathen chief'.[24]

In the Orange Free State, the commercial economy was more firmly established in this period than in its northern neighbour. The Free State had already begun to claw its way out of an abyss of depression in the late 1860s, in part by its conquest of the rich grain lands of the Southern Sotho and in part by increased production of merino wool. Prior to the conquest of the Sotho grain lands, the Free State was largely dependent for maize upon imports from the Sotho kingdom; white *trekboers* in the republic could not compete with the African peasants of an area already famous for its corn growing as early as 1841.[25] This fact was reflected in the trade between the two areas: the chief exports from the Free State to Basutoland before the war of 1865–8 were cotton goods, woollen goods and bags for the export of grains; Sotho grain went largely to the Free State.[26] Next door to the diamond fields, the republic was well sited to prosper further, and a considerable amount of agricultural commercialization and economic recovery took place between 1870 and 1875.[27]

During the seventies, the persistent litany of farmers for labour was answered by the benison of proclamations and laws, notable for their unambiguous determination to force Africans onto the labour market.[28] The statutes undoubtedly made life difficult for their targets, especially those who were effectively denied access to land. But for a majority of Africans in the republic, quasi-feudal relationships were secured, and squatter-peasants on fertile state and private lands were able to resist the pressures of the market and the tax collector. Sir John Fraser gave evidence forty years later that half-sharing had occurred in the Orange Free State as early as 1872, and that 'this had continued all through the history of the country':[29] this particular relationship will be discussed more fully later on.

Angry farmers denounced the idle existence of the squatter-peasants, protesting that '*de kaffers te rijk zijn om zich eenig zints met werken to vermoijen*' (the Kaffirs are too rich to trouble themselves with anything to do with labour), and that they congregated upon unoccupied farms while white farmers were starved of servants. Absentee landlords were content to receive rents in cash or kind; a Mr Green in the Harrismith district held 50,000 morgen (or 106,000 acres) on which there lived over 100 kraals, or more than 800 squatter-peasants.[30] Anti-squatting laws and other legislation designed to promote the flow of labour were enacted year after year (especially 7–1866, 2–1871, Masters and Servants Law of 1873, 7–1881, 11–1883), yet the same years saw considerable settlement by African peasants on government and private lands. Anti-squatting measures remained dead letters as long as collection of tribute from African peasants remained the easiest means of appropriating surplus: the rent paid by Africans 'was profitable, so they would not remove the natives'.[31]

2 AFTER GOLD: 1886–1913

In the Transvaal, purchase of land by Africans – almost all communally owned and farmed – increased after 1886. Burghers 'were found willing to sell them farms because they could thereby get a better price than from Europeans' and so 'a good deal of land changed hands'. One tribe leased no fewer than twenty-two farms for grazing; others bought eighteen and eleven farms respectively. Population pressure on purchased land was less than half that on government locations, and by the outbreak of the South African War, Africans in the Transvaal owned just under a quarter of a million acres of land, a figure which is open to revision upwards, as some purchases were in all likelihood concealed.[32]

The gold boom gave new outlets to the rural population of the Transvaal, black and white. In particular, the period prior to the arrival of the rail system saw an enormous increase in the demand for transport riding, as well as for foodstuffs. The markets for meat, maize and forage boomed, and it seems likely that Africans were able to put gains accruing from this period towards land purchases and hirings. The years 1886 to 1900 saw land concentration intensify, both in the hands of a class of Afrikaner 'notables' and in those of mining and land companies.[33] (Early in 1899 one F. Young wrote to the Colonial Office in the name of a Committee representing companies owning some eight million acres of land in the Transvaal.)[34] This was of vital significance to the peasant population of the country: over half of their number lived upon privately owned lands. They did so in return for the payment of rents: indeed, says Denoon, land companies refused to rent to white *bywoners* (squatters) who were 'uninterested in farming for profit and paid no rent', but found African peasants profitable tenants. Describing this phenomenon, as well as the willingness of the peasantry to participate in the produce market, Horwitz concluded that African peasants 'showed a keener insight into the functions of capital and the market ... than did the whites'.[35]

The corollary to the existence of quasi-feudal relations, and the class of squatter-peasants that these gave rise to, was unvarying. In English and Dutch, in the Free State and Transvaal as in the Cape and Natal, came cries of anguish and annoyance by white farmers anxious to put their own lands to profit; their hostility to 'kaffir-farming' and their fury at the 'indolence' of squatters were ubiquitous and enduring. The reports of the 'Superintendent of Natives' in the Transvaal for the 1890s bear annual testimony to the prevalence of squatting and the ineffectuality of even the sternly worded new Act of 1895. In 1897 he lamented:

> *Wil een burger zijne dienstboden werkelik als zoodanig gebruiken, dan opebaart zich de treklust al spoedig en het duurt niet lang of zulk een burger zit zonder hulp, of moet weer van zijn woonkaffers verdragen dan wenschelihk is.*

> (If a citizen really wants to use his servants [labour-tenants] as such, then wanderlust speedily shows itself and it is not long before such a farmer is sitting without assistance, or has to carry more 'kaffir-tenants' than is legal.)[36]

In the Orange Free State, a pocket of individual land ownership by Africans was created by the annexation in 1884 of the Republic's former allies, Moroka's (Baralong) territory. The Raad recognized a total of 95 farms in Baralong hands, of which only 60, by the 1890s, and 51 by 1903–5, remained unalienated. The nineties saw another sharp rise in the number of protests and petitions to the Raad against the *luilekkerlewe* [idle existence] of squatters and the difficulties of obtaining labour on farms. A frustrated Dutch farmer wrote in September 1890 to *De Express*:

Op sommige plaatsen liggen van 10 tot 20 kaffers en boer lekker zonder hunne handen in het koud water te steeken; zaaien zooveel als zy verkies, en als hun baas hen dit alles niet wil toelaten dan komen zij, zoodra hunne oogst ingezamel is en zonder dat zij iets voor hun baas deded, met te seggen 'Baas, mijn pas; ik wil trek.'

(On some farms there lie from ten to twenty Kaffirs who farm happily without having to stick their hands in cold water [i.e., without being in any discomfort]; they sow as much as they choose, and if their employer won't permit all this, then they come, as soon as their harvest is reaped, and without having done anything for their employer, to say 'Boss, my pass, I want to move on.')[37]

The 1890s also saw a wider incidence in the Free State of farming-on-the-halves.*

This was a form of share-cropping in which the white proprietor usually provided the seed and the land, African peasants farmed the grain, and the returns were shared. The division of the crop varied between the eponymous 'halves' and greater or lesser proportions; particularly in the years before the South African War, share-cropping agreements sometimes overlay or were intertwined with other forms of quasi-feudal relations: thus, the African 'sharer' might also have to render a number of days' labour upon a separate field, set aside as his employer's alone. The relationship was one which afforded the share-cropping peasant a decided advantage in the security of his tenure; inasmuch as his landlord was looking to the same crop for his own share of the returns, he was most unlikely suddenly to terminate the squatter-peasant's lease.

The practice provoked the specific complaint, from those who did not indulge in it, that it posed an economic threat to white farmers. One petition to the Volksraad in 1894 was signed by 100 farmers of the Ladysmith-Ficksburg region, and called for a restriction of share-cropping, as '*zoodanige kleurlingen in competitie komen met die blanke zaai of graan boeren*' (in that way coloureds [Africans] come into competition with white tillers or grain farmers) so that it was '*onmogelyk ... voor onze graanboeren tegen kleuringen en wel nog in*

---

* According to one correspondent, (*The Friend*, 2 April 1895) it was 'the general practice' by 1895. It is, however, clear that the incidence of sharing increased greatly after the war. See below, pp. 213–14.

ons eigen land te wedyveren' (impossible . . . for our white grain-farmers – and this even in our own country – to compete against coloureds). In the Raad, a member confessed himself 'perturbed' (*bevreesd*) that Africans '*de boeren langzamerhand zullen uitboeren. Kleuringen word nu al langzamerhand rijker dan blanken. Wij moeten onze burgers te hulp komen'* (would gradually outfarm the white farmers. Coloureds were gradually becoming richer than whites. We must come to the aid of our citizens).[38]

Africans in the Transvaal and Orange Free State were affected directly by the South African War in greater numbers than in the British colonies. Tens of thousands experienced enforced removals, the requisition of foodstuffs and stock, and the destruction of homes and crops. Over 108,000 Africans were settled by April 1902 in sixty-six refugee camps set up by the British military authorities. These camps were set up near railway lines, and the Africans encouraged to raise foodstuffs, with the intention of making the camps as nearly self-sufficient as possible. Surplus grain and forage were sold out of the camps to the military commissariat, and this offered many Africans in these camps an opportunity to accumulate cash during the war.[39] It was reported in August 1901 that 13,000 out of 46,000 refugee Africans were completely self-supporting, and that the remainder were producing enough food to have reduced the British Government's expenditure upon their welfare from $4\frac{1}{2}$d per head per day to less than 2d per head per day. The refugee peasants had been established upon deserted Boer farms along the railway line, where nearly 12,000 acres of maize and sorghum were sown. The officer in charge of 'Native Refugees' in the two republics explained that:

All mealies and kaffir corn grown are the property of the natives exclusively, and should naturally assist towards their own maintenance throughout the ensuing year, thus relieving the administration of a very large expenditure next year.

The natives have . . . been partially compensated for the loss of their crops, and for the hardships which state of war must inevitably bring about, by receiving free land, agricultural implements, seed, and a certain number of cattle on loan. Thus they have a fair chance of growing sufficient to enable them to return to their homes on the cessation of hostilities, with enough food to last them until the succeeding year's crop.[40]

A substantial number of Africans – the total varies from estimate to estimate, but may have been as high as 100,000 – simply settled during the war upon land vacated by 56,000 whites.[41] Their belief that after a British victory they would have access to the lands, and the dashing of these expectations, was a major factor in the 'restlessness and unusual excitement', the 'rather hostile attitude' and the 'unrest' that the Milner administration encountered immediately after the war.[42]

Another war-time experience shared by thousands of Africans was the opportunity for wage employment at greatly increased rates: reports frequently state that the wages were double or treble those prevailing in the Transvaal before the outbreak of war. This included work for the military authorities – as teamsters, drivers, grooms, ploughmen, police, porters and so on – as well as other employment.

Finally, Africans in the 'large locations' (notably in the Soutpansberg and in Lydenburg and Rustenburg-Marico) – who numbered perhaps half of the black population of the republic – had their experience of war confined to excitement, rumour, reports and disruptions in the routines of traders, tax-collectors and company rent-agents.

The opportunities for accumulation during the war – either from sales of produce at enhanced prices, or from the inflated wages – and the dissatisfaction with the political aftermath of war operated together with a cut in African wage-rates on the mines (from 50s to 30-35s a month) to precipitate an acute labour shortage in the Transvaal, lasting from 1901 to 1906.[43] The difficulty encountered by the Chamber of Mines recruiters was compounded by the availability of alternative and more attractive employment during the construction and transport boom of 1903–4. Many observers at the time ascribed the shortage of labour to the 'wealth' and 'independence' of the African peasantry. Milner's Commissioner for Native Affairs, Sir Godrey Lagden, wrote that 'from all reports made to me I now gather that the natives are in possession of means wherewith to purchase if required any food sufficient for their wants'. Even more emphatically, Beak argued that according to their 'own standards', Africans had become 'rich and independent' during the war, and 'sufficiently flush with cash to take a holiday'; by war's end, 'the position of the native on the whole was a more or less independent one. He was possessed of the wherewithal to purchase his requirements and he could afford to pick and choose in the kind of employment he was prepared to undertake.'[44] While one accepts Denoon's *caveat* that descriptions of the wealth of Africans were often exaggerated and sometimes groundless, it is patent that Africans in the Transvaal were granted a measure of extra economic leverage immediately after the war; they were more able to resist demands for their labour, especially labour in unattractive circumstances. The main complainants of labour shortage were white farmers and the mine-owners (and also Milner's own administration, for Africans refused to undertake the low-paid jobs on the agricultural repatriation schemes).

Certain other factors in the Transvaal also served to maintain the 'independence' of the peasantry. The first of these was the continued prevalence – indeed, the hey-day – of absentee proprietorship, and the opportunities this offered to squatter-peasants. The replacement of the Boer republic administrative system by the Milner 'reconstruction' government had as one of its by-products an increased freedom of movement for Africans; peasants responded to this by moving, in significant numbers, out of labour tenancies into rent-paying tenancies on the land of absentee proprietors, whether companies or individuals. (Of an African population of over 900,000 by 1904, no fewer than 438,000 were renting privately owned land; another 180,000 leased Crown Lands, and 130,000 farmed land that they owned. In other words, three-quarters of a million peasants in the Transvaal had access to land on terms more favourable than the 123,000 on Government locations or the 50,000 Africans in full-time employment.)

Further, the Milner administration, solicitous as it was of the needs of mining capital, was less sensitive to the demands of Afrikaner farmers in the Transvaal. Most notably, the administration actually made 'squatting' on Crown Lands more attractive and more accessible to Africans than it had been, presenting an alternative to labour tenancies on white farms. The liability to work was less onerous than for labour tenants, and the rent (£1 per annum) was considerably lower than the rent in cash, kind or labour paid to farmer landlords. H. H. Hall, a farmer in the Barberton district, said that no fewer than fifteen families had left his farm after the war and gone to 'government grounds': 'They say, why should they stay on my farm where they have to pay me 20s for living on my ground and work for me, and pay Government 40s as well, when they can simply go to the Government ground, where they pay 40s and work for nobody.'[45] Moreover, the Government was less diligent in collecting rents on Crown leases than Kruger's officials had been: spokesmen for the landowners Association protested to the Native Affairs Commission that many tenants were leaving private lands to settle on Crown Lands. As one official put it, 'the great complaint (of the Boers) has been ... that we have not compelled the native families to go out and live on the farms as they did before the war'.[46] Finally, Lagden did away with the tax differential that had discriminated in favour of farm labourers and against tenants.

Lagden's expressed reasons for refusing to apply existing anti-squatting provisions to tenants on Crown Lands are an interesting commentary upon the role of the peasantry within the Transvaal's economy: apart from the risk of driving Africans out of the territory, he explained, 'it would tend to place a good deal of land out of cultivation which is now of benefit to the country;' and, 'moreover the peasants produce a considerable amount of cereals, especially mealies, used for consumption in this country'.[47]

In the decade following the end of the war, several aspects of the rural economy of the Transvaal are noteworthy. There was clearly an upsurge in peasant agricultural activity, especially in the western, central and northern Transvaal; there are reports of large quantities of grain raised for consumption and sale. In addition to a general increase in production, there were also signs of specific responses to transport and market opportunities: these included transporting goods by wagon to rail heads, adopting a new strain of maize, and diversifying crops.[48] In one instance, peasants took political action to improve their access to a favourable market: in Pretoria, African food sellers protested about two unscrupulous produce dealers, and were rewarded by the appointment of two special constables in the market. Since that appointment – it was reported in 1910 – 'the Natives have regained confidence and, whereas in the past there were seldom more than six native waggons on the market, it is now not uncommon to see thirty or forty with native produce'.[49]

Another theme of the period was the keenness of Africans to hire or to purchase additional land. The ban on African land ownership was lifted; farms came onto the market because of losses or deaths during the war, and there was a flurry of purchases by Africans. General Piet Cronje understood the urge by peasants to acquire land, even while he disapproved of it; if an African could get a farm by paying £15 a year for it, and could earn £30, £40 or £50 out of that farm in the year, then they would see – he said – 'that it is much better for them to remain on the farm under these conditions rather than work for £1/10s per month'.[50] Others commented upon the determination by individual peasant farmers, particularly in the central and western Transvaal, to assert claims to individual tenure and to challenge the authority of the chiefs.[51]

The decade saw a growing awareness of the dangers to whites inherent in success by African agriculturists, both in terms of labour shortage and of competition. The Labour Commission concluded in 1904 that agricultural production by Africans 'would not only with-hold labour from industry, but will also bring them into competition with white agricultural producers', and warned that higher taxation was not an automatic response to the labour shortfall: 'It appears that the native meets pressure of this character in many instances by a greater output of agricultural produce.' Another succinct statement of the relationship between peasant production and white labour requirements was made by farmer-politician P. G. W. Grobler, MLA for Rustenburg: 'The natives at Mabalane hired land all over the place because the land was too small, and in that way they were absolutely independent and not compelled to go and work on a farm. There was no necessity for them to give their labour to a farmer.'[52] The threat of competition was expressed most often in terms of the plight of 'poor whites'. The status of the white *bywoner* declined and his access to land became increasingly precarious, as land became more commercially viable and as class differentiation in Afrikaner society deepened.[53] Fears were voiced that the black peasant, 'with his more thrifty habits and small wants is gradually ousting the poor white'; and failed white farmers sold out their property to Africans from whom they could get better prices than from struggling whites.[54] Officials and farmers said that Africans were doing 'decidedly' better at farming than poor whites; that 'taking them all round, the black man ... made the best living in the district;' and that at Haenertsberg, Africans had taken over the agricultural lots originally surveyed for whites to supply the gold fields with farm and garden produce.[55]

In short, the evidence for the years 1902–13 does confirm the impression, noted at the beginning of that decade, that 'the natives own large herds of cattle, and they are by far the greatest cultivators of land in the Transvaal', and that some squatter-peasants had 'become almost as rich as their masters'.[56] In years that favoured the spread of rent-paying tenancies, squatter-peasants enjoyed the advantages that their status gave them – advantages summed up by one W. A. King, Native Commissioner for the Pretoria district:

> My experience is that native squatters are invariably better off than natives living under service conditions: they pay, in many cases as much as £10 a year rent and they generally have lots of stock, whereas you find in the case of natives who are living and working on farms that they very rarely have any stock at all.[57]

Understandably, many peasants moved off 'labour farms' onto 'rent farms'.[58] In years during which the legal prohibition on African land purchases was briefly lifted, peasants sought every opportunity to buy land so that they could live by agriculture rather than labour for others: as the chief Mogale of Rustenburg district told the South African Native Affairs Commission:

> Mogale: ... we are trying to buy the farm we live on....
> Commissioner: How do you live: do you plough and get crops and sell the crops?
> M: If we have enough crops we sell, and when we have not enough we have nothing to sell.
> C: Then how do you live?
> M: We labour.
> C: Where?
> M: All over the towns, wherever we can obtain work....
> C: Why do you want to purchase land?
> M: So that we may live.
> C: In what way?
> M: By cultivation and farming, and so as to be able to build.[59]

In years during which the reconstruction administration relaxed certain of the controls imposed by the Boer state over the Transvaal's black population, African peasants were swift to pursue opportunities and to reap what gains they could. Witness after witness told the 1904 Commission that peasants were 'independent', had access to 'an undue amount of arable land', and so on.[60]

Nevertheless, the impression should not be derived that the African peasantry was enjoying a period of uninterrupted prosperity and progress. Apart from those already proletarianized, and apart from the 25,000 or so who left the land each year to seek work on a temporary basis, many peasants were keenly aware of other pressures during this decade. One common form of pressure and source of insecurity (bitterly attested to by African witnesses in these years) was the danger that lay in improving lands that were only rented, and not owned: all too often this led either to higher rents or to expropriation. 'When they have built their houses and improved the land, they are ejected at a month's notice. This has been done again and again. I know this to be true' wrote a missionary.[61]

Another source of pressure upon peasants was the desire of some white farmers to commercialize their holdings and operations. 'Now times are changed,' wrote a magistrate in 1913, 'and the method of farming already having become more advanced ... the white farmers will want their own land more and more for their own operations.' This meant that such 'improving' white farmers would wish to see any Africans resident upon their lands there as labourers or labour tenants, and not as lessees or share-croppers: 'Before the war the farmers farmed with stock – sheep and cattle – but now they are ploughing and growing cereals, and ... as agriculturists they require more labourers than they do as pastoralists.'[62]

In the first half dozen years after the end of the War, black peasants profited from the conflict of interests between the owners of 'rent estates' (the companies and other absentee proprietors) and Boer producers, inasmuch as the desire of the former for a rent income offered to the peasantry a wide choice of land on quasi-feudal terms. The 1907 electoral victory for Louis Botha and *Het Volk* in the Transvaal was also a victory for Afrikaans farmers, most especially, the wealthier and modernizing amongst them. The scales of political influence in the Transvaal countryside were tipped in their favour in 1907, and the new balance confirmed in the accommodation – in the form of Union in 1910 – between the Imperial Government and South Africa's new rulers. The re-assertion by Afrikaans farmers in the Transvaal of political power was marked almost immediately, by a series of moves against the independence of the share-cropper and the rent-paying squatter-peasant. The 1908 Natives Tax Act imposed a levy of £2 on 'squatters', while labour tenants were wooed with a tax of only £1.[63] In the northern districts, rent squatters were removed from some farms by direct governmental action in 1909 and 1910. (Significantly, these and other anti-squatting measures in the Transvaal were welcomed by farmers but opposed by absentee landowners.)[64] In 1911 and 1912, the revived anti-squatter legislation of 1895 as well as the 1908 Act were pressed in central and northern districts, and by their very nature they attacked those squatter-peasants who had most to lose. A. Burnett, a Methodist missionary and active participant in Transvaal politics, wrote in September 1912 that: 'In the Vereeniging and Heidelberg districts it will at once break up some of our most prosperous Native churches.'[65]

All this sniping was succeeded by the heavy artillery of the 1913 Natives Land Act. Despite the concentration by most historians upon the prohibition of land purchase by Africans in 'white' areas, and the demarcation of 13 per cent of the surface area as 'Native Reserves', an extremely important function of the Act was the reduction of rent-paying squatters and share-croppers to the level of labour tenants. Pressure for the Act, Francis Wilson has found, came almost entirely 'from those who wished to ensure a cheap supply of labour, by eliminating squatters and by doing away with the system of farming-on-the-half'.[66]

The Act and its intentions are of virtually unparalleled importance in twentieth-century South African history. Apart from the pursuit of the aim already described, the transformation of quasi-feudal relations 'from above', the framers of the law served several other interests. The closing of the free market in land served to soothe white fears – expressed frequently throughout the previous decade – about the amount of land purchased by Africans. (Nor is it correct to suggest, as is sometimes done, that they were empty fears: as Horwitz said of SANAC's warnings on land purchases by Africans, they reflected the reality that the process of economic development was facilitating acquisition by *some* Africans of white-owned land.)[67] In addition, the ban on purchases outside the Reserves had important implications for the population within the Reserves. By preventing the most obvious form of accumulation open to successful black peasants, it sought to apply a brake to the process of class differentiation in African rural areas, thus inhibiting the growing group of small commercial farmers (potential competitors with white farmers, as well as displacers of indigent *bywoners*). It sought to 'freeze' social relations in the Reserves, so as to avoid the creation of a permanently landless majority of Africans, whose urbanization would have further drained the supply of rural labour, as well as posing a potential political threat.

A separate chapter on the 1913 Act specifically outlawed farming-on-the-halves in the Orange Free State; wrote Goodfellow fifteen years later, ' "To put it quite bluntly," as was said at the time, "the natives have become too rich." '[68] It has already been mentioned that share-cropping in the Free State was well established in the 1890s; but the major flowering of the system took place immediately after the South African war. White Free Staters were impoverished;[69] many African peasants, on the other hand, returned – from Basutoland and other non-combatant areas, or from wage labour, or from their farming operations along the rail line to Bloemfontein – with ploughs and with cattle. Two Ladybrand farmers explained to the 1903–5 Commission that (although they personally disapproved of sharing) they would not call for its prohibition 'because ... there are hundreds of boys

[Africans] that have gone to Basutoland with their wagons and things... and their masters are only too glad to have them back' as in many cases the African's cattle would be the only span of oxen upon the farm.[70] There was, writes Van Rensburg, an almost total labour shortage in the Orange Free State until 1903 or 1904;[71] farmers, unable to get Africans to work for them as labour tenants, entered instead into share-cropping arrangements.

It is impossible to assess exactly how many of the 224,000 Africans in the Orange Free State were share-cropping by 1913 (although only 17,000 of that total lived in the two 'reserved' areas, and perhaps 5,000 in towns, so that the great bulk of the black population lived on white-owned farms in some or other capacity). Few white owners of land would admit to official enquiries that they were permitting the system; but, as the most authoritative commission on the subject concluded, there was 'a considerable body of Natives who have for years – some of them for all their lives' farmed on shares.[72] In some districts, but most particularly the entire eastern Orange Free State – the districts of Ficksburg, Ladybrand, Harrismith, Winburg, Vrede, Bothaville and Bethlehem – the share-cropping system was the pre-dominant social relationship; half-sharing was the experience of the majority of Africans there.

Individual share-croppers, in the words of the policeman quoted by Sol Plaatje, grew 'fairly comfortable, if not rich and enjoyed the possession of their stock, living in many instances just like Dutchmen'.[73] Other contemporary evidence confirms this impression. Africans were using 'up-to-date machinery' in their agriculture in most districts of the Free State, it was reported in 1910; from Bethlehem, Edenburg, Ficksburg, Harrismith, Ladybrand, Bothaville and Vrede came details of the sales of surplus crops. Share-croppers sold directly to produce merchants, and received the same prices as European growers; they ran large flocks of sheep and goats and herds of cattle.[74] (Thirty-nine well off squatter-peasants who protested in person to the Heilbron magistrate against the operations of the 1913 Act owned, between them, 858 cattle, 111 horses and 2,000 sheep.)[75] While maize and sorghum were also reaching the produce dealers from African peasants, the trend was observed from several districts that wheat was being grown as a cash crop, and maize and sorghum for consumption. The ability of the squatter-peasant to withhold his labour, except in return for higher wages, and his ability to choose upon which lands to live, contributed directly to the punitive measures of the Native Lands Act.

In the Orange Free State as elsewhere in South Africa, a crucial source of change in the years immediately before and immediately after 1910 was the desire of white farmers to commercialize their own farming – to alter the form of surplus expropriation on their lands from quasi-feudal to capitalist. Share-cropping had offered a modicum of income to both whites and blacks in an area savagely dealt with by the war; the attractiveness of the relationship – to whites – declined *pari passu* with the rise of opportunities to profit from commercial agriculture. The objections to the shares system in the Free State came overwhelmingly from commercializing farmers: as R. Harley, magistrate of Winburg, summed it up, 'It is the progressive farmer who objects to the system.' He did so because he appreciated that 'the land is getting more valuable', because since the war the agricultural department had been bringing to his notice the advantages of intensive farming, and because there was 'less and less inclination to allow natives with appreciable herds to come on his farm'.[76] White maize farmers responded more urgently than any other producers, and this was largely due to the reduction, in 1907, of the rail rates to the ports for export maize. This was the first in a series of incentives and subsidies to white maize farmers that was to transform their agriculture.[77] The portion of the Orange Free State that was to become part of the 'maize triangle' (celebrated in South African school geography books) was the same area that had seen a particular form of quasi-feudal relations most widely developed, and African squatter-peasants most firmly and prosperously established.

The transformation of the maize-producing Free State was in essence the transformation of its African population from squatter-peasants of substance to farm labourers: a process in which 'a man was reduced from being a farmer in his own account to a servant at one stroke'.[78] It was perhaps the most dramatic instance of the rise and fall of a peasant community in South Africa, and one of the clearest illustrations of the role of extra-economic coercion in the accumulation and control of capital by white interests in the country. It also demonstrates a more general phenomenon: the greater rapidity of capitalist development in the Transvaal and the Orange Free State in comparison to that of the Cape. Social and economic processes described in the Cape were replicated in the northern provinces in speeded-up form, and this had a dual consequence. First, for those peasants who were affected by economic and political changes, the decline in their fortunes would be sudden and dramatic, as for the share-croppers in the Free State. On the other hand, the very rapidity of capitalist development (particularly in the Transvaal) meant that it was often very difficult for the whites concerned – be they mine-owners or farmers – to effect the social changes they desired. There was a 'lag', for instance, between much of the anti-squatting legislation (and including the 1913 Act) and its effective implementation in large portions of the Transvaal where quasi-feudal relationships enjoyed so tenacious an existence.

In conclusion and recapitulation, much of what has been outlined in this chapter of the history of the peasantry in the Transvaal and the Free State is encapsulated in a single case history. In it one can observe the existence of a small peasant community, upon a farm in the

215

neighbourhood of Springs, in the central Transvaal: the peasants' initial establishment upon the land of absentee proprietors, their ability to raise agricultural output to meet rent obligations, their participation in the produce market, the rising cost of their existence as changes in land tenure reflected changes in the locus of political power, the burden that the 1913 Act imposed upon squatter-peasants, and, finally, the dispersal and decline of the community.

> The farm is the property of a land company. Before the South African war about twenty Bakgatla families lived on the farm and each paid £10 per annum in rent. By arrangement among themselves they ploughed the arable lands and were allowed the rest of the farm for pasturage. In a good year an industrious tenant could raise two hundred bags of mealies and sell them at fifteen to eighteen shillings a bag. Between 1903 and 1913 the Company rented the farm to European farmers and the Natives were retained on the half-share system. They still continued to plough with their own ploughs and oxen, but the result of the new arrangement was that in a good year their rent of half-share went up to the neighbourhood of £70 or £80 instead of the £10 previously paid. In 1913 or soon afterwards the farmers called the Natives together and told them that the half-share system had come to an end, and if they wished to remain on the farm they would be given a few morgen to plough for themselves, but that they must now plough the rest of the lands for the farmers with their own ploughs and oxen and that for the pasturage of their cattle they must be prepared to do the transport of produce to the market.
>
> This was a great blow to all the Natives. Half of them refused the new arrangement and went off to seek better terms on other farms. We have traced the history of one of the most prosperous of them. He first found a place as a squatter for two years until new terms of service were dictated to him, and he went to another farm for three years and then to the Vischkuil Colliery farm for another three years. He is now on another farm as a servant giving 90 days service, not consecutive days, but spread out over half the year. He gets no wage. His own ploughing and skoffeling has to be done after he has done the farmer's and often too late to secure a decent harvest. He is not allowed to keep any cows, sheep or goats, and only such oxen as are useful to the farmer....
>
> Some of the Natives remained on the farm to see how the new arrangement would work. Very few of the original occupants are there today. There are ten families there at present but they come and go. In a bad year food is short and the people have to borrow food from the farmer and pay for it by extra labour in the following year.
>
> There has been a steady decline in the last 25 years in the economic status and condition of the farm Natives.[79]

NOTES

1 L. Thompson, 'Co-operation and Conflict: The High Veld', OHSA, I, 414–15, 424.

2 S. Marks, 'African and Afrikaner History', *Journal of African History*, XI, 3 (1970), 435–47.

3 P. Bonner, 'Aspects of the Political Economy of the Transvaal, 1846–1873', unpublished paper delivered at Roma Conference on Southern African Historiography, summer 1977.

4 Thompson, OHSA, I, 435.

5 L. Thompson, 'The Subjection of the African Chiefdoms, 1870–1898', OHSA, II, 245–84, especially 281–4.

6 Roy. Comm. Soc. Lib., Mss 55V, F. J. Newnham, 'Transvaal Native Locations History', unpublished typescript, 1908. (Newnham was Secretary to the Native Locations Commission of 1905–6.)

7 M. Legassick, 'South Africa: Capital Accumulation and Violence', *Economy and Society,* 3 (August 1974), 253–91, 261.

8 S. Trapido, 'The South African Republic: Class Formation and the State, 1850–1900', ICS, CSP, No. 16, Vol. 3 (London, 1973), 53–65.

9 PRO, CO 879/13, Conf. Print Afr. No. 156, 'Report on the Province of Transvaal' by W. C. Sargeaunt, 15.

10 SPG Arch., D MSS, T. E. Wilkinson to Secty, USPG, 10 June 1874. For details of Sotho-Tswana trade prior to the Great Trek, see M. Legassick, 'The Sotho-Tswana peoples before 1800' in L. Thompson (ed.), *African Societies in Southern Africa* (London, 1969), 86–125, esp. 107–9.

11 R. J. Atcherley, *A Trip to Boerland, Or a Year's Travel, Sport and Gold-digging in the Transvaal and Colony of Natal* (London, 1879), 190–1.

12 MMS Arch., Box Transvaal 1885, J. W. Underwood to Kilner, 22 August 1885.

13 SPG Arch., E MSS, E39, C. Clulee to Secty, USPG, 30 June 1884 (emphasis in the original).

14 E. Holub, *Seven Years in South Africa* 2 vols. (London, 1881), I, 164–6.

15 Mrs Heckford, *A Lady Trader in the Transvaal* (London, 1882), 249–50, 256, 258, 289–90.

16 PRO, CO 879/16, Conf. Print Afr. No. 204, encl. No. 6 in desp. No. 4, 14 March 1879. (Rustenburg continued to be the Transvaal district in which Africans bought most land; by 1904, 387,730 acres were held there by black proprietors; see *Transvaal Annual Reports*, Nat. Aff. Dept., 1903–4.)

17 *Report by the Commissioner for Native Affairs relating to the acquisition and tenure of Land by Natives in the Transvaal, July 1904* (Pretoria, 1904), 22.

18 MMS Arch., Box Transvaal 1881–4, G. Weavind, 9 April 1883, and J. G. Benson, 17 September 1884.

19 Newnham, 'Transvaal Native Locations History', loc. cit., p. 3. Cf. Newnham, 'Native Land Tenure in South Africa', *United Empire*, Vol. 1, 721–8, 797–804, p. 797: missionaries sometimes claimed that the assistance that they had rendered gave them freehold right of usufructuary interests over parts of the farm.

20 SPG Arch., E 38, 1883, 21 March 1883.

21 Diocese of Pretoria, *Occasional Paper No. XII*, February 1887 (Pretoria 1887), 22–9.

22 SPG Arch., E MSS, E41, 1886, C. Clulee, 30 June 1886.

23 SPG Arch., E MSS, E45, 1890, T. A. Thompson, Springvale, Natal, 31 December 1890.
24 SPG Arch., E MSS, 1892, Vol. II, 24 December 1892; 1893, Vol. II, 31 March 1893; 1894, Vol. II, 31 March 1894.
25 W. C. Holden, *A Brief History of Methodism and of Methodist Missions in South Africa* (London, 1877), 387.
26 G. J. Lamprecht, 'Die Ekonomiese Ontwikkeling van die Vrystaat van 1870–1899' (Stellenbosch University, D.Phil. thesis, 1954), 140.
27 ibid., 3–40.
28 H. J. Van Aswegen, 'Die Verhouding tussen Blank en nie-Blank in die Oranje-Vrystaat, 1854–1902' (University of O.F.S., D.Phil. thesis, 1968), 340–45, 469–506.
29 U.G. 22–'14, *Beaumont Commission,* 41.
30 Van Aswegen, op. cit., 492 (and see also 493–500), 535.
31 ibid., 544.
32 Newnham, 'Transvaal Native Locations History', 3, 4, 5, 19.
33 Trapido, 'The SAR: Class Formation and the State'.
34 J. S. Marais, 'African Squatting on European Farms in South Africa, with Particular Reference to the Cape Colony (1892–1913)' (Inst. Comm. Stud. Library, London, unpublished seminar paper).
35 D. J. N. Denoon, *A Grand Illusion: The Failure of Imperial Policy in the Transvaal Colony during the period of Reconstruction, 1900–1905* (London, 1973); R. Horwitz, *The Political Economy of South Africa* (London, 1967), 39.
36 *Rapport van den Superintendent van Naturellen, 1892–1898,* State Library Pretoria Reprint No. 14 (Pretoria, 1969), report for 1897, 2. Cf. 1893, 3, and appendices E and F; 1894, 3; 1895, 3.
37 Van Aswegen, op. cit., 362–6, 508–56, 556–7.
38 ibid., 576, 580–81.
39 G. B. Beak, *The Aftermath of War: An Account of the Repatriation of Boers and Natives in the Orange River Colony, 1902–1904* (London, 1906), 26–8, and P. Warwick, 'The African Refugee Problem in the Transvaal and Orange River Colony, 1900–1902', *Southern African Research in Progress: Collected Papers,* 2, (Centre for Southern African Studies, University of York, 1977), 61–81.
40 PRO, CO 224/7, 25144, Milner to Chamberlain, 30 May 1902, encl. No. 7 in report by Maj. G. J. de Lotbiniere, Officer i/c Native Refugees.
41 *Report . . . relating to the acquisition and tenure of land by Natives, 1904,* 2.
42 The phrases are taken from the Transvaal NAD's Annual Reports for 1903–4, A1, B18.
43 See D. J. N. Denoon, 'The Transvaal Labour Crisis, 1901–06', *Jnl. Afr. Hist.,* VII, 3 (1967), 481–94. For a contemporary enquiry and voluminous evidence on the shortage, see BPP, XXXIX, 1904, *Reports of the Transvaal Labour Commission,* Cd. 1896, and *Minutes of the Proceedings and Evidence,* Cd. 1897.
44 Colony of the Transvaal, NAD, *Report by the Commissioner for Native Affairs,* Transvaal Admin. Reports for 1902, Part I (Pretoria, 1903), 8; Beak, *Aftermath,* 137, 160.
45 *Transvaal Labour Commission,* Cd. 1897, 199.

46 SANAC, IV, 455.
47 Report . . . relating to the acquisition and tenure of land by Natives, 4; NAD, Report for 1903–4, B18.
48 See NAD, Report for 1908–9, 32–5; U.G. 17–'11, Dept. Nat. Aff. Bluebook for 1910, 149–52.
49 U.G. 17–'11, BBNA for 1910, 152 (and compare the description of African marketing procedures in Pretoria during 1885, quoted p. 201, note 12).
50 Transvaal Labour Commission, Cd. 1897, 277.
51 SANAC, IV, 427–30; Transvaal NAD, Report 1905–6, B44, B54.
52 Transvaal Labour Commission, Cd. 1896, 41, 38; Beaumont Commission, 264.
53 See Trapido, 'SAR: Class Formation and State'.
54 U. G. 17–'11, BBNA for 1910, 341, 48, 340; Beaumont Commission, 333.
55 T. G. 13–'08, Report of the Transvaal Indigency Commission, 1906–08, (evidence of the Native Commissioner for Rustenburg and the Manager of Beerlaagte Settlement): SANAC, IV, 80 (evidence of G. G. Munnik of Zoutpansberg Boeren Vereeninging).
56 W. Bleloch, The New South Africa and its Development (London, 1902), 226–7.
57 Beaumont Commission, 274.
58 ibid., 340–68.
59 SANAC, IV, 650–2.
60 Transvaal Labour Commission, Cd. 1897, 217, 233, 234, 277, 294, 346, et al.
61 MMS Arch., Box Transvaal 1881–86, 1885 file, O. Watkins, 28 July 1885; cf. U.G. 17–'11, BBNA for 1910, 152.
62 Beaumont Commission, 261, 289
63 Marais, 'African squatting on European farms'.
64 U.G. 17–'11, BBNA for 1910, 48.
65 MMS Arch., Box 1913–18, 1913 file, A. Burnett, 16 September 1912.
66 F. Wilson, 1866–1966', OHSA, II, 129. And cf. P. G. Dickson, 'The Native Lands Act, 1913: Its Antecedents, Passage, and Reception' (University of Cape Town, M.A. thesis, 1970), esp. 119–24: in January 1913, 13 petitions from the Orange Free State and Transvaal called for a law making half-sharing or leasing of land to Africans illegal.
67 Horwitz, Political Economy of South Africa, 39.
68 D. M. Goodfellow, A Modern Economic History of South Africa (London, 1931), 232.
69 For details of the devastation caused by the war in the Free State, see Beak, op. cit., 14–20.
70 Beaumont Commission, 41; SANAC, IV, 339.
71 A. P. T. Van Rensburg, 'Die Ekonomiese Herstel van die Afrikaner in die Oranjerivier-Kolonie, 1902–1907' (University of O.F.S., D.Phil. thesis, 1964), 362–4.
72 U.G. 26–'16, Report of the Beaumont Commission (Minute), 3–4.
73 S. T. Plaatje, Native Life in South Africa (London, n.d.), 66.
74 U.G. 17–'11, BBNA for 1910, 53, 127–9; cf. Beaumont Commission, 9, 10, 35, App. XI, 3, 4, 6, 7; SANAC, IV, 309.
75 Beaumont Commission, 35.

76 ibid., 2.
77 Wilson, 'Farming', OHSA, II, 135, 138, 165.
78 *Beaumont Commission,* 36 (evidence of H. Reading, magistrate of Heilbron).
79 U.G. 22–1932, *Report of the Native Economic Commission, 1930–32,* 199–200 (statement submitted to Commission by Archdeacon Hill, of Springs).

8

Aftermath and Conclusions

1 AFTER 1913: RESERVES BECOME BANTUSTANS

The narrative has been carried to 1913, and the passage of the Natives Land Act. The argument has been advanced that by that date African peasant areas showed serious signs of agrarian degeneration, and that their transformation into teeming rural slums – or the process of their underdevelopment – was well under way. Areas that had been able to provide for themselves, and in favourable seasons to export foodstufs, were being reduced to a state of precarious self-reliance or already to a dependence upon imported food and the remittance of wages by migrant labourers. There exists a vast and depressing body of evidence as to the nature and extent of underdevelopment in the Reserves (and particularly the Ciskei and Transkei) in the forty years that followed the 1913 Act:[1] the details abound of infant mortality, malnutrition, diseases and debility; of social dislocation expressed in divorce, illegitimacy, prostitution and crime; of the erosion, desiccation and falling fertility of the soil; and of the ubiquity of indebtedness and material insufficiency of the meanest kind. The cumulative effect of these features is not easily described; life moulded by them was not lightly endured. It is small wonder that the past is invoked as an idealized and golden age:

> Before the white man came, we had plenty of land and stock. Our children were obedient to us. ... We lived according to our customs and were healthy and strong. It is only since the white men came to rule over us that things have changed, that everything is death for us now. We speak of the dead as those who have run away from the Poll Tax.[2]

In the light of the body of evidence already mentioned, it is not necessary strenuously to argue the case for the underdevelopment of the African Reserve areas: it remains only to illustrate and identify its main characteristics.

There was in the 1920s a shocked, and in the 1930s a widening, realization of the state of the Reserve areas; a series of graphic descriptions (and rather less precise prescriptions) appeared. In his pioneering articles for the *Cape Times* and in several other writings, Macmillan summarized his own findings in unambiguous and sombre language: 'The Natives of the Union as a whole are dragging along at the very

221

lowest level of bare subsistence.' In his *Complex South Africa,* he documented a wide range of social and economic ills in the Reserves. Africans there were 'immeasurably poorer' than they had been; they lived in 'poverty congestion and chaos', blighted by 'ill-health, and starvation, endemic typhus, and almost chronic scurvy'; they suffered 'an often appalling mortality rate among infants'; they lived in 'heavily over-populated' and 'grossly neglected' areas where they were 'utterly dependent on wage-earning outside' to relieve 'a dead level of poverty' inside.[3]

Macmillan's assertions were underlined and his warnings reiterated by the Native Economic Commission of 1932: the commissioners (commented Hancock) 'could not find adjectives enough' to describe the desolation. They spoke of the descent of the Reserves 'at a rapid pace' towards 'desert conditions', and said that the 'process of ruination' threatened 'an appalling problem of Native poverty'.[4] When the focus was narrowed to the study of individual districts, the images remained constant. Macmillan's survey of Herschel has been summarized already; in another Ciskei district, Victoria East, a senior official told Henderson of Lovedale in 1928 that

> I have no hesitation in saying that the Natives of this district are not making any progress. They are steadily going back, and I should say that their economic condition as people is deplorable, and, as a whole, they are hopelessly in debt. Most of them live in a state of semi-starvation.[5]

A study of Elliotdale, in the Eastern Transkei, concluded that 'Poverty, a bare subsistence at a low level', was 'the outstanding fact in the present economic situation', and that that situation was 'moving steadily in the direction of greater and greater poverty'.[6] Economists,[7] missionaries and educationists,[8] and also physicians[9] and others bore corroborative witness.

If one moves from general descriptions of the process taking place to some details of the actual changes observed, a valuable starting point is the survey in Victoria East (and it was stressed that the district was typical of the Ciskei as a whole) carried out by James Henderson.[10] He compared the available statistics of African consumption and production in the district for the year 1875 (figures collected by an unusually energetic and articulate magistrate, Percy Nightingale) with details provided by the Civil Commissioner in 1925. Henderson's abridged conclusions are set out in Table 5. The financial returns from peasant agricultural production (as Table 5 shows) had fallen by 46 per cent while the population engaged in agriculture had more than doubled. The sale of produce had ceased to provide the bulk of the income for those living on the land; it also failed by 1925 to provide sufficient food for subsistence: the proportion of the income spent on food had risen from under 20 per cent to over 60 per cent. In 1875 traders told Nightingale that the 'Native trade is for cash ... they put down their money for what they want to buy. A Native will very rarely ask for credit.' In 1925 (Henderson learnt from a trader) Africans bought on credit by preference; only fifteen per cent were really creditworthy; 'this is mainly due to poverty'.[11]

TABLE 5

Declining peasant production in Victoria East, 1875–1925

	1875	*1925*
Total African population	6,900	15,800
Population with access to land	5,600	12,000
Sales of peasant produce:		
wool	£12,541	£6,471
hides, skins, horns	2,457	1,728
grains	4,275	2,177
total	19,273	10,376
Average sales per (average) family of six:	£20/12/0	£4/8/9
Purchases of traders' goods:		
clothes, blankets	£12,000	£4,792
farm tools, furniture, etc.	4,784	2,508
food, groceries	4,289	12,748
total	21,073	20,048
Average purchases per (average) family of six:	£20/2/0	£9/5/5

(Abridged from *South African Outlook,* 1 July 1927)

How firmly embedded these tendencies were in the Ciskei was confirmed by the *Keiskammahoek Rural Survey,* carried out between 1949 and 1951. Traders in that district sold goods worth £136,000 to Africans – and peasant produce earned only £8,000. Even an 'exceptionally good year's harvest' provided only enough food for half the nutritional requirements of the district; in poor years it provided one-twentieth. Four of the five villages surveyed spent an average of 62 per cent of their income on food; the sample as a whole just under 60 per cent.[12] (An unpublished study of trade in the district, carried out alongside the major survey, established that over 90 per cent of all expenditure by Ciskeians was on 'the bare necessaries of life'; and that investment in any forms of agricultural improvement was negligible: building materials, metals and wire, machinery and tools, and chemicals and fertilizers *together* amounted to 2 per cent of all spending.)[13]

Studies based upon Transkei data during the 1930s strongly suggested that agriculture there was stagnant or in decline, that peasant families spent an average of a fifth to a quarter of their income on food,[14] that debt was endemic,[15] and that migrant labour persisted at a high, steady level. When a Native Commissioner was sent from Kenya in 1931 to examine the workings of the Glen Grey system in the Transkei with a view to introducing a similar system in Kikuyu areas, he was quite obviously taken aback by the low level of productivity and the high rate of migrancy in the Transkei. He sat in on a couple of sessions of the 1932 Native Economic Commission's hearings, and referred several times in his own report to evidence that made it plain that without migrant wages the entire economy of the Transkei would collapse. He concluded that in the 'straight jacket' of the 'one man one lot' system 'no considerable or permanent improvement in the standard of living' was possible, and anticipated 'an intensification rather than an alleviation of the difficulties of subsistence'.[16]

Underlying this pattern (its features even more deeply etched in the Ciskei than in the Transkei) were three mutually reinforcing and fundamentally unfavourable factors: falling yields, an increasing scarcity of resources and heightened competition for them, and a migrant labour level so high as seriously to deplete the agricultural work force. Various estimates of the fall in African peasant production use different bases or criteria, but from them a broadly consistent picture emerges. A 1944 Union Government report showed that in the African Reserves in all four provinces production of both the staple grains, maize and sorghum, declined in the period between the end of the First and the beginning of the Second World War. Another report published in 1946 detailed the fall in production of both grains between 1934 and 1939.[17] Roux expressed the same truth in a different form. For the decade 1921–30, the annual average production of maize by Africans on Reserve and mission lands was 640 million lb; for the decade 1931–9, it was 490 million lb. In the same periods, the annual average production of white farmers rose from 2,900 million lb to 3,300 million lb.[18] In the Transkei alone, the production of grain was estimated to have declined by about 25 per cent during the 1930s. Between 1939 and 1942, the Transkei had to import an average of 187,000 bags of grain (about 13 per cent of its total requirements) per year.[19]

The scarcity of resources was most urgently felt, and is most dramatically illustrated, in the pressure on arable land. R. W. Norton, who had been Assistant Director of Native Agriculture for the Ciskei, offered this judgement: 'Nearly one third of all families have no arable land. The average land-holder works what is, under the climatic conditions obtaining in the Ciskei, a sub-economic unit of land. He owns ... sub-economic numbers of stock. Above him is a relatively small favoured class of bigger owners.'[20] While some men owned over a hundred cattle and as many as a thousand sheep (he continued), over

60 per cent of the population owned five or fewer cattle, and 29 per cent owned no cattle at all. Jokl's estimate for the Transkei* suggested that about 5 per cent of the population owned one third of the livestock; a Government report in 1946 found that 44 per cent of the families in the Transkei owned no cattle. 'Thousands of families in the Reserves,' it said, 'not only own no land, but also possess no stock.'[21] (In seven Transkei districts, all of which had been surveyed under the provisions of the Glen Grey Act, over 11,000 married hut owners paid tax and owned no land.)[22] Ten years after the 1946 report, the Tomlinson Commission reported that 12·7 per cent of the families in the Reserves earned 46·3 per cent of the total income accrued inside these areas.[23]

Finally, the high level of migrant labour among adult males in peasant communities meant that the level of economic activity possible upon family holdings was seriously depleted. According to the 1936 Census Report, about 54 per cent of the adult male population of the Reserves was absent; or, expressed another way, in the Transkei 'practically every available fit labourer enters upon a term of employment within a period of two years'.[24] In the Ciskei, the sharp rise in the migration of adult women workers between 1936 and 1946 meant that the 'home' population became even more skewed: over half of the 'permanent' Keiskammahoek population consisted of those too old, too young or too ill to earn wages. In all the Reserve areas, those who remained at home *and* were fit bore an added burden of dependency; those not fully able, but pressed into agricultural work, performed fitfully and feebly. Ploughing with cattle, in areas where the masculinity ratio was abnormally low, was neglected so that arable land again fell under the hoe and *skoffel*.[25]

It was by the 1940s almost impossible to be unaware of the dearth in the Reserves. (But only 'almost': the Chamber of Mines, in its evidence to the Mine Wages Committee, was assiduously constant to an image of the 'attractive and healthy individual existence of the Native and his family in the reserves'. The Native's 'independent position as peasant farmer and stock holder', the Chamber explained, assured him of 'his prolonged holiday at home'; was there, ran the statement's peroration, 'any other body of workers in the world so fortunately placed?')[26] By the 1940s the indices of falling crop production, rising pressures on resources, and shrinking per capita real income were also manifested in terms of deficiencies, diseases and deaths. The first report of the National Nutritional Council stated that:

> The pellagra ... group of diseases is on the increase. ... There are also more general signs of the lack of food. The thin, round-shouldered, flat-chested, pot-bellied child with spindly legs was such a common sight that it could only be concluded that many were on the borders of starvation.

* Cited on p. 128, n. 56.

There was a 40 per cent *higher* death rate in the Reserve areas in 1936 than there had been in 1921, and the same report commented:

> One of the most striking features about health conditions in the Native reserves is the prevalence of debilitating conditions. ... It is also noteworthy that practically all diseases prevalent in the Native reserves are associated with malnutrition and personal poverty ... they are all preventable.[27]

In the Umtata district, nearly 50 per cent of the babies born died before reaching the age of two years; in Keiskammahoek, the mortality rate was 453 deaths per 1000 births: of the total deaths in the district, no fewer than 94 per cent were of children of sixteen years and younger.[28]

In sum, by the time that the Tomlinson Commission was appointed and made its lengthy investigation during the early fifties, a crisis point had been reached in the Reserve areas. The Tomlinson recommendations (discussed below) sought to ensure at least some level of subsistence for migrant workers, and to revivify agricultural production: these aims had already been pursued in the late 1930s and 1940s, and the manner in which Professor Tomlinson proposed to extend them was a measure of the urgency of the crisis. Certainly, the 'homelands' or 'Bantustan' policies of the Verwoerd-Vorster years cannot adequately be explained without reference to the necessity of controlling, halting or reversing an underdevelopment so severe that it menaced even the Reserves' capacity to maintain and reproduce a migrant labour force.

The policy of the National Party since 1948 with respect to agriculture in the Reserve areas is inextricably bound up with the development of its programme that began with the Bantu Authorities Act (1951) and has matured in the Bantustan schema. The Bantu Authorities Act was the corollary to the dismantling of the Natives Representative Council, and its implementation during the fifties was a logical accompaniment to the state's determination to defeat the African nationalist movement and to deny its leadership's claim to represent the black majority. The Act delegated a good deal of local administrative authority to 'traditional' African leadership through a formal hierarchy of chiefs and headmen. These latter became an arm of the governmental apparatus; their power and status were no longer derived from nor checked by* the workings of a redistributive economy. Although individual chiefs were to provide leadership in acts or campaigns of resistance to aspects of state policy, the tendency was for these 'uncooperative' chiefs to be disciplined or set aside. The rest became salaried officers of the white state.

* 'Many of the chiefs who gained power under the new system have been extremely unpopular. Charges of corruption are continually made. The control of the commoners over the chiefs which existed traditionally diminished ... formerly an unpopular chief lost his following. ... The unpopular chief is maintained in office by force exercised by the Government of the Republic.' (M. Wilson, OHSA.)

The Promotion of Bantu Self-Government Act (1959) and the subsequent articulation of Bantustan policy elevated the local administrative authorities into semi-autonomous 'governments'; transferred the burden of certain social welfare costs and of unemployment from 'white' urban areas to the homelands; and provided the framework for a specific form of economic development and modernization. At the ideological level it legitimized bureaucratic violence, a grievous level of regionalized poverty and a continuing monopoly by whites of participation in the Republic's politics by the concepts of Separate Development and the rodomontade of 'independence' celebrations in Umtata and Mafeking.[29]

The use of a (transformed and untraditional) traditional elite to exercise social control of the mass of the Reserve population has occurred alongside the state's efforts to improve the parlous economic state of the Reserves. Wolpe has defined *apartheid,* including separate development, as the 'mechanism specific to South Africa in the period of secondary industrialization, of maintaining a high rate of capitalist exploitation through a system which guarantees a cheap and controlled labour-force, under circumstances in which the condition of reproduction (the redistributive African economy in the Reserves) of that labour-force is rapidly disintegrating'.[30]

The steps taken to halt the disintegration of the rural economy included, first, the division of the land into arable, grazing and residential sites, and the relocation of people and livestock; and secondly, limited spending on a programme of agrarian reform: stock-culling, fencing, contour ploughing, water conservation and erosion control. The first steps in these directions were taken in the late 1930s; in particular, however, Proclamation 116 of 1949 instituted the Betterment or Closer Settlement schemes. These were attempts to stabilize and increase crop production and to improve land use and animal husbandry. At the same time, intervention of this nature had implications for social relations in the Reserves. The South African state flirted intermittently with the idea of creating and consolidating a kulak or rich peasant class in the Reserves, and of completing the proletarianization of those marginal men who clung tenaciously to small and unproductive plots of land. Such proposals were made most explicitly in the form of the recommendations of the Tomlinson Commission. These called for the abandonment of the one-man-one-plot formula, countenanced the removal of fully half of those who had claims to agricultural land, sought the development of a class of stable farmers, and accepted the creation of a large class of landless workers.

As is well known, the Tomlinson recommendations were rejected in part by the Government in its subsequent White Paper, and the economic restructuring of the Bantustans has been a far more hesitant process of decentralization and rehabilitation than that proposed by the Commission. Nevertheless, the operation of the Betterment

Schemes and some of the rehabilitation reforms during the fifties and sixties appear to have reduced the income available to small or marginal peasants. Rehabilitation 'did not herald economic units and in many ways reinforced the status quo in the reserves although it has certainly made some contribution to the fight against erosion. The pattern of inadequate plots, poor farming methods and mass migrancy has continued.'[31] The Betterment Schemes have limited the rights of stock ownership and defined availability to arable lands in terms that favour the haves at the expense of have-nots. While those with enough land qualified for rehabilitation schemes, those without arable allotments were removed to the closer settlement villages ('work colonies for the landless, which the government prefers to call Bantustan towns').[32]

The relationship between the two processes outlined above ('indirect rule' through an elite of chiefs and headmen, and agricultural reforms that could at best check degeneration and often accentuated rather than alleviated the hardships of the poorest) was clearly indicated in the incidence of rural resistance in the 1950s and early 1960s. In a series of clashes political action centred either upon resistance to stock-culling or resettlement schemes or on hostility to the imposition of 'Bantu Authorities'. Or both: typically, the two were fused when the local headman would accept and try to implement a Betterment scheme and was opposed by the majority of 'his' tribespeople. The largest instances of rural discontent and resistance were at Witzieshoek in the Orange Free State in 1950; in Marico district in the Transvaal in 1957 when a large-scale revolt among the Bafurutse broke out over the extension of pass laws to women (superintended by the new Bantu Authorities); in Sekhukhuneland in the northern Transvaal in 1958; in Zululand and Natal in 1959; and in 1960 when several years of simmering discontent welled over in the Pondoland risings.[33]

In the 1970s, the Republic's agricultural policy for the Bantustans again looks to the fostering of a class of better-off peasants or small farmers. The number of families with a claim to smallholdings in the homelands, say the planners, is to be reduced from 500,000 to 50,000.[34] That process is already under way in the Transkei. It involves the re-allocation and concentration of land, the 'rationalization' of agriculture, and a subsidized rise in cash crop production by the few, while the yields of 'subsistence' agriculture by the many fall even lower. In April 1977, the Transkei government of K. D. Matanzima included in its budget proposals for a swingeing tax upon livestock: the levy ranged from R2 (about £1-30) for each sheep and goat to R10 (about £6-50) for each donkey and head of cattle. While larger stockholders could have met the expenses by the sale of one or a few beasts, the tax would have hit the owners of small herds or flocks particularly hard. Certainly, it would have increased the concentration of agricultural resources into the hands of a minority: it was 'a step towards concentration of herds, a step towards the creation of a "farmer class" and of a larger group with no stock at all'.[35] Opposition to the measure forced a radical scaling-down of the taxation rates, illustrating – among other things – the insecure nature of the economic base of the ruling groups in the Transkei.

Finally, a recent survey conducted in the Transkei establishes in valuable detail the pervasive level of poverty in the first of the 'independent' Bantustans. Over 750 rural households in three different areas of the Transkei provided the sample; the findings amply justify the conclusion that the mass of the population in the Reserves is trapped 'in processes of relentless economic regression' – to the point where the position of the inhabitants of the Bantustans is 'worse than that of the inhabitants of any other part of Africa, except perhaps the "Sahel" countries'.[36] Leeuwenberg demonstrates in particular how exiguous is the role of agriculture in providing an income or even feeding Transkei families. In 1974, 2,800,000 bags of maize were imported while only 1,250,000 bags were produced locally. Only 62 of the 757 households surveyed (or 8·4 per cent) regularly produced sufficient food to feed the members of the household; in 61·9 per cent of the total, the household is *never* able to produce enough to feed or reproduce itself; while in 30 per cent of the households, enough food could be raised in favourable years. Even the 8·4 per cent who produced enough for consumption and for sale marketed only a tiny surplus; the maximum reported sale was R50 (about £30) a year, and the mean was R15 (about £9). Almost half the households surveyed owned no cattle at all; 55 per cent owned no sheep. Of the households with stock, half held very small numbers (five or fewer cattle, ten or fewer sheep). Leeuwenberg's impression was that many of the owners of larger herds were 'chiefs' or 'sub-headmen'.[37]

Conditions in the Transkei are desperate – but they are not peculiar to that Bantustan. Between 1947–8 and 1967–8, the production of maize in the Bantustans fell from 3·8 million bags to 3·7 million bags while the production of maize in white farming areas rose from 30·4 to 105·2 million bags. The shifts in the other great staple, sorghum, were even more pronounced; Bantustan production fell from 1·2 to 0·7 million bags, while white farmers stepped up production from 1·8 to 9·5 million bags. Although official figures released in 1974 indicate that the total crop and pastoral production increased in the Bantustans between 1968 and 1973, it is clear that this improvement 'was concentrated in a limited number of areas ... with little or no participation by the general population'.[38] Agricultural degeneration is not merely measured in shrinking wool clips and falling crop yields, however; it is also expressed in the most exaggerated social dislocation, and in – literally – shocking details of ill-health and mortality.* There are a

* As to social dislocation, consider the implications for family life of the 'masculinity ratio' (the number of men per 100 women) in the Transkei: for *all* age groups, the ratio

number of milieus in which poverty is experienced by black South Africans today. There are the polyglot mine compounds of the Reef and the dehumanized existence[39] of their recruits; there are the notorious and depressing single-sex migrant 'hostels' being built in the 'townships' fringing every major city; there are the townships themselves, whose grid streets and endlessly repeated 'housing units' so inadequately convey to the outsider the strains, insecurity, volatility and violence of life within them.[40] It might be asked, however, whether in any of these the experiential knowledge of underdevelopment and poverty is as numbingly, inescapably arrived at as in the rural Bantustans.

2 AFTER 1913: OUTSIDE THE RESERVES

One cannot speak of the history of black peasants outside the Reserves since 1913 without also describing the development of capitalist agriculture in South Africa since Union. They can be distinguished for the purpose of exposition as separate processes, but were historically necessarily interlocked; they were different planes or aspects of the transformation of the mode of production and of social relationships in rural South Africa. As far as the peasantry is concerned, it is a chronicle of irresistible economic pressures bearing upon people politically right-less, unorganized and unrepresented; it is an account of the actual elimination of various categories of peasant: share-croppers, cash tenants and labour tenants, and peasant proprietors who owned land outside the Reserves. On another plane, it is an account of the particular manner in which capitalist agriculture developed and of the political pursuit by white farmers of their interests; due to the uneven development of capitalism in South Africa, agriculture has depended in the twentieth century upon the state not only for subsidies, tax relief, tariff protection, credit, price stabilization, marketing controls and training, but also for large-scale intervention in the supply, distribution and retention of labour.[41]

Among the first victims of these processes were the share-croppers or 'men-on-the-halves'. The Natives Land Act was in part aimed at the immediate removal of this type of squatter-peasant, and in this respect came close to achieving its aims. Social transformation was swift, sweeping and severe. In the Orange Free State especially share-croppers were faced with the choice between becoming farm servants, or moving off with their stock in the desperate hope of finding land

---

has fallen from 73 (1946) to 66 (1974); for the age group 25–29 years, the decline in the same years is from 36·1 to 28·9. (See L. Clark and J. Ngovese, *Women without Men* (Institute for Black Research, Durban, 1975). For ill-health and mortality, see B. Rogers, *Divide and Rule: South Africa's Bantustans* (International Defence and Aid Fund, London, 1976), 29–30.)

elsewhere. The 'roving pariahs' who chose the latter course have been memorably depicted by Plaatje. He makes telling use of individual cases of hardship and bewilderment, but keeps reminding his readers that they are instances of a wider process – the 'sickening procedure of extermination, voluntarily instituted by the South African Parliament'[42] – and the cumulative effect is reminiscent of contemporary descriptions of the enclosure movement in late eighteenth-century England.

The great majority of the share-croppers were dispersed (they travelled into the Reserves, or into Basutoland and Bechuanaland) or translated into farm servants (as wage labourers, or much more frequently as labour tenants). Studies of rural change in many different places have remarked upon the tenaciousness of its victims: institutions, relationships and attitudes linger on in the crevices or at the margins of succeeding epochs and social formations. Share-cropping persisted in South Africa, despite its contravention of the law, in pockets of the Eastern Cape and of the Orange Free State itself, and in a broad swathe of the south-eastern Transvaal.[43] And, as was the case before 1913, it appears that peasants enjoying this form of access to the means of production could win a tolerable living. As late as 1945 it was remarked that in the Transvaal 'share-farmers seem able to live on a good scale and educate their children', that they enjoyed a better diet and a 'comfortable income'.[44]

Apart from share-croppers, there were two other forms of squatter-peasant: tenants, paying in cash or kind for the use of a white proprietor's land, and labour tenants. Many of the former category were directly affected by the 1913 Act, and became labour tenants in its immediate aftermath; hostility to the existence of cash-paying tenants (increasingly the use of the term 'squatter' came to be reserved for such peasants) remained one of the most consistently and frequently reiterated expressions of white farm interests. The prohibition on cash leases of the 1913 Act was flouted in all four provinces (a Supreme Court decision ruled in 1916 that the Act was not applicable to the Cape) and although statistics are almost impossible to come by, a small stratum of better-off squatter-peasants continued to rent land clandestinely. They existed in largest numbers upon some of the four and a half million acres of land still in possession of the land companies by 1925. Chapter IV of the Natives Land and Trust Act (18/1936) outlawed cash tenancies even more rigorously than the 1913 Act: it divided Africans on white farms into servants (wage labour), labour tenants and squatters (rent tenants), and was designed to exert pressure on the latter categories to become members of the former. As the office of the Chief Native Commissioner of Kingswilliamstown put it, the statute was 'designed primarily to effect an even distribution of labour for the farming community'.[45] Its chief weakness was that it applied only to certain districts, and could be resisted by 'non-progressive' white landowners. The final phase in the opposition to 'squatters' (cash tenants) commenced on 1 September 1956, when the provisions of Chapter IV of the 1936 Act were applied to the whole of the Union; it was in the late 1960s and early 1970s that the full effects were felt and thousands of squatters were evicted.

Labour tenancy was, of course, the form of securing and exploiting a labour force specifically protected by the 1913 Act. *Hiring* land was defined as payment of 'a rent in money' or 'a share of the produce of that land', and outlawed; but 'farm labourer' was construed to include 'a native who resides on a farm and is *bona fide* but not necessarily continuously employed . . . [i.e.] he renders ninety days' service at least in one calendar year'. All existing contracts in Natal and the Transvaal might remain unchallenged at the landowner's choice; and future restrictions upon labour tenancy in the Transvaal were disavowed. In a sense, the retention, transformation and finally the abolition of labour tenancy are at the centre of the whole nexus of changes being described in this section.

M. L. Morris has recently drawn attention, most pertinently, to the transformation that took place in the nature of labour tenancy as capitalist agriculture asserted its dominance in the countryside during the early portion of the twentieth century. The typical nineteenth-century form of labour tenancy was a semi-feudal or precapitalist form (corresponding to feudal *corvée* labour). It was characterized by 'free' labour (the absence of any wages), labour dues that were required the year round (for 'two days a week'), and the availability and use of the labour tenant's own livestock and implements (which he used on his own and his landlord's plots). By the 1920s, however, most labour tenants were being contracted to work for a definite period (usually three or four months) and were mainly using the white farmers' ploughs and animals on their own and their landlords' land.[46] Although the older forms persisted in certain localities (so that 'free' labour service still occurred in places in the 1930s and 1940s), the prevailing tendency was 'the transformation from above of labour service peasants into labour tenant farm workers'. As Morris indicates, the 'transformed' labour tenant no longer owned his own means of labour; moreover, by 1932 everywhere except in the Northern Transvaal labour tenants received the bulk of their subsistence in the form of wages (whether cash or kind) and not from their endeavours on their own land. The relationship between employer and labour tenant was capitalist in nature.[47] These 'transformed' labour tenants, quite clearly then, had ceased to be peasants.

Labour tenancy in the nineteenth century was a quasi-feudal arrangement that reflected the political superiority of British colonists or Boer republicans and their limited ability to expropriate a surplus: it secured for the squatter-peasants, however tenuously, access to the means of production. Why was it retained, albeit in its altered form, even after the development of capitalist agriculture? Labour tenancy, in brief, was retained at the desire of those white agriculturists who doubted their own ability to bid for African labour in competition with urban employers. It has been remarked in earlier chapters that white food producers were relatively slow to respond to possibilities of commercial agriculture. Even after the 1913 Act and after the bounties towards the agrarian sector granted by the Pact Government in the 1920s, agriculture remained short of cash and technologically back-ward; farmers felt threatened by the capacity of the mines and other urban employers to offer higher cash wages. Farmers attempted to meet the competition for labour in a variety of ways, including calls for restrictions on mobility, stricter influx controls and pass laws, and so on, but also by retaining labour tenancy. For the African labour tenant, the practice offered an alternative to full-time labour for a white employer; it could, where conditions were favourable, also provide opportunities for a modest annual income through the sale of wool, grain or vegetables. It was the weakness of the agricultural sector within the capitalist economy as a whole, as well as the determination by Africans in the countryside to retain access to land, even on deteriorating terms, that affected the development of 'capitalist labour tenancy'.[48]

A distinctive form of labour tenancy that emerged in the 1920s and 1930s, mainly in the northern and eastern Transvaal, was the major exception to the changes detailed above. This was the 'labour farm', where squatter-peasants lived on one piece of land, but performed the required stint of labour on another, often many miles away. They were common where whites owned land in different regions; one property might be near markets and farmed relatively intensively; another (the 'bushveld farms') distant from markets and left entirely in the occu-pation of labour tenants who were collected in droves by the farmer as required.

The 1930s were years of acute crisis for capitalist agriculture in South Africa. The international depression forced agricultural com-modity prices down in South Africa as elsewhere; and a searing drought in 1932–3 killed thousands of animals and parched standing grain fields. At the same time, as manufacturing and mining recovered fairly quickly from the initial slump, 'the sectoral terms of trade between agriculture and industry moved ... against the former'.* Finally, the farming community's most acute problem was the shortage of labour which was itself an expression of the unprofitability of farming and also of the uneven development between sectors of the capitalist economy. By the end of the 1930s, the sectoral imbalance

---

* 'Between 1932 and 1937 the GNP rose from £217 million to £370 million.' 'Simul-taneously with the drought ... came a rise of 50 per cent in the price of gold which sparked off an enormous industrial expansion ... in the mines ... [and] in the manufac-turing sector.' (*Oxford History of South Africa*, II, 32, 142.)

and the labour shortage had acted upon each other and 'in their concentrated form they threatened to shatter the already tenuous security of the capitalist farming class'.[49]

Farmers and their politically powerful representatives sought solutions to both 'sides' of the problem. The economic debility of agriculture was treated by a massive programme of protection and of state control over marketing: Francis Wilson concludes that 'the primary aim of the Marketing Act was not so much the short-term stabilization of prices' but rather 'the long-term social aim of keeping farming incomes more in line with those in towns'.[50] Remedies for easing the labour shortage were sought, first, through alternative sources of labour, and secondly, in ways of preventing the drift of working hands away from the land. In the quest for alternative supplies, two steps were pursued most strenuously. Farmers called for the provisions of the 1913 and 1936 Acts to be directed against 'squatters' on company and private farms so that these rent-payers should be ejected, denied entry to the towns and forced into labour on white farms. In addition, there was a great increase in the use of prison labour on farms. At the height of the scheme, in 1957–8, some 200,000 convicts were hired to white farmers annually, at 9d per day.[51]

The means most relied on to prevent migrancy (especially by members of the labour tenant's family away from the farm) during the 1930s was to strengthen the legislation and machinery of 'influx control': the 1930 and 1937 amendments to the 1923 Native (Urban Areas) Act both reflected pressures from white agricultural interests.[52] Yet the most striking feature of these attempts was the extent to which they failed.* By the mid-1940s, instead of futilely seeking to stem the flow of labour tenants or their dependants, some farmers came to criticize the institution of labour tenancy directly, and to call for its abolition and replacement by full-time agricultural labour. Morris cites a number of farm lobby calls for the full and effective implementation of Chapter IV of the 1936 Act, for the clear division of the black workforce into industrial and full-time agricultural labourers, and the ending of labour tenancy. During the 1950s, under the National Party, all these were met: the changes brought about in that decade and the next 'effectively ended the migration from white agricultural districts to the towns, settling the farm labour force', and 'finally led to the total destruction of the labour tenant system'.[53] The 1936 legislation had created Labour Tenant Control Boards, and their power to emend or terminate contracts between farmers and labour tenants drastically reduced the latter's security of tenure; the major weakness of the Boards (that they were operative only in 'proclaimed areas') was

* Between 1936 and 1951 (the period of the most rapid urban population growth in South Africa in the twentieth century) the largest single source of newly urbanized Africans was the 'white' rural sector: five times as many of the urban newcomers came from white farms as from the Reserves in this period.

overcome with the extension of the Act to all areas in 1956. It was, in addition, the establishment of labour bureaux in 1951 and their greatly increased powers in terms of amending legislation in 1964 that provided the implements for the final assault on labour tenants. In 1936, perhaps as many as a million Africans on white farms were labour tenants and their families; in 1964, there were still 163,000 in South Africa (mainly in Natal). By 1970, there remained only 27,585 labour tenants, and in 1973 it was announced that 16,000 labour tenants in Natal were the last survivors of the system, and that their stay was to be brief. Throughout this lengthy process that transformed various sorts of squatter-peasants into agricultural labourers, it should be remembered that black workers on white farms in South Africa were indeed 'at the bottom of the pile'[54] as far as wage earners were concerned. Low wages, harsh treatment and heavy work won a reputation to match.

There was another category of peasants whose elimination – or in some cases physical relocation – took its own distinct form. These were peasant communities established on pockets of land outside those areas delimited in 1913 and 1936 as Native Reserves. Such peasant proprietors lived on a farm or on several adjacent farms in 'white' South Africa; there they survived all the economic blows and blood-letting dealt to small farmers over two or three generations, only to be done to death by the most direct form of political intervention by the state. Such peasant communities were of various sorts, but their defining characteristic was that they were established upon land held in freehold; in almost all cases title had been secured during the period covered in detail in the chapters above, between 1870 and 1913.

These holdings – relics of the era of a peasantry's expansion – were named (when their removal was deemed necessary) Black Spots. It was estimated in the early 1960s that there were some 350 Black Spots in South Africa, of which 250 were in Natal, comprising about half a million acres in all. Some Black Spots were farms owned by individual African farmers; some had been purchased originally by groups of enterprising men (the Natal 'syndicates' are an obvious example). In both of these sorts, original title-holders or their descendants frequently subdivided their property and leased it out to other black tenants. (Thus a survey of nineteen Black Spots in Natal in 1958 showed that they carried about 30,000 people, of whom some 1100 were title-holders, and the majority tenants.) A third type of Black Spot was the communally or 'tribally' held farm, often purchased originally by a chief whose followers all contributed towards the cost. Other Black Spots were 'Mission farms', owned by missionary societies, and subdivided amongst often quite large numbers of tenants. Examples of the creation of each of these types have already been encountered in this book: the following are merely a few of those whose destruction was described by Cosmas Desmond or by Liberal Party researchers in Natal.

In 1908, a syndicate (including J. H. and T. Kumalo and E. Lutango) bought 250 acres of land. Mr Matsheni Hlomuka, the only living member of the original syndicate when the Bantu Affairs Department bulldozers demolished the settlement in 1963, remembered how each individual had dropped his five-pound contribution into one of two enamel basins, until they were both full of coins. The land was particularly attractive in that it adjoined the railway line, an advantage shared by no other African-owned land in the area. About a hundred plot-holders won a living out of the Kumalosville land up till the time of the demise of the settlement.[55] In Tzaneen district in the Northern Transvaal, about 500 families of the Mamahlola people attracted attention in the late 1950s for their resistance to being removed under ultimatum from a farm originally allocated to them by President Kruger in the 1880s. In the Central Transvaal, three Lutheran mission farms, Botsabelo (founded by Merensky), Walmansthal and Middelfontein (founded in 1869 and 1868 respectively), supported over a thousand families. These included 400 tenant families, leasing from the Lutherans, 600 families who had bought their land at Walmansthal, as well as tenants paying rent to the Walmansthal proprietors. Upon their removal, these communities have been dispersed, with a majority relocated at Syferkuil farm. There, Desmond adjudged them to be 'more fortunate than most others who have been moved from Mission farms': they have access to some land (though less than before), keep some cattle and cultivate. But Syferkuil's area, with only some 350 agricultural plots of a proposed 800 filled when Desmond visited it, was already clearly inadequate to support the families living there.[56]

The Black Spot communities were moved 'voluntarily' (that is, after lengthy persuasion and pressure from Bantu Affairs Department officials). When people resisted the moves, the Government expropriated the lands involved and then charged the inhabitants with illegal squatting. Larger proprietors were compensated in cash or by provision of land inside a Bantustan; smaller peasants were allocated lots in 'closer settlement' or Trust villages. The frequent assertions by official spokesmen that the new land provided was the equal of Black Spots land are not merely unconvincing, but in the light of descriptions by Desmond and others are seen to be callous and threadbare deception.*

---

* A group of 140 Barolong peasants farmed near Potchefstroom, on land originally granted them during Kruger's presidency. Between 1959 and 1971, they were subject to great pressure by the Potchefstroom Town Council and the Bantu Affairs Dept. to leave: fees were raised, their school closed, and the access road barred. They were eventually forced to leave Machaviestad and were reported in 1971 to be living in an area with 'no land for ploughing, no schools or clinics, no work available locally, and social pensions had not been paid since they moved'. (South African Institute of Race Relations, *Survey 1971*, 116–18.)

3 CONCLUSIONS

What are the connections between the state of penury and agricultural debility sketched above – the lot of peasants inside and outside the Reserve areas established in 1913 – and the incidence of peasant enterprise delineated in earlier chapters? And what conclusions can be reached about the connections? Connections and conclusions are most usefully introduced by restating the arguments of the book, reduced to their bare essentials. Thus filleted out, the arguments stand free of the fleshy surrounds of qualifications and details: skeleton-like, they are starker than, yet are the essential core to, the body of the whole.

The earliest involvement of African pastoralist-cultivators in the mercantilist colonial economy took the form of the exchange of cattle and hunt products for European trade goods. With the expansion of trade and of imperial authority eastwards, the Cape Nguni came into increasingly close contact with white pastoralists, farmers, traders and missionaries in the eastern portions of the Cape. The imposition in 1806 of long-term British rule hastened the penetration of trade, of mission stations, and of administrative control into Nguni societies. At the same time, the wars of Zulu conquest had introduced into the eastern Cape the Mfengu who proved particularly receptive to opportunities for small-scale accumulation as well as to political collaboration.

In the 1820s and 1830s, the abandonment of a policy of 'non-intercourse' between colonists and Nguni, the encouragement of white settlement, the abolition of slavery, the withdrawal of a sizeable proportion of Afrikaner pastoralists and a qualitatively increased volume of frontier trade all had important bearings upon the emergence of an African peasantry. The merchants of Cape Town and Port Elizabeth sought an expanded market; missionary ideologues equated the spread of Christianity with the spread of metropolitan economic influences and 'habits of industry'; administrators sought allies or 'buffers' against hostile kingdoms to the north, and they also looked to an increased production in African areas as a means of making the colony pay its way. This constellation of economic and political interests favoured the creation of an African peasantry, of a class of cash-cropping small proprietors, producer-consumers within a providentially ordered system of burgeoning prosperity.

Some Africans – especially those whose place within the prevailing Nguni political structure and/or economic system had been affected – came to terms with increased imperial authority over them through participation in the produce market. On and near mission stations at first, and very soon elsewhere as well, innovative and enterprising peasant producers appeared.

The population movements and wars of the middle third of the nineteenth century – 1836 to 1867 – saw the annexation by Britain of Natal and new portions of the Eastern Cape, and the formation of the Afrikaner Republics. Where the indigenous African population was relatively small, or was weakened by political and military circumstances, there were numbers of cultivator-pastoralists who lost access to land and cattle, and who were compelled to enter the service of white landowners and other employers. At the same time, the majority of Africans displayed a tenacious preference for a life that drew subsistence from a family plot rather than from labour at low levels of remuneration. This preference could be pursued in those areas of Southern Africa where the redistributive economy had either not been destroyed or where it had been modified to meet novel pressures on land and other resources.

There existed, that is, by the beginning of the final third of the nineteenth century, African peasants of three broad types. First, in areas designated as African reserves or locations peasants lived in political and social structures little altered; the rule of chiefs and headmen, the ties of kinship, even where these had been diluted or distorted, provided the framework for these peasant communities. Traditional production methods, modified at points (and particularly by the introduction of the ox-drawn plough), were used by peasants who sought to produce agricultural surplus (over subsistence requirements) sufficient to meet the demands of the state as well as their own rising consumer needs.

Secondly, there were peasants wherever land nominally owned by whites remained in occupation and under production by Africans: whites were able to seize tracts of land by virtue of military superiority, but less capable of separating Africans from the means of production, or of engaging in significant agricultural production on their own behalf. These peasants paid rent – in cash, kind, or in labour service – and used their own livestock and implements in their agricultural efforts, frequently stepping up production to the level necessary to meet the landlord's demands. In the long run, the access to the land enjoyed by these squatter-peasants were to prove more vulnerable than that of peasants on communally held (Reserve) land; they could be more directly influenced by the actions of either individual white landlords or of legislators.

Thirdly, a numerically smaller group of peasants is identifiable: those who had to some extent departed from the traditional economic and social structure. These peasants directed their activities to a greater degree towards the market and towards accumulation; their most successful representatives may be said to have passed beyond peasant agriculture and become small-scale commercial farmers. Typically, peasants of this type held land on some form of individual tenure, their farming methods and implements represented a considerable adaptation of Nguni agriculture, and a sizeable proportion of them would have commenced their agricultural careers on mission stations. Many made money in other ventures, particularly transport riding, which they then invested in land, in stock and in improvements.

After 1870, mineral discoveries and the economic changes that they generated created conditions that permitted a rapid spread of peasant production, but that also set in train forces that ultimately inhibited and suppressed peasant production. Before 1870, mercantile capital was dominant in Southern Africa, and was primarily interested in extracting commodities produced within the precapitalist sector. After 1870, mining capital (and after 1900 agrarian capital) was primarily interested in extracting labour power from the region in which pre-capitalist elements had been perpetuated.

Peasants responded swiftly to opportunities for participation in the enlarged market and entrepreneurial activities; innovation, diversification and a modest level of accumulation marked the efforts of the more successful peasants. (Others were less successful. Peasant communities became increasingly stratified: some peasants consolidated their gains, a few set up as small farmers, others survived grimly, and others were extruded – seasonally, temporarily or permanently – as labourers.) Most freely in the Cape and Natal, and in disguised forms in the Republics, Africans entered the land market as purchasers; by the early twentieth century it was clear that black peasants 'were beginning to challenge for land, even on terms dictated by white legislators'.[57] In certain areas and at certain levels of the economy, peasant production played a part that has subsequently been underestimated by historians: the trade in wool and grain in the market towns of the Eastern Cape, the production of foodstuffs in nineteenth-century Natal, the share-cropping peasants in the Orange Free State, and the market production in the western and central Transvaal are examples. Throughout Southern Africa, African petty producers possessed certain advantages over white producers: African societies were rather more efficient in land use than the white, and peasants responded more effectively to economic opportunities and pressures than most white pastoralist-cultivators.

A hypothetical projection, then, of trends in the closing years of the nineteenth century might envisage that class formation and differentiation among African agriculturists would lead to: the emergence of a class of black farmers, a diminishing 'traditional' peasantry, and a growing permanently proletarianized urban working force. But various forces, interests and interventions operated to inhibit, check and distort the direction of economic changes in peasant areas, a phenomenon that found its most graphic expression in the 1913 Native Lands Act.

The competing needs of 'Gold' and 'Maize' (mining and agricultural capital) for African labour were a major source of pressure upon an 'independent' peasantry. Mine-owners and white farmers alike sought legislative measures designed to dislodge labour from African areas; they vied for fierceness in their railing against an image of idle young men lolling at home amidst fields of corn and herds of cattle. White farmers also objected to peasant production on the grounds of competition; by 1913 white food producers in all four provinces were aware of a growing and potentially even greater economic challenge from African producers. The desire to reduce competition by peasant producers was one of the motives behind the Natives Land Act. It has been argued in the context of the 'agrarian counter-revolution' in the Transvaal that the South African Native Affairs Commission's report of 1905 should be seen as the 'first step in a political response to the economic and political challenge' being made by Africans in that province; and that the 'most important of these was the economic challenge presented by the growth of groups of peasant farmers'.[58]

Whereas mercantile capital was interested in imports to southern Africa as well as exports, mining capital was in its early years very little concerned with the development of a local market. There was, as the nineteenth century ended, a diminution in the numbers and sway of such political elements as had favoured the creation of an African peasantry, and more influence by those who had come to define the desirable future in terms of the creation of a mass labour force. Even the spokesmen of – broadly – the mercantile-missionary liberal tradition in the Cape had considerably diluted their own enthusiasm for a class of black consumer-producers. In part, this reflected a shift in metropolitan attitudes and interests, away from 'assimilation' and towards 'segregation'; locally, it was related to the fact that with the completion of conquest and the decisive tilt of power in favour of white colonists there was no longer need for a peasantry as buffer;[59] the South African Native Affairs Commission of 1903–5 took a lengthy and portentous step towards the selective preservation of 'traditional' institutions and structures and their manipulation instead of their abolition.

This cluster of political and economic forces, evident in the years 1890 to 1913, underlay a series of legislative pressures upon the peasantry. Access to land was made more difficult; taxes, rents, and other fees were raised; the control of various forms of 'squatting' was intensified. During precisely this period, the belated commercialization of white agriculture meant that land values rose and land usage altered: squatter-peasants were evicted or offered stiffer terms. State aid for agriculture, the provision of credit facilities, and especially the development of a modern economic structure in 'white' areas by the spread of the rail network, adversely affected the competitiveness of peasant production. The relations between peasant and market, in the shape of peasant/trader dealings, the peasant's distance from markets, his exaggerated vulnerability to depression, and the spread of debt, further diminished the peasant's ability to generate a surplus.

Peasant production was also subject to natural setbacks. Droughts were a recurrent threat, and probably the most feared climatic penalty; but they could be cruelly punctuated by flash floods, hailstorms that battered crops, or grass fires that consumed them. Rinderpest and East Coast Fever were the most punitive outbreaks of animal disease between 1890 and 1913, but not the only ones: cattle were weakened in the 1880s and 1890s by redwater; horses died in thousands in the Cape between 1888 and 1890 of horse sickness; sheep were affected by scab. Crops were also visited by disease, or worse, by pests. The locust infestations of the middle 1890s were particularly harsh. Indeed, the 'ecological disaster' of the 1890s identified by historians of Eastern and Central Africa may justly be said to have hit peasant production in South Africa too. Some critics appear to believe that the demonstration of natural disasters calls into doubt or disrepute an explanation of peasant difficulties that stresses changes in the political economy.* Of course the peasant household could be stricken by lack of rain, animal diseases and deaths, and the like; but that was not the end of its troubles. These hardships were not experienced 'separately' from the exactions of landlord, trader or state. Precolonial economic systems were also prey to natural disasters, but developed a range of compensatory mechanisms that operated at such times to blunt their impact. By the late nineteenth century, however, it was not merely that these mechanisms were no longer always available (especially, new land was much harder to come by) but also that a range of other, insistent pressures co-existed with those generated by locusts or drought. The same is true of overpopulation. The overcrowding of the peasant regions was not *only* due to conquest, expropriation, and the political and economic barriers erected to acquisition of land by blacks; demographic increase also stemmed from the ending of warfare in rural areas, medical advances, and so on; but the pressure of population increase in peasant areas already underdeveloped and disadvantaged very rapidly became one of the most oppressive features of rural poverty.

The whole question of political intervention – of efforts by other social groups to curtail, deflect or prevent peasant production – raises a range of questions. Take the 1913 Act: it sought not only to suppress successful squatter-peasants and to shield white agriculture from competition by black farmers, but also to 'freeze' social relations in the Reserve areas. How does one explain the 'incomplete' form of proletarianization in South Africa, or the preservation of certain precapitalist forms and relationships? The question can be answered in several ways. Howard Pim's catalogue of the benefits to the developed economy of the preservation of an underdeveloped region has already

* Thus, H. Wright lists 'rinderpest, ... scab, redwater fever, horse sickness, locusts, and periodic drought' as 'devastating afflictions', and adds that they 'were not, presumably, a result of white capitalist influences' (!). (H. M. Wright, *The Burden of the Present: Liberal-radical Controversy over South African History* (Cape Town, 1977), 81.)

241

been cited (p. 126). More bluntly (and, in its blend of the callous and ingenuous so typical of its author) Sir Godfrey Lagden stated the case for preserving areas solely for African occupation. Should not, he was asked, the Transvaal authorities greatly reduce the land available to the African, and thereby 'throw him on to the labour market?' No, responded Lagden:

> This would throw him out of the country.... A man cannot go with his wife and children and his goods and chattels on to the labour market. He must have a dumping ground. Every rabbit has a warren where he can live and burrow and breed, and every native must have a warren too.[60]

Several commentators have recently analysed the relationship between the Reserves and the specific interests of different groups of employers in South Africa; but it may be worth recalling a much earlier formulation of the argument. (Interestingly, it was arrived at in the course of a review of Alfred Hoernle's *South African Native Policy and the Liberal Spirit.*)[61]

> The mines want healthy and vigorous workers who would have to have higher wages to attend to their own health and diet. It is therefore cheaper to give them hospitals, balanced diets, and even games and cinemas upon a collective and dictated basis.... 'Married quarters' for Africans on the mines would be more expensive than homes in the Reserves.... The vast spaces available in South Africa are a fine substitute for doles and unemployment relief as well as 'married quarters'. They serve as the sponge that absorbs, and returns when required, the reserve army of African labour. Tribal tenure is a guarantee that the land will never be properly worked and will never really belong to the natives. Cheap labour must have a cheap breeding place, and so it is furnished to the Africans at their own expense. Our dominators do not *say*, and some of them do not even *think*, that they have these motives. None the less, their conduct is to be so explained, and not by the high rhetoric we hear on the topic of segregation.[62]

The 1913 Land Act sought to arrest the tendency towards a bipolar stratification (farmers and workers) and to preserve instead an under-developed peasantry: a peasantry whose productive capacity had been so inhibited, whose access to land so confined, whose access to markets rendered so unfavourable, that its members must have recourse to labour for white employers even at the very low wage levels prevailing. The principle of one-man-one-lot, the closing of the free market in land, and the limit on the size of the surveyed plots all served the purpose of preventing the rise of a class of black farmers.[63] At the same time, the retention of Reserve areas, the preservation of low-level peasant production, served important ends for other elements of the white ruling classes than agrarian capitalists. While the under-development of the peasant sector ensured a vast reservoir of migrant labour, at the same time the ability of the Reserve inhabitants to supply a portion of their subsistence through peasant production conferred direct benefits upon urban employers – particularly the mines – in the form of low wages, cheap housing, the avoidance of welfare considerations for workers' dependants, and a brake on the growth of an urban proletariat.

The capitalist economy based upon the Cape (before 1870) had begun to transform the precolonial economies in South Africa; but the transformation in location, composition and direction of capitalist development in South Africa after the mineral discoveries also involved a different set of demands upon the indigenous economic systems. Meillasoux, in an influential passage published in 1971, noted that capitalism works in two ways upon precapitalist sectors. On the one hand 'it elicits a sector of production built up in its own image. . . . On the other hand it feeds off the precapitalist sectors through the mechanism of primitive accumulation – with the contradictory results of both perpetuating and destroying them at the same time.'[64] This last concept – the simultaneous perpetuation and destruction of the Reserves – is enlarged upon by Lionel Cliffe:

> Side by side with the establishment of a capitalist mode, a contradictory set of forces operated against neighbouring indigenous modes: on the one hand, their production of commodities for labour was held in check so as to eliminate any productive alternative to labour migration ... but, on the other hand, the tendency to destruction of the indigenous mode had to be halted before the point where it ceased to provide for the reproduction of labour power itself. Thus the relationships of production, notably with respect to access of land and the division of labour within the family, were held back from the differentiation process which would have promoted rapid internal proletarianization, but at the same time the productive forces of this indigenous agriculture remained stunted in their development in order to promote an exodus of semiproletarianized labour.[65]

This book, in common with other recent work, has argued that racially 'defined' exploitation is most fruitfully explained in terms of the particular historical features of economic growth (and not in terms of its opposition to a rational and colour-blind development). It has suggested that the underdevelopment of an African peasantry can only be understood within the framework of the development, severally, of agrarian, mining and industrial capital in South Africa. The underdeveloped sector of the South African economy is not 'separate' from the developed sector: the economy of the former is firmly integrated with that of the latter. The emergence and decline of the peasantry was a necessary component of, and not distinct from, the process of capitalist development in South Africa: the structural underdevelopment of the peasantry was the other side of the coin of capitalist development in South Africa.

The case argued in earlier chapters that South Africa's historians have overlooked or underestimated a period of early prosperity, and the evidence led in support of this, should not be misinterpreted to mean that 'left alone' all members of an African peasantry would have prospered. Demographic factors, as well as long-term price trends for agricultural produce, were of themselves sufficient to militate against any widespread peasant prosperity. Nevertheless, it is true of the upper strata of the peasantry that they 'had managed to begin to win back the land and their independent means of livelihood',[66] and for even greater numbers of peasants that the living they won enabled them to resist entry into full-time agricultural employment for whites at very low wage levels. The importance of the early prosperity argument resides also in that it renders untenable explanations of contemporary poverty couched in terms of a fundamental or inherent backwardness of the traditional sector. Moreover, an awareness of the extent and nature of peasant participation in the produce market, as well as of the degree of adaptability and innovation displayed, greatly illuminates any account of the actions taken and policies propagated by groups or interests with access to political power.

Mention of this last point prompts a further observation about the relationship between capitalist and peasant agriculture: the extent to which the success of the former was secured by the curbing of the latter. Trapido has suggested that a simple truth about economic development in South Africa is that 'no economic group can continue to accumulate capital in the South African agricultural sector' without the diversion of capital from other sectors and without some recourse to coerced labour. (Before him, de Kiewiet arrived at an essentially similar conclusion: 'Agriculture in South Africa is poor and precarious.... Without subsidy and under conditions of free competition much of the land could not be economically cultivated.')[67] It is important to realize how vulnerable South Africa's white farmers were at the turn of the century. Those who had already adjusted, or were then trying to adjust, their methods to those of commercial agriculture were menaced by competition in two forms: first, in imported agricultural produce, and secondly, in agricultural production by African peasants. The first of these threats was considerably blunted by the Union government's 'aggressive policy of bounties and protection'[68] made possible by the redirection of revenue from mines and industries. Secondly, capitalist agriculture was encouraged and bolstered at the direct expense of potential peasant production: there was mounting pressure upon direct producers, and access to the means of production was made increasingly more difficult for peasants. Once peasants had been squeezed into limited Reserves, the subsidization of capitalist agriculture, the effective segregation of transport and other resources, and the deeply imbedded features of underdevelopment in the peasant regions all operated to drive peasants out of competition in the market place. By that time – by the years described in the first two sections of this chapter – political mechanisms were no longer of crucial importance in closing the gaps between the demand and supply of labour to mines and to farms; with the competitive position of capitalist agriculture enhanced and peasant production hampered and harassed, the operations of the market itself perpetuated the dominance of the former.

The social processes of peasantization and proletarianization have been described in the Cape, Natal, Transvaal and Orange Free State. It should be clear that broadly similar pressures (with specific local differences) brought about broadly similar outcomes. Although in one sense there were many different peasantries in South Africa, whose historically individual and regional characteristics need to be established, their differences and peculiarities were not generic, but were various aspects of the experience of *the* South African peasantry. Nor is this all, for economic pressures and social transformation carry no passports and easily cross political boundaries. A striking feature of the rise and fall of the South African peasantry is the way in which the process was subsequently replicated throughout much of Southern and Central Africa.

The experience was 'exported' in two ways. First, at the empirical level, legislative and administrative practices were examined, emended, copied and re-enacted; secondly, at the structural level, the South African pattern was repeated elsewhere not merely as conscious mimicry but also as involuntary variations of processes at work within 'a regional economic system which embraced a large part of the geographical area of South and Central Africa'.[69] The reliance on South African precedents, precepts and prejudices is encountered in various ways. Individuals with South African experience were regarded elsewhere as 'experts' on matters affecting land, labour and Africans; civil servants from farther north in British Africa travelled to South Africa to study land tenure or the Transkei council system or anti-squatting procedures. In what was then Southern Rhodesia, South African ends and means (Robin Palmer's work clearly shows) were echoed in a number of ways. Consider the 'unmistakably South African focus' of the 1914 Native Reserves Commission: its members had all served in South Africa, and many of the 'unspoken assumptions in the report are clearly of white South African origin'. More than this, the crucial discriminatory devices in Rhodesia – denying good land and market access to black peasants by zoning the territory into Reserves and 'white' areas – drew closely on South African models.[70] Rennie, in a comparative study of anti-squatting legislation in southern and eastern Africa, displays in detail how land sales were banned, tenancies and share-cropping prohibited, and forms of labour tenancy restricted in Kenya, Northern and Southern Rhodesia and – to a lesser extent – in Nyasaland. South African (and very often Cape Colony/Province) legislation was the ready-made exemplar, to be adapted to local needs and circumstances.[71]

At the second level – and a growing body of scholarship is broadening our understanding of the processes involved – the formula used for the political components of South Africa (local variations upon a basic pattern) holds true for the different political components of the Southern African economic region. The economic region was really defined by the development of capitalism along the Witwatersrand: capital in that hub entrenched and much more fully developed could exert pressures along radials that extended into Basutoland, Bechuanaland and Swaziland, the Rhodesias, Mozambique and Nyasaland. (This is not to suggest that historical changes in these areas were simply tugged along resistlessly by the needs of the South African 'core'. When Van Onselen describes the flow of migrant labour southwards from Nyasaland he locates it 'against a background of *local and regional* demands for the proletarianisation of the African peasantry to meet the requirements of a growing capitalism'[72], and it is necessary in the study of every society in the economic region to unravel and distinguish the local and the regional pressures.) In each of a number of areas, the overall pattern was broadly similar: Palmer and Parsons speak of the 'stimulation, then strangulation, of peasant production under early colonial capitalism' and the way in which 'enclaves of capitalist agriculture knock[ed] out peasant competition to supply the industrial enclaves'.[73] For Rhodesia, Arrighi, Palmer, Phimister and others have all studied aspects of 'a process of involution, of gradually falling productivity modelled closely on the South African pattern'.[74]

This provides a suitable point and perspective with which to close this study: the reach and ramification of capitalism in Southern Africa, and a sense of social and economic change viewed against a wide historical and geographical back drop. I find it difficult, however, to permit the curtains to swish shut without a final glimpse of individual peasants and a last echo of their voices. When the Beaumont Commission reached Soutpansberg in the Transvaal, a number of local Africans gave evidence, eloquent in the sharpness of their distress and graphic in their identification of a whole range of interlocking pressures and problems. Mpefu complained of the high tax levels ('I am all by myself because little children have been made to pay taxes; they have to go out and work'); Mapafuri described how economic losses weakened Africans politically ('We have lost our herds, and the only thing you can do is to say "Do this! Take that away!" and we obey your orders'); Senthimula and Mayemo discussed the aims of the 1913 Act ('I think that the Government fears that the natives would, in the future, become white men'), and so on. These witnesses were then scolded by one of the Commissioners in a speech of profound, unintended irony:

I can judge by your answers that you did not quite understand. You have talked about your children at work, about the punishments inflicted upon

246

them, about dog taxes and other taxes – all matters to which Sir William Beaumont made no reference whatever. He told you we were here about land.[75]

NOTES

1 Especially the following: *Report of the Native Economic Commission*, 1930–32, U.G. 22–1932; *Social and Economic Planning Council Report No. 4*, 'The Future of Agriculture in South Africa', U.G. 10–1945; *Social and Economic Planning Council Report No. 9*, 'The Native Reserves and their place in the Economy of the Union of South Africa', U.G. 32–1946; *Report of the Witwatersrand Mine Native Wages Commission, 1943*, U.G. 21–1944; *Report of the Native Laws Commission* (The Fagan Report), U.G. 28–1948; *Report of the Commission for the Socio-Economic Development of the Bantu Areas* (The Tomlinson Report), U.G. 61–1955. See also Reports of the Native Affairs (later Bantu Affairs) Department since 1913; Reports by the Native Affairs Commission; *Proceedings and Reports* of the Transkeian Territories General Council (later United TTGC) and the Ciskeian Territories General Council; the journal (*Race Relations*) and other publications of the South African Institute of Race Relations (see *Classification of Publications of the SAIRR*, Johannesburg, 1962, and supplements). The *Keiskammahoek Rural Survey*, 4 vols. (Pietermaritzburg, 1952) is a valuable case study of a Ciskei district. Corroborative details and local data are available in a number of other briefer studies, a few of which are cited in this chapter.
2 Cited in M. Wilson *et al.*, 'Social Structure', Vol. 3 of *Keiskammahoek Rural Survey*, 178.
3 W. M. Macmillan, 'Natives and the Land', in J. D. Taylor (ed.), *Christianity in South Africa* (Lovedale, 1928), 12; *Complex South Africa* (London, 1930), 121, 137, 138, 38–9, *et passim*.
4 W. K. Hancock, *Survey of British Commonwealth Affairs*, II, part 2, 'Problems of Economic Policy, 1918–1939' (London, 1940), 69; U.G. 22–1932, 18, 10, 13, *et passim*.
5 *South African Outlook*, 2 January 1928.
6 P. A. W. Cook, *The Education of a South African Tribe* (Cape Town, 1934), 31.
7 S. H. Frankel, 'The Position of the Native as a Factor in the Economic Welfare of the European Population in South Africa', *Jnl. Econ. Soc. of SA*, II, 1 (February 1928); N. N. Franklin, 'Economic Welfare and the Development of the Native Reserves', *SA Jnl. Econ.*, 10, 1 (1942); D. Hobart Houghton, 'Some Economic Problems of the Bantu in South Africa' (SAIRR Monograph Series No. 1, Johannesburg, 1938).
8 *The Evangelisation of South Africa: Report of the Sixth General Missionary Conference of South Africa* (Cape Town, 1925); *The Re-alignment of Native Life on a Christian Basis: The Report of the Seventh General Missionary of South Africa* (Lovedale, 1928); J. D. Taylor (ed.), op. cit.
9 N. MacVicar, 'The Problem of Native Ill-health', in *Seventh General Missionary Conference Report*; Dr Fox and Mr Back, 'Nutritional Survey of the Transkei and Ciskei' (cited in U.G. 22–1932).

10 J. Henderson, 'The Economic Condition of the Native People', *South African Outlook*, 1 July 1927.

11 ibid.

12 *Keiskammahoek Rural Survey*, II, 68, 74–5, 177.

13 A. B. Forsdick, 'The Role of the Trader in the Economy of a Native Reserve: A Study of the Traders in the Keiskama Hoek District' (Rhodes University, M. Comm. thesis, n.d.), 7–12.

14 E. S. Haines, 'The Transkei Trader', *SA Jnl. Econ.*, 1, 1933, 216.

15 H. Pim, *A Transkei Enquiry* (Lovedale, 1934), 21.

16 S. H. Fazan, 'Report of a Visit made to the Union of South Africa for the purpose of comparing the methods of land tenure in the Native Reserves there with the systems obtaining in Kikuyu Province' (Rhodes House Library, typescript), 41.

17 U.G. 10–1945, 'The Future of Agriculture in SA', 8; U.G. 32–1946, 'The Native Reserves ... of South Africa'.

18 E. Roux, 'Land and Agriculture in the Reserves', in E. Hellmann and L. Abrahams (eds.), *Handbook on Race Relations in South Africa* (London, 1949), 183–4.

19 U.G. 21–1944, *Mine Native Wages Commission*.

20 U.G. 28–1948, *The Fagan Report*, 15.

21 U.G. 32–1946, 'The Native Reserves ... of South Africa', 23.

22 T. M. Makiwane, 'Agricultural and Pastoral Conditions', in *Christian Students and Modern South Africa* (Lovedale, n.d.).

23 U.G. 61–1955, *Tomlinson Commission Report*.

24 Cited in U.G. 32–1946, 'The Native Reserves ... of South Africa', 44; U.G. 22–1932, *Native Economic Commission*, 182.

25 *Keiskammahoek Rural Survey*, II, 34; National Union of South African Students Research Journal, *The Transkei Survey*, ed. P. V. Tobias (Cape Town, 1951), 26–9, 33. The evidence on these topics in U.G. 22–1932, 21–1944, *et al.*, is usefully summarized in H. Suzman, 'Rural Areas', *Race Relations*, XIV, 2 (1947), 67–8.

26 Cited in M. Webb, 'Vanishing Lands and Migrant Labour', *Race Relations*, XI, 3 and 4 (1944), 46–7.

27 Cited in U.G. 32–1946, 'The Native Reserves ... of South Africa', 29, 34. Cf. U.G. 22–1932, *Native Economic Commission*, 182, for similar observations a decade earlier.

28 *Keiskammahoek Rural Survey*, II, 45.

29 See M. Legassick, 'Legislation, Ideology and Economy in Post-1948 South Africa', *Journal of Southern African Studies*, 1, 1 (1974), 5–35, esp. 26.

30 H. Wolpe, 'Capitalism and cheap labour-power in South Africa: from segregation to apartheid', *Economy and Society*, I, 4 (1972), 433.

31 W. Beinart, 'The Livestock Levy in Transkei', unpublished seminar paper, University of Cape Town, May 1977, 13 (this paper is shortly to be published in a collection of essays).

32 G. Mbeki, *South Africa: The Peasants' Revolt* (Harmondsworth, 1964), 97.

33 The fullest account of the Pondoland risings is in Mbeki, op. cit., 95–134; the Bafurutse resistance is movingly recorded in C. Hooper, *Brief Authority* (London, 1960); U.G. 26–1951, *Report of the Commission of Enquiry into the Disturbances in the Witzieshoek Native Reserve* is the starting point

for enquiry on the Witzieshoek resistance. Two recent short papers have re-opened to investigation aspects of rural unrest in the 1950s: S. Moroney, 'The 1950 Witzieshoek Rebellion', and J. Yawitch, 'Rural Natal 1959 – The Women's Riots', both in *Africa Perspective* (published by Students African Studies Society, Witwatersrand University), issues February 1976, and No. 5, 1977, respectively.

34 D. Innes and D. O'Meara, 'Class Formation and Ideology: The Transkei Region', *Review of African Political Economy*, No. 7 (1976), 73.

35 Beinart, 'Livestock Levy', 13.

36 J. Leeuwenberg, *Transkei: A Study in Economic Regression* (The Africa Bureau, London, 1977), 2.

37 ibid., 7–8, 15–17.

38 B. Rogers, *Divide and Rule: South Africa's Bantustans* (International Defence and Aid Fund, London, 1976), 32.

39 See F. Wilson, *Migrant Labour in South Africa* (Johannesburg, 1972), and South African press reports in December 1976 of the details contained in 'Another Blanket', a booklet on mine compounds experience, published by a church group, and based on reports from 23 Basotho theology students, eight of whom had been employed as migrant mineworkers.

40 See J. Sikakane, *A Window on Soweto* (International Defence and Aid Fund, London, 1977).

41 See F. Wilson, OHSA, II, 104–71, especially 136–53, for the growth of 'white' agricultural output and of state aids and control. The full story of land and labour relations on white-owned areas after 1913 is complex and intricate: it remains to be told. Stanley Trapido and Peter Delius are currently engaged in research on farmers, labour, land and the state (mainly in the Transvaal) for the period 1900–36.

42 S. T. Plaatje, *Native Life in South Africa* (London, n.d.), especially Chapters IV and V. The quotations are from pp. 77 and 71.

43 For the Eastern Cape, see U.G. 22–'32, *Native Economic Commission*, 53; for the OFS see *Farm Labour in the Orange Free State* (South African Institute of Race Relations, Johannesburg, 1939); for the Transvaal, see E. B. Rheinallt-Jones, 'Farm Labour in the Transvaal', *Race Relations*, XII, 1 (1945), 5–14.

44 Rheinallt-Jones, 'Farm Labour', 11, 12.

45 M. Roberts, *Labour in the Farm Economy* (South African Institute of Race Relations, Johannesburg, 1958), 127.

46 M. L. Morris, 'The development of capitalism in South African agriculture: class struggle in the countryside', *Economy and Society*, 5 (1976), 296 *et passim*.

47 ibid., 309, 304.

48 ibid., 308–11.

49 F. Wilson, 'Farming, 1866–1966', OHSA, II, 139, 142; Morris, op. cit., 313–15, 318.

50 Wilson, OHSA, II, 140.

51 R. Ainslie, *Masters and Serfs: Farm Labour in South Africa* (London, 1973), 22; and see Wilson, OHSA, II, 146–9.

52 D. Welsh, 'The Growth of Towns', OHSA, II, 198.

53 Morris, op. cit., 335, 338.

54 The title of a chapter in Ainslie, *Masters and Serfs*.

55 *Blackspots: A Study of Apartheid in Action* (Liberal Party of South Africa, Pietermaritzburg, n.d.), 2, 13.

56 C. Desmond, *The Discarded People* (Harmondsworth, 1971), 130–34.

57 D. Denoon (with B. Nyeko), *Southern Africa since 1800* (London, 1972), 131.

58 P. Rich, 'The Agrarian Counter-Revolution in the Transvaal and the Origins of Segregation: 1902–1913', in P. L. Bonner (ed.), *Working Papers in Southern African Studies* (Johannesburg, 1977), 72. I came across this paper too late to make use of it in the preparation of Chapter 7.

59 On 'the decisive tilt of power in favour of white colonists' see A. Atmore and S. Marks, 'The Imperial Factor in South Africa in the Nineteenth Century: Towards a Reassessment', *Journal of Imperial and Commonwealth History*, III (October 1974), 105–39.

60 *Transvaal Labour Commission*, Cd. 1897, 399.

61 See M. Legassick, 'Race, Industrialization and Social Change in South Africa: the case of R. F. A. Hoernle', *African Affairs*, 75, 299 (1976), 224–39.

62 G. Findlay, 'Review of R. F. A. Hoernle, *South African Native Policy and the Liberal Spirit*', *Race Relations*, VII, 2 (1940).

63 U.G. 54–1939, *Report of the Native Affairs Commission*, pointed out: 'The seven and a quarter million morgen . . . set aside . . . was intended to serve the needs of all the people and not a comparatively small section of advanced natives. . . . The broad rule . . . is that the communal claims of the mass of the native people must have first consideration.' (Cited by S. T. Van der Horst, *Native Labour in South Africa* (London, 1942), 309.)

64 C. Meillasoux, *The Development of Indigenous Trade and Markets in West Africa* (London, 1971), 76.

65 L. Cliffe, 'Political Economy of Rural Africa', in P. C. W. Gutkind and I. Wallerstein (eds.), *The Political Economy of Contemporary Africa* (London, 1976), 115.

66 Denoon, *Southern Africa since 1800*, 134.

67 S. Trapido, 'South Africa and the Historians', *African Affairs*, 71 (October 1972), 446; C. W. de Kiewiet, *A History of South Africa: Social and Economic* (London, 1940), 259.

68 See de Kiewiet, *History of South Africa*, 253–61, for details.

69 C. Van Onselen, *Chibaro: African Mine Labour in Southern Rhodesia 1900–1933* (London, 1976), 227.

70 R. Palmer, *Land and Racial Domination in Rhodesia* (London, 1977), 104–5, 135–6. (And see 19–20, 99, 213, 241, *et passim*.)

71 J. K. Rennie, 'White farmers and labour tenants: the formation of tenant legislation in southern and eastern Africa in the early colonial period, with particular reference to the Southern Rhodesia Private Locations Ordinance (1908)' (unpublished paper, presented at 12th Social Sciences Conference, Dar es Salaam, December 1976).

72 Van Onselen, *Chibaro*, 121.

73 N. Parsons, 'The Economic History of Khama's Country in Botswana, 1844–1930', 114; R. Palmer and N. Parsons, 'Introduction: Historical Background', 11; both in Palmer and Parsons, *The Roots of Rural Poverty in Central and Southern Africa* (London, 1977).

74 The quotation is from Palmer, *Land and Racial Domination*, 213. See also G. Arrighi, 'Labour Supplies in Historical Perspective: A Study of the Proletarianization of the African Peasantry in Rhodesia', in G. Arrighi and J. Saul, *Essays on the Political Economy of Africa* (London, 1973); and the essays by Palmer, Phimister, and Kosmin in Palmer and Parsons, *Roots of Rural Poverty*.
75 U.G. 22–1916, *Report of the Native Land Commission* (The Beaumont Report), 378–81.

Abbreviations

The following abbreviations have been used in the notes that follow:

BBNA	Blue Book of Native Affairs
BPP	British Parliamentary Papers
CPP	Cape (of Good Hope) Printed Papers
ICS, CSP	Institute of Commonwealth Studies (University of London), *Collected Seminar Papers on the Societies of Southern Africa in the 19th and 20th Centuries*, 8 vols., 1969–77
MMS Arch.	Archives of the Methodist Missionary Society
NAD	Native Affairs Department
NNAC 1906–7	Natal Native Affairs Commission of 1906–7
OHSA	*Oxford History of South Africa*
PRO	Public Record Office
SANAC	South African Native Affairs Commission, 1903–5
SPG Arch.	Archives of the Society for the Propagation of the Gospel

Selected Bibliography

The bibliography has been set out under the following heads:

I   MANUSCRIPT SOURCES
    (A) Mission archives
    (B) Public Record Office
    (C) Miscellaneous

II OFFICIAL PUBLICATIONS
    (A) Cape of Good Hope Official Papers
    (B) British Parliamentary Papers
    (C) Other Official Papers

III NEWSPAPERS AND PERIODICALS

IV CONTEMPORARY ACCOUNTS

V   SECONDARY SOURCES
    (A) Books
    (B) Articles and Unpublished Papers

VI THESES

1 Manuscript Sources

(A) Mission Archives

Archives of the Society for the Propagation of the Gospel in Foreign Parts, United Society for the Propagation of the Gospel, Tufton Street, London:

    D MSS   (Original letters received; mainly diocesan matters)
    E MSS   (Reports from missionaries in the field; annually bound after 1858; 1858–1913)
    C.L.R. MSS (Collected Letters Received, Copied and Bound: Grahamstown, 1858–1927, 3 vols. Kaffraria, 1874–1927, 3 vols.)

Archives of the Methodist Missionary Society, Wesleyan Methodist Missionary Society, Marylebone Road, London:

    Box XI South Africa (Miscellaneous)
    Box XV South Africa (Queenstown 1868–76)
    Box XVI South Africa (Queenstown 1877–85)
    Box XVII South Africa (Bechuanaland 1838–57)
    Box XVIII South Africa (Bechuanaland 1858–76)

Box XXIV South Africa (Kaffraria 1858–64)
Box XXV South Africa (Grahamstown 1868–76)
Box XXVII South Africa (Grahamstown and Queenstown 1864–67);
Box Transvaal 1881–6
Box Transvaal 1886–90
Box Transvaal 1891–6
Box Transvaal 1899–1901
Box Transvaal 1901–3
Box Transvaal 1903–5
Box Transvaal 1905–12
Box Transvaal 1913–18

(The archives and libraries of both missionary societies, in addition, contain a number of useful pamphlets, periodicals, reports and books, printed in the nineteenth century, and those relevant appear elsewhere in this bibliography.)

(B) Public Record Office

Colonial Office papers:

Series 48, Vols. 449 (Jan. 1870) to 606 (1910), Cape correspondence.
Series 386, Vols. 132–3, 164–6 (Lands and Emigration Commission correspondence).
Series 879, Vols. 9 to 24 (Confidential Prints, African, Nos. 86, 142, 147, 150, 151, 154, 162, 188, 204).
Series 224, Vols. 3 to 12 (Orange River Colony correspondence, 1901–4).
C.O. 181, 62 (16 and 17), Colony of Natal, Report of the Native Affairs Commission, 1906–7 (Report and Evidence in 2 vols.).

(C) Miscellaneous

Cape of Good Hope Archives, Cape Town:
G.H. 8/48, *Letters from Native Chiefs and others, 1854–1884.*
Jagger Library, University of Cape Town:
Walter Stanford Papers (a few extracts).
Rhodes House Library, Oxford:
MSS Afr. r8, Lumley Graham and Alex. Barclay, Cape Journal, Vol. III, Jan. 1853–Sept. 1853.
MSS Afr. s54, Collected letters of Francis George Hall.
MSS Afr. s212, Papers of Sir Godfrey Lagden (selected files).
Royal Commonwealth Society Library, London:
MSS 55, F. J. Newnham, 'Transvaal Native Locations'.
MSS 55V, F. J. Newnham, 'Transvaal Native Locations History'.

2 OFFICIAL PUBLICATIONS

(A) Cape of Good Hope Official Papers

Votes and Proceedings of the House of Assembly with Annexures, 1854–1910 (The most important series of publications in the *Votes and Proceedings,* for this book, was the *Blue Book of Native Affairs,* annually 1874–1910. Until 1904, *Blue Books of Native Affairs* were dated according to their year of publication, and the reports in them dealt with the previous year – i.e., CPP, G.8–1883, BBNA, contained reports for 1882. After 1904, they were dated as to the year for which they carried information. The sequence was 'bridged' by G.12*–1904 between G.12–1904 and G.22–1905.).

Index to the Annexures and Printed Papers of the House of Assembly and also the Principal Resolutions adopted, and to the Bills and Printed Select Committee and Commission Reports, 3 vols., 1854–97, 1898–1903, 1904–10.

Blue Book for the Colony of the Cape of Good Hope, annually 1870–85, thereafter continued as *Statistical Register of the Colony of the Cape of Good Hope*, 1886–1909.

Cape of Good Hope Census 1875 (G.42–1876).

Cape of Good Hope Census 1891 (G.5–1892).

Cape of Good Hope Census 1904 (G.19–1905).

Various Commissions, Reports, and Memoranda (on aspects of 'Native Affairs', the administration of the Transkei, land tenure, labour, trade, etc.):

Report of Surveyor General, annually 1876–1908.

Report and Proceedings of the Committee of the Legislative Council on the Annexation of the Transkeian Territory (C.3–'61).

Proceedings of, and Evidence taken by, the Commission on Native Affairs 1865 (Grahamstown, 1865).

Report of the Select Committee on the Native Question (C.3–'69).

Reports, Correspondence, Returns, etc., of the Frontier Armed and Mounted Police for the Year 1872 (G.30–'73).

Report on the Social and Political Condition of Natives in the Transkeian Territory, 1872 (G.34–'73).

Report on the Social and Political Condition of Natives in Tambookieland, 1872 (G.35–'73).

Statistics collected ... of the weight of traffic between King Williams Town, East London, and other places during the Year 1872 (A.22–'73).

Report on Immigration and Labour Supply for the Year 1875 (G.8–'76).

Report of a Commission to Inquire into the Affairs of the territory of Griqualand East (G.37–'76).

Report of S. A. Probart (M.L.A.) of his Mission to Tambookieland in January 1876 (G.39–'76).

Report of the Select Committee on the Supply of the Labour Market (A.26–'79).

Return shewing No. of Titles to Garden and Building Lots in the several Mission Stations in the King Williams Town Division which have been taken up (A.33–'80).

Correspondence on Encouragement to Natives to Engage in Agricultural and Other Labour (C.8–'81).

Reports and Returns of Inspectors of Native Locations in the Colony (A.16–'81).

Report of the Commission to Enquire and Report upon the Losses sustained by farmers and other residents upon the Eastern Frontier of the Colony during the late war and rebellion of 1877–78 (G.76–'81).

Report and Proceedings of the Government Commission on Native Laws and Customs (G.4–'83).

Report and Proceedings of the Tembuland Commission (G.66–'83).

The Report of the Griqualand East Commission (G.2–'84).
Report of the Commission on the Labour Question, 3 vols., (Vol. 1 G.39–'93, Vols. 2 and 3, G.3–'94).
Report of the Select Committee on the Glen Grey Act (A.33–'98).
Report of the Chief Inspector of Sheep and Superintendent Sheep Inspector for the Transkei, 1897 (G.35–'98).
Report of the Chief Inspector of Sheep, 1898 (G.20–'99).
Report of the Select Committee on the Glen Grey Act (A.1–'03).
Report of the Chief Inspector of Sheep (G.37–'03).
Report on Trade with the Native Territories (G.22–1905).
Report of the Select Committee on the Location Act (A.20–'06).
Report of the Select Committee on Farm Labour (C.2–'07).
Memorandum on Estimates of Expenditure of the Native Affairs Department (A.3–'07).
Report of a Departmental Commission on the Occupation of Land by Natives in Unreserved Areas (G.46–1908).
Reports of the Select Committee on Native Affairs (A.2–1909).

(B) British Parliamentary Papers

Reports on the Present State of Her Majesty's Colonial Possessions (Transmitted with the Blue Books) for the year 1869, (C.334), XLVII.
Correspondence Respecting the Affairs of the Cape of Good Hope, 1871 (C.459), XLVII, 397; and *Further Correspondence ... 1872* (C.508), XLIII, 163; and *Further Correspondence ... 1873* (C.732) XLIX, 423.
Correspondence relating to the Colonies and States of South Africa, 1875 (C.1342), LII, 149; and *Further Correspondence ... 1876* (C.1401), LII, 9.
Correspondence respecting the war between the Transvaal Republic and the neighbouring native tribes, and generally with reference to native affairs in South Africa, 1877 (C.1814), LX, 529; (C.1883), LX, 545.
Further correspondence respecting the affairs of South Africa, 1878 (C.1961), LV, 481; (C.2000), LV, 735; (C.2079), LVI, 1; (C.2144), LVI, 373.
Further Correspondence respecting the affairs of South Africa, 1878–9, (C.2220), LII,1; (C.2222), LII, 427.
Correspondence respecting the affairs of Basutoland, and the territories to the eastward of the Cape Colony, including Pondoland, Transkei, and St. John's River, 1882 (C.3112), XLVII, 133.
Royal Commission on the Natural Resources, Trade, and Legislation of Certain Portions of his Majesty's Dominions, Minutes of Evidence taken in the Union of South Africa, in 1914, 2 vols., (Cd. 7706, 7707).
Reports of the Transvaal Labour Commission, 1903–4, (Cd. 1896), and *Minutes of the Proceedings and Evidence* (Cd.1897), XXXIX, 1904.

(C) Other Official Papers

(i) Natal

Blue Books for the Colony of Natal, 1861–91/2 (of these, until 1878, evidence about African agriculture is contained in the magistrates' reports on agriculture; from 1879 magistrates' reports for each division contain a section on 'native affairs').

Colony of Natal, *Departmental Reports,* 1892–3, 1893–4.
Colony of Natal, *Department of Native Affairs, Annual Reports,* for 1904–1909.
Report and Evidence of the Natal Native Commission, 1881–2.
Report of the (Natal) Trade Commission, 1885–6.
Report of the Native Affairs Commission, 1906–7.

(ii) South African Republic/Transvaal

Rapport van den Superintendent van Naturellen, 1892–1898, (Z.A.R.) State Library Pretoria Reprints, No. 14 (Pretoria, 1969).
Report by the Commissioner for Native Affairs relating to the Acquisition and tenure of land by Natives in the Transvaal (Pretoria, 1904).
A Short History of the Native Tribes of the Transvaal, Native Affairs Department, (Pretoria, 1905).
Report of the Transvaal Indigency Commission 1906–08, T.G. 13–'08 (Pretoria, 1908).
Colony of the Transvaal, Native Affairs Department, Annual Reports, 1903/4 to 1909/10.

(iii) Government of the Union of South Africa

Blue Book on Native Affairs for 1910 (U.G. 17–1911).
Report of the Native Affairs Department for 1912 (U.G. 33–1913).
Report of the Native Land Commission (Beaumont Commission) (U.G. 19–1916, 22–1916, 25–1916).
Report and Schedule of Areas Recommended for Native Occupation (U.G. 81–1918).
Report of the Native Affairs Department for 1913–1918 (U.G. 7–1919).
Report of the Native Affairs Department for 1919–1921 (U.G. 34–1922).
Report of the Native Affairs Department for 1922–1926 (U.G. 14–1927).
Report of the Native Economic Commission, 1930–32 (U.G. 22–1932).
Social and Economic Planning Council, Report No. 4, 'The Future of Agriculture in South Africa' (U.G. 10–1945).
Social and Economic Planning Council, Report No. 9, 'The Native Reserves and their place in the Economy of South Africa' (U.G. 32–1946).
Department of Native Affairs, *Report of the Native Laws Commission* (The Fagan Report) (U.G. 28–1948).
Report of the Commission for the Socio-Economic Development of the Bantu Areas (Summary of Report of the Tomlinson Commission) (U.G. 61–1955).

(iv) Miscellaneous official publications

South African Native Affairs Commission, 1903–1905, Minutes of Evidence together with written replies to questions and supplementary memoranda, 5 vols. (Cape Town, 1905).
Transkeian Territories General Council, *Annual Meeting and Report of Proceedings, 1904* (East London, 1904).
Transkeian Terr. Gen. Coun., *Report of Proceedings of Annual Meeting 1906, Annual Reports 1905, and estimates of revenues and expenditure, 1906* (Cape Town, 1906).
Transkeian Territories General Council, *Reports ... for 1909* (Umtata, 1909).

257

Reports ... for 1910 (Umtata, 1910).
Reports ... for 1911 (Umtata, 1911).
Reports ... for 1912 (Umtata, 1912).
Reports ... for 1913 (Umtata, 1913).

3 NEWSPAPERS AND PERIODICALS

(Including missionary publications)

Bedford Enterprise
Cape and Natal News
The Cape Mercury
Cape Monthly Magazine
Cape Quarterly Review
Christian Express (began as *Kaffir Express*, 1870–75, continued as *Christian Express*, 1876–April 1923, then as *South African Outlook*)
Eastern Province Herald
Fort Beaufort Advocate and Adelaide Opinion
Grahamstown Church Chronicle
The Mission Chronicle
The Mission Field
The Natal Witness
Queenstown Free Press (later *Queenstown Free Press and Representative*)
Umtata Herald
Wesleyan Missionary Notices

4 CONTEMPORARY ACCOUNTS

(In this section are included books, pamphlets, and articles written before 1913.)

R. J. Atcherley, *A Trip to Boerland, or a Year's Travel, Sport, and Gold-digging in the Transvaal and the Colony of Natal* (London, 1879).

J. Ayliff and J. Whiteside, *History of the Abambo, Generally Known as Fingos* (Butterworth, 1912, reprinted Cape Town, 1962).

A. Aylward, *The Transvaal of Today* (Edinburgh, 1878).

A. G. Bain, *Journals of Andrew Geddes Bain*, ed. M. H. Lister (Cape Town, 1949).

.T. Baines, *Journal of Residence in Africa, 1842–1853*, ed. R. F. Kennedy, 2 vols. (Cape Town, 1961).

G. B. Beak, *The Aftermath of War: An Account of the Repatriation of Boers and Natives in the Orange River Colony, 1902–1904* (London, 1906).

W. Bleloch, *The New South Africa and its Development* (London, 1902).

W. L. Blore, *Statistics of the Cape Colony* (Cape Town, 1871).

H. R. F. Bourne, *Blacks and Whites in South Africa* (London, 1900).

H. R. F. Bourne, *Forced Labour in South Africa: Notes on the Conditions and Prospects of South African Natives under British Control* (London, 1903).

J. H. Bovill, *Natives under the Transvaal Flag* (London, 1900).

W. B. Boyce, *Notes on South African Affairs, from 1834 to 1838, with refer-*

ence to the Civil, Political, and Religious Condition, of the Colonists and Aborigines (Grahamstown, 1838, reprinted Cape Town, 1971).

A. Brigg, *'Sunny Fountains' and 'Golden Sands': Pictures of Missionary Life in the South of the Dark Continent* (London, 1888).

C. Brownlee, *Reminiscences of Kaffir Life and History* (Lovedale, 1896).

A. T. Bryant, *A Description of Native Foodstuffs and their Preparation* (Pietermaritzburg, n.d.)

J. Bryce, *Impressions of South Africa* (3rd ed., London, 1899, first printed 1897).

H. Calderwood, *Caffres and Caffre Missions* (London, 1858).

G. Callaway, *Sketches of Kafir Life* (London, 1905).

J. A. Chalmers, *Tiyo Soga: A Page of South African Mission Work* (2nd ed., London, 1878).

J. S. Christopher, *Natal, Cape of Good Hope, A Grazing, Agricultural, and Cotton-Growing Country* (London, 1850).

G. St. V. Cripps, 'Highlands and Lowlands of Kafirland', *Cape Monthly Magazine*, 2nd series, Vol. XIV (1877), 310–17, 325–34.

W. Dower, *The Early Annals of Kokstad and Griqualand East* (Port Elizabeth, 1902).

M. S. Evans, *The Problem of Production in Natal* (Durban, 1905).

A. F. Fox *et. al.,* 'The Native Labour Question in South Africa', *Contemporary Review*, LXXXIII (1903), 540–53.

A. G. S. Gibson, *Eight Years in Kaffraria, 1882–1890* (London, 1891).

A. G. S. Gibson, (ed.), *Reminiscences of the Pondomisi War of 1880* (Edinburgh, 1890).

W. Govan, *Memorials of the Missionary Career of the Rev. James Laing* (Glasgow, 1875).

E. M. Green, 'Native Unrest in South Africa', *Nineteenth Century*, XLVI (1899), 708–16.

(Mrs) Heckford, *A Lady Trader in the Transvaal* (London, 1882).

J. Hemming, 'A Narrative of the Proceedings in the Tambookie Location during the Kafir War of 1877–78', *Cape Quarterly Review*, Vol. II; No. 6 (1882).

C. J. Henkel, *The Native or Transkeian Territories (History, Resources, and Productions of the Country between Cape Colony and Natal, or Kaffraria Proper)* (Hamburg, 1903).

W. C. Holden, *The Past and Future of the Kaffir Races* (London, 1866).

W. C. Holden, *A Brief History of Methodism and of Methodist Missions in South Africa* (London, 1877).

W. C. Holden, *British Rule in South Africa* (London, 1879).

E. Holub, *Seven Years in South Africa: Travels, Researches, and Hunting Adventures, between the Diamond-fields and the Zambesi (1872–79)*, transl. E. Frewer, 2 vols. (London, 1881).

W. Irons, *The Settlers Guide to the Cape of Good Hope and Colony of Natal* (London, 1858).

S. Kay, *Travels and Researches in Caffraria* (London, 1833).

S. Kay, *A Succinct Statement of the Kaffer's Case* (London, 1837).

B. Key, 'On the Management of the Native Tribes in South Africa', *The Contemporary Review*, XXXIX (1881), 516–28.

J. Lennox, *The Story of Our Missions in South Africa* (Edinburgh, 1911).

Lovedale: Past and Present, A Register of Two Thousand Names (Lovedale, 1887).

J. Maclean, *A Compendium of Kafir Laws and Customs* (Mt. Coke, 1858).

F. MacNab, *On Veldt and Farm: In Bechuanaland, Cape Colony, The Transvaal, and Natal* (London, 1897).

C. H. Malan, *Rides in the Mission Field of South Africa, Between the Kei and Bashee Rivers, Kaffraria* (London, 1872).

J. Mann, 'The Black Population of the British Colony of Natal', 'Wild Kaffir Life and Wild Kaffir Intelligence', 'Kaffir Promise and Capability', *The Intellectual Observer, Review of Natural History* (London, 1867), 184–94, 189–98, 428–41.

R. J. Mann, *The Colony of Natal* (London, 1860).

M. H. Mason, 'Dearth in the Transkei', *Nineteenth Century (and After)*, LXXIII (March 1913), 667–81.

J. X. Merriman, *Selections from the Correspondence of John X. Merriman*, 4 vols., ed. P. Lewsen (Cape Town, 1960–9).

N. J. Merriman, *The Kafir, the Hottentot, and the Frontier Farmer: Passages of Missionary Life from the journals of the Venerable Archdeacon Merriman* (London, 1853).

F. J. Newnham, 'Native Land Tenure in South Africa', *United Empire*, Vol. 1, 721–8, 797–804.

J. Noble, *Descriptive Handbook of the Cape Colony: Its condition and resources* (Cape Town, 1875).

J. Noble, *The Cape and South Africa* (Cape Town, 1878).

J. M. Orpen, *Reminiscences of Life in South Africa, From 1846 to the Present Day, with Historical Researches* (Cape Town, 1964).

J. Philip, *Researches in South Africa Illustrating the Civil, Moral, and Religious Condition of the Native Tribes*, 2 vols. (London, 1828).

T. Phipson, *Letters and Other Writings of a Natal Sheriff (Thomas Phipson, 1815–1876)*, ed. R. N. Currey (Cape Town, 1968).

H. M. Prichard, *Friends and Foes in the Transkei: An Englishwoman's Experiences during the Cape Frontier War of 1877–8* (London, 1880).

R–, 'Native Labour and Native Policy', *Cape Monthly Magazine*, 2nd series, X (January 1875), 1–13.

C. Rae, *Malaboch, or Notes from my Diary on the Boer Campaign of 1894 against the Chief Malaboch* (London, 1898).

J. Robinson (ed.), *Notes on Natal: An Old Colonist's Book for New Settlers* (London, 1872).

H. A. Roche, *On Trek in the Transvaal: or Over Berg and Veldt in South Africa* (London, 1878).

R. W. Rose-Innes, *The Glen Grey Act and the Native Question* (Lovedale, 1903).

'A Run to Nomansland', *Cape Monthly Magazine*, 2nd series, XII (February 1876), 104–14.

V. Sampson, 'A Letter on Frontier and Natal Travelling', *Cape Monthly Magazine*, 3rd series, Vol. II (June 1880), 333–44.

V. Sampson, 'A Trip through Pondoland to the Mouth of the St. John's River', *Cape Quarterly Review*, Vol. II (1882), 100–19.

E. F. Sandeman, *Eight Months in an Ox-waggon: Reminiscences of Boer Life* (London, 1880).

W. C. Scully, *Reminiscences of a South African Pioneer* (London, 1913).

W. C. Scully, *Further Reminiscences of a South African Pioneer* (London, 1913).

W. Shaw, *The Story of my Mission in South-Eastern Africa* (London, 1860).

S. W. Silver & Co's Handbook to South Africa (3rd ed., London, 1880).

E. Smit, *The Diary of Erasmus Smit,* ed. H. F. Schoon (Cape Town, 1971).

South African Native Races Committee (ed.), *The Natives of South Africa: Their Economic and Social Condition* (London, 1901).

South African Native Races Committee (ed.), *The South African Natives: Their Progress and Present Condition* (London, 1908).

W. E. Stanford, *The Reminiscences of Sir Walter Stanford,* 2 vols., ed. J. W. MacQuarrie (Cape Town, 1958).

A. Steedman, *Wanderings and Adventures in the Interior of Southern Africa,* 2 vols. (London, 1835).

F. N. Streatfield, *Reminiscences of an Old 'Un* (London, 1911).

Tabular View of Mission Work in South Africa 1884 (Report of the United Missionary Conference) (Lovedale, 1884).

H. T. Tamplin, 'Native Development in South Africa', *United Empire,* Vol. I, 398–403.

W. Taylor, *Christian Adventures in South Africa* (London, n.d.).

O. Thomas, *Agricultural and Pastoral Prospects of South Africa* (London, 1904).

'A Trip Through Kafirland', *Cape Monthly Magazine,* 2nd series, IX (September 1874), 204–9 and X (1875), 36–43, 152–5, 211–25.

A. Trollope, *South Africa,* 2 vols. (London, 1878).

R. Wallace, *Farming Industries of Cape Colony* (London, 1896).

C. Warren, *On the Veldt in the Seventies* (London, 1902).

5 SECONDARY SOURCES

A Books

T. Adler (ed.), *Perspectives on South Africa,* African Studies Institute Communication No. 4 (Johannesburg, 1977).

J. F. A. Ajayi, *Christian Missions in Nigeria 1841–1891: The Making of a New Elite* (London, 1965).

W. Allan, *The African Husbandman* (London, 1965).

C. Board, *The Border Region: Natural Environment and Land Use in the Eastern Cape* (Cape Town, 1962).

P. Bonner (ed.), *Working Papers in Southern African Studies,* African Studies Institute Communication No. 5 (Johannesburg, 1977).

E. A. Brett, *Colonialism and Underdevelopment in East Africa* (New York, 1973).

E. H. Brookes, *The History of Native Policy in South Africa from 1830 to the Present Day* (2nd ed., Pretoria, 1927).

E. H. Brookes and N. Hurwitz, *The Native Reserves of Natal,* The Natal Regional Survey, Vol. 7 (Cape Town, 1957).

E. H. Brookes and C. de B. Webb, *A History of Natal* (Pietermaritzburg, 1965).

F. Brownlee, *The Transkeian Native Territories: Historical Records* (Lovedale, 1923).

G. Callaway, *South Africa from Within: Made Known in the Letters of a Magistrate* (London, 1930).

Cambridge History of the British Empire, VIII, 'South Africa, Rhodesia, and the Protectorates', ed. E. A. Walker (2nd ed., Cambridge, 1963).

W. A. Campbell, *The South African Frontier, 1865–1885: A Study in Expansion*, Archives Year Book for South African History, 1959, I (Pretoria, 1960).

The Ciskei: A Bantu Homeland – A General Survey (Fort Hare, 1971).

H. Davies and R. H. W. Shepherd (eds.), *South African Missions 1800–1950* (London, 1950).

C. W. de Kiewiet, *The Imperial Factor in South Africa: A Study in Politics and Economics* (Cambridge, 1937).

C. W. de Kiewiet, *A History of South Africa: Social and Economic* (London, 1941).

M. H. de Kock, *Selected Subjects in the Economic History of South Africa* (Cape Town, 1924).

M. H. de Kock, *The Economic Development of South Africa* (London, 1936).

P. de Schlippe, *Shifting Cultivation in Africa* (London, 1956).

D. J. N. Denoon (with B. Nyeko), *Southern Africa since 1800* (London, 1972).

D. J. N. Denoon, *A Grand Illusion: The Failure of Imperial Policy in the Transvaal Colony during the period of Reconstruction 1900–1905* (London, 1973).

M. Dobb, *Studies in the Development of Capitalism* (London, 1946).

J. Du Plessis, *A History of Christian Missions in South Africa* (London, 1911).

A. E. Du Toit, *The Cape Frontier: A Study of Native Policy with special reference to the years 1847–1866,* Archives Year Book for South African History, 1954, I (Pretoria, 1954).

A. E. Du Toit, *The Earliest South African Documents on the Education and Civilization of the Bantu* (London, 1963).

M. S. Evans, *Black and White in South East Africa* (2nd ed., London, 1916).

G. G. Findlay and W. W. Holdsworth, *The History of the Wesleyan Methodist Missionary Society,* 5 vols. (London, 1921).

Fifth National European-Bantu Conference, Reports, minutes, findings, and addresses (Johannesburg, 1934).

A. G. Frank, *Capitalism and Underdevelopment in Latin America* (New York, 1969).

C. Furtado, *Development and Underdevelopment* (Berkeley, 1964).

D. M. Goodfellow, *A Modern Economic History of South Africa* (London, 1931).

D. M. Goodfellow, *Principles of Economic Sociology: The Economics of Primitive Life as Illustrated by the Bantu Peoples of South and East Africa* (London, 1939).

J. F. W. Grosskopf, 'Economic Report: Rural Impoverishment and Rural Exodus', Vol. I of *The Poor White Problem in South Africa,* Report of the Carnegie Commission (Stellenbosch, 1932).

P. C. W. Gutkind and I. Wallerstein (eds.), *The Political Economy of Contemporary Africa* (London, 1976).

W. D. Hammond-Tooke (ed.), *The Bantu-Speaking Peoples of South Africa* (2nd ed. of I. Schapera (ed.), q.v., London, 1974).

W. K. Hancock, *Survey of British Commonwealth Affairs*, II, Part 2, 'Problems of Economic Policy, 1918–1939' (London, 1940).

E. Hellmann and L. Abrahams (eds.), *Handbook on Race Relations in South Africa* (London, 1949).

P. Hinchcliffe, *The Anglican Church in South Africa* (London, 1963).

D. Hobart Houghton, *Some Economic Problems of the Bantu in South Africa*, South African Institute of Race Relations Monograph Series: No. 1 (Johannesburg, 1939).

D. Hobart Houghton, *Life in the Ciskei (A Summary of the findings of the Keiskammahoek Rural Survey)* (Johannesburg, 1955).

D. Hobart Houghton, *The Tomlinson Report: A Summary* (Johannesburg, 1956).

D. Hobart Houghton, *The South African Economy* (2nd ed., Cape Town, 1967).

D. Hobart Houghton (ed.), *Economic Development in a Plural Society* (Cape Town, 1960).

D. Hobart Houghton and J. Dagut, *Source Material on the South African Economy 1860–1970,* 3 vols. (Cape Town, 1972).

D. Hobart Houghton and E. M. Walton, *The Economy of a Native Reserve,* Vol. 2 of the Keiskammahoek Rural Survey (Pietermaritzburg, 1952).

M. Horrell, *The African Reserves of South Africa* (Johannesburg, 1969).

R. Horwitz, *Political Economy of South Africa* (London, 1967).

M. Hunter, *Reaction to Conquest* (London, 1936).

N. Hurwitz, *Agriculture in Natal 1860–1950,* Vol. 12, Natal Regional Survey (Cape Town, 1957).

D. D. T. Jabavu, *The Black Problem* (Lovedale, n.d.).

F. A. Johnstone, *Class, Race and Gold* (London, 1976).

B. M. Jones, *Land Tenure in South Africa: Past, Present and Future* (Pietermaritzburg, 1965).

Z. A. Konczacki, *Public Finance and Economic Development of Natal, 1893–1910* (Durham, N.C., 1967).

C. Lewis and G. E. Edwards (eds.), *Historical Records of the Church of the Province of South Africa* (London, 1934).

U. Long, *An Index to Authors of Unofficial, Privately Owned Manuscripts relating to the History of South Africa 1812–1920* (London, 1947).

J. B. Loudon, *White Farmers and Black Labour-tenants,* African Social Research Documents, Vol. 1 (Cambridge, 1970).

W. M. Macmillan, *The Land, the Native, and Unemployment* (Johannesburg, 1924).

W. M. Macmillan, *Complex South Africa – An Economic Footnote to History* (London, 1930).

W. M. Macmillan, *Bantu, Boer and Briton: The Making of the South African Native Problem* (2nd rev. ed., Oxford 1963).

N. Majeke, *The Role of the Missionaries in Conquest* (Johannesburg, 1952).

S. Marks, *Reluctant Rebellion: The 1906–8 Disturbances in Natal* (Oxford, 1970).

G. Mbeki, *The Peasants' Revolt* (Harmondsworth, 1963).

Natal Regional Survey, Additional Report Number 1, 'Experiment at Edendale' (Pietermaritzburg, 1951).

S. D. Neumark, *Economic Influences on the South African Frontier* (Stanford, 1957).

J. D. Omer-Cooper, *The Zulu Aftermath: A Nineteenth Century Revolution in Bantu Africa* (London, 1966).

R. Palmer and N. Parsons (eds.), *The Roots of Rural Poverty in Central and Southern Africa* (London, 1977).

H. Pim, *A Transkei Enquiry* (Lovedale, 1934).

S. T. Plaatje, *Native Life in South Africa* (London, n.d.).

N. C. Pollock and S. Agnew, *An Historical Geography of South Africa* (London, 1963).

R. Redfield, *Peasant Society and Culture* (Chicago, 1956).

J. Rutherford, *Sir George Grey* (London, 1961).

M. D. Sahlins, *Tribesmen* (Englewood Cliffs, 1968).

C. C. Saunders and R. Derricourt (eds.), *Beyond the Cape Frontier: Studies in the History of the Transkei and Ciskei* (Cape Town, 1974).

I. Schapera, *Migrant Labour and Tribal Life* (London, 1947).

I. Schapera (ed.), *Western Civilization and the Natives of South Africa* (London, 1934).

I. Schapera (ed.), *The Bantu-Speaking Tribes of South Africa* (London, 1937).

C. G. W. Schumann, *Structural Changes and Business Cycles in South Africa* (London, 1938).

T. Shanin (ed.), *Peasants and Peasant Societies* (London, 1971).

H. J. Simons, *African Women: Their Legal Status in South Africa* (London, 1968).

H. J. and R. E. Simons, *Class and Colour in South Africa, 1850–1950* (London, 1969).

R. H. Smith, *Labour Resources of Natal* (Cape Town, 1960).

T. Szentes, *The Political Economy of Underdevelopment* (Budapest, 1971).

C. M. Tatz, *Shadow and Substance in South Africa: A Study in Land and Franchise Policies affecting Africans* (Pietermaritzburg, 1962).

J. D. Taylor (ed.), *Christianity and the Natives of South Africa: A Yearbook of South African Missions* (Lovedale, 1928).

L. Thompson (ed.), *African Societies in Southern Africa* (London, 1969).

University of London Institute of Commonwealth Studies, *Collected Seminar Papers on the Societies of Southern Africa in the 19th and 20th Centuries* (Vols. 1–8, 1969–77).

S. T. Van der Horst, *Native Labour in South Africa* (London, 1942).

D. Welsh, *The Roots of Segregation: Native Policy in Colonial Natal, 1845–1910* (Cape Town, 1971).

J. Whiteside, *History of the Wesleyan Methodist Church of South Africa* (London, 1906).

D. Williams, *When Races Meet (The Life and Times of William Ritchie Thomson, Missionary, Government Agent, and Dutch Reformed Church Minister, 1794–1891)* (Johannesburg, 1967).

F. Wilson, *Labour in the South African Gold Mines, 1911–1969* (Cambridge, 1972).

M. Wilson and M. E. Elton Mills, *Land Tenure,* Vol. IV, IV, *Keiskammahoek Rural Survey* (Pietermaritzburg, 1952).

M. Wilson and L. Thompson (eds.), *The Oxford History of South Africa*, 2 vols. (Oxford, 1969, 1971).

E. R. Wolf, *Peasants* (Englewood Cliffs, 1966).

M. Yudelman, *Africans on the Land* (Cambridge, Mass., 1964).

(B) Articles and Unpublished Papers

G. Arrighi, 'Labour Supplies in Historical Perspective: A Study of the Proletarianization of the African Peasantry in Rhodesia', *Journal of Development Studies,* Vol. 6, 3 (April 1970), 197–235; also in G. Arrighi and J. Saul, *Essays on the Political Economy of Africa* (New York, 1973).

E. J. Berg, 'Backward Sloping Labour Supply Functions in Dual Economies – the Africa case', *Quarterly Journal of Economics* (August 1961).

H. Bley, 'Social Discord in South West Africa, 1894–1904', in P. Gifford and W. R. Louis (eds.), *Britain and Germany in Africa* (New Haven, 1967).

H. Blumer, 'Industrialization and Race Relations', in G. Hunter (ed.), *Industrialization and Race Relations: A Symposium* (London, 1965), 220–53.

N. Bromberger, 'Economic Growth and Political Change in South Africa', in A. Leftwich (ed.), *South Africa: Economic Growth and Political Change* (London, 1974).

C. J. Bundy, 'The Emergence and Decline of a South African Peasantry', *African Affairs,* Vol. 71, No. 285 (October 1972), 369–88.

C. J. Bundy, 'The Response of African Peasants to Economic Changes in the Cape, 1870–1910', ICS, CSP, Vol. 3.

C. J. Bundy, 'The Transkei Peasantry, c. 1890–1914: "Passing through a period of stress" ', in R. Palmer and N. Parsons, *The Roots of Rural Poverty in Central and Southern Africa* (London, 1977), 201–20.

S. Chodak, 'The Birth of an African Peasantry', *Canadian Journal of African Studies,* V, iii (1971), 327–47.

L. Cliffe, 'Rural Class Formation in East Africa', *Journal of Peasant Studies,* Vol. 4, No. 2 (January 1977), 195–224.

R. Cloete, 'Black Farmers in Natal, 1850–1913', *African Perspective,* No. 4 (July 1976).

G. Dalton, 'The Development of subsistence and peasant economies in Africa', *International Social Sciences Journal,* XVI, 3 (1964), 378–89.

G. Dalton, 'Peasantries in Anthropology and History', *Current Anthropology,* Vol. 13 (1972), 385–415.

D. J. N. Denoon, 'The Transvaal Labour Crisis, 1901–1906', *Journal of African History,* VII, 3 (1967), 481–94.

L. A. Fallers, 'Are African Cultivators to be called "Peasants"?' *Current Anthropology,* II (1961), 108–10.

L. A. Fallers, 'Social Stratification and Economic Processes', in M. J. Herskovitz and M. Harwitz (eds.), *Economic Transition in Africa* (London, 1964).

N. N. Franklin, 'Economic Welfare and the Development of the Reserves', *South African Journal of Economics,* Vol. 10, 1 (March 1942).

E. S. Haines, 'The Transkei Trader', *South African Journal of Economics,* Vol. 1, No. 2 (June 1933), 201–16.

J. Henderson, 'The Economic Life of the Native in Relation to his Evangelisation', in *The Evangelisation of South Africa: Report of the Sixth General Missionary Conference of South Africa* (Cape Town, 1925).

J. Henderson, 'The Economic Condition of the Native People', *South African Outlook*, 1 July 1927.

J. Hertslet, 'The African Peasant', *Race Relations*, XXVI, 4 (1959).

D. Hobart Houghton, 'Economic Development in the Reserves', *Race Relations*, XXIX, 1 (1962).

M. Horrell, 'The Economic Development of the "Reserves"', South African Institute of Race Relations, Fact Paper No. 3 (Johannesburg, 1959).

B. Hutchinson, 'Some Social Consequences of Nineteenth Century Missionary Activity among the South African Bantu', *Africa*, XXVII, 2 (April 1957), 160–77.

C. Hutton and R. Cohen, 'African Peasants and Resistance to Change', in I. Oxaal *et al.*, *Beyond the Sociology of Development: Economy and Society in Latin America and Africa* (London, 1975).

J. R. L. Kingon, 'The Economic Consequences of East Coast Fever', *Christian Express*, 45 (1915), 46 (1916), Nos. 539–42.

J. R. L. Kingon, 'The Transition from Tribalism to Individualism', *South African Journal of Science*, XVI (1919–20), 113–57.

M. Legassick, 'South Africa: Capital Accumulation and Violence', *Economy and Society*, III (1974), 253–91.

M. Legassick, 'Legislation, Ideology and Economy in post-1948 South Africa', *Journal of Southern African Studies*, I, 1 (October 1974), 5–35.

M. Legassick, 'South Africa: Forced Labour, Industrialization, and Racial Differentiation', in R. Harris (ed.), *The Political Economy of Africa* (Cambridge, Mass., 1975), 229–70.

M. Legassick, 'Race, Industrialization, and Social Change in South Africa: the case of R. F. A. Hoernle', *African Affairs*, 75, 299 (April 1976), 224–39.

P. Lewsen, 'The Cape Liberal Tradition – Myth or Reality?' *Race*, XIII, 1 (July 1971).

C. T. Leys, 'Politics in Kenya: the development of peasant society', *British Journal of Political Science*, I, 3 (1971), 307–37.

N. MacVicar, 'The Health of Africans in Rural Areas', *Race Relations*, IX, 4 (1942).

B. Magubane, 'A Critical Look at Indices used in the study of change in Colonial Africa', *Current Anthropology*, XII, 4–5 (October–December 1971), 419–45.

T. M. Makiwane, 'The Agricultural and Pastoral Conditions of the Bantu Population of South Africa', in *Christian Students and Modern South Africa* (Lovedale, n.d.).

S. Marks, 'African and Afrikaner History', *Journal of African History*, XI, 3 (1970), 435–47.

S. Marks, 'Liberalism, Social Realities and South African History', *Journal of Commonwealth Political Studies*, X, 3 (November 1972).

S. Marks, 'The Ambiguities of Dependence: J. L. Dube of Natal', *Journal of Southern African Studies*, 1, 2, (1975).

S. Marks, 'South African Studies since World War Two', in C. Fyfe (ed.), *African Studies since 1945* (London, 1976).

C. Meillasoux, 'The Social Organization of the Peasantry: The Economic Basis of Kinship', *Journal of Peasant Studies*, I, 1 (October 1973), 82–90.

C. Meillasoux, 'From Reproduction to Production: A Marxist Approach to Economic Anthropology', *Economy and Society*, I, 1 (1972), 93–105.

S. W. Mintz, 'A Note on the Definition of Peasantries', *Journal of Peasant Studies,* I, 1 (October 1973), 91–106.

M. L. Morris, 'The development of Capitalism in Southern African Agriculture: class struggle in the countryside', *Economy and Society,* Vol. 5 (1976), 292–343.

J. Phillips, 'Could Traditional Agriculture in South Africa be Modernized?' (unpublished paper; originally a series of broadcast lectures, 1972).

I. R. Phimister, 'Peasant Production and Underdevelopment: Southern Rhodesia, 1890–1914', *African Affairs,* Vol. 73, No. 291 (April 1974), 217–28.

K. Post, ' "Peasantization" and Rural Political Movements in Western Africa', *European Journal of Sociology,* XIII (1972), 223–54.

D. H. Reader, 'A Survey of Economic Activities among the Peoples of Africa', *Africa,* XXXIV, 1 (January 1964), 28–45.

J. Rex, 'The Plural Society: The South African case', *Race,* XII, 4 (April 1971), 401–15.

H. M. Robertson, '150 Years of Economic Contact between Black and White in South Africa: A Preliminary Survey', 2 parts, *South African Journal of Economics,* II, 4 (December 1934), 403–25, and III, 1 (March 1935), 3–25.

I. Schapera, 'Economic Changes in South African Native Life', *Africa,* Vol. 1, No. 2 (April 1928), 170–88.

D. Seddon, 'The Origins and Development of Agriculture in Eastern and Southern Africa', *Current Anthropology,* IX, 5 (December 1968), 489–509.

T. Shanin, 'Peasantry: Delineation of a Sociological Concept and a field of Study', *European Journal of Sociology,* XII (1971), 289–300.

T. Shanin, 'The Nature and Logic of the Peasant Economy', *Journal of Peasant Studies,* I, 1 (October 1973), 63–79.

H. Slater, 'Land, Labour and Capitalism: The Natal Land and Colonisation Company, 1860–1948', *Journal of African History,* XVI, 2 (1975), 257–83.

H. Slater, 'Peasantries and Primitive Accumulation in Southern Africa', in C. R. Hill and P. Warwick (eds.), *Southern African Research in Progress: Collected Papers, 2* (University of York, 1977), 82–94.

R. H. Smith, 'Native Farm Labour in Natal', *South African Journal of Economics,* IX, 2 (June 1941).

W. H. Tooke, 'The Natives and Agriculture', *South African Journal of Science,* XVII (1921–2), 419–29.

S. Trapido, 'South Africa in a Comparative Study of Industrialization', *Journal of Development Studies,* Vol. 7, No. 3 (April 1971), 309–22.

S. Trapido, 'South Africa and the Historians', *African Affairs,* Vol. 71, No. 285 (October 1972), 444–8.

S. T. Van der Horst, 'The Effects of Industrialization on Race Relations in South Africa', in G. Hunter (ed.), *Industrialization and Race Relations: A Symposium* (London, 1965), 97–140.

C. Van Onselen, 'Reactions to Rinderpest in South Africa, 1896–97', *Journal of African History,* XIII, 3 (1972), 473–88.

M. Wilson, 'Conditions in the Ciskei', *Race Relations,* XXI, 1 (1954).

M. Wilson, 'The Early History of the Transkei and Ciskei', *African Studies,* 18, 4 (1959).

M. Wilson, 'Effects on the Xhosa and Nyakyusa of Scarcity of Land', in D. Biebuyck (ed.), *African Agrarian Systems* (London, 1963).

H. Wolpe, 'Industrialism and Race in South Africa', in S. Zubaida (ed.), *Race and Racialism* (London, 1970), 151–79.

H. Wolpe, 'Capitalism and Cheap Labour-power in South Africa: from segregation to apartheid', *Economy and Society,* I (1972), 425–56.

D. Yudelman, 'Industrialization, Race Relations, and Change in South Africa: an ideological and academic debate', *African Affairs,* Vol. 74, No. 294 (January 1975), 82–96.

6 THESES

W. Beinart, 'Peasant Production, Underdevelopment, and the Traditionalist Response in Pondoland, c. 1880–1930' (University of London, M.A. thesis, September 1973).

A. F. Conradie, 'The Life and Work of the Methodist Missionary Peter Hargreaves in the land of Sigcau, Chief of the AmaPondo, 1882–1901' (University of Pretoria, M.A. thesis, 1967).

D. G. L. Cragg, 'The Relations of the AmaPondo and the Colonial Administration (1830–1886) with special reference to the role of the Wesleyan Missionaries' (University of Oxford, D.Phil. thesis, 1959).

P. G. Dickson, 'The Native Lands Act, 1913: Its antecedents, passage and reception' (University of Cape Town, M.A. thesis, 1970).

N. A. Etherington, 'The Rise of the Kholwa in South-east Africa: African Christian communities in Natal, Pondoland, and Zululand, 1835–1880' (Yale University, Ph.D. thesis, 1971).

R. B. Ford, 'The Frontier in South Africa: A Comparative Study of the Turner thesis', (University of Denver, Ph.D. thesis, 1966).

A. B. Forsdick, 'The Role of the Trader in the Economy of a Native Reserve: A Study of traders in the Keiskama Hoek District' (Rhodes University, M. Comm. thesis, n.d.)

S. J. Jenkins, 'The Administration of Cecil John Rhodes as Prime Minister of the Cape, 1890–1896' (University of Cape Town, M.A. thesis, 1951).

P. G. J. Koornhof, 'The Drift from the Reserves among the South African Bantu' (University of Oxford, D.Phil. thesis, 1953).

G. J. Lamprecht, 'Die Ekonomiese Ontwikkeling van die Vrystaat van 1870 tot 1899' (Stellenbosch University, D.Phil. thesis, 1954).

C. C. Saunders, 'The Annexation of the Transkeian Territories (1872–1895) with particular reference to British and Cape policy' (University of Oxford, D.Phil. thesis, 1972).

S. Trapido, 'White Conflict and Non-white Participation in the Politics of the Cape of Good Hope 1853–1910' (University of London, Ph.D. thesis, 1970).

H. J. Van Aswegen, 'Die Verhouding tussen Blank en Nie-Blank in die Oranje-Vrystaat 1854–1902' (University of the Orange Free State, D.Phil. thesis, 1968).

A. P. J. Van Rensburg, 'Die Ekonomiese Herstel van die Afrikaner in die Oranjerivier-Kolonie, 1902–1907' (University of the Orange Free State, D.Phil., 1964).

W. A. Venter, 'Die Geşkiedenis en Invloed van die Wesleyaanse Sending in die Transvaal Gedurende die 19e Eeu' (University of the Orange Free State, D.Phil. thesis, 1961).

Index

In this index the Notes numbers have been italicized